W9-BOA-875

BARRON'S

GRE®
巴朗词表

ESSENTIAL WORDS
FOR THE GRE®

[美] Philip Geer, Ed.M. 编著

 北京语言大学出版社
BEIJING LANGUAGE AND CULTURE
UNIVERSITY PRESS

图书在版编目(CIP)数据

GRE 巴朗词表 /（美）吉尔（Geer, P.）编著. 一北京：北京语言大学出版社，2010（2014.4 重印）
ISBN 978-7-5619-2887-5

Ⅰ.①G… Ⅱ.①吉… Ⅲ.①英语—词汇—研究生—入学考试—美国—自学参考资料 Ⅳ.①H313

中国版本图书馆 CIP 数据核字（2010）第 192215 号

版权登记：图字 01－2009－6225 号

ESSENTIAL WORDS FOR THE GRE BY PHILIP GEER, ED. M.
Copyright:©2007 BY BARRON'S EDUCATIONAL SERIES, INC.
This edition arranged with BARRON'S EDUCATIONAL SERIES, INC.
through BIG APPLE TUTTLE-MORI AGENCY, LABUAN MALAYSIA.
Simplified Chinese edition copyright:
2010 Beijing Language and Culture University Press
All rights reserved.

书　　名：GRE 巴朗词表
　　　　　ESSENTIAL WORDS FOR THE GRE
编　　著：（美）Philip Geer Ed. M.
译　　者：吴春晓　芦　莹
责任编辑：李　亮
封面设计：贾臻臻

出版发行：北京语言大学出版社
社　　址：北京市海淀区学院路 15 号　邮政编码：100083
网　　站：www.blcup.com
电　　话：发行部　（010）62605588 /5019 /5128
　　　　　编辑部　（010）62418641
　　　　　邮购电话　（010）62605127
　　　　　读者服务信箱　bj62605588@163.com
印　　刷：北京慧美印刷有限公司
经　　销：全国新华书店
版　　次：2014 年 4 月第 1 版第 6 次印刷
开　　本：720 毫米×960 毫米　1/16　印张：25
字　　数：498 千
书　　号：ISBN 978-7-5619-2887-5
定　　价：45.00 元

新东方图书策划委员会

前　言

　　众所周知，所有准备参加 GRE 考试的考生都需要训[...]
结构以及分析篇章信息的能力。要具备上述能力，不光需[...]
实战技巧，还需要大量广泛地阅读，拓宽知识面，并进行批[...]
科学箴言报》《大西洋月刊》《纽约客》《时代》《经济学[...]
外，考生还应该经常阅读一些极具批判性的著作，如著名科[...]
融通》、颇具影响力的现代思想家 B. F. 斯金纳的论著《超越自[...]
于提高理解复杂句子和进行缜密逻辑推理的能力，不仅可[...]
GRE，而且还可以为考生以后的学术生涯打下坚实的基础。考[...]
不认识的单词查字典的习惯，久而久之，词汇量将会大幅增加。[...]

　　词汇在 GRE 考试中起着举足轻重的作用。考生若想在 GR[...]
习 GRE 语言测试部分最有可能会出现的词汇，这就是本书所[...]

本书内容简介

掌握 GRE 考试高频词汇

　　本书重点讲解了 800 个 GRE 考试高频词汇，包括 300 个基础核心词汇(见[...]
选词时，编者严格按照历次 GRE 考试题目，参考已有的 GRE 词汇列表（包括[...]
Master Word List、Barron's High-Frequency Word List 等），并结合多年的教学经验精[...]
词，力求打造最权威、最实用的 GRE 词表。本部分共分为 80 个单元，每单元 10 个单词，[...]
单词在历次考试中出现的含义进行中英双语释义，并提供与真实考试难度相当的例句帮助[...]
生在仿真语境中记忆与理解单词。同时，书中还针对例句中出现的重要学科术语进行中英双[...]
释义，丰富考生的背景知识，拓宽知识面，更好地理解 GRE 考试中的阅读文章。

　　每单元后均附有针对本单元所学单词的精编练习，包括单词释义连线题、选词填空题[...]
单词用法判断题三种题型，题型难度逐级增加，步步为"赢"，帮助考生逐步巩固对已学单词的[...]
理解与掌握。

　　下面我们通过美国教育考试服务中心(ETS)最近公布的一套样题，来了解一下本书收[...]
的权威性。下表列出了该样题语言测试部分的核心词汇，表中加粗部分是过去这 20 多年[...]

目　录

Pretest

It's time to test your readiness for graduate-level reading. Don't worry. If you aren't familiar with the GRE words tested below, you can be sure you will learn them in Essential Words for the GRE.

Choose the best word or set of words to fill in the blanks in each of the sentences below.

1. The statement "India has recently made great progress in _____ poverty" should be seen in the context of India's vast population of one billion, of which 320 million remain in _____ poverty.
    (A) mitigating .. discordant
    (B) palliating .. ephemeral
    (C) parrying .. doleful
    (D) ameliorating .. equivocal
    (E) alleviating .. abject

2. In his book *Knowledge and Wisdom*, the distinguished twentieth-century philosopher Bertrand Russell said, "Although our age far surpasses all previous ages in knowledge, there has been no _____ increase in wisdom."
    (A) correlative
    (B) articulate
    (C) analogous
    (D) prodigious
    (E) imminent

3. Increased tariffs in the 1930s _____ a collapse in world trade, _____ the Great Depression.
    (A) started .. augmenting
    (B) incited .. ridiculing
    (C) instigated .. forgiving
    (D) caused .. ameliorating
    (E) precipitated .. exacerbating

4. The main impetus behind America's development of the hydrogen bomb was Edward Teller, a Hungarian refugee who had fled Nazism and who _____ the _____ system that was in

place in the former Soviet Union and the Eastern Bloc countries.

(A) disparaged .. innocuous

(B) loathed .. totalitarian

(C) nurtured .. authoritarian

(D) castigated .. benevolent

(E) maligned .. meritorious

5. Physicists now believe that what had been considered the most basic constituents of the universe are in turn comprised of even more fundamental units, called quarks— _____ given that _____ by a physicist familiar with James Joyce's novel, *Finnegan's Wake*.

(A) jocularly .. epitome

(B) flamboyantly .. alias

(C) flippantly .. epigram

(D) whimsically .. appellation

(E) pedantically .. anomaly

6. The English expert regards concern about slight redundancies as _____ and senseless _____ .

(A) pedantic .. quibbling

(B) cryptic .. aggrandizing

(C) sophistical .. elucidating

(D) sophomoric .. tempering

(E) sordid .. abrogation

7. According to the view of the nineteenth-century apologist for capitalism, _____ was an unfortunate but unavoidable _____ of both capitalism and of the natural order of the world.

(A) abnegation .. ramification

(B) subjugation .. precept

(C) indigence .. concomitant

(D) privation .. grandiloquence

(E) penury .. transgression

8. In the final stage in the impeachment process of an American President, the Chief Justice of the Supreme Court presides over the Senate, which sits as a body _____ to a jury to decide whether to convict the President.

(A) idealistic

(B) malevolent

(C) prurient

(D) concomitant

(E) analogous

9. The geological theory of uniformitarianism is the antithesis of the geological theory of catastrophism; it asserts that it is _____ that natural law and processes do not fundamentally change, and that what we observe now is essentially the same as what occurred in the past.

(A) benevolent

(B) ludicrous

(C) relevant

(D) blatant

(E) axiomatic

10. It is interesting to _____ the bromide*, "Haste makes waste" and the _____, "Better safe than sorry."

(A) coalesce .. axiom

(B) obfuscate .. sobriquet

(C) circumvent .. maxim

(D) juxtapose .. platitude

(E) consolidate .. aphorism

Read the following passage carefully. Then answer the questions that follow.

    The term "the arts," when used to classify a group of academic disciplines at schools and universities, subsumes the study of languages, history, and literature, while universities use the term "fine arts" to refer to painting and sculpture as an object of study. Elsewhere the term "the arts" includes painting and sculpture (usually grouped

(5) together as "the plastic arts"), music and literature, and is often extended to embrace dance, mime, and cinema; the word "artist" being used to refer to a practitioner of any of these. Art is commonly opposed to science (as "subjective," where science is "objective") and its sense is distinguished from etymologically related words such as "artifact," "artificial," and "artisan."

11. The word "subsumes" as it is used in line 2 most nearly means

(A) assumes to be true

(B) makes inferior to

A bromide is a commonplace remark or idea.

(C) undermines

(D) includes in a less comprehensive category

(E) incorporates in a more comprehensive category

12. The word "plastic" as it is used in line 5 most nearly means

(A) artificial

(B) superficial

(C) malleable

(D) related to performance

(E) whimsical

13. The word "etymologically" as it is used in line 8 most nearly means

(A) related to insects

(B) related to the study of the relationship between art and language

(C) related to the study of the connotations of words

(D) concerned with the dichotomy between art and science

(E) related to the origin of words

14. Based on the information in lines 7—9 ("Art ... artisan."), which statement would the author be most likely to agree with?

(A) Two words can be related etymologically but have different meanings.

(B) The word "art" has only an accidental and tangential similarity to the words "artifact," "artificial," and "artisan," since it originated from a different word.

(C) Artifacts can only be studied subjectively.

(D) "Artisan" is an older word than the modern word "artist."

(E) The words "artifact," "artificial," and "artisan" are not cognate.

Read the following passage carefully. Then answer the questions that follow.

You may have heard the cynic's version of the golden rule, namely, he who has the gold makes the rules. That is the thrust of this treatise on power by 75-year-old Noam Chomsky, a professor of linguistics at the Massachusetts Institute of Technology (MIT). He has written more than 30 books on linguistics and current affairs, including

(5) the best-selling *Language and Politics* (1990), *Manufacturing Consent* (1994), and *911* (2001). Once called "arguably the most important intellectual alive" by *The New York Times*, this very politically incorrect academic has taught at MIT since 1955, immediately after graduating with a Ph.D. in linguistics from the University of

Pennsylvania. He is currently one of MIT's institute professors, which means he can

(10) teach in any department of the university. But, as he notes wryly in this book, "If I

even get near political science, you can feel the bad vibes starting."

The book is an edited collection of his lectures and tutorials from 1989 to 1999.
Published as a book for the first time, his talks offer high-definition snapshots of the
ills of the twentieth century, even as he slices through history to serve up unpalatable

(15) truths—like how America's founding fathers actually loathed the idea of democracy,
why the United States hires rogue states to fight its wars, and why nation-states are the
wrong political model for a postmodern world.

He reserves one of his biggest knives for the media, which he takes methodical
stabs at for being dictated by the desires of the elite. With the same vigor, the gleeful

(20) iconoclast tells his students why there is not only no such thing as a free lunch, but also
no such thing as a free market. As he puts it: "Of course, the 'free market' ideology is
very useful—it's a weapon against the general population (in the U.S.), because it's an
argument against social spending, and it's a weapon against poor people abroad,
because we can hold it up to them and say, 'You guys have to follow these rules,' then

(25) just go ahead and rob them."

He also sees the world's current economic star, China. Still, conceding that its
ascendance to power is unstoppable, he says, "I don't think we should be asking the
question, 'How do we improve relations with China?' We should be asking other
questions like, 'What kind of relations do we want to have with China?'"

(30) Eyebrow-raisers aside, the question-and-answer format of this book captures the
rhythm of intellectual repartee between Chomsky and his audience but, more
importantly, breaks the monotony of what would otherwise be his marathon soliloquy
on the world's ills. Indeed, his mind is such a ragbag of ideas that it is not above
pondering such things as the validation of vegetarianism. Yet, in the end, his brilliance

(35) falls prey to a certain kind of intellectual snobbery, the sort which asserts that heroes
are not to be found "mentioned in the newspapers." As he puts it: "If they're there, you
know probably they're not heroes, they're antiheroes."

Still, love him or hate him, there are not many thinkers around who can proffer
credible alternative perspectives on how power corrupts today. This book is as much

(40) an antidote to apathy as it is a counterweight to elitist thought. As in this paradox he
surfaces: "You'll see that so long as power remains privately concentrated, everybody,
everybody, has to be committed to one overriding goal: To make sure that the rich folk
are happy—because unless they are, nobody else is going to get anything.

"So, if you're a homeless person sleeping in the streets of Manhattan, let's say,

(45) your first concern must be that the guys in the mansions are happy—because if they're

happy, then they'll invest, and the economy will work, and things will function, and then maybe something will trickle down to you somewhere along the line. But if they're not happy, everything's going to grind to a halt...basically, that's a metaphor for the whole society."

15. The word "linguistics" as it is used in line 4 most nearly means
   (A) rhetoric
   (B) the study of language
   (C) political science
   (D) alchemy
   (E) aesthetics

16. The word "unpalatable" as it is used in line 14 most nearly means
   (A) arcane
   (B) shocking
   (C) insipid
   (D) unpleasant
   (E) jejune

17. The phrase "rogue states" as it is used in line 16 most nearly means
   (A) American states that seceded from the United States in the nineteenth century
   (B) states with purely mercenary motives
   (C) states with a high proportion of rogues in their population
   (D) nation-states that don't adhere to rules agreed to and followed by most modern nation-states
   (E) nation-states founded on egalitarian principles

18. The word "iconoclast" as it is used in line 20 most nearly means
   (A) a conformist
   (B) a person who attacks views held sacrosanct by most people
   (C) a misanthrope
   (D) a person with orthodox views
   (E) a cynic

19. The word "soliloquy" as it is used in line 32 most nearly means
   (A) inanity
   (B) stupidity
   (C) criticism

(D) harangue

(E) literary or dramatic speech by one character

20. The word "apathy" as it is used in line 40 most nearly means

(A) disease

(B) corruption

(C) absence of a consensus

(D) lack of concern

(E) demagoguery

End   of   Pretest

ANSWERS

1. E	2. A	3. E	4. B	5. D
6. A	7. C	8. E	9. E	10. D
11. E	12. C	13. E	14. A	15. B
16. D	17. D	18. B	19. E	20. D

YOUR PRETEST SCORE

1—3   CORRECT ANSWERS: VERY POOR

4—6   CORRECT ANSWERS: POOR

7—9   CORRECT ANSWERS: BELOW AVERAGE

10—12   CORRECT ANSWERS: AVERAGE

13—15   CORRECT ANSWERS: GOOD

16—18   CORRECT ANSWERS: VERY GOOD

19—20   CORRECT ANSWERS: EXCELLENT

300 Absolutely Essential GRE Words

aberrant	bombastic	desultory	effrontery
abeyance	boorish	diatribe	elegy
abscond	burgeon	dichotomy	elicit
abstemious	burnish	diffidence	embellish
admonish	buttress	diffuse	empirical
aesthetic	cacophonous	digression	emulate
aggregate	capricious	dirge	endemic
alacrity	castigation	disabuse	enervate
amalgamate	catalyst	discerning	engender
ambiguous	causality	discordant	ephemeral
ambivalence	chicanery	discredit	equanimity
ameliorate	coagulate	discrepancy	equivocate
anachronism	coda	discrete	erudite
analogous	commensurate	disingenuous	esoteric
anomalous	compendium	disinterested	eulogy
antipathy	complaisant	disjointed	euphemism
apprise	conciliatory	dismiss	exacerbate
approbation	confound	disparage	exculpate
appropriate	connoisseur	disparate	exigency
artless	contention	dissemble	extraneous
ascetic	contentious	disseminate	facetious
assiduous	conundrum	dissolution	facilitate
assuage	conventional	dissonance	fallacious
attenuate	convoluted	distend	fatuous
audacious	craven	distill	fawning
austere	decorum	doctrinaire	felicitous
autonomous	deference	dogmatic	flag
aver	delineate	dupe	fledgling
banal	denigrate	ebullient	flout
belie	derivative	eclectic	foment
beneficent	desiccate	efficacy	forestall

frugality	insinuate	officious	propriety
gainsay	insipid	onerous	proscribe
garrulous	insularity	opprobrium	pungent
goad	intractable	oscillate	qualified
gouge	intransigence	ostentatious	quibble
grandiloquent	inundate	paragon	quiescent
gregarious	inured	partisan	rarefied
guileless	invective	pathological	recalcitrant
gullible	irascible	paucity	recant
harangue	irresolute	pedantic	recondite
homogeneous	laconic	penchant	refractory
hyperbole	lassitude	penury	refute
iconoclastic	laud	perennial	relegate
idolatry	lethargic	perfidious	reproach
immutable	levee	perfunctory	reprobate
impair	levity	permeable	repudiate
impassive	log	pervasive	rescind
impede	loquacious	phlegmatic	resolution
impermeable	lucid	piety	reticent
imperturbable	magnanimity	placate	reverent
impervious	malingerer	plasticity	sage
implacable	malleable	platitude	salubrious
implicit	maverick	plethora	sanction
implode	mendacious	plummet	satiate
inadvertently	metamorphosis	pragmatic	saturate
inchoate	meticulous	precarious	secrete
incongruity	misanthrope	precipitate	shard
inconsequential	mitigate	precursor	skeptic
incorporate	mollify	presumptuous	solicitous
indeterminate	morose	prevaricate	soporific
indigence	mundane	pristine	specious
indolent	negate	probity	spectrum
inert	neophyte	problematic	sporadic
ingenuous	obdurate	prodigal	stigma
inherent	obsequious	proliferate	stint
innocuous	obviate	propensity	stipulate
insensible	occlude	propitiate	stolid

9

striated	tangential	truculence	vituperative
strut	tenuous	vacillate	volatile
subpoena	tirade	venerate	warranted
substantiate	torpor	veracious	wary
supersede	tortuous	verbose	welter
supposition	tractable	viable	whimsical
tacit	transgression	viscous	zealot

800 High-Frequency GRE Words

UNIT 1

音频

abate / əˈbeɪt / *v.* to decrease; reduce 削减，减少；减轻，缓和

NASA announced that it would delay the launch of the manned spacecraft until the radiation from the solar flares *abated*. 美国航空航天局宣布将延迟发射载人航天器，直至太阳耀斑辐射有所减弱。

abdicate / ˈæbdɪkeɪt / *v.* to give up a position, right, or power 离职，离任；放弃

Romulus Augustus, the last Western Roman emperor, was forced to *abdicate* the throne in 476 A.D., and the Germanic chieftain Odovacar became the de facto ruler of Italy. 西罗马最后一位皇帝罗慕路斯·奥古斯都被迫在公元476年退位，而日耳曼首领奥多瓦卡成为意大利真正的统治者。// The appeals judge has *abdicated* his responsibility to review the findings of the high court. 上诉法庭法官已放弃其对高级法院的裁决进行再审的责任。

─── ● 常见学科术语 ● ───

de facto: in fact, whether by right or not; exercising power without being legally established (Latin: from the fact)
事实上（的），实际上（的）：事实上，无论合法与否；在合法确立权力之前即行使（拉丁文，相当于英语的from the fact）

aberrant / æˈberənt / *adj.* deviating from what is normal 偏离正常的，反常的

When a person's behavior becomes *aberrant*, his or her peers may become concerned that the individual is becoming a deviant. 当一个人的行为离经叛道时，其同伴就会担心这个人会成为异类。

【派】**aberration** *n.* something different from the usual or normal 失常，反常

For centuries, solar eclipses were regarded as serious *aberrations* in the natural order. 几个世纪以来，人们一直认为日食是严重违背自然规律的异常现象。

─── ● 常见学科术语 ● ───

deviant: a person whose behavior differs from the accepted standards of society
离经叛道的人，异类：在行为上与社会公认的准则相去甚远的人

abeyance / əˈbeɪəns / *n.* temporary suppression or suspension 暂时中止；临时搁置

A good judge must hold his or her judgment in *abeyance* until all the facts in a case have been presented. 在案件的事实未被全部陈述之前，一名好法官应该暂搁自己的判决。

abject / ˈæbdʒekt / *adj.* miserable; pitiful 痛苦的，悲惨的；非常可怜的

John Steinbeck's novel *The Grapes of Wrath* portrays the *abject* poverty of many people during the Great Depression. 约翰·斯坦贝克在其小说《愤怒的葡萄》中描绘了很多人在大萧条时期的悲惨窘迫的生活。

abjure / əbˈdʒʊr / *v.* to reject; abandon formally 拒绝；正式放弃，摈弃

Most members of the Religious Society of Friends (commonly known as the Quakers or Friends) *abjure* the use of violence to settle disputes between nations. 大部分公谊会（即人们常说的贵格会或教友会）成员都不赞同武力解决国家间争端的做法。// For a foreigner to become a U.S. citizen, he or she must take an oath *abjuring* allegiance to any other country and pledging to take up arms to defend the United States. 一个外国人若要成为美国公民，则必须宣誓不再效忠他国，并起誓在必要时拿起武器保卫美国。

abscission / æbˈsɪʒən / *n.* ① the act of cutting 切割 ② the natural separation of a leaf or other part of a plant 剥离，脱落

Two scientists, Alan G. Williams and Thomas G. Whitham, have hypothesized that premature leaf *abscission* is an adaptive plant response to herbivorous attack. 艾伦·G·威廉姆斯和托马斯·G·惠瑟姆两位科学家猜测，有些植物过早落叶是植物本身为应对食草性动物攻击的适应性反应。

【派】**abscise** *v.* to cut off or away 切断，去除

The surgeon *abscised* a small growth on the patient's hand. 外科医生切除了病人手上的一块小小的赘生物。

● 常见学科术语 ●
---

hypothesize: form a hypothesis, that is a proposition put forward as a starting point for further investigation

假设，假说：形成假说，即为日后的研究提出作为起点的命题

adaptive: relating to adaptation, an alteration in structure or habits by which a species improves its condition in relationship to its environment

适应性的：和适应性有关的，适应性即物种为改善自身与外部环境的关系而在结构或习性上所作的改变。

herbivorous: feeding mainly on plants

食草的，草食性的：主要以植物为食的

---

abscond / əbˈskɑːnd / *v.* to depart secretly 潜逃，逃匿

A warrant is out for the arrest of a person believed to have *absconded* with three million dollars. 警方对一个被怀疑携带300万美金潜逃的人发出通缉令。

abstemious / əbˈstiːmiəs / *adj.* moderate in appetite 饮食有度的，有节制的

Some research suggests that people with an *abstemious* lifestyle tend to live longer than people who indulge their appetites. 一些研究结果表明，饮食有度的人往往比那些饮食无度的人更长寿。

abstinence / ˈæbstɪnəns / *n.* the giving up of certain pleasures 节制，节欲；戒除

The monk's vow of *abstinence* includes all intoxicating substances. 修道士禁戒誓言中包括戒除所有酒精饮品。

REVIEW 1

Matching

Match each word with its definition:

1. abate
2. abdicate
3. aberrant

a. to abandon formally

b. temporary suppression

c. to give up a position or power

4. abeyance   d. giving up of certain pleasures

5. abject   e. to depart secretly

6. abjure   f. miserable; pitiful

7. abscission   g. to decrease

8. abscond   h. moderate in appetite

9. abstemious   i. the act of cutting

10. abstinence   j. deviating from what is normal

Fill-ins

Choose the best word to fill in the blank in each sentence.

abate	abdicated	aberrations	abeyance	abject
abjured	absconded	abscission	abstemious	abstinence

1. The 90-year-old monarch _____ the throne to allow his son to become king.

2. Psychotherapy relies on psychological rather than physiological approaches to curing mental _____.

3. Implementation of the new plan has been held in _____ pending an investigation of its effectiveness to date.

4. Ms. Johnson's _____ lifestyle helped her to amass a fortune.

5. The crew of the vessel waited for the storm to _____ before going on deck to make repairs.

6. The alcoholic's physician recommended total _____ from liquor for her patient.

7. The documentary filmmaker was accused of using misleading footage to make it appear that nearly everyone in the country lived in _____ conditions.

8. The judge said he would reduce the convicted woman's sentence if she _____ all association with those convicted of treason.

9. The senior surgeon performed the difficult _____.

10. The audit of the bank's financial records led investigators to suspect that someone had _____ with $100,000.

Sense or Nonsense

Indicate whether each sentence makes good sense or not.
Put S (SENSE) if it does, and put N (NONSENSE) if it does not.

1. The doctor decided to let her patient's fever abate before ordering further clinical tests. _____

2. The university's plans for expansion have been put in abeyance until the economic outlook is more favorable. _____

3. Ruth's abstemious appetite has caused her to put on ten pounds in the last month. _____

4. The senator announced that he formally accepted and abjured all of his past statements on the issue. _____

5. The judge instructed the members of the jury that they would be abdicating their responsibilities if they did not reach a verdict in the case. _____

UNIT 2

abysmal / ə'bɪzməl / *adj.* very bad 非常糟糕的

The *abysmal* failure of the free market system in Russia has led some people to argue that the planned economy of the Soviet Union, while not perfect, was better suited to Russia's history and culture than Western-style capitalism. 俄罗斯自由市场制度的惨痛失败使很多人认为，较之西方的资本主义制度，苏联的计划经济尽管不尽完善，但可能更适合俄罗斯的历史和文化。

• 常见学科术语 •

free market: an economic market in which the demand and supply of goods and services is either not regulated or is slightly regulated
自由市场： 一种经济市场。在该市场中，商品与服务的供求关系完全不受调控，或只受稍许调控。

planned economy: an economic system in which the production, allocation, and consumption of goods and services is planned in advance. Another term for planned economy is "command economy."
计划经济： 一种经济体制。在该体制下，商品和服务的生产、分配与消费都是预先计划好的。计划经济的另一种说法是"指令性经济"。

capitalism: an economic and political system in which a country's industry and trade are controlled by private owners rather than the government
资本主义： 一种政治经济体制。在该体制下，国家的工业和贸易受私营业者而非政府的掌控。

---

accretion / ə'kriːʃn / *n.* growth in size or increase in amount（体积上的）增大，（数量上的）增多

In the 1960s, the American geophysicist Harry Hess conceived the idea of sea-floor spreading, a process in which the new crust in the ocean is continually generated by igneous processes at the crests of the mid-oceanic ridges, causing a steady *accretion* of the crust. 20世纪60年代，美国地球物理学家哈里·赫斯提出了海床扩张的构想。在这一过程中，大洋中脊顶部的火成过程不断产生新的地壳，导致海底新的地壳稳步生成，从而形成海床扩张。（译者注：增厚的地壳对两侧板块，即海床，形成挤压，导致海床扩张。）

• 常见学科术语 •

geophysicist: one who specializes in the physics of the earth and its environment
地球物理学家： 专门研究地球及其环境的物理特征的人

igneous: in geology, relating to the formation of rocks by solidification from a molten state. The word igneous is from Latin ignis (fire).
火成的，火成岩的： 在地质学上指由熔化岩石固化而形成的。该词源于拉丁语ignis（火）。

---

accrue / ə'kruː / *v.* to accumulate; grow by additions 积累，增加；自然增长

Regulating the growth of large companies when they begin to become monopolistic is a difficult task for government in a capitalist county; if it limits monopolies too much, the nation's firms could become less competitive than foreign companies that enjoy the advantages *accruing* from greater monopolies. 在资本主义国家，当一些大公司开始表现出垄断的苗头时，政府却很难限制其发展壮大。因为如果过度限制垄断，那么较之国外的大公司，本国的大公司就可能变得缺乏竞争力，因为国外大公司可以获益于更大的垄断积累的优势。

• 常见学科术语 •

monopolistic: having exclusive control over a commercial activity
垄断的：对商业活动独享控制权的

---

adamant / ˈædəmənt / *adj.* uncompromising; unyielding 不屈服的，不妥协的；固执的

Despite widespread opposition to his plan, the political party's leader is *adamant* that the party must move to the center to appeal to moderate voters. 尽管那位政党领导人的计划遭到不少反对，但他仍坚持认为该政党应不遗余力地去吸引中间选民。

adjunct / ˈædʒʌŋkt / *n.* something added, attached, or joined 附加的东西，附属物

Speed walking, cross-country running, and marathons are normally regarded as *adjuncts* of track and field athletics since races in these sports are not normally held on a track. 竞走、越野跑与马拉松通常被归为田径运动的附属项目，因为这些比赛通常不在跑道上进行。

admonish / ədˈmɑːnɪʃ / *v.* to caution or reprimand 提醒；警告，告诫

The judge *admonished* the jury to discount testimony that had been ruled inadmissible. 法官提醒陪审团不要理会已经宣布无效的证词。

adulterate / əˈdʌltəreɪt / *v.* to corrupt or make impure 掺假，使不洁

The unscrupulous company sells an *adulterated* version of the drug, and doesn't inform consumers that they are getting a less efficacious drug than they think they are getting. 那家见利忘义的公司出售假药，而且并不告知消费者他们购买的药品并不像他们预期的那样有效。

aesthetic / esˈθetɪk / *adj.* relating to beauty or art 有关美的，审美的；美学的；艺术的 *n.* a conception of what is artistically beautiful 美感

Members of the English *aesthetic* movement, such as Oscar Wilde, were proponents of the doctrine of art for art's sake, which is the belief that art cannot and should not be useful for any purpose other than that of creating beauty. 奥斯卡·王尔德等一些英国唯美主义运动倡导者倡导"为艺术而艺术"的理念，即艺术不能也不应该用于除产生美以外的任何其他目的。// The Gothic *aesthetic* dominated European art and architecture from approximately the twelfth to the fifteenth century. 约从12世纪至15世纪，哥特式美学一直在欧洲的艺术和建筑中占据主导地位。

【派1】**aesthetics** *n.* ① a conception of what is beautiful 美感 ② a branch of philosophy dealing with beauty and art, and standards in judging them 美学（对美的认识，研究美和艺术及其评判标准的一个哲学分支）

【派2】**aesthete** *n.* someone who cultivates a special sensitivity to beauty, especially the person whose interest in beauty and art is regarded as excessive or superficial 审美家，唯美主义者

• 常见学科术语 •

Gothic: a style of architecture that was very popular in the late Middle Ages characterized by such features as pointed arches, soaring spaces, and light. In literature the term refers to a genre of fiction that was popular in the eighteenth and early nineteenth centuries. Gothic novels have an atmosphere of gloom, mystery, and horror.

---

affected / əˈfektɪd / *adj.* pretentious, phony 假装的，矫揉造作的；赝品的

It has been argued that the emphasis on so-called "proper English" leads to unnatural and *affected* speech. 有人认为对所谓的"正式英语"的强调会催生不自然的、矫揉造作的英语。

affinity / əˈfɪnəti / *n.* ① fondness; liking 亲切；喜爱 ② similarity 相似性，相似处

The female students in the class felt an *affinity* for the ancient Greek playwright Euripides because he sympathized with women, slaves, and other despised members of his society. 班上的女生都喜欢古希腊剧作家欧里庇得斯，因为他同情妇女、奴隶以及其他被他那个社会所鄙弃的人。

REVIEW 2

Matching

Match each word with its definition:

1. abysmal		a.	to grow by additions
2. accretion		b.	very bad
3. accrue		c.	relating to beauty or art
4. adamant		d.	something added
5. adjunct		e.	to corrupt or make impure
6. admonish		f.	increase in amount
7. adulterate		g.	pretentious
8. aesthetic		h.	fondness
9. affected		i.	uncompromising
10. affinity		j.	to caution

Fill-ins

Choose the best word to fill in the blank in each sentence.

abysmal	accretion	accrued	adamant	adjunct
admonished	adulterated	aesthetic	affected	affinity

1. The film is marred by the actor's _____ English accent.

2. In Emily Bronte's *Wuthering Heights* the characters Heathcliff and Catherine feel such an _____ for each other that they almost literally cannot live without each other.

3. Over the years the university's computer system has grown so much by _____ that no one person has a complete understanding of it.

4. The committee on education reform recommended that the school introduce more art courses to develop students' _____ awareness.

5. The poet _____ the critic for failing to appreciate the subtle changes in his poem's meter.

6. Tom's savings account has ＿＿＿＿＿＿＿ $3,000 in interest over the last ten years.

7. The band's playing was so ＿＿＿＿＿＿＿ that they were booed off stage.

8. The English teacher is ＿＿＿＿＿＿＿ about one thing: students must correct all the errors in written work that she returns to them.

9. Over the last 20 years or so consumers have increasingly demanded food that is not ＿＿＿＿＿＿＿ with additives.

10. Nearly half of the college courses in America are taught by ＿＿＿＿＿＿＿ professors.

Sense or Nonsense

Indicate whether each sentence makes good sense or not.
Put S（SENSE）if it does, and put N（NONSENSE）if it does not.

1. In many ways Aristotle's aesthetic dictums have never been surpassed. ＿＿＿＿＿＿＿

2. Beth is so adamant about the plan that she is willing to give it up at the first opportunity. ＿＿＿＿＿＿＿

3. The waiters in the expensive restaurant were told to affect a French accent to impress customers. ＿＿＿＿＿＿＿

4. Most students love to be admonished for their good work. ＿＿＿＿＿＿＿

5. State law requires that whole milk be 100% adulterated. ＿＿＿＿＿＿＿

UNIT 3

aggrandize / əˈgrændaɪz / *v.* to make larger or greater 扩大；增多；提高
One of the concerns of the framers of the U.S. Constitution was that one branch of government would try to *aggrandize* itself at the expense of the others. 当初美国宪法的缔造者们的担忧之一是政府的某一分支会以牺牲其他分支为代价来壮大自己。

aggregate / ˈægrɪgət / *adj.* amounting to a whole; total 合计的，累计的；全部的 *n.* collective mass or sum 集合体 / ˈægrɪgeɪt / *v.* to collect into a mass 累计；积累
The *aggregate* wealth of a country includes private as well as public resources and possessions. 一个国家的全部财富包括私人的和公共的资源和财产。// Portals are Web sites designed to *aggregate* information and are used as a starting point on the Web. 门户网站是为收集信息而设计的网站，通常被用作上网畅游的起点。

alacrity / əˈlækrəti / *n.* ① cheerful willingness; eagerness 欣然同意，乐意；渴望 ② speed 轻快
The football coach was pleased to see the team get to work on the task of improving its tackling skills with *alacrity*. 橄榄球教练很高兴看到他的队员们欣欣然地去改进铲球技术。

alchemy / ˈælkəmi / *n.* ① a medieval chemical philosophy based on changing metal into gold 炼金术（中世纪时的一种化学哲学，其根本目标是将金属变成黄金）；② a seemingly magical power or process of transmutation 魔力；神秘变化

Alchemy was the forerunner of the modern science of chemistry. 炼金术是现代化学的前身。// None of their friends could understand the mysterious *alchemy* that caused two people as different from one another as Rob and Barbara to fall in love. 他们的朋友中没人能理解是什么魔力使鲍勃和芭芭拉这样截然不同的两个人坠入爱河。

● 常见学科术语 ●
---

alchemy: Modern scientists believe alchemy was not a true science since there's no evidence that anyone succeeded in turning a base metal into gold. Interestingly, however, the word for the modern science of "chemistry" is derived directly from the word "alchemy."

炼金术: 现代科学家认为炼金术并不是一门真正的科学，因为没有证据证明曾有人成功地把贱金属变成金子。然而有趣的是，现代科学的chemistry(化学)一词却直接来源于alchemy(炼金术)。

allay / əˈleɪ / *v.* to lessen; ease; soothe 减弱；安慰，使安静

Improvements in antivirus software have *allayed* many people's fears of having their computers "infected" with malicious software. 杀毒软件的改进减轻了不少人对自己的电脑受恶意软件攻击的担心。

alleviate / əˈliːvieɪt / *v.* to relieve; improve partially 舒缓，减轻；部分改善

According to some commentators, one of the weaknesses of capitalism is that, although it is very efficient at increasing absolute wealth, it is not as successful at *alleviating* relative poverty; thus, a person living in a slum in America may be reasonably well off by historical standards, but he might perceive himself to be poor compared to members of the bourgeoisie, whom he sees regularly buying luxury goods that he is not able to afford. 据一些评论员分析，资本主义的一个弱点是：尽管它能高效地增加绝对财富，但却不能同样成功地减轻相对贫困。因此，一个住在美国贫民窟的人尽管按照历史标准来看可能相当富裕，但和中产阶级相比，他仍会认为自己很贫困。因为中产阶级经常购买奢侈品，他却负担不起。

● 常见学科术语 ●
---

bourgeoisie: the social order dominated by the property-owning class. The term is associated with Marxism, the political and economic philosophy of Karl Marx and Friedrich Engels, but today it is often used disparagingly to suggest materialism and philistinism (an unenlightened and smug attitude toward culture).

中产阶级: 由有产阶级占统治地位的社会秩序。这个词经常与由卡尔·马克思和弗雷德里克·恩格斯创立的马克思主义政治经济哲学联系在一起。但现在这个词通常含有贬抑的意味，暗示着物质主义和市侩主义(对文化无知却自以为是的态度)。

alloy / ˈælɔɪ / *n.* ① a combination 混合物，合成 ② a mixture of two or more metals 合金

Scientists formulate *alloys* to create properties that are not possessed by natural metals or other substances. 科学家按比例制成合金以创造出自然金属或其他物质不具备的特性。

allure / əˈlʊr / *n.* the power to entice by charm 吸引力；迷惑 *v.* to entice by charm 吸引，诱惑

Political groups in the United States often lobby Congress to use the *allure* of America's vast market as an incentive for countries to pursue policies in accordance with American policies. 美国的政治团体经常游说国会用美国巨大的国内市场当作诱饵，诱使他国政府在采取政策时以美国的政策为榜样。

【派】**alluring** *adj.* 迷人的，吸引人的，诱惑的

The idea of a clockwork universe is very *alluring* to some people because it explains how the universe was created, yet allows human beings to live in it without believing in supernatural intervention. 机械式宇

宙论对很多人来说极具吸引力，因为它既解释了宇宙的形成，又允许人类不必相信超自然干预也能生活在宇宙之中。

• 常见学科术语 •

lobby: a group whose members share certain goals and work to bring about the passage, modification, or defeat of laws that affect these goals

游说团体：为了某些共同目标而一起工作的团体，他们通常会影响法律的制定和修正，或废除那些影响他们目标实现的法律。

clockwork universe: a theory of the origin of the universe that compares the universe to a mechanical clock created by God. According to this theory, once created, the universe continues to run according to the laws of nature and does not require further Divine intervention. This idea was very popular in the Enlightenment, an eighteenth-century philosophical movement that emphasized the use of reason to examine accepted beliefs and traditions.

机械式宇宙论：一种解释宇宙起源的理论，它把宇宙比作上帝创造的一个机械式钟表。该理论认为，宇宙一旦被创造出来，就将继续根据自然法则运转而无需上帝的进一步干预。该理论在启蒙运动时期非常流行。启蒙运动是发生于18世纪的一场哲学运动，强调用理性去重新审视公认的信念或传统。

---

amalgamate / əˈmælɡəmeɪt / *v.* to combine into a unified whole 合并，结合

In early 1999, six municipalities were *amalgamated* into an enlarged city of Toronto, Canada. 1999年初，6个自治市（译者注：即5个近郊市加多伦多城区）合并成一个扩大了的加拿大多伦多市。

ambiguous / æmˈbɪɡjuəs / *adj.* unclear or doubtful in meaning 不清楚的，意义含糊的

The gender of the Mahayana Buddhist deity Avalokitesuara, the god of infinite mercy, is *ambiguous* in both China and Japan, where the god is sometimes called a goddess. 大乘佛教的神观世音菩萨，即大慈大悲观世音，其性别在中国和日本都不明确，有时被视为女神。

• 常见学科术语 •

Mahayana Buddhist: one of the three major traditions of Buddhism. It regards the historical Buddha as a manifestation of the celestial Buddha.

大乘佛教：佛教三大宗派之一，它认为现世的佛是传说中的佛的显灵。

REVIEW 3

Matching

Match each word with its definition:

1. aggrandize
2. aggregate
3. alacrity
4. alchemy
5. allay
6. alleviate

a. cheerful willingness
b. a combination
c. the power to entice by charm
d. to make larger or greater
e. to combine into a unified whole
f. to lessen; ease

7. alloy   g. amounting to a whole

8. allure   h. to relieve; improve partially

9. amalgamate   i. unclear or doubtful in meaning

10. ambiguous   j. a medieval chemical philosophy

Fill-ins

Choose the best word to fill in the blank in each sentence.

aggrandize	aggregate	alacrity	alchemy	allay
alleviate	alloys	allure	amalgamate	ambiguous

1. The _____ of France is great; millions of people around the world study its language and culture.

2. With the organic chemistry test coming up soon, Maria knew she had to start studying for it with _____ .

3. The computer manufacturer donated 100 computers to the inner-city school to _____ the problem of children not having access to the Internet.

4. The corporation's CEO claimed that his purchase of a personal jet airplane was not meant to personally _____ him.

5. By what remarkable artistic _____ did the interior decorator transform the drab living room into a room of vibrant color and light?

6. John's role in the affair is _____ ; it is not clear whether he took an active part in it or was merely an advisor.

7. The final plan is an _____ of the ideas of everyone in the class.

8. Modern _____ have helped make cars lighter and more resistant to corrosion.

9. To _____ the public's fears that his health was failing, the prime minister played tennis every day and invited reporters to be present.

10. Now separate entities, the 12 colleges will _____ to create a single university.

Sense or Nonsense

Indicate whether each sentence makes good sense or not.
Put S (SENSE) if it does, and put N (NONSENSE) if it does not.

1. The allure of gold is so great that hardly anyone is buying it. _____

2. The governor is concerned that one agency of government is aggrandizing itself at the expense of other agencies. _____

3. The judge instructed the witness to make an ambiguous statement so that everyone could be clear about what she meant. _____

4. The alacrity of John Milton's *Paradise Lost* makes it one of the great epic poems in English.
_____

5. The charity was set up to alleviate the suffering of the poor. _____

UNIT 4

ambivalence / æmˈbɪvələns / *n.* a state of having conflicting emotional attitudes 矛盾情绪；犹豫不决

John felt some *ambivalence* about getting married before finishing college. 约翰对完成大学学业前就结婚感到很矛盾。

【派】**ambivalent** *adj.* 矛盾的，举棋不定的

In public opinion surveys in the United States, scientists rank second only to physicians in public esteem, yet much of the public is increasingly *ambivalent* about some of the implications for society of "Big Science" and its related technology. 美国公众意见调查显示，在最受公众尊敬的职业中科学家排在第二位，仅次于医生，然而很多民众对"大科学"及其相关技术带来的社会影响的态度日益矛盾(译者注：大科学是国际科学界近年来提出的新概念，其主要特点为：投资强度大、多学科交叉、需要昂贵且复杂的实验设备、研究目标宏大等)。

ambrosia / æmˈbrouziə / *n.* ① the food of the gods 神的食物 ② something delicious 美味食品

The combination of flavors in the Moroccan baked eggplant was pure *ambrosia*. 摩洛哥烤茄子中混合了各种调料的风味，简直就是人间美味啊。

【派】**ambrosial** *adj.* 美味的；神的

The food critic praised the chef for preparing what he called an "*ambrosial* meal." 那位美食评论家赞扬了大厨，称其做出了"神食般的佳肴"。

● 常见学科术语 ●

In Greek mythology, **ambrosia** and **nektar** were the delicious and fragrant food and drink of the gods that gave them immortality. The English word **nectar** (from Greek nektar) means a sweet liquid secreted by flowers, or a delicious drink.

在希腊神话中，神食和蜜露是供神享用的美味香馨的食物和饮品，食用后可长生不老。英语单词nectar(蜜露，甘露)来源于希腊语nektar，指从花中提取的甜美饮品或非常好喝的酒。

---

ameliorate / əˈmiːliəreɪt / *v.* to improve 提高，改善

Knowing they could not stop the spread of a contagion in a few days, health authorities worked to inhibit its spread and to *ameliorate* its effects by issuing warnings to the public and initiating immunization programs. 考虑到难以在几天内遏制住这种传染病的传播，卫生部门开始向民众通告其危害性并开始实施免疫计划以控制其传播，并减少其造成的影响。

amenable / əˈmenəbl / *adj.* agreeable; cooperative; suited 同意的，乐意的；合作的；适合的

The young writer is *amenable* to suggestions for improving her prose style to make it more interesting. 那位年轻作家很乐于听取能改善其文风使之更有趣的建议。

amenity / əˈmenəti / *n.* something that increases comfort 便利设施；舒适

Many *amenities* considered normal and necessary by people in developed countries, such as indoor plumbing, were luxuries only a few generations ago. 在发达国家被当作普通而必要的生活便利设施，如室内管道，在短短几代前还是奢侈品。

amulet / ˈæmjʊlət / *n.* ornament worn as a charm against evil spirits 护身符

The early Christian Church forbade the use of *amulets*, which had become common in the Roman Empire at the time the Christian Church began to develop. 早期基督教会禁止佩戴护身符，而这一习俗早在基督教会刚刚兴起时在罗马帝国就已经很普遍了。

anachronism / əˈnækrənɪzəm / *n.* something out of the proper time 时代错误；不合时宜的事

Some experts regard the retirement age of 65 as an *anachronism* at a time when people in the developed world have much longer life expectancies than previously. 很过专家认为规定65岁退休非常不合时宜，因为在发达国家，现代人的平均寿命比以前长得多。

analgesic / ˌænəlˈdʒiːzɪk / *n.* medication that reduces or eliminates pain 止痛药，镇痛剂

Aspirin (the trademark of the drug acetylsalicylic acid) is a powerful *analgesic* that was introduced in 1899 and is still one of the most effective medicines available to alleviate pain, fever, and inflammation. 阿司匹林(药品乙酰水杨酸的商用名称)是一种强效镇痛剂，诞生于1899年，至今仍是现有药物中最能有效缓解疼痛、退烧和消炎的药物之一。

analogous / əˈnæləgəs / *adj.* comparable 可比的；相当的

The psychology researcher's experiment postulates that the brain is *analogous* to a digital computer. 心理学家在实验中把人脑假定为数字计算机。

【派1】**analogy** *n.* a similarity in some ways between things that are otherwise dissimilar 类比；相似，类似
The idea of evolution in nature is sometimes misconstrued and applied by *analogy* to other areas in which there is scant evidence for its existence; a notable example of this is Social Darwinism, in which it is argued that society is like nature, and thus people, like animals, are competing for survival, with those who are genetically superior at surviving and reproducing. 自然界中的进化论有时被曲解，并用于同其他领域进行类比，但在这些领域还没有足够的证据表明进化论的存在。一个著名的例子就是社会达尔文主义，该理论认为，社会就像自然界，因此人就像动物一样，为生存而竞争，结果是基因优越的人才获得生存和繁衍的权利。

【派2】**analog** *n.* something that is comparable to something else 类似物，相似体
Some commentators have posited the existence of an *analog* to the Protestant work ethic in Chinese culture, which they call the "Confucian work ethic," to explain the economic success of some countries with large Chinese populations. 有评论家认为已经在中国文化中找到了与新教的职业道德相对应的理念，他们称之为"儒家职业道德"。他们据此来解释为什么一些有着大量华裔人口的国家能在经济上取得成功。

● 常见学科术语 ●

Social Darwinism: a theory in sociology that individuals or groups achieve advantage over others as the result of genetic or biological superiority
社会达尔文主义：一种社会学理论，认为社会中的一些个体或团体因其基因或生物学上的优越性而获得优势

Protestant work ethic: a view of life that encourages hard work and a rational view of the world as a way to achieve material success
新教的职业道德：一种鼓励勤勉工作的人生观，一种以获得物质成功为目的的理性世界观。

Confucian: a system or ethics based on the teachings of the ancient Chinese sage Confucius. It places a high value on family relationships.
儒家思想：依据中国古代圣贤孔子的说教而形成的一套思想体系和道德规范，高度推崇家族关系。

anarchy / ˈænərki / *n.* ① absence of government 无政府状态 ② a state of disorder 混乱

The American philosopher Robert Nozick does not advocate *anarchy*; rather, he argues for the merits of a minimal state that would not violate the natural rights of individuals. 美国哲学家罗伯特·诺齐克并不赞同无政府状态，而是为不会侵犯个人自然权利的"最低限度的国家"进行辩护。

【派1】**anarchic** *adj.* lacking order or control 无秩序的，混乱的

The student of mythology speculated that Dionysos was created as a projection of the pleasure-loving, *anarchic* aspect of human nature. 学习神话学的人会产生这样的推断，人们创造出酒神狄厄尼索斯是为了折射人性中纵欲、混乱的一面。

【派2】**anarchism** *n.* ① a theory that all forms of government are oppressive and should be abolished 无政府主义（认为任何形式的政府都是一种压迫，应该废除）② the advocacy of this theory or the attempt to bring about anarchism 反政府活动

Most political scientists do not believe *anarchism* to be a tenable theory of government. 很多政治学家认为无政府主义这种关于政府的理论是站不住脚的。

—— • 常见学科术语 • ——

Dionysos: known as Bacchus to the Romans, Dionysos was the son of Zeus and Selene. He was the Greek god of agriculture, fertility, wine, and ecstasy, and later regarded as a patron of the arts. Dionysos was worshipped by an emotional cult that held secret rites called Bacchanalia—wild orgies of frenzied revelry, drunkenness, and debauchery.

狄厄尼索斯：在罗马神话中名为巴克斯，是宙斯和塞勒涅之子。他是希腊神话中的农神、丰饶之神、酒神以及狂欢之神，后被尊为艺术之神。狂热的人们举行秘密的仪式来祭拜他，即"酒神节"，在这天人们纵情狂欢，开怀畅饮，放浪形骸。

REVIEW 4

Matching

Match each word with its definition:

1. ambivalence
2. ambrosia
3. ameliorate
4. amenable
5. amenity
6. amulet
7. anachronism
8. analgesic
9. analogous
10. anarchy

a. agreeable; cooperative
b. medication that reduces pain
c. a state of having conflicting emotional attitudes
d. absence of government
e. ornament worn as a charm against evil spirits
f. something out of the proper time
g. to improve
h. comparable
i. something delicious
j. something that increases comfort

Fill-ins

Choose the best word to fill in the blank in each sentence.

ambivalent	ambrosia	ameliorate	amenable	amenities
amulet	anachronism	analgesic	analogy	anarchy

1. Many people have an _____ attitude to war: it causes great suffering, yet appears at times to be the only solution to a serious problem.
2. During the revolution the country began to slip toward _____.
3. The soldier attributed his survival through three battles to an _____ he had found in Borneo.
4. After fasting for 24 hours, Wayne said that his first bite of steak tasted like _____.
5. "I'm afraid all I can do for your headache is prescribe an _____ to relieve the pain," the doctor told her patient.
6. The governor drew an _____ between a family and society, pointing out that both need a leader if they are to function smoothly.
7. The antithesis of the principle of art for art's sake is social realism, which feels a heavy responsibility to identify, and even _____, social ills.
8. The history professor is _____ to student suggestions for the topic of the term paper.
9. The editor discovered an _____ in the script; set in 1944, it contained a reference to the atomic bombing of Hiroshima in 1945.
10. Many modern tourists like to have all the _____ of home when they travel.

Sense or Nonsense

Indicate whether each sentence makes good sense or not.
Put S (SENSE) if it does, and put N (NONSENSE) if it does not.

1. Amulets have been used for centuries to generate electric power. _____
2. The economist drew an analogy between a family spending beyond its means and a government running a deficit. _____
3. Although the government program was intended to help the poor, in reality it has only ameliorated their situation. _____
4. John is ambivalent about whether to apply to graduate school or look for a job after receiving his degree. _____
5. A group of anarchists called for the overthrow of the government. _____

UNIT 5

anodyne / ˈænədaɪn / *n.* something that calms or soothes pain 止痛剂，镇痛剂 *adj.* relaxing, or capable of soothing pain 止痛的；安慰的，舒缓的

Some people use alcohol as an *anodyne* to numb their emotional pain. 一些人用酒精来麻醉他们感情上的伤痛。// The public relations officer is remarkably *anodyne*; all he does is mouth comforting, politically correct platitudes, saying nothing of substance. 那位公关主任以善于舒缓大家的情绪而著称，说的全是些口头上给人安慰、政治上正确的老生常谈，没有一点实质性内容。

anomalous / əˈnɑːmələs / *adj.* irregular; deviating from the norm 不规则的；反常的

The psychologist discounted the *anomalous* behavior of the soldier, saying it was merely a short-term effect of the stress of battle. 那位心理学家对那名士兵的反常行为不以为然，表示那只不过是战争压力的短期影响。

【派】**anomaly** *n.* 不规则；反常

A moral dilemma that arises with humanity's ability to clone is posed in the following hypothetical scenario: a pig that produces much more meat than a normal pig can be cloned, but the pig's life span would be cut in half because of *anomalies* in the cloning process: Is it right to clone such an animal? 人类克隆能力引发的道德困境被置于以下的假想情景：如果能克隆出一头比平常的猪产肉量高的猪，但由于克隆过程的反常性，这头猪的寿命会减半，那么克隆这样的动物是否正确呢？

antecedent / ˌæntɪˈsiːdnt / *n.* something that comes before 先前发生的事，先例

Historical factors, such as the increased emphasis on the individual, the invention of printing, and the rise of the bourgeoisie, contributed to make the Reformation, which had its *antecedents* in the reform movement within the Roman Catholic Church, into a much broader phenomenon that created powerful churches that grew to rival the original church. 诸如对个体的日渐注重、印刷术的发明和资产阶级的兴起等历史因素促使宗教改革发展成一种影响更为广泛的现象。这场改革在罗马天主教改革运动中已有先例，使得很多有权势的教会出现并开始和原有教会相抗衡。

> ──── ● 常见学科术语 ● ────
>
> **Reformation:** a sixteenth-century movement aimed at reforming abuses in the Roman Catholic Church. It led to the establishment of new churches.
> 宗教改革：发生于16世纪的一场旨在改革罗马天主教会种种弊端的运动，促使新教会的兴起。

antediluvian / ˌæntɪdɪˈluːviən / *adj.* prehistoric 史前的

Most of our knowledge of *antediluvian* times has been built up as a result of one of humanity's grandest collaborative endeavors—the gathering, identification, dating, and categorization of fossils as they are discovered. 我们对史前时代的了解基于人类最庞大的集体努力之———对所发现的化石进行收集、标注、确定年代以及分类。

antipathy / ænˈtɪpəθi / *n.* dislike; hostility 不喜欢，厌恶；敌意

Heathcliff, the protagonist of Emily Bronte's novel *Wuthering Heights*, feels great *antipathy* for Edgar Linton, the man who marries the woman he loves. 艾米莉·勃朗特的小说《呼啸山庄》中的主人公西斯克利夫对娶走了他心上人的埃德加·林顿怀有深深的敌意。

> —— ● 常见学科术语 ● ——
>
> **protagonist:** the main character in a work of literature
> 主人公：文学作品中的主要人物

apathy / ˈæpəθi / *n.* indifference 冷漠

Apathy was high in the election because there was no major controversy or issue to arouse voter interest. 人们对选举的态度非常冷淡，因为没有什么重大争议或问题能引起他们的兴趣。

【派】**apathetic** *adj.* 冷漠的

One criticism of the welfare state is that it makes people overly reliant on government, with the result that democracy is gradually weakened as citizens take a more *apathetic* and detached view of politics. 对福利国家的一个批评是它使人们过度依赖政府，结果是公民对政治越来越漠不关心，从而导致民主的逐渐削弱。

> —— ● 常见学科术语 ● ——
>
> **welfare state:** the provision of welfare services by the state (that is, the government)
> 福利国家：国家(即政府)提供福利的社会

apex / ˈeɪpeks / *n.* the highest point 顶点，最高点

In English literature, classicism reached its *apex* in the poetry of Alexander Pope and the other Augustans. 在英国文学史上，亚历山大·蒲柏和其他奥古斯都文学家的诗歌使古典主义达到巅峰。

> —— ● 常见学科术语 ● ——
>
> **classicism:** an aesthetic tradition that values simplicity, elegance, restraint, and order
> 古典主义：一种美学传统，推崇简洁、优雅、克制以及秩序。
>
> **Augustan:** a period of English literature from around 1700 to 1789. Satire was a feature of the writing of many authors of this period. Two notable authors of the Augustan Age were Alexander Pope and Jonathan Swift.
> 奥古斯都时期：英国文学史上一段时期，约从1700年到1789年。"讽刺文学"是该时期很多作家的写作特征，亚历山大·蒲柏和乔纳森·斯威夫特是两位著名的代表作家。

apogee / ˈæpədʒi: / *n.* ① the point in an orbit most distant from the body being orbited 远点地 ② the highest point 最高点

The Ottoman Empire reached its *apogee* in the seventeenth century, when it controlled a territory running from Budapest to North Africa. 奥斯曼帝国在17世纪达到巅峰，其疆土从布达佩斯延伸到北非。

> —— ● 常见学科术语 ● ——
>
> **Ottoman Empire:** an empire that arose in Anatolia (which corresponds to the Asian portion of modern Turkey) in the fourteenth century, destroying the Byzantine Empire.
> 奥斯曼帝国：公元14世纪从安那托利亚(小亚细亚，今土耳其的亚属部分)兴起的帝国，摧毁了拜占庭帝国。

apothegm / ˈæpoʊθem / *n.* a terse, witty saying 格言，箴言，警句（可拼作apophthegm）

One of the best-known political *apothegms* was written by the British historian Lord Acton: "Power tends to corrupt and absolute power corrupts absolutely." 英国历史学家阿克顿勋爵写下这样一条著名的政治格言："权力滋生腐败，绝对强权滋生绝对腐败。"

appease / əˈpiːz / *v.* to calm; pacify; placate 使镇静，使安静，安抚；绥靖

Many historians have criticized British Prime Minister Neville Chamberlain for trying to *appease* Adolf Hitler in the 1930s. 很多历史学家批判英国首相内维尔·张伯伦在20世纪30年代时竭力对阿道夫·希特勒采取绥靖政策。

REVIEW 5

Matching

Match each word with its definition:

1. anodyne		a.	indifference
2. anomalous		b.	prehistoric
3. antecedent		c.	something that comes before
4. antediluvian		d.	to pacify
5. antipathy		e.	hostility
6. apathy		f.	point in orbit most distant from body being orbited
7. apex		g.	something that soothes pain
8. apogee		h.	the highest point
9. apothegm		i.	irregular
10. appease		j.	terse, witty saying

Fill-ins

Choose the best word to fill in the blank in each sentence.

anodyne	anomalous	antecedents	antediluvian	antipathy
apathy	apex	apogee	apothegms	appease

1. The transistor was the result of a collaborative effort by researchers at Bell Laboratories in New Jersey, one of the world's most advanced scientific and technological laboratories, which had its _____ in the great laboratories created in the late nineteenth century by people like Thomas Edison.

2. In "Strange Meeting," one of Wilfred Owen's poems about World War I, the speaker says that he has no _____ for the foe he killed in battle.

3. The students are trying to overcome public _____ on the issue by setting up exhibitions about it in shopping centers.

4. The scientist asked the lab technician to check the _____ results again.

5. To _____ angry voters the legislature approved a tax cut.

6. The English teacher showed his class the classic film *On the Beach*, but many of the students had trouble appreciating it because of what one student called its "_____ black and white film technology."

7. The eighteenth-century British writer Samuel Johnson is famous for his sage _____, such as "If you are idle, be not solitary; if you are solitary, be not idle."

8. The pastor's comforting words at the child's funeral were an _____ for the grieving family.

9. When the spacecraft reaches its _____ in its orbit around Earth, another craft will be launched from it on a voyage to Mars.

10. Many religions view human beings as standing at the _____ of creation.

Sense or Nonsense

Indicate whether each sentence makes good sense or not.
Put S (SENSE) if it does, and put N (NONSENSE) if it does not.

1. The simple electric circuit consists of a battery and an anodyne. _____

2. Although the scientist's career as a researcher had long since reached its apex, she continued to give valuable guidance to younger scientists. _____

3. The gun is capable of firing deadly apothegms that can rip enemy soldiers apart. _____

4. The anomalous test results mean that the rocket is ready to launch. _____

5. Anthropologists believe that the tribe used animal sacrifice to appease the angry gods. _____

UNIT 6

appellation / ˌæpəˈleɪʃn / *n.* name 命名；名字

The discovery of the bones of a person with the *appellation* Kennewick Man in the state of Washington in 1996 has raised important questions about who the earliest people to populate America were. 1996年在华盛顿州出土并被命名为"肯尼维克人"的遗骨引发了到底谁才是美洲最早居民的重要问题。

apposite / ˈæpəzɪt / *adj.* strikingly appropriate and relevant 非常合适的，非常贴切的

The writer searched two dictionaries and a thesaurus before finding the perfectly *apposite* word he was looking for. 那位作家在找到他想要的最贴切的单词之前，翻阅了两本词典和一本同义词词典。

apprise / əˈpraɪz / *v.* to inform 知会，告知；披露

Nadine Cohodas's biography of the blues singer Dinah Washington keeps the reader *apprised* of the racism black Americans had to endure. 奈丁·科霍达斯在布鲁斯歌手蒂娜·华盛顿的传记中向读者披露了美国黑人不得不忍受的种族歧视。

approbation / ˌæprəˈbeɪʃn / *n.* praise; approval 赞扬，嘉许；认可，批准

The Congressional Medal of Honor is the highest *approbation* an American soldier can receive. 国会荣誉勋章是美国士兵能够获得的最高荣誉。

appropriate / əˈproʊprieɪt / *v.* to take possession for one's own use; confiscate 盗用，挪用；侵占；没收

The invading army *appropriated* supplies from the houses of the local people. 入侵的军队从当地人的房子中掠夺财物。

apropos / ˌæprəˈpoʊ / *adj.* relevant 相关的

Apropos of nothing, the speaker declared that the purpose of life is to love. 那位演说人毫无铺垫地宣称人生的目的在于去爱。

arabesque / ˌærəˈbesk / *n.* ① ornate design featuring intertwined curves 阿拉伯花饰（以互相交织的曲线图案为特色）② a ballet position in which one leg is extended in back while the other supports the weight of the body 阿拉贝斯克舞姿（一脚站立，另一只脚向后伸平的芭蕾舞姿）

The ballerina stunned the audience with her perfectly executed *arabesque*. 那位芭蕾舞女演员以完美的阿拉贝斯克舞姿令所有观众赞叹不已。

archeology / ˌɑːrkiˈɑːlədʒi / *n.* the study of material evidence of past human life 考古学

Carbon-14 dating is of great use in *archeology* because it can determine the age of specimens as old as 35,000 years, but it is of less use in geology because most of the processes studied in this field occurred millions of years ago. 碳-14断代法在考古学上用处非常大，因为它能测定3.5万年前标本的年代，但在地质学上用处就不大，因为地质学领域研究的大都是几百万年前的事。

─── ● 常见学科术语 ● ───

Carbon-14 dating: determining the actual or relative age of an object, of a natural phenomenon, or of a series of events through the use of the isotope carbon-14, which occurs naturally.

碳-14断代法： 通过利用自然界中的碳-14同位素测定一个物体、某种自然现象或某系列事件的真实年代或相对年代。

ardor / ˈɑːrdər / *n.* great emotion or passion 激情，狂热

The twentieth-century American poet Wallace Stevens said, "It is the unknown that excites the *ardor* of scholars, who, in the known alone, would shrivel up with boredom." 20世纪美国诗人华莱士·史蒂文森曾说："未知能激起学者的激情，这些人如果只待在已知世界中就会因厌倦而枯萎。"

arduous / ˈɑːrdʒuəs / *adj.* extremely difficult; laborious 非常困难的；艰辛的

The task of writing a research paper is *arduous*, but if it is broken down into logical steps it becomes less daunting. 写研究论文是非常艰辛的，但如果把这个过程分成几个有逻辑的步骤，就不会那么令人生畏了。

REVIEW 6

Matching

Match each word with its definition:

1. appellation
2. apposite
3. apprise
4. approbation
5. appropriate
6. apropos

a. relevant
b. to confiscate
c. great emotion or passion
d. ornate design
e. name
f. laborious

7. arabesque
8. archeology
9. ardor
10. arduous

g. strikingly appropriate and relevant
h. praise
i. the study of material evidence of past human life
j. to inform

Fill-ins

Choose the best word to fill in the blank in each sentence.

appellation	apposite	apprised	approbation	appropriated
apropos	arabesque	archeology	ardor	arduous

1. Some people felt the remarks were out of place, but others thought they were perfectly _____ .

2. The president ordered his chief of staff to keep him _____ of any changes in the situation.

3. The English professor has started on the _____ task of writing book-length commentaries on all 37 of William Shakespeare's plays.

4. During an economic "bubble" there is a great _____ for speculative investing.

5. _____ provides anthropologists with important information about prehistoric cultures.

6. The city _____ private land to build low-cost housing.

7. The _____ is one of the fundamental ballet poses.

8. Former U.S Supreme Court Justice Byron White was given the _____ "Whizzer" when he played football in college.

9. The fashion book contains the perfect, _____ image to represent 100 famous designers.

10. The young scientist is working 80 hours a week to gain the _____ of her peers.

Sense or Nonsense

Indicate whether each sentence makes good sense or not.
Put S (SENSE) if it does, and put N (NONSENSE) if it does not.

1. The judge rejected the witness' testimony because nothing in it was apropos to the case. _____

2. One of the major questions in modern archaeology is whether God exists or not. _____

3. A comet with the appellation Shoemaker-Levy 9 collided spectacularly with Jupiter in July 1994. _____

4. The group plans to make the arduous ascent of Mt. Everest without oxygen supplies. _____

5. "Jack hit Jim." has an apposite meaning from "Jim was hit by Jack." _____

UNIT 7

argot / ˈɑːrgət / *n.* a specialized vocabulary used by a group 行话，黑话

Writers of crime fiction often use the *argot* of criminals and detectives to create a realistic atmosphere. 犯罪小说作家经常用罪犯和侦探们的行话营造真实的氛围。

arrest / əˈrest / *v.* ① to stop 停止 ② to seize 逮捕 *n.* 停止

Temporary *arrest* of the patient's respiration made it easier for the doctor to perform surgery on him. 令那位病人暂时停止呼吸有利于医生对他实施手术。

artifact / ˈɑːrtɪfækt / *n.* item made by human craft 人工制品；手工艺品

Marxists contend that appreciation of art has declined because capitalism has trained people to perceive human *artifacts* as commodities, and has alienated people from nature, their true humanity, and their creations. 马克思主义者认为人们对艺术的鉴赏力已经大不如前，因为资本主义使人们把手工艺品看作商品，而且使人们远离自然、真正的人性以及人类创造物。

● 常见学科术语 ●

Marxist: a follower of Marxism, the political and economic philosophy of Karl Marx and Friedrich Engels. In Marxism the concept of class struggle plays a central role in understanding society's inevitable development from bourgeois oppression under capitalism to a socialist and ultimately classless society.

马克思主义者：马克思主义政治经济哲学的追随者。马克思主义政治经济哲学是卡尔·马克思和弗里德里克·恩格斯创立的，在这一主义中，阶级斗争这个概念起着主要的作用，有助于理解社会从资本主义下的资产阶级压迫发展到社会主义并最终走向无阶级社会的必然过程。

---

artless / ˈɑːrtləs / *adj.* guileless; natural 纯洁的；真实的；自然的

The source of the meaning of *artless* as guileless is the poet John Dryden, who wrote of William Shakespeare in 1672: "Such *artless* beauty lies in Shakespeare's wit..." 最初赋予artless一词"纯洁的"之意是诗人约翰·德莱顿，他在1672年这样描写莎士比亚："莎士比亚的机智有天然去雕饰之美……"

ascetic / əˈsetɪk / *n.* one who practices self-denial 清心寡欲的人，禁欲者 *adj.* self-denying or austere 禁欲的，清心寡欲的，苦行的

Muslim *ascetics* consider the internal battle against human passions a greater jihad than the struggle against infidels. 穆斯林禁欲者认为同人类欲望所作的内心斗争是一场比针对异教徒的斗争更伟大的圣战。// The writer's *ascetic* lifestyle helped her to concentrate on finishing her novel. 那位作家清心寡欲的生活使她能够专注于完成小说。

【派】**asceticism** *n.* 禁欲主义

One tradition of *asceticism* derives from the belief that the body is fundamentally bad and must be subjugated to the soul. 禁欲主义的一个传统来源于这样一种信仰，即人的肉体从根本上来说是邪恶的，必须用灵魂征服它。

> **jihad:** the religious duty of Muslims to defend their religion (Islam) by war or spiritual struggle against nonbelievers
> 圣战：穆斯林的宗教职责，通过对非伊斯兰教信徒采取武力或精神上的斗争来保卫伊斯兰教。

asperity / æˈsperəti / *n.* severity; harshness; irritability 严厉，严肃；严酷

In his autobiography Gerald Trywhitt, the British writer, composer, artist, and aesthete, recounts a humorous incident: "Many years later, when I was sketching in Rome, a grim-looking Englishwoman came up to me and said with some *asperity*, 'I see you are painting MY view.'" 英国作家、作曲家、画家及审美家杰拉尔德·特来怀特在其自传中，讲述了一件很幽默的事："多年以后当我在罗马写生时，一个表情严肃的英国妇女走到我跟前，严厉地说：'我看到你在画**我的**风景。'"

aspersions / əˈspɜːrʒnz / *n.* slander; false rumor 诽谤，中伤

The republic is a young democracy, and its leaders often respond strongly to journalists and others who cast *aspersions* on their integrity. 该共和国是个年轻的民主国家，其领导人经常激烈回应记者以及其他诽谤他们清白的人。

assiduous / əˈsɪdʒuəs / *adj.* diligent; hard-working 勤勉的，努力工作的

The *assiduous* people of Hong Kong live in a district with one of the highest per capita incomes in the world. 勤勉的香港人使香港成为世界上人均收入最高的地区之一。

assuage / əˈsweɪdʒ / *v.* to make less severe 减轻；缓和

On November 21, 1864, during the Civil War, President Abraham Lincoln wrote the following in a letter to Mrs. Bixby of Boston, who had lost five sons in battle: "I pray that our Heavenly Father may *assuage* the anguish of your bereavement and leave you only the cherished memory of the loved and lost, and the solemn pride that must be yours to have laid so costly a sacrifice upon the altar of freedom." 1864年11月21日美国内战期间，总统亚伯拉罕·林肯在一封写给波士顿那位在战争中失去五个儿子的比克斯柏夫人的信中这样写道："我，祈求天父抚平您的丧子之痛，心中只留下对深爱的已故之人的珍贵回忆，您在自由祭坛前如此昂贵的献祭必为您带来无上的光荣。"

astringent / əˈstrɪndʒənt / *adj.* ① tending to draw together or constrict tissues （能使皮肤或伤口）收敛的，止血的 ② harsh; severe 辛辣的，尖刻的

Bob tends to nick himself when he shaves, so he uses an *astringent* aftershave to stop the bleeding. 鲍勃总在刮脸时划伤自己，所以他用须后收敛水止血。

REVIEW 7

Matching

Match each word with its definition:

1. argot
2. arrest
3. artifact
4. artless
5. ascetic

a. guileless; natural
b. slander
c. item made by human craft
d. to make less severe
e. to stop; seize

6. asperity   f. hard-working

7. aspersion   g. harshness

8. assiduous   h. a specialized vocabulary used by a group

9. assuage   i. harsh; severe

10. astringent   j. one who practices self-denial

Fill-ins

Choose the best word to fill in the blank in each sentence.

argot	**arrest**	**artifact**	**artless**	**ascetic**
asperity	**aspersions**	**assiduously**	**assuage**	**astringent**

1. The young actor's brilliant portrayal of the _____ young boy was the result, paradoxically, of many hours of careful rehearsal.

2. Considering that the two men had been such good friends for so long, we were surprised by the _____ of their attacks on each other.

3. In his book *Confessions*, Saint Augustine tells of his sinful life before he was converted to Christianity and began to live an _____ and virtuous life.

4. Mate, a popular beverage in South America, is similar to tea but is less _____ and often contains more caffeine.

5. Some scholars have argued that the idea of romantic love is an _____ of culture, unique to the West, with its origin in the European tradition of courtly love; however, sociological research has shown that romantic love exists in most cultures.

6. The new drug is able to _____ the development of cancerous cells.

7. That country's leaders talked with a group of American congressional representatives to _____ fears that they plan to threaten American military preeminence.

8. The study's conclusion is that more females attend college than males because girls tend to apply themselves more _____ to their studies than boys.

9. Much of the _____ from the field of information technology that previously was familiar only to experts in the field is now used in everyday conversation ("Internet Service Provider," for example).

10. The report in the newspaper cast _____ on the candidate.

Sense or Nonsense

Indicate whether each sentence makes good sense or not.
Put S (SENSE) if it does, and put N (NONSENSE) if it does not.

1. The hungry people gratefully received the aspersions from the charity. _____

2. The crew of the submarine bid their families farewell before setting off on their long argot. _____

3. The poet Walt Whitman quotes John Burroughs's comment on the writer Henry David Thoreau: "He improves with age—in fact, it requires age to take off a little of his asperity, and fully ripen him." _____

4. "My comments on your book were merely astringent, not venomous," the critic said to the author. _____

5. The writer James Boswell is so famous for his assiduous recording of Samuel Johnson's words that the word "Boswell" now refers to a person who admires another so greatly that he or she records their words and deeds. _____

UNIT 8

asylum / əˈsaɪləm / *n.* a place of refuge or shelter 避难所；庇护

The Stoic, accused of seeking *asylum* in the consolations of philosophy, rebutted this charge, saying that Stoicism is simply the most prudent and realistic philosophy to follow. 人们批评斯多葛学派是在哲学的慰藉中寻找避难所，但他们反驳说，斯多葛哲学是最审慎、最现实的哲学，理当追随。

• 常见学科术语 •

Stoic: follower of Stoicism, a pantheistic philosophy emphasizing submission to divine will and freedom from emotion

斯多葛派：斯多葛哲学的追随者。斯多葛哲学是一种泛神论哲学观，强调顺从神圣的意志并消除个人情感。

---

atavism / ˈætəvɪzəm/ *n.* ① in biology, the reappearance of a characteristic in an organism after several generations of absence 【生】隔代遗传，返祖现象 ② individual or a part that exhibits atavism 返祖体 ③ return of a trait after a period of absence 重现

Some modern political theorists reject nationalism as a tribal *atavism*. 一些现代政治理论家不接受民族主义是部落返祖现象的观点。

attenuate / əˈtenjueɪt / *v.* to weaken 变小，变细；减弱

Modern digital radio equipment allows even signals that have been greatly *attenuated* to be transmitted by one station and received by another station. 现代数字无线电装置甚至能让已经变得非常微弱的信号从一个电台发出并被另一个电台接收。

audacious / ɔːˈdeɪʃəs / *adj.* bold; daring 大胆的，勇敢的

The German army commander Erwin Rommel was known as the "Desert Fox" as a result of his *audacious* surprise attacks on Allied forces in World War II. 德军统帅埃尔温·隆梅尔，因其在二战中屡次大胆突袭盟军而赢得"沙漠之狐"的称号。

austere / ɔːˈstɪr / *adj.* ① stern 严肃的，苛刻的 ② unadorned 朴素的，不加装饰的

Deism is an *austere* belief that reflects the predominant philosophy of the Age of Enlightenment: a universe symmetrical and governed by rationality. 自然神论是一种朴素的信仰，反映了启蒙运动时期盛行的哲学观：宇宙是对称的，并由理性统治。

deism: the belief in a God who created the universe and then abandoned it, assuming no control over life or natural phenomena, and giving no supernatural revelation

自然神论：该理论认为神在创造了世界后就遗弃了世界，不对生命及自然现象进行掌控，也不给出超自然的启示。

Age of Enlightenment: a period in European philosophy during the eighteenth century that emphasized reason

启蒙运动时期：18世纪欧洲哲学史上的一个时期，强调理性。

autonomous / ɔːˈtɑːnəməs / *adj.* self-governing; independent 自治的；自主的，独立的

Some biologists have theorized that our belief in our ability to act as *autonomous* agents is in conformity with the theory of evolution because it gives us a sense of meaning and purpose in our lives that helps us to survive. 一些生物学家提出这样的理论：人类对"自己是自治的主体"这一观点的信仰和进化论是一致的，因为它给了我们人生一种意义感和目标感，让我们得以生存。

theory of evolution: the theory that living things originate from other similar organisms and that differences between types of organisms are due to modifications in successive generations. A central tenet of Darwinian evolution is that surviving individuals of a species vary in a way that enables them to live longer and reproduce, thus passing this advantage to future generations (Natural Selection).

进化论：该理论认为所有的生物都是从其他相似的生物进化而来，各种生物间的区别是由连续数代的演化造成的。达尔文进化论的一个核心思想是一个物种中存活下来的个体会产生变异，从而使它们活得更长，并进行繁衍，把这一优势遗传给后代（这就是所谓的自然选择）。

avarice / ˈævərɪs / *n.* greed 贪婪

Successful investment bankers are sometimes accused of *avarice*; their defenders, however, say that they are simply very good at what they do and should be rewarded accordingly. 成功的投资银行家们经常被指摘为过于贪婪，而他们的捍卫者则说，他们只不过是精于本职工作，理应获得相应回报。

aver / əˈvɜːr / *v.* to affirm; declare to be true 断言；宣布⋯真实；确认

Yogis *aver* that everyone has a guru, whether it be a person, God, or the experiences of the world, that helps him or her practice the yoga that is in accordance with his or her nature, and assists on the path toward enlightenment. 瑜伽士认为每个人都有属于自己的古鲁，不论它是人、神还是对世界的体验，都能帮助他们练习符合自己天性的瑜伽，从而实现开悟。

yogi: a yogi is the Sanskrit (an ancient Indian language) name for a man who practices yoga. A woman who practices yoga is a yogini.

瑜伽士：瑜伽士是梵语（古印度语言）中对练习瑜伽的男子的称呼。女人则叫瑜伽女。

guru: a personal spiritual teacher. The term is also used to refer to a trusted advisor or an authority.

古鲁：个人精神导师，也用于指令人信任的指导者或权威人士。

> **yoga:** spiritual practices in the Hindu and Buddhist religions that are believed to help one to attain higher awareness and union with God
>
> **瑜伽：** 盛行于印度教和佛教地区的一种修行，人们认为它能帮助人实现更高的觉悟从而与神灵融汇。

avocation / ˌævoʊˈkeɪʃn / n. secondary occupation 第二职业，副业；业务爱好

Dan became so proficient at his *avocation* — computer programming — that he is thinking of giving up his job as a teacher to do it full time. 电脑编程原本是丹的副业，但他现在已经很精通了，以至于他正在考虑放弃教师一职，而将此作为自己的全职工作。

avuncular / əˈvʌŋkjələr / adj. like an uncle, benevolent and tolerant 像叔叔(伯伯)那样的；谆谆长辈风范的；慈祥的；宽容的

Walter Cronkite, who was the anchorman of Columbia Broadcasting System (CBS) News during much of the 1970s and 1980s, had an *avuncular* manner that made him one of America's most trusted personalities. 沃尔特·克朗凯在1970–1980年间的大部分时间里都担任美国哥伦比亚广播公司的新闻主持人，其如谆谆长者的主持风格，使他成为美国最受信任的知名人士之一。

REVIEW 8

Matching

Match each word with its definition:

1. asylum		a.	stern; unadorned
2. atavism		b.	return of a trait after a period of absence
3. attenuate		c.	greed
4. audacious		d.	secondary occupation
5. austere		e.	bold; daring
6. autonomous		f.	like an uncle
7. avarice		g.	self-governing; independent
8. aver		h.	a place of refuge
9. avocation		i.	to affirm
10. avuncular		j.	to weaken

Fill-ins

Choose the best word to fill in the blank in each sentence.

asylum	**atavism**	**attenuate**	**audacious**	**austere**
autonomous	**avarice**	**avers**	**avocation**	**avuncular**

1. It is important to have an _____ judiciary so that laws can be interpreted free of political influence and considerations.
2. The monks live in _____ quarters.
3. Scientists examining the whale discovered an _____ : it had two legs.
4. The _____ teacher is popular with students.
5. Many people prefer to pursue an _____ that is very different from their occupation.

6. The United States and Britain have long histories of offering _____ to victims of persecution.

7. The plan to eliminate hunger in the world is an _____ one, but it can be achieved if all the nations of the world cooperate.

8. A criticism that has been made of capitalism is that it encourages _____ .

9. Materialism is a philosophy that _____ that matter is the only reality and denies the existence of idealism and spiritualism.

10. Aspirin has the power to _____ a fever.

Sense or Nonsense

Indicate whether each sentence makes good sense or not.
Put S (SENSE) if it does, and put N (NONSENSE) if it does not.

1. The doctor is considering surgery because of the atavism in the patient's left eye. _____

2. Before giving testimony at a trial, each witness must solemnly aver that he or she is telling the truth. _____

3. Shortly after taking office in 1977, President Jimmy Carter fulfilled his campaign promise to pardon young men who had sought asylum in Canada because of their opposition to the war in Vietnam and to the military draft. _____

4. There is a strong tradition that physicians should practice medicine to ease human suffering rather than be motivated by avarice. _____

5. The singer's voice was so attenuated by the PA system that she could be heard even outside the stadium. _____

UNIT 9

axiomatic / ˌæksɪə'mætɪk / *adj.* taken for granted 理所当然的，想当然的

In nineteenth-century geology, uniformitarianism was the antithesis of catastrophism, asserting that it was *axiomatic* that natural law and processes do not fundamentally change, and that what we observe now is essentially the same as what occurred in the past. 在19世纪地质学研究中，均变说一直和灾变说针锋相对，前者想当然地认为自然法则和自然进程并没有发生质变，我们现在所观察到的实际上和过去所发生的是一样的。

• 常见学科术语 •

uniformitarianism: a geological theory popular in the nineteenth century. Uniformitarianism holds that geological processes have slowly shaped the Earth and continue to do so.
均变说：盛行于19世纪的一种地质理论，认为地质进程缓慢地塑造着并将继续塑造着地球。

catastrophism: a theory that was a rival to uniformitarianism. It postulates an Earth formed in a series of unique, catastrophic events.
灾变说：和均变说相抗衡的一种地质理论，认为地球是在一系列独特的、灾难性的事件中形成的。

bacchanalian / ˌbækəˈneɪliən / *adj.* ① pertaining to riotous or drunken festivity 酒神节的 ② pertaining to revelry 狂饮作乐的

For some people New Year's Eve is an occasion for *bacchanalian* revelry. 对很多人来说，新年除夕夜是纵情狂饮的时候。

● 常见学科术语 ●

Bacchus: known as Dionysos to the ancient Greeks, Bacchus was the god of agriculture, fertility, and wine. He was worshipped by an emotional cult that held secret rites called Bacchanalia—wild orgies of frenzied revelry, drunkenness, and debauchery. Bacchanalian is derived from Bacchanalia.

巴克斯：古希腊人称之为狄厄尼索斯，是农神、丰饶之神、酒神以及狂欢之神。狂热的人们举行秘密的仪式来祭拜他，这仪式即"酒神节"，在这天人们纵情狂欢，开怀畅饮，放浪形骸。bacchanalian就是从Bacchanalia 派生而来。

---

banal / bəˈnɑːl / *adj.* commonplace; trite 平常的，平庸的；陈腐的，老套的

The writer has a gift for making even the most *banal* observation seem important and original. 那位作家很有天分，能让看上去最平淡无奇的评论都显得至关重要而且颇具匠心。

banter / ˈbæntər / *n.* playful conversation 戏谈，打趣

The governor engaged in some *banter* with reporters before getting to the serious business of the news conference. 严肃的新闻发布会开始前，州长与记者们打趣着说些什么。

bard / bɑːrd / *n.* poet（游吟）诗人

The great *bards* of English literature have all been masters of the techniques of verse. 英国文学史上那些伟大的诗人都擅长写韵文。

bawdy / ˈbɔːdi / *adj.* obscene 淫秽的

Geoffrey Chaucer's *Canterbury Tales* is the story of a group of Christian pilgrims who entertain one another with stories, ranging from the holy to the *bawdy*, on their journey to Canterbury Cathedral. 杰弗里·乔叟的《坎特伯雷故事集》讲述了一群基督朝圣者在前往坎特伯雷大教堂的路上讲故事以互相娱乐，故事内容从神圣的到淫秽的都有。

beatify / biˈætɪfaɪ / *v.* to sanctify; bless; ascribe a virtue to 为…行宣福礼；使神圣化；祈福；赋予（美德等）

In the year 2000 Pope John Paul II traveled to Fatima in Portugal to *beatify* two of the three children who said they saw the appearance of the Virgin Mary there in 1917. 2000年，教皇约翰·保罗二世前往葡萄牙的法蒂玛市为三位自称1917年在该地见到圣母显灵的儿童中的两位行宣福礼。

【派】**beatification** *n.* 赐福；宣福礼

Beatification is the second and next to last step on the path to sainthood. 宣福礼是成为圣人之路上的第二步，也是封圣前的最后一步。

bedizen / bɪˈdɪzn / *v.* to dress in a vulgar, showy manner 过分地打扮

Paul went to the costume party *bedizened* as a seventeenth-century French aristocrat. 保罗把自己打扮成了一个招摇的17世纪贵族去参加化装舞会。

behemoth / bɪˈhiːməθ / *n.* a huge creature; anything very large and powerful 巨兽；庞然大物

In the 1980s and 1990s, the trend in American business was toward increased privatization of government industries (such as power generation), partly because it was believed that private industry is more efficient and partly because foreign private companies were becoming commercial *behemoths*, outstripping government-owned companies in competitiveness. 二十世纪八九十年代，美国的商业发展趋势是国有经济日益私有化（如电力部门），部分原因是人们认为私有经济更高效，还有部分原因是外国私营公司逐渐成为商业巨擘，比民营企业更有竞争力。

belie / bɪˈlaɪ / *v*. ① to contradict 同…相抵触 ② to misrepresent; give a false impression 掩饰，给以假象

The boxer's childlike face *belies* the ferocity with which he can attack opponents in the ring. 那名拳击手孩子般的面孔掩饰了他在拳台上攻击对手时的凶狠。

REVIEW 9

Matching

Match each word with its definition:

1. axiomatic		a.	playful conversation
2. bacchanalian		b.	to give a false impression
3. banal		c.	pertaining to riotous or drunken activity
4. banter		d.	dress in a vulgar, showy manner
5. bard		e.	obscene
6. bawdy		f.	commonplace
7. beatify		g.	a huge creature
8. bedizen		h.	taken for granted
9. behemoth		i.	poet
10. belie		j.	to bless; sanctify

Fill-ins

Choose the best word to fill in the blank in each sentence.

axiomatic	**bacchanalian**	**banal**	**banter**	**bard**
bawdy	**beatification**	**bedizen**	**behemoths**	**belie**

1. The comedian dropped the _____ jokes from his routine for his appearance on national television.
2. The _____ Ted Hughes was appointed Britain's Poet Laureate in 1984.
3. Women in nonpolygamous societies often express amazement that several women could share one husband without friction, taking it as _____ that couples are the norm, and that any departure from it must be wrong.
4. At first, college seemed to _____ all the good things Steve had heard about it in high school; gradually, however, he came to like it.
5. First IBM, next Microsoft and then Google became the _____ of the computer industry.
6. The TV show's producer tries to steer a middle path between making a typical _____ program and being so original that much of the audience is lost.

7. The queen decided to _____ herself with expensive jewelry for the ball.

8. In the Roman Catholic Church, the final stage in the path to sainthood is canonization, which occurs after _____ .

9. The college's annual spring break party in Florida is a/an _____ affair.

10. The world leaders enjoyed some friendly _____ before getting down to the serious business of the negotiations.

Sense or Nonsense

Indicate whether each sentence makes good sense or not.
Put S (SENSE) if it does, and put N (NONSENSE) if it does not.

1. The prisoner was beatified by the jury and sentenced to ten years imprisonment. _____

2. The band's backstage crew often exchange banter during long rehearsals. _____

3. The principle that every person has certain fundamental rights is regarded by most people as axiomatic. _____

4. The ascetic monks regularly hold bacchanalian parties. _____

5. The question of whether the Greek bard Homer was a single individual or the name given to several authors is still hotly debated by scholars. _____

UNIT 10

beneficent / bɪˈnefɪsnt / *adj.* kindly; doing good 慈善的，仁爱的；行善的

The theologian discussed the question of why a *beneficent* and omnipotent God allows bad things to happen to good people. 那位神学家论述了为什么仁慈的、无所不能的上帝会让好人落难。

bifurcate / ˈbaɪfərkeɪt / *v.* to divide into two parts 分支，分叉；分开

Contemporary physicists generally *bifurcate* their discipline into two parts—classical physics and modern physics; the former are the fields of study that were already well developed before the momentous breakthroughs of the early twentieth century by scientists such as Albert Einstein, Niels Bohr, and Werner Heisenberg, which inaugurated the age of modern physics. 现代物理学家通常将物理学分为两部分——经典物理学和现代物理学。在20世纪早期，阿尔伯特·爱因斯坦、尼尔斯·波尔以及维尔纳·海森堡等科学家在物理学上取得了重大突破，宣告现代物理学的开始；而在此之前已经发展得比较完善的研究领域则属于经典物理学的范畴。

【派】**bifurcation** *n.* 分支，分叉；分开

Some people regard the Hindu-Buddhist philosophy on animals as more in accordance with the modern scientific view than the traditional Western view, since it does not posit a radical *bifurcation* of man and nature. 一些人认为印度佛教关于动物的看法较传统的西方观点更符合现代科学理念，因为它们并不假定人与自然的彻底分离。

blandishment / ˈblændɪʃmənt / *n.* flattery 奉承

Despite the salesperson's *blandishments*, Donna did not buy the car. 尽管销售人员不停阿谀奉承，唐娜还是没买那辆车。

【派】**blandish** *v.* to coax with flattery 哄骗；奉承

blasé / blɑːˈzeɪ / *adj.* bored because of frequent indulgence; unconcerned 饱享生厌的；不关心的

We were amazed by John's *blasé* attitude toward school; he seems to have made it a rule never to open a book. 约翰对学校生活极端厌倦，我们对此非常惊讶，他似乎把不看书当成了常规。

bolster / ˈboʊlstər / *v.* to give a boost to; prop up; support 给予支持；支撑

The President has visited the state several times to *bolster* his sagging popularity there. 总统数次访问该州，以挽回他不断下降的支持率。

bombastic / bɑːmˈbæstɪk / *adj.* pompous; using inflated language 夸夸其谈的，言辞浮夸的

Nearly lost in the senator's long, *bombastic* speech were several sensible ideas. 那个参议员冗长的、夸夸其谈的演讲险些埋没了几个合理的观点。

boorish / ˈbʊrɪʃ / *adj.* ① rude 粗野的，笨拙的 ② insensitive 不敏感的，迟钝的

Bob apologized for his *boorish* behavior at the party, saying he hadn't realized that it was such a formal occasion. 鲍勃对他在宴会上的粗鲁行为表示歉意，他说自己并未意识到那是个如此正式的场合。

bovine / ˈboʊvaɪn / *adj.* cowlike 像牛的；愚笨的；反应迟钝的

Following the slow-moving group of students up the long path to the school's entrance, the word "*bovine*" popped into the English teacher's mind. 跟在缓慢移动的学生队伍后面，走在通往学校正门的漫漫长路上，那位英语教师脑海中闪现出"bovine(像牛的)"这个词。

brazen / ˈbreɪzn / *adj.* bold; shameless 胆大妄为的；厚颜无耻的

The *brazen* student irritated his teacher by saying that he could learn more from a day spent "surfing" the World Wide Web than a day spent in school. 那个大胆的学生说他在网上冲浪一天学到的东西要比在学校待一天学到的多，这让老师大为恼火。

broach / broʊtʃ / *v.* to mention for the first time 初次谈起

Steve's boss knew that she couldn't put off warning him about his poor performance and decided to *broach* the subject the next time she saw him. 史蒂夫的老板明白她不能再拖了，一定要对他在工作中的糟糕表现给予警告，并决定下次跟史蒂夫见面时谈论此事。

REVIEW 10

Matching

Match each word with its definition:

1. beneficent	a.	flattery
2. bifurcate	b.	cowlike
3. blandishment	c.	kindly; doing good
4. blasé	d.	bold
5. bolster	e.	bored because of frequent indulgence
6. bombastic	f.	to mention for the first time
7. boorish	g.	to give a boost to

8. bovine   h. rude; insensitive
9. brazen   i. to divide into two parts
10. broach   j. pompous; using inflated language

Fill-ins

Choose the best word to fill in the blank in each sentence.

beneficence	bifurcation	blandishments	blasé	bolstered
bombastic	**boorish**	**bovine**	**brazen**	**broached**

1. The coach warned the lacrosse team not to become _____ even though they had won a school record 20 matches the previous season.

2. There is a _____ in American politics between a tradition that believes that interference in the affairs of other countries is imprudent, and an idealistic streak that seeks to use American power to help other countries.

3. Bill Gates showed his _____ by setting up with his wife Melinda a foundation to provide financial help to, among other things, fight disease in the Third World.

4. Amanda went out with her boyfriend for two years before she _____ the subject of marriage.

5. The audience listened to the boring speech with _____ expressions on their faces.

6. Russian historians have shown how the Soviet leader Joseph Stalin used a mixture of arguments, _____ , and threats to overcome resistance to his repressive policies among his fellow Politburo members.

7. The small company startled investors by its _____ takeover of a company with three times its assets.

8. Many people in the audience were annoyed at the _____ behavior of the two men who talked loudly to each other through the entire movie.

9. The President's speechwriter told him that she was doing her best to write a speech that was serious and solemn but not _____ .

10. The prosecutor's case was _____ by the new testimony of a credible witness.

Sense or Nonsense

Indicate whether each sentence makes good sense or not.
Put S (SENSE) if it does, and put N (NONSENSE) if it does not.

1. Satan is often portrayed as the embodiment of malevolence and beneficence. _____

2. The actor is admired by everyone for her boorish behavior. _____

3. The brazen student demanded that the teacher postpone the test so she would have more time to study for it. _____

4. The general visited the troops to bolster their morale before the crucial battle. _____

5. Jim is so blasé about the upcoming GRE test that he is studying six hours a day for it. _____

42

UNIT 11

音频

bucolic / bjuːˈkɑːlɪk / *adj.* characteristic of the countryside; rustic; pastoral 田园风光的；乡村的

The south end of Toronto's beautiful High Park is a *bucolic* expanse of land that is perfect for anyone wanting a quiet walk. 多伦多市南端的高地公园面积广阔，富有田园气息，是安静散步的理想去处。

burgeon / ˈbɜːrdʒən / *v.* to flourish 迅速发展；苗壮成长

After World War II, the increased speed of industrialization and the *burgeoning* world population resulted in such an increase in pollution that it began to be recognized by some people as a threat to the human habitat, Earth. "二战"后，全球工业化进程加速，人口激增，导致污染的加剧，使得很多人开始认识到这将威胁人类生活的家园——地球。

burnish / ˈbɜːrnɪʃ / *v.* to polish 擦亮；磨光

The poet T. S. Eliot *burnished* his reputation as one of the master poets of the twentieth century with *Four Quartets*, four long poems published between 1936 and 1942. T.S.艾略特的《四个四重奏》——四首发表于1936年至1942年间的长诗为他20世纪伟大诗人的声誉增光添彩。

buttress / ˈbʌtrəs / *v.* to reinforce; support 加强；支持

Some critics of the American legal system argue that the requirement of proving guilt "beyond a reasonable doubt" is too difficult a criterion to use, and *buttress* their case by citing the fact that objective studies suggest that only a very small number of criminals are successfully prosecuted. 美国立法体系的批评者们认为要求证明任何罪行"无合理疑问"这一原则非常难以付诸实践，而且他们引用下述事实来支撑他们的论点，即客观研究表明只有一小部分罪犯最终被成功起诉。

cacophonous / kəˈkɑːfənəs / *adj.* unpleasant or harsh-sounding 刺耳的，声音不和谐的

The dissonant harmonies of the great jazz pianist and composer Thelonious Monk might seem *cacophonous* to some listeners, but to many jazz aficionados they are sublime. 对一些听众来说，伟大的爵士乐钢琴家和作曲家赛隆尼斯•蒙克毫不协调的协奏曲听起来刺耳不堪，可对于爵士乐发烧友来说那却是天籁之音。

【派】**cacophony** *n.* a jarring, unpleasant noise 刺耳嘈杂的噪音

● 常见学科术语 ●

aficionados: people who are enthusiastic admirers or followers

发烧友：狂热的崇拜者和追随者

---

cadge / kædʒ / *v.* to beg; sponge 行乞，乞讨；请求，索取

An enduring image of the Great Depression in America is the out-of-work man *cadging* money with the line, "Hey, mister, can you spare a dime for a cup of coffee?" 美国大萧条时期的一个经典画面是：一个失业的男人沿街乞讨："嘿，先生，赏几个子儿让我喝杯咖啡吧！"

callous / ˈkæləs / *adj.* thick-skinned; insensitive 起茧的；不敏感的；冷漠的

Jim's terrible experiences in the war have made him *callous* about the suffering of others. 战争中的可怕经历使吉姆对他人的痛苦漠不关心。

calumny / ˈkæləmni / *n.* false and malicious accusation; slander 诽谤，中伤；谣言

"Be thou chaste as ice, as pure as snow, thou shalt not escape *calumny*."

—William Shakespeare, Hamlet Act III, Scene 1

(Hamlet addressing Ophelia)

"也许你坚贞如冰，纯洁如雪，但仍逃不过他人的诽谤。"

——威廉·莎士比亚，《哈姆雷特》第三幕第一场

(哈姆雷特对奥菲利娅如是说)

canard / kəˈnɑːrd / *n.* false, deliberately misleading story 谎言，谣传

Most politicians do not want to be associated with the old *canard* that big government in Washington can solve all of America's problems. 多数政治家都不愿意与那句古老的谎言——位于华盛顿的强大政府能解决美国一切问题——联系在一起。

canon / ˈkænən / *n.* ① an established principle; a basis or standard for judgment 标准，准则 ② the works of a writer that have been accepted as authentic 真作 *adj.* 教会的

Canons of aesthetic taste vary over the years; the Rococo period, for example, valued ornate art. 人们的审美标准随着年代变化而变化，比如洛可可时代就推崇装饰艺术。// The 60-volume *Great Books of the Western World* is an attempt to gather the central *canon* of Western civilization into one collection. 60卷本的《西方世界的伟大著作》试图囊括西方文明的核心作品。// The system of civil law originated in the Roman Empire and was kept alive in the Middle Ages in the *canon* law of the Church. 民法体系起源于罗马帝国时期，并通过中世纪教会的教会法得以保存下来。

【派】canonical *adj.* 真经的；权威的

The English professor is trying to persuade the chairperson of her department to let her teach some writers that are not *canonical.* 英文教授正在试图说服系主任允许她在课上介绍几位非主流作家。

REVIEW 11

Matching

Match each word with its definition:

1. bucolic
2. burgeon
3. burnish
4. buttress
5. cacophonous
6. cadge
7. callous
8. calumny
9. canard
10. canon

a. to polish
b. to reinforce
c. to beg
d. false, misleading story
e. an established principle
f. characteristic of the countryside
g. insensitive
h. to flourish
i. unpleasant or harsh-sounding
j. false, malicious accusation

Fill-ins

Choose the best word to fill in the blank in each sentence.

bucolic	burgeoning	burnish	buttress	cacophonous
cadge	callous	calumny	canard	canon

1. The _____ of modern communications has made fiber optics nearly indispensable because of its ability to transmit vast amounts of information.

2. The link between economic boom and war is used by Marxists to _____ their view that capitalism thrives on war, and to some degree, encourages it in periods of low economic activity.

3. How many times have you heard the old _____ "Those who can, do; those who can't, teach"?

4. A traditional olive farm is a _____ sight: big trees spaced fairly far apart providing good cover for grass and grazing animals.

5. The student is well known for his tendency to _____ money from his friends.

6. The company's new advertising campaign is intended to _____ its image as a dynamic, forward-looking firm.

7. The movie star sued the newspaper for printing _____ about him.

8. The task the poultry farm worker looked forward to the least was going into the _____ hen yard at feeding time.

9. The public relations director's comments that the inmates had hanged themselves as a public relations stunt was widely regarded as showing a _____ disregard for life.

10. The nineteenth-century French composer Hector Berlioz has become a central figure in the Western musical _____.

Sense or Nonsense

Indicate whether each sentence makes good sense or not.

Put S (SENSE) if it does, and put N (NONSENSE) if it does not.

1. It may sound odd, but I actually enjoy the cacophonous sound of an orchestra tuning up. _____

2. The artist is painting a bucolic rush hour scene in Manhattan. _____

3. We sailed our canard around the world last year. _____

4. Government officials in China are concerned about the burgeoning numbers of old people in their country. _____

5. Steve buttressed his position in the pharmaceutical company by earning a Ph.D. in chemistry. _____

UNIT 12

cant / kænt / *n.* ① a insincere talk 伪善的言辞 ② language of a particular group 术语，行话

Many of the beat artists of the 1950s reacted against what they regarded as the *cant* of bourgeois society. 20世纪50年代，许多垮掉一代艺术家对他们认为的资产阶级社会伪善言辞进行反抗。

• 常见学科术语 •
---

bourgeois: both bourgeois and bourgeoisie come from Old French burgeis, citizen of a bourg （town）. Bourgeois refers to a person who belongs to the middle class or has middle-class attitudes. It can be used in a neutral way. However, it is frequently used to suggest that someone is not sophisticated.

资产阶级：bourgeois和bourgeoisie都是从古法语burgeis演变而来，原指城镇（bourg）的居民。bourgeois指资产阶级或持有资产阶级观点的人。这个词是中性的，但人们经常用它描述不够有教养的人。

cantankerous / kæn'tæŋkərəs / *adj.* irritable; ill-humored 急躁的；坏脾气的

Many of us have in our mind the stereotype of the *cantankerous* old man who is constantly complaining about something or other. 在我们很多人的脑海中，那个坏脾气的老人都是一个不停抱怨这抱怨那的僵化形象。

capricious / kə'prɪʃəs / *adj.* fickle 易变的，无常的

The rule of law is regarded by many historians as one of humanity's great achievements because since its inception citizens are no longer subject to *capricious* decisions and penalties of rulers. 很多历史学家认为，法治是人类最伟大的成就之一。自它创立伊始，人们就不再受制于统治者反复无常的决定和惩罚。

【派】**caprice** *n.* an inclination to change one's mind compulsively 反复无常；任性

Styles in high fashion seem governed by *caprice* as much as anything else. 与其他任何事物一样，高级时装的式样似乎也变化无常。

captious /ˈkæpʃəs/ *adj.* ① faultfinding 吹毛求疵的 ② intended to entrap, as in an argument 糊弄人的

The pedantic and *captious* critic seems incapable of appreciating the merits of even the most highly regarded books. 那位学究气十足、吹毛求疵的批评家似乎连最受推崇的书籍的优点都难以体会。

cardinal /ˈkɑːrdɪnl/ *adj.* of foremost importance 最重要的

The *cardinal* rule of any weight-loss diet must be limiting the intake of calories. 任何减肥食谱都要遵循的首要原则就是限制热量的摄入。

carnal /ˈkɑːrnl/ *adj.* of the flesh or body; related to physical appetites 身体的，肉体的；和肉欲有关的

The yogi's goal is to achieve nirvana through, among other things, the overcoming of *carnal* desires. 瑜伽修行者的目标是实现涅槃，这首先要克服身体的欲望。

● 常见学科术语 ●

nirvana: ideal condition of rest, harmony, or joy. Nirvana is from Sanskrit nirvanam（a blowing out）, as in the blowing out of a flame. According to Buddhism and Hinduism, in order to reach nirvana one must extinguish the fire fueled by the ego, which causes suffering, ignorance, delusion, and greed.

涅槃：平静、和谐或快乐的理想境界。该词来自梵语nirvanam（火焰熄灭）。佛教和印度教认为，要达到涅槃，人必须熄灭由自我燃起的欲望之火，它是痛苦、无知、妄想和贪欲的源泉。

---

carp /kɑːrp/ *v.* to find fault; complain 找茬儿，吹毛求疵；抱怨

Cost-benefit analysis owes much of its origin to utilitarian thought; despite the *carping* of critics that such analysis is based on faulty premises, the technique has proved useful in many areas. 成本效益分析在很大程度上源于功利主义的思想。尽管有一些吹毛求疵的批评家声称这种分析是基于错误的前提，但这种方法已被证实在很多领域都有用。

● 常见学科术语 ●

cost-benefit analysis: the process of weighing the total expected costs against the total expected benefits of one or more actions in order to choose the best option

成本效益分析：为了做出最好选择，对一个或多个行为预期的总成本与总收益进行权衡的过程。

utilit arian: the ethical philosophy that human activity should be aimed at achieving the greatest good for the greatest number. Jeremy Bentham was the founder of the theory and his student John Stuart Mill was its most famous proponent. Mill used the theory to argue for social reform and increased democracy.

功利主义：道德哲学中的一个概念，认为人类的行为应以实现最多数人的最大的善为目标。杰里米·边沁是功利主义的创始人，他的学生约翰·斯图尔特·穆勒是其最著名的支持者。穆勒利用这个理论支持社会改革并推进民主事业。

---

cartography /kɑːrˈtɑːgrəfi/ *n.* science of making maps 制图学

Satellites in Earth orbit take pictures of topography that have greatly aided *cartography*. 地球轨道上的卫星所拍摄的地貌图给制图学提供了莫大的帮助。

caste /kæst/ *n.* ① any of the hereditary social classes of Hindu society 印度的世袭阶级 ② social stratification 种姓制度；社会等级制度 *adj.* 等级的

The dalits, formerly known as untouchables, are at the bottom of the thousands of *castes* that make up Indian society. 印度的"贱民"（达利特人），以前被叫作"不可接触者"，处于组成印度社会的几千个种姓的最底层。// Most modern corporations employ a sort of *caste* system, with senior executives at the top and ordinary workers at the bottom. 大多数现代公司都采用这样一种等级制度——高级执行者高高在上，普通员工处于底层。

● 常见学科术语 ●

There are four main **castes** or hereditary groups （and thousands of subcastes）in Hindu society that restrict the occupations of members and limit their interaction with members of other castes.

There are four main castes:

    Brahmans （priests and teachers）

    Kshatriyas （noblemen）

    Vaisyas （merchants and traders）

    Sudras （laborers）

A fifth group, called "Harijans" or "untouchables" are considered impure and are discriminated against. They toil in lowly occupations such as cleaning up waste and leatherworking.

印度社会中有四大种姓(也称世袭集团，下有数千个次种姓)，这些种姓限制了其成员所从事的工作，同时也限制了他们与其他种姓人间的接触。这四大种姓分别是：

    婆罗门(祭司和教师)

    刹帝利(贵族)

    吠舍(商人和手工业者)

    首陀罗(劳动者)

第五类叫作"贱民"或"不可接触者"，他们被认为是不纯洁的，饱受歧视，只能从事垃圾清理或皮革制作之类的低等职业。

---

castigation / ˌkæstɪˈɡeɪʃn / *n.* punishment; chastisement; criticism 惩罚；指责

Many British writers recall with loathing the *castigation* they received at school. 许多英国作家一回想起他们在学生时期受到的惩罚就感到憎恶。

REVIEW 12

Matching

Match each word with its definition:

1.	cant	a.	of foremost importance
2.	cantankerous	b.	fickle
3.	capricious	c.	science of making maps
4.	captious	d.	insincere talk
5.	cardinal	e.	of the flesh or body
6.	carnal	f.	hereditary social class of Hindu society
7.	carp	g.	to complain
8.	cartography	h.	punishment
9.	caste	i.	irritable
10.	castigation	j.	faultfinding

Fill-ins

Choose the best word to fill in the blank in each sentence.

cant	cantankerous	capricious	captious	cardinal
carnal	carping	cartography	caste	castigated

1. The military employs a type of _____ system with generals at the top and privates at the bottom.
2. Commentators dismissed the speech as the mere _____ of someone desperately trying to be reelected.
3. The English teacher is so pedantic and _____ in her marking that her students have become discouraged.
4. It is a postulate of science that the laws of nature are not _____ and that the universe is not chaotic.
5. According to this book the _____ rule of good writing is to be clear.
6. Rococo painting often reflects the great pleasure the French aristocracy took in all things _____.
7. The ability of modern _____ to produce very accurate maps of the Earth's surface has been a boon to navigators.
8. The boss _____ the worker for losing the important client's file.
9. The band decided to continue to play in their new style despite the _____ of critics who said it was a sell-out to commercial interests.
10. The _____ old man is always getting into arguments with people.

Sense or Nonsense

Indicate whether each sentence makes good sense or not.
Put S (SENSE) if it does, and put N (NONSENSE) if it does not.

1. The judge is respected by legal scholars for her capricious rulings. _____
2. The cantankerous old man seems to like nothing better than arguing with the checkout clerk in the supermarket. _____
3. Cartography has helped scientists gain a good understanding of the fundamental workings of the human brain. _____
4. A cardinal rule of hiking is to never hike alone. _____
5. The painting's caste gives it the mood of a Rembrandt. _____

UNIT 13

cataclysm / ˈkætəklɪzəm / *n.* a violent upheaval that causes great destruction and change 巨变；暴动；大灾难

The French Revolution of 1789 was a *cataclysm* whose effects are still felt today. 1789年的法国大革命是一场巨变，其影响一直延续至今。

catalyst / ˈkætəlɪst / *n.* something causing change 催化剂

Among the *catalysts* of the Romantic movement were the libertarian ideals of the French Revolution. 法国大革命中的自由主义理想是引发浪漫主义运动的催化剂之一。

● 常见学科术语 ●

Romantic movement: a late eighteenth- and nineteenth-century movement in literature and the arts. The movement was a very varied one, and so is not easily described in a few words. Romanticism was a revolt against classicism and reason and emphasized the individual and the emotional. The Romantics also stressed the inherent goodness of man and nature and valued freedom highly. Important Romantic poets in England include William Blake, John Keats, William Wordsworth, and P. B. Shelley. Famous Romantic composers include Hector Berlioz, Franz Liszt, and Frederic Chopin.

浪漫主义运动： 发生于18世纪晚期至19世纪的一场文艺运动。该运动包罗万象，难以三言两语进行总结。浪漫主义思潮是对古典主义和理性的反叛，强调个体和情感。浪漫主义者强调人性和自然固有的善，赋予自由崇高的地位和价值。英格兰重要的浪漫主义诗人有威廉·布莱克、约翰·济慈、威廉姆·华兹华斯和P.B. 雪莱。著名的浪漫主义作曲家包括埃克托尔·柏辽兹、弗朗茨·李斯特和费雷德里克·肖邦。

libertarian: libertarians place great importance on individual freedom. They believe that no limitations should be placed on a person's freedom unless that person's actions limit the freedom of others.

自由论者： 自由论者极为注重个人自由。他们认为人们不应该对个体的自由加以干涉，除非其影响到了他人的自由。

French Revolution: a crucial period (1789–1799) in French, and more generally, Western civilization. France's absolute monarchy was replaced by republicanism. It is regarded by most historians as a major turning point in Western civilization, ushering in the era of citizens as the major force in politics.

法国大革命(1789–1799)： 法国乃至西方文明的关键时刻，使法国的君主专制被共和制所取代。多数历史学家认为这是西方文明的重大转折点，开辟了公民成为政治主体的时代。

---

categorical / ˌkætəˈɡɔːrɪkl / *adj.* absolute; without exception 绝对的；完全的；彻底的

Although incest is *categorically* forbidden by every state, recent evidence that marriage between cousins is no more likely to produce abnormal offspring than "normal" marriages may allow the constitutionality of bans on marriage between cousins to be challenged. 尽管美国各州完全禁止近亲结婚，但最新证据表明，堂/表亲结婚生育出非正常子嗣的概率并不比"正常"婚姻的概率高，而宪法对堂/表亲间结婚所施加的禁令也将因此遭到挑战。

caucus / ˈkɔːkəs / *n.* a smaller group within an organization（政党等决定政策或推举竞选人的）核心成员，决策班子

The workers formed an informal *caucus* to discuss their difficulties. 工人们组成了一个非正式的决策小组来讨论面临的困难。

causal / ˈkɔːzl / *adj.* involving a cause 原因的；具有因果关系的

The philosopher Plato believed there is a *causal* relationship between income inequality, on the one hand, and political discontent and crime, on the other hand: in his *Laws* he quantified his argument, contending that the income of the rich should be no more than five times that of the poor, and he proposed policies to limit extremes of wealth and poverty. 哲学家柏拉图认为收入不均和对政治的不满和犯罪这二者之间是有因果关系的。他在《法律篇》里将这一看法量化了，主张富人的收入不应多于穷人的五倍，还提出了限制贫富两极分化的政策。

caustic / ˈkɔːstɪk / *adj.* sarcastically biting; burning 辛辣而讽刺的；感情强烈的；腐蚀性的

The columnist's *caustic* comments on government policy did not win her any friends among government officials. 这个专栏作家对政府政策的辛辣评价使她在政府官员中没有一个朋友。

celestial / səˈlestʃl / *adj.* ① concerning the sky or heavens 天空的，天体的；天国的 ② sublime 高尚的 *n.* a heavenly being 天神

Astronomers make use of the Doppler effect to measure the velocities and distance from Earth of stars and other *celestial* objects. 天文学家利用多普勒效应测定恒星与其他天体的速率以及它们与地球间的距离。

● 常见学科术语 ●

Doppler effect: change in the wavelength and frequency of a wave as a result of the motion of either the source or receiver of the waves

多普勒效应：由波源或波观测者的移动而产生的波长或波频的变化

---

centrifugal / ˌsenˈtrɪfjəgl / *adj.* moving away from a center 离心的

As the empire expanded, there was an ever increasing *centrifugal* stress as remote colonies sought autonomy. 随着帝国的扩张，偏远的殖民地寻求自治，政府面临的离心应力也越来越大。

centripetal / senˈtrɪpɪtl / *adj.* moving or directed toward a center 向心的

Astronomers calculate that the *centripetal* force exerted by the Earth's gravity on the Moon will keep the Moon in orbit around the Earth for billions of years. 天文学家计算出地球的万有引力对月球产生的向心力，将使月球在其轨道上绕地球旋转几十亿年。

champion / ˈtʃæmpiən / *v.* to defend or support 捍卫；拥护，支持

Robin Hood is famous for *championing* the underdogs of England. 罗宾汉因捍卫英格兰的受压迫者而享有盛名。

REVIEW 13

Matching

Match each word with its definition:

1.	cataclysm	a.	involving a cause
2.	catalyst	b.	absolute
3.	categorical	c.	concerning the sky or heavens
4.	caucus	d.	moving toward a center
5.	causal	e.	a violent upheaval
6.	caustic	f.	moving away from a center
7.	celestial	g.	to defend or support
8.	centrifugal	h.	something causing change

9. centripetal
10. champion

i. sarcastically biting
j. a smaller group within an organization

Fill-ins

Choose the best word to fill in the blank in each sentence.

cataclysm	catalysts	categorical	caucus	causal
caustic	celestial	centrifugal	centripetal	championed

1. Since its founding in 1966, the National Organization for Women （NOW） has _____ the rights of women.

2. A study finds that people who exercise more tend to be healthier: Its authors raise the question, "Are these individuals healthier because they exercise—a _____ link—or do they exercise more because they are healthier to begin with?"

3. "My position is _____," the CEO said. "I will not allow this company to be bought out."

4. Biochemical _____, called enzymes, occur naturally in cells, changing one molecule into another.

5. Scientists say that the impact of a large meteor with the Earth would cause a _____ that might end all life on our planet.

6. Japanese sociologists are studying the _____ effects of a homogenous population on society.

7. Theoretically, a space station could be rotated to create artificial gravity as a result of _____ force.

8. Gothic cathedrals place a great importance on light and a sense of space that seems to lift one toward the _____.

9. The parliament's minority _____ issued a report condemning government policy.

10. Wear protective gloves when working with _____ substances in the laboratory.

Sense or Nonsense

Indicate whether each sentence makes good sense or not.
Put S （SENSE） if it does, and put N （NONSENSE） if it does not.

1. Laboratory centrifuges make use of centrifugal force to separate substances according to their relative masses. _____

2. A study in Western Australia established a causal relationship between talking on a cell phone while driving and an increased likelihood of having an accident. _____

3. Catalysts for change on the school board blocked attempts to implement reforms. _____

4. In 1054, ancient Chinese astronomers recorded their observation of many important celestial events, such as the supernova that created the Crab Nebula. _____

5. The newly discovered species of caucus is remarkable for its ability to survive for months with almost no water. _____

UNIT 14

chasten / ˈtʃeɪsn / *v.* ① to correct by punishment or reproof（通过惩罚而使坏习惯等）改正；斥责 ② to restrain or subdue 遏制

The child's behavior improved after she had been *chastened* by punishment. 受到惩罚后，那个小姑娘的行为有所收敛。

chicanery / ʃɪˈkeɪnəri / *n.* trickery; fraud 哄骗；欺诈（行为）

The governor ordered an audit to investigate alleged financial *chicanery*. 州长下令进行一次审计，以调查涉嫌的金融欺诈行为。

chivalry / ˈʃɪvəlri / *n.* the qualities idealized by knighthood such as bravery and gallantry toward women 骑士精神，骑士品质

Chivalry was rooted in Christian values, and the knight was bound to be loyal to Christian ideals; the Crusades enhanced this idea, as knights vowed to uphold Christianity against heathens. 骑士精神深深植根于基督教价值观，骑士必须效忠于基督理想。十字军东征强化了这一思想，出征的骑士都发誓捍卫基督教，排斥异教徒。

【派】chivalric *adj.* 有骑士风范的

● 常见学科术语 ●
---

chivalry: The code of chivalry dictated how a knight should act; this code enjoined the knight to defend the Church, make war against infidels, perform scrupulously feudal duties, and in general champion virtue against evil.

骑士精神：骑士应该遵守的行为准则，它规定骑士必须捍卫教会，对异教徒发动战争，一丝不苟地执行封建职责，总之要捍卫正义，抑制邪恶。

Crusade: military expeditions by Christians in the Middle Ages to win the Holy Land from the Muslims

十字军东征：中世纪时基督徒为从穆斯林手中夺回"圣地"而发起的军事远征。

---

churlish / ˈtʃɜːrlɪʃ / *adj.* rude; boorish 粗鲁的，粗野的，粗暴的

According to the chivalric code, a knight was never supposed to be *churlish*, especially toward noble ladies, to whom he was supposed to be unfailingly gentle and courteous. 根据骑士准则，骑士绝对不能言行粗鲁，对待贵妇时，他们尤其应该温柔殷勤。

circuitous / sərˈkjuːɪtəs / *adj.* roundabout 迂回的；绕路的

According to Hindu philosophy, some souls take a *circuitous* path through many births to reach God. 印度哲学认为，一些灵魂要经历多次生死轮回才能到达神那里。

clairvoyant / klerˈvɔɪənt / *n.* one who can predict the future; psychic 有预见的人；透视者；通灵者

Edgar Cayce was a famous *clairvoyant* who some people believe was able to go into a trance during which he was in touch with a spiritual realm. 埃德加·凯斯是一位著名的通灵者，一些人相信他能进入一种入定状态从而与精神世界（的人或物）进行沟通。

clamor / ˈklæmər / *n.* noisy outcry 叫嚣，喧哗；大声叫喊 *v.* to cry out noisily 叫嚷，大声呼叫

Over the past 12 years or so the voices *clamoring* for better protection of the Earth's rain forests have increased dramatically. 在过去的12年左右的时间里，要求更好地保护热带雨林的呼声一浪高过一浪。// The crowd *clamored* their disapproval of the plan. 群众大声呼喊着反对那个计划。

clique / kliːk / *n.* a small, exclusive group 朋党，派系

The principal of the high school is concerned that one *clique* of students is dominating the student council. 那所高中的校长很担心学生会会被一小帮学生控制。

cloister / ˈklɔɪstər / *v.* to confine; seclude 使隔绝，隐退 *n.* a monastery or convent 修道院，女修道院

The writer *cloistered* herself in a country house to finish her novel. 那位女作家为完成她的小说而隐居到了乡村小屋里。

【派】**cloistered** *adj.* shut away from the world 与世隔绝的；脱离现实的

The journalist described the large American philanthropic foundations as arrogant, elitist, and *cloistered*. 那名记者把美国庞大的慈善机构说成是傲慢无礼、高高在上而且脱离现实。

coagulate / koʊˈæɡjuleɪt / *v.* to thicken; congeal 凝固，使结块

In normal individuals, blood begins to *coagulate* about 20 seconds after a wound is sustained, thus preventing further bleeding. 对于正常人来说，受伤后约20秒血液就会开始凝固以防止继续出血。

REVIEW 14

Matching

Match each word with its definition:

1. chasten		a.	rude; boorish
2. chicanery		b.	to confine
3. chivalry		c.	trickery; fraud
4. churlish		d.	roundabout
5. circuitous		e.	to correct by punishment
6. clairvoyant		f.	noisy outcry
7. clamor		g.	to thicken; congeal
8. clique		h.	qualities idealized by knighthood
9. cloister		i.	a small, exclusive group
10. coagulate		j.	psychic

Fill-ins

Choose the best word to fill in the blank in each sentence.

chastened	**chicanery**	**chivalric**	**churlish**	**circuitous**
clairvoyant	**clamor**	**clique**	**cloistered**	**coagulates**

1. The idea of the gentleman is derived from the _____ ideal that a man should be honorable, courteous, brave, and loyal, especially to women.
2. Egg white _____ when heated.

3. The college newspaper is dominated by a ＿＿＿＿＿＿＿ of students who seem to be interested mainly in sports.

4. Over the last few years there has been a ＿＿＿＿＿＿＿ in the media about increased global warming.

5. After robbing the store, the thief took a ＿＿＿＿＿＿＿ route back to his house in case anyone was following her.

6. Mr. Jones tends to be ＿＿＿＿＿＿＿ before he has had breakfast.

7. The government's budget deficit was covered up by ＿＿＿＿＿＿＿ ; several items were moved off-budget and unrealistically high revenues were projected.

8. The dictator of the small country was ＿＿＿＿＿＿＿ by the great power's show of naval strength in the harbor of his country's capital city.

9. We all said that Claire must be a ＿＿＿＿＿＿＿ after she predicted the exact score of the football game.

10. The scholar lives a ＿＿＿＿＿＿＿ life among his books.

Sense or Nonsense
Indicate whether each sentence makes good sense or not.
Put S (SENSE) if it does, and put N (NONSENSE) if it does not.

1. The chivalric code commanded knights to be brave, generous, and faithful. ＿＿＿＿＿＿＿

2. Blood is coagulating around the wound. ＿＿＿＿＿＿＿

3. The United States is an open, cloistered society that prides itself on being tolerant of a wide range of views. ＿＿＿＿＿＿＿

4. Herb's boss chastened him with a raise of $10,000 dollars a year. ＿＿＿＿＿＿＿

5. Stage magicians often use clever tricks to make it appear that they are clairvoyants. ＿＿＿＿＿＿＿

UNIT 15

coalesce / ˌkoʊə ˈles / *v.* to cause to become one 联合，合并
President John F. Kennedy said that Americans must be vigilant so that the interests of business and the military do not *coalesce* and thus undermine those of society as a whole. 美国总统约翰·F·肯尼迪曾说美国人一定要保持警觉，以防止商业和军事利益相互勾结，从而损害社会的整体利益。

coda / ˈkoʊdə / *n.* ① the concluding part of a literary or musical composition（文学或音乐作品的）结尾部，终结句 ② something that summarizes or concludes 尾声，结局
The *coda* of the Danish composer Per Norgard's Sixth Symphony seems to return to the serene sounds of the opening. 丹麦作曲家佩尔·内尔高《第六交响曲》的尾声部分似乎又回归到了开场部分的平静。

codify / ˈkɑːdɪfaɪ / *v.* to systematize 使法律成文化；使系统化，规范化
The state legislature voted to *codify* regulations governing banking fraud. 州立法机构投票立法以杜绝银行诈骗。

【派1】codification *n.* 法律成文化

The most influential *codification* of civil law was the *Napoleonic Code* in France, which became the paradigm for law in the non-English-speaking countries of Europe and had a generally civilizing influence on most of the countries in which it was enacted. 最有影响力的民法立法莫过于法国的《拿破仑法典》，它已经成为欧洲非英语国家的立法典范，并对大多数实施该法典的国家起到了教化作用。

【派2】codified *adj.* 编撰成法的

Common law is the system of laws that originated in England; it is based on court decisions and on customs rather than on *codified* written laws. 普通法源自英格兰的法律体系，它基于法庭判决和风俗习惯，而不是成文法。

● 常见学科术语 ●

civil law: a system of law developed from Roman law that is used in continental Europe, the U.S. state of Louisiana, and several other places. The basis of civil law is statute rather than custom and precedent, which are the basis of common law.

民法：由罗马法律演变而来的一个法律体系，用于欧洲大陆、美国路易斯安那州和其他一些地区。民法的成法基础是法律条文，而不是风俗习惯和判例，后两者是普通法的判决基础。

Napoleonic Code: French legal code enacted by Napoleon in 1804. It made uniform the private law of France.

《拿破仑法典》：拿破仑于1804年制定的法国法典，统一了法国的私法体系。

common law: body of law that includes many nonstatutory laws based on many years of precedent derived from rulings by judges

普通法：一种包括很多不成文法在内的法律体系，基于法官多年来的判例而形成。

---

cognizant / ˈkɑːɡnɪzənt/ *adj.* informed; conscious; aware 被告知的；清楚的，明白的；认知的

O. Henry's "The Gift of the Magi" is a simple evocation of a young couple's love for one another, a story in which a husband and wife in straitened circumstances each sacrifices to buy a Christmas present for the other, not *cognizant* of what the other is doing. 欧·亨利的《麦琪的礼物》以朴实的笔触再现了一对年轻夫妇之间的爱情，故事中的这对经济拮据的年轻夫妇为了给对方买圣诞礼物而不得不忍痛割爱，但彼此却并不知情。

collage / kəˈlɑːʒ / *n.* ① artistic composition of materials pasted over a surface 拼贴画 ② an assemblage of diverse elements 杂烩，汇集

The cubist Juan Gris is noted for his use of *collage* to create trompe l'oeil effects—the illusion of photographic reality. 立体派画家胡安·格里斯因采用拼贴手法创造的错觉效果——平面图画的立体视觉幻象——而闻名于世。

● 常见学科术语 ●

cubism: a movement in art in the twentieth century that represented subjects from several points of view rather than from a single perspective. Pablo Picasso and Georges Braques were the two most influential cubist artists.

立体画派：发生于20世纪的一场艺术运动，主张多角度表现事物，而非从单一视角出发。巴勃罗·毕加索和乔治·勃拉克是该流派最有影响的两位艺术家。

> **trompe l'oeil:** a French term meaning "deceive the eye." It refers to a style of portraying objects in a way that deceives the observer into believing it is the object itself.
> 错觉效果：法语术语，指"欺骗眼球"。它指一种绘画风格，用这种风格所描绘的物体能使观察者相信自己所看到的是物体本身而不是画作。

commensurate / kə'mensərət / adj. proportional 相称的；相当的；相对应的

In the United States, malpractice suits have raised the cost of medicine because doctors must pay more for insurance, and thus increase their fees *commensurately*. 在美国，医疗纠纷导致医疗费用增加，因为医生们必须支付更多的保险费用，因此他们的收费也就相应提高了。

compendium / kəm'pendiəm / n. a brief, comprehensive summary 摘要，概要

The Mozart Compendium: A Guide to Mozart's Life and Music by H. C. Robbins Landon is a convenient reference for finding information about the life and music of Wolfgang Amadeus Mozart. H. C. 罗宾斯·兰登编著的《莫扎特概览：生平与音乐》一书为人们了解沃尔夫冈·阿马多伊斯·莫扎特的生平和音乐创作提供了便利的参考。

complacent / kəm'pleɪsnt / adj. self-satisfied 自满的

Although Tom received an "A" on his exam, Professor Donovan warned him not to become *complacent* since the work in the second term would be harder. 虽然汤姆在考试中得了一个A，但多诺万教授警告他切忌自满，因为第二学期的课会更难。

complaisant / kəm'pleɪzənt / adj. overly polite; willing to please; obliging 过于礼貌的；顺从的；殷勤的

Although France and Germany have a close relationship, neither would consider the other a *complaisant* ally. 尽管法德两国关系密切，但双方都不愿视对方为顺从的盟友。

complement n. / 'kɑːmplɪmənt / something that completes or makes up a whole 补充部分，补充物 v. / 'kɑːmplɪment / 补充，补足

Some people envision chess developing into a game played at the highest levels between teams of humans and computers, each *complementing* the other and providing investigators with insight into the cognitive processes of each. 有些人想象让象棋成为人类与电脑之间进行的最高级别较量，这样的较量可以令双方相互取长补短，而且还能让研究者洞察二者的认知过程。

REVIEW 15

Matching

Match each word with its definition:

1. coalesce
2. coda
3. codify
4. cognizant
5. collage
6. commensurate
7. compendium
8. complacent

a. to systematize
b. to cause to become one
c. an assemblage of diverse elements
d. overly polite
e. proportional
f. self-satisfied
g. something that makes up a whole
h. something that summarizes

9. complaisant   i. a brief, comprehensive summary

10. complement   j. informed; conscious

Fill-ins

Choose the best word to fill in the blank in each sentence.

coalesced	coda	codification	cognizant	collage
commensurate	compendium	complacent	complaisant	complement

1. The final chapter of the scientist's book is a _____ in which the author reflects on her life and the important role science played in it.

2. The former chain-smoker describes herself as "Now a _____, passive nonsmoker."

3. A recent theory of how the Earth got its moon is that a very large object collided with the Earth about 4.5 billion years ago to cause iron-free material that gradually _____ into the Moon.

4. One of the cornerstones of capitalism is the conviction that a worker's rewards should be _____ with his or her contribution.

5. Another important _____ of modern civil law in addition to the *Napoleonic Code* is the *German Civil Code* (German Bürgerliches Gesetzbuch) that went into effect in the German Empire in 1900.

6. When one is studying a complex novel, it is helpful to have a _____ that gives information about characters, setting, plot, etc.

7. Traditionally, white wine is considered a good _____ to fish, whereas red wine is considered to be more suitable for meat.

8. The company's CEO is worried that this quarter's record profits will make his employees _____.

9. It is important that a person accused of a crime be _____ of his or her legal rights.

10. Modern Singapore is a multiethnic _____ of Malays, Indians, Chinese, and many other groups.

Sense or Nonsense

Indicate whether each sentence makes good sense or not.
Put S (SENSE) if it does, and put N (NONSENSE) if it does not.

1. After three months of training, the battalion coalesced into a formidable fighting force. _____

2. The collage portrays the university's history since its founding in 1766. _____

3. A widely held belief is that an employee's pay should be commensurate with his or her qualifications and experience. _____

4. It is unwise to become complaisant and assume you will do well on the GRE just because you did well on the SAT or ACT. _____

5. During World War II German naval commanders radioed codas to their submarines containing the location of Allied ships. _____

UNIT 16

compliant / kəmˈplaɪənt / *adj.* yielding 顺从的，依从的；唯唯诺诺的

The young negotiator is trying to learn the skill of being open to proposals by the other side without seeming too *compliant*. 那个年轻的谈判家正在努力学习技巧，使他坦诚地接受对方的意见但又不显得过于顺从。

compunction / kəmˈpʌŋkʃn / *n.* uneasiness caused by guilt 懊悔，良心不安

The American psychiatrist Frank Pittman said, "Men who have been raised violently have every reason to believe it is appropriate for them to control others through violence; they feel no *compunction* over being violent to women, children, and one another." 美国心理学家弗兰克·皮特曼曾说："那些在暴力环境下长大的人有充分的理由相信，通过暴力来掌控他人并无不妥。向妇女、儿童以及其他人施暴，他们也不会感到丝毫愧疚。"

concave / kɑːnˈkeɪv / *adj.* curving inward 凹的，凹面的

Concave lenses are used in glasses to compensate for myopia(nearsightedness). 凹透镜通常用于眼镜，以弥补近视造成的缺陷。

conciliatory / kənˈsɪliətɔːri / *adj.* overcoming distrust or hostility 抚慰的，安抚的；调和的

The leader of the country made *conciliatory* statements assuring the world that his country did not intend to acquire nuclear weapons. 该国领导人发表了安抚性的声明，他向全世界保证自己的国家绝无获取核武器的意图。

concoct / kənˈkɑːkt / *v.* to invent 发明，创造；编造

The various human cultures have *concocted* a great many explanations to describe the beginning of the Earth, life, and humanity. 人类丰富多彩的文化为地球、生命和人类的起源提供了多种解释。

concomitant / kənˈkɑːmɪtənt / *n.* one that occurs or exists concurrently 伴随物

A rebuttal of the argument that homo sapiens's higher cognitive functions could not be the result solely of evolution is that such abilities arose as *concomitants* of language, which gave early hominids a tremendous advantage over other species. 对于"智人更高级的认知功能不可能仅仅是进化的结果"一说，有人反驳说，这种认知能力是作为语言的伴随物而产生的，这就使得早期原始人相比于其他物种具有了极大的优势。

• 常见学科术语 •
---

hominid: a hominid is any member of the biological family Hominidae(the "great apes"), which include chimpanzees, gorillas, orangutans, and humans.

人科动物：指所有类人生物(巨猿)，包括黑猩猩、大猩猩、猩猩以及人类。

---

condone / kənˈdoʊn / *v.* to overlook voluntarily; forgive 主动原谅；宽恕；谅解

Mahatma Gandhi believed in the principle of ahimsa and refused to *condone* violence of any kind, even if used in a just cause. 圣雄甘地坚信非暴力主义，并拒绝原谅任何形式的暴力，甚至在正义事业中所用的暴力。

confound / kən'faʊnd / *v.* to baffle; perplex; mix up 使困惑，使疑惑

Everyone but astrophysicists seems to be *confounded* by the question, "What happened before the Big Bang?" 除天体物理学家外，似乎每个人都会对"宇宙大爆炸之前都发生了什么？"这一问题感到困惑。

congenial / kən'dʒiːniəl / *adj.* ① similar in tastes and habits; friendly 兴趣相投的；同类的；友好的 ② suited to 适合的，适宜的

The physicist Freeman Dyson has expressed his awe at how *congenial* the universe is to intelligent life and consciousness. 物理学家弗里曼·戴森对于宇宙是多么适宜智慧生命和意识存在表示敬畏。

conjugal / 'kɑːndʒəgl / *adj.* pertaining to marriage agreement 结婚的；配偶的

The goal of the Bennett sisters in Jane Austen's *Pride and Prejudice* is to find a suitable man to marry with whom they can live in *conjugal* happiness. 在简·奥斯汀的《傲慢与偏见》中，贝内特姐妹们的目标就是嫁给一个理想的男人，过上美满幸福的婚姻生活。

REVIEW 16

Matching

Match each word with its definition:

1. compliant
2. compunction
3. concave
4. conciliatory
5. concoct
6. concomitant

a. curving inward
b. yielding
c. baffle; perplex
d. to invent
e. to overlook voluntarily
f. pertaining to marriage agreement

7. condone
8. confound
9. congenial
10. conjugal

g. overcoming distrust or hostility
h. similar in tastes or habits
i. uneasiness caused by guilt
j. existing concurrently

Fill-ins

Choose the best word to fill in the blank in each sentence.

compliant	**compunction**	**concave**	**conciliatory**	**concocted**
concomitant	**condoned**	**confounded**	**congenial**	**conjugal**

1. It appears that bureaucracies are today a necessary evil, a _____ of modern society.
2. Amateur radio operators must be _____ with federal laws as administered by the Federal Communications Commission.
3. The novel's plot centers around a woman's search for _____ bliss.
4. One of the main goals of military training is to train soldiers to kill without _____.
5. The dating service matches men and women with _____ interests.
6. For centuries, Fermat's last theorem _____ mathematicians.
7. The story Bud _____ about having been abducted by Vegans in search of Earth's greatest knowledge was not deemed by his professor an acceptable excuse for not handing in his term paper.
8. A lens with two _____ surfaces is called a biconcave lens.
9. Some people believe that the use of nuclear weapons should never be _____.
10. After ten years of feuding with her neighbor, Mrs. Clampett decided enough was enough: as a _____ gesture, she baked a cake and brought it over to her neighbor.

Sense or Nonsense

Indicate whether each sentence makes good sense or not.
Put S (SENSE) if it does, and put N (NONSENSE) if it does not.

1. Since the enemy had made a number of conciliatory gestures, we had no option but to attack them in return. _____
2. The prison allows conjugal visits on weekends. _____
3. This amateur radio transceiver's complex menu system has me completely confounded. _____
4. How the mind concocts new ideas is still a mystery to both psychologists and philosophers. _____
5. The optical telescope's complex system of lenses contains both concave and convex lenses. _____

UNIT 17

connoisseur / ˌkɑːnəˈsɜːr / *n.* ① a person possessing expert knowledge or training 专家，行家 ② a person of informed and discriminating taste 鉴赏家

The art *connoisseur* selected works by Van Gogh, Rembrandt, and Picasso for the exhibition. 那位艺术鉴赏家精心挑选了梵高、伦勃朗以及毕加索的作品作为这次展览的展品。

conscript *n.* / ˈkɑːnskrɪpt / a person compulsorily enrolled for military service 义务兵，应征入伍者 *v.* / kənˈskrɪpt / to enroll a person for military service 征兵，征召入伍

The position of NOW (The National Organization for Women) is that having male-only *conscripts* violates the principle of gender equality. 美国全国妇女组织坚持认为只招收男兵是违反男女平等的原则的。// The French writer Andre Breton was *conscripted* into the artillery and had to put his medical studies in abeyance for the duration of World War I. 法国作家安德烈·布雷东曾被征入炮兵部队，因此他不得不在一战期间中止医学学习。

【派】**conscription** *n.* 征兵

During the War of 1812, American political leaders considered national *conscription* to augment state militias, but Daniel Webster successfully argued before Congress that such a measure would be unconstitutional and thus the proposal was rejected. 在1812年战争期间，美国政治领袖提出通过全国征兵来扩充国民卫队，但丹尼尔·韦伯斯特成功说服国会此举违宪，该提案因此被驳回。

● 常见学科术语 ●

War of 1812: a war fought between the British Empire and the United States from 1812 to 1815. The war ended in a stalemate.

1812年战争：发生于1812至1815年，交战双方为大英帝国和美利坚合众国，最后双方陷入僵局。

con scription: forced enlistment of people in the military. Modern conscription originated during the French Revolution.

征兵：强制征召入伍。现代征兵源于法国大革命。

Daniel Webster: American lawyer and political leader during the period before the Civil War, which he tried to avert

丹尼尔·韦伯斯特：美国内战爆发之前的律师和政治领袖，他努力试图避免内战。

---

consecrate / ˈkɑːnsɪkreɪt / *v.* to declare sacred 宣称…是神圣的；使神圣化

In his Gettysburg Address, President Abraham Lincoln said of the soldiers who died in the Battle of Gettysburg in July, 1863: "We have come to dedicate a portion of that field, as a final resting place for those who here gave their lives that that nation might live...But, in a larger sense, we cannot dedicate—we cannot *consecrate*—we cannot hallow— this ground. The brave men, living and dead, who struggled here, have *consecrated* it, far above our poor power to add or detract." 在葛底斯堡演说中，亚伯拉罕·林肯总统如此评价在1863年7月的葛底斯堡战役中牺牲的士兵："烈士们为使这个国家能够生存下去而献出了自己的生命，我们来到这里，是要把这个战场的一部分奉献给他们作为最后安息之所……但是，从更广

泛的意义上来说，对于这块土地，我们不能够奉献，不能够圣化，也不能够神化。因为那些曾在这里奋战的勇士们，活着的和去世的，已经把这块土地圣化了，这远不是我们微薄的力量所能增减的。"

contend / kən'tend / v. to assert 声称；主张

One of the most famous philosophers to argue for ethical relativism was the German Friedrich Nietzsche, who *contended* that the rightness of a particular action is dependent on the circumstances of the time and culture in which it occurs. 为道德相对主义据理力争的哲学名家之一是德国的弗里德里希·尼采，他主张某一行为是否正当应取决于该行为发生时的客观环境以及文化背景。

【派】contention *n*. an assertion 主张，声称，断言

The study's *contention* is that obesity is America's biggest health problem. 这项研究宣称肥胖症是美国最大的健康问题。

--- ● 常见学科术语 ● ---

ethical relativism: the view that there is no objective truth in issues of what is right or wrong
道德相对主义：该观点认为是与非并没有绝对的判断标准。

Friedrich Nietzsche: nineteenth-century German philosopher. Nietzsche is best known for his doctrine of "the Superman," which held that superior people should reject the "slave morality" of traditional Christianity in favor of a new morality centered on the individual.
弗里德里希·尼采：19世纪德国哲学家。其"超人"学说最为著名，主张"超人"(品格高尚的人)应该反对传统基督教义中的"奴隶道德(被动式道德观)"，并支持以个人为中心的新道德观。

contentious / kən'tenʃəs / adj. quarrelsome; causing quarrels 好争论的；引起争论的

When genetic engineering began in the 1970s, there was a *contentious*, and sometimes acrimonious, debate among scientists themselves about its dangers. 在基因工程刚刚兴起的20世纪70年代，科学家内部就其可能带来的风险进行了激烈的、有时甚至是唇枪舌剑般的争论。

--- ● 常见学科术语 ● ---

genetic engineering: the use of various methods to manipulate the DNA (genetic material) of cells to change hereditary traits or produce biological products
基因工程：通过各种方法来操纵细胞的DNA(遗传物质)，从而改变遗传特征或生产生物产品。

contiguous / kən'tɪgjuəs / adj. touching; neighboring; connecting without a break 互相接触的；相接的；相邻的

There are 48 *contiguous* states in the United States of America. 美国本土包含48个州。

continence / 'kɑːntɪnəns / n. self-control; abstention from sexual activity 自制，节制；性欲的控制

Saint Augustine's famous line "Give me chastity and *continence*, but not yet" is sometimes used to highlight the idea that action is desirable at some point, but not at present. 圣奥古斯丁的名言"请赐予我忠贞和节制，但不是现在"有时被用来说明某些行为在某些时候是恰当的，但并不是现在。

contrite / kən'traɪt / adj. very sorrowful for a wrong 悔悟的，忏悔的

In sentencing the convicted man to a life sentence, the judge took into consideration the fact that he did not seem to be at all *contrite* about his crime. 考虑到那个罪犯对其所犯的罪行未有丝毫悔过之意，法官决定对他处以无期徒刑。

contumacious / ˌkɑːntuˈmeɪʃəs / *adj.* disobedient; rebellious 拒不服从的；反叛的

In the late eighteenth century, Great Britain tried unsuccessfully to put down the uprising against their rule by *contumacious* Americans, leading eventually to the establishment of a separate nation. 18世纪晚期，大不列颠试图镇压反叛的美国人发动的起义，但失败了，最终一个独立的国家诞生了。

conundrum / kəˈnʌndrəm / *n.* riddle; puzzle with no solution 谜；复杂难解的谜

The paradoxical statement "This statement is false" presents us with a *conundrum*. 这句似非而是的表述"这段陈述是错误的"给我们出了一道难题。

REVIEW 17

Matching

Match each word with its definition:

1. connoisseur	a. self-control
2. conscript	b. to declare sacred
3. consecrate	c. touching; neighboring
4. contend	d. disobedient; rebellious
5. contentious	e. a person compulsorily enrolled for military service
6. contiguous	f. quarrelsome
7. continence	g. a person of informed and discriminating taste
8. contrite	h. puzzle with no solution
9. contumacious	i. very sorry for a wrong
10. conundrum	j. to assert

Fill-ins

Choose the best word to fill in the blank in each sentence.

connoisseur	conscripted	consecrated	contends	contentious
contiguous	continence	contrite	contumacious	conundrums

1. The appropriate function of literary criticism is a _____ issue, even among critics themselves.

2. The art critic _____ that the art of what are called less sophisticated cultures has an immediacy that is often lacking in civilized art, perhaps because it is less self-conscious, intellectual, and stylized.

3. In Israel, women as well as men are _____ into the armed forces; however, men can be made to serve in combat, whereas women serve in a noncombat capacity.

4. One of the great _____ in economics is how to achieve full employment without high inflation.

5. The monk pledged himself to a life of _____.

6. The dream holiday of the wine _____ is a trip to France to visit famous chateaux in the region of Bordeaux.

7. The king ordered his army to quell the rebellion by his _____ subject.

8. The landowner had the abandoned house _____ to his house torn down.

9. The Cardinal _____ the cathedral in 1676.

10. The _____ sinner prayed every day for God to forgive her.

Sense or Nonsense

Indicate whether each sentence makes good sense or not.

Put S (SENSE) if it does, and put N (NONSENSE) if it does not.

1. There is nothing that a connoisseur of fine cigars hates more than smoking the finest Cuban cigars. _____

2. Conscription is seen by many people as a last resort to be used when an army must absolutely be raised and sufficient forces cannot be provided by a volunteer army. _____

3. Canada and the United States are contiguous. _____

4. The meeting was so contentious that the proposal was passed in a few minutes and without objection. _____

5. Cynthia contends that jogging is the best way to keep physically fit. _____

UNIT 18

convention / kən'venʃn / *n.* ① practice widely observed in a group; custom 惯例，常规，习俗 ② accepted technique or device 传统手法

The work of French artist Henri Rousseau demonstrates a naiveté that many people find more attractive than the sophistication of highly complex works that make use of all the *conventions* of their genre. 法国画家亨利·卢梭的作品展示出一种纯真质朴，许多人觉得这比那些用尽各种常规手法创作出来的复杂精致的作品更吸引人。

【派】**conventional** *adj.* customary or commonplace 常规的；俗套的

Guerrilla war presents a dilemma for framers of rules of war: should guerrilla fighters be subject to the same rules as those imposed on soldiers who fight *conventional* wars? 游击战的出现令战争规则的制定者陷入两难的境地：游击队员是否应该与常规战的士兵遵守同样的战争规则呢？

● 常见学科术语 ●

Henri Rousseau: French painter (1844–1910) famous for his paintings, often of jungles, done in a Primitive manner

亨利·卢梭(1844–1910)：法国画家，以油画著称，经常以一种原初主义的方式描绘丛林。

guerrilla war: a war involving small groups of soldiers that are flexible and mobile. In guerrilla war there is no front line as there is in conventional war.

游击战：由灵活多变的若干小队士兵进行战斗。与常规战不同的是，游击战没有所谓的前线。

---

converge / kən'vɜːrdʒ / *v.* to approach; come together; tend to meet 接近；汇集，汇合

Although the People's Republic of China and India are rivals in many ways, in certain areas their interests *converge*. 尽管中印双方在很多方面都是竞争对手，但在某些特定领域，双方的利益也有交集。

convex / ˈkɑːnveks / *adj.* curved outward 凸面的

The term for a lens with one *convex* and one concave side is "*convex*-concave." 一面为凸透镜、一面为凹透镜的镜子被称为凸凹透镜。

convivial / kənˈvɪviəl / *adj.* sociable 好交际的；随和的，友好的

One of the jobs of an ambassador is to provide a *convivial* atmosphere for diplomats to meet. 大使的工作职责之一就是为外交官们营造一种愉快友好的会面氛围。

convoluted / ˈkɑːnvəluːtɪd / *adj.* twisted; complicated 盘绕的；错综复杂的，晦涩难懂的

Unraveling the *convoluted* genetic code is one of the great achievements of modern science. 破解错综复杂的遗传密码是现代科学的一项重大成果。

copious / ˈkoʊpiəs / *adj.* abundant; plentiful 大量的，充裕的，丰富的

The *copious* rainfall was welcomed by farmers in the parched land. 这场透雨让土地久旱的农夫喜不自禁。

coquette / koʊˈket / *n.* a woman who flirts 卖弄风情的女人

After she had played the part of a *coquette* in the college play, Pam's boyfriend felt that he needed to remind her that real life was quite different from the theater. 帕姆在学校戏剧节上饰演一位风情万种的女子之后，她的男友觉得有必要提醒她现实生活与舞台是完全不同的。

cornucopia / ˌkɔːrnjuˈkoʊpiə / *n.* ① a horn overflowing with fruit and grain 丰饶之角（装满水果、谷物等象征富饶的羊角）② a state of abundance 丰饶，丰富

The U.S. economy has produced a *cornucopia* of employment opportunities. 美国经济创造了大量就业机会。

cosmology / kɑːzˈmɑːlədʒi / *n.* ① study of the universe as a totality 宇宙学 ② theory of the origin and structure of the universe 宇宙论

Albert Einstein downplayed the strength of the evidence for quantum theory because a universe governed by laws that are inconsistent in their application was not congruent with his personal *cosmology*. 阿尔伯特·爱因斯坦并不十分认可量子理论证据的可靠性，因为一个受应用中就存在矛盾的定律支配的宇宙，是违背他个人的宇宙观的。

【派1】**cosmos** *n.* the physical universe regarded as a totality 宇宙

Shakespeare embodies the incredible confidence and vitality of Renaissance artists and writers, depicting the entire *cosmos*, not intimidated by its vastness. 莎士比亚体现了文艺复兴时期艺术家和作家身上那种令人难以置信的自信与活力，他们试图描绘整个宇宙，绝不因其浩渺无垠而却步。

【派2】**cosmic** *adj.* relating to the physical universe, especially as distinct from Earth, and suggests infinite vastness 宇宙的；无限的

The gods of ancient Greece were concerned not only with *cosmic* events, but also with the ordinary events of everyday life. 古希腊的众神们不但要处理一些宇宙大事，而且还要为生活琐事而操心。

• 常见学科术语 •

quantum theory: a theory in physics based on the principle that matter and energy have the properties of both particles and waves

量子理论：物理学上的一种理论，基于物质与能量都具有粒子和波两种属性这一原理。

Renaissance: the period of revival in art and learning that occurred in Europe during the fourteenth to the seventeenth century

文艺复兴：14–17世纪欧洲艺术和知识的复兴时期。

covert / ˈkoʊvɜːrt / *adj.* hidden; secret 隐蔽的，秘密的

Central Intelligence Agency (The CIA) gathers information about foreign intelligence through many means, including *covert* ones. 美国中央情报局通过多种手段收集外国情报，其中包括一些秘密手段。

REVIEW 18

Matching

Match each word with its definition:

1. convention		a.	complicated
2. converge		b.	curved outward
3. convex		c.	study of the universe
4. convivial		d.	to approach; come together
5. convoluted		e.	a horn overflowing with fruit and grain
6. copious		f.	practice widely observed in a group
7. coquette		g.	abundant
8. cornucopia		h.	a woman who flirts
9. cosmology		i.	hidden; secret
10. covert		j.	sociable

Fill-ins

Choose the best word to fill in the blank in each sentence.

conventions	converges	convex	convivial	convoluted
copious	coquette	cornucopia	cosmology	covert

1. One need not know anything of medieval Christian _____ to appreciate the great Gothic cathedrals, edifices that are a supreme legacy of that age.
2. A work of art may seem contrived to a person who is unfamiliar with the _____ of the form of art he is observing.
3. Fyodor Dostoevsky's *The Possessed* has a fascinating, though _____, plot.
4. _____ lenses are used to correct farsightedness.
5. Politicians are often _____ individuals who are comfortable with a wide variety of people.
6. Stella takes _____ notes in all of her classes.
7. In Robert Frost's famous poem "The Road Not Taken" the speaker must choose which path to take after the one he is on _____ with another.
8. The plainclothes detective took part in a _____ operation.
9. Sarah has a reputation as a bit of a _____.
10. Tropical rain forests contain a _____ of plant substances that have proven to be effective medicines.

Sense or Nonsense

Indicate whether each sentence makes good sense or not.

Put S (SENSE) if it does, and put N (NONSENSE) if it does not.

1. Every Sunday morning Steve buys half a dozen fresh coquettes at the corner bakery. _____

2. After the technician replaced the damaged convex lens in my 5″ reflector telescope, it worked fine. _____

3. The government launched the covert operation amid great fanfare. _____

4. The convivial host helped make sure everyone enjoyed the party. _____

5. Cosmology has helped poetry to become more popular among the public. _____

UNIT 19

covetous / ˈkʌvətəs / *adj.* desiring something owned by another 垂涎的，觊觎的；贪婪的

The astronomer is *covetous* of the time that his colleague gets for research using the Hubble Space Telescope. 这位天文学家渴望能像同事那样拥有用哈勃太空望远镜进行研究的时间。

【派】**covet** *v.* 垂涎，觊觎；渴望

The latest model cellphone is designed to make people *covet* it so much that they go out and buy it even though their present phone is perfectly adequate. 最新款的手机旨在勾起人们对它的强烈渴望，使大家竞相购买，尽管他们现有的手机已完全够用了。

cozen / ˈkʌzn / *v.* to mislead by trick or fraud; deceive 误导；欺骗

The writer H. L. Mencken pointed out that a common strategy of politicians is to *cozen* the people by exaggerating the seriousness of a problem and then offering a solution that, conveniently, only they can provide. 作家H. L. 门肯披露政客们惯用的一个伎俩是，先夸大问题的严重性，然后不失时机地给出一个只有他们能提供的解决方案来欺骗人民。

craven / ˈkreɪvn / *adj.* cowardly 胆怯的，胆小的 *n.* coward 懦夫

In the Hindu epic poem *Bhagavad-Gita*, Lord Krishna warns the hero, who is reluctant to fight, that refusing to fight would be a *craven* act. 在印度史诗《薄伽梵歌》中，克利希纳神警告不愿去战斗的男主人公，称拒绝战斗是一种懦夫行为。

credence / ˈkriːdns / *n.* acceptance of something as true 相信，信任

One of the lessons in Aesop's fable "The Shepherd Boy and the Wolf" is that if a person "cries wolf" too many times without real danger being present（that is, raises too many false alarms）people will be less likely to give *credence* to future alarms raised by that person. 《伊索寓言》中的《牧童和狼》给人们的一则教训是，如果一个人喊了太多次"狼来了"，实际上并没有危险（也就是给了太多的假警报），人们就不太可能相信他以后发出的警报了。

credo / ˈkriːdoʊ / *n.* statement of belief or principle; creed 信条

The *credo* of Google is "Don't be evil." 谷歌的信条是"不作恶。"

daunt / dɔːnt / *v.* to discourage; intimidate; dishearten 使泄气；威吓，使胆怯

Do not let the difficulty of learning the essential words for the GRE *daunt* you. 不要被学习GRE必备词汇的困难所吓倒。

【派1】**daunting** *adj.* discouraging or disheartening 让人害怕的；令人气馁的

Earning a Ph.D. is a *daunting* task, but it can be done. 获得博士学位是一项令人生畏的任务，但并非不可实现。

【派2】**dauntless** *adj.* fearless 无畏的

dearth / dɜːrθ / *n.* scarcity 缺乏，不足

In his book *The Affluent Society*, published in 1958, the economist J. K. Galbraith pointed out that in America affluence is located disproportionately in the private sector, leaving a *dearth* of resources available for the public sector. 经济学家J. K. 加尔布雷思在其1958年出版的《富人社会》一书中指出，美国的财富分配不均，在私人领域比例过大，从而导致公共部门可用资源不足。

debauchery / dɪˈbɔːtʃəri / *n.* corruption 放荡；堕落，纵情声色

The prince lived a life of *debauchery* until he discovered a spiritual dimension to life. 在发现生活的精神层面以前，王子一直过着声色犬马的生活。

decorum / dɪˈkɔːrəm / *n.* proper behavior 举止得体，礼貌；礼节

When addressing the nation, the President generally has an air of *decorum*. 在向民众致辞时，该总统总是表现出得体的风范。

【派】**decorous** *adj.* 得体的，有礼貌的

defame / dɪˈfeɪm / *v.* to malign; harm someone's reputation 诽谤，中伤；损害（某人的）名誉

The ancient Greek philosopher Socrates was *defamed* as a teacher who corrupted the morals of his students. 古希腊哲学家苏格拉底被人诽谤成一个腐蚀学生思想的老师。

REVIEW 19

Matching

Match each word with its definition:

1. covetous		a.	cowardly
2. cozen		b.	scarcity
3. craven		c.	to intimidate; discourage
4. credence		d.	desiring something owned by another
5. credo		e.	acceptance of something as true
6. daunt		f.	to harm someone's reputation
7. dearth		g.	corruption
8. debauchery		h.	to mislead by trick or fraud
9. decorum		i.	statement of belief or principle; creed
10. defame		j.	proper behavior

Fill-ins

Choose the best word to fill in the blank in each sentence.

covets	cozens	craven	credence	credo
daunting	dearth	debauchery	decorum	defaming

1. Because so many young men were killed in the war, there is a _____ of potential husbands for the young women of the village.

2. The general called his advisor's suggestion that he surrender "the _____ proposal of a coward."

3. The sales pitch _____ potential customers by omitting the fact that the product has been superseded by far superior products available at the same price.

4. To make the task of writing the book less _____, the author broke the task into a number of small tasks he could do one at a time.

5. I admit that the professor's statement is baffling; however, it should be given some _____ because of his towering reputation in the field.

6. The principal reminded the students to conduct themselves with _____ during the guests' visit.

7. The amateur radio operator _____ a new ICOM 7800 high-frequency transceiver costing more than $10,000, but his wife says he can afford only the Kenwood 570D costing about $1,000.

8. The novelist follows the _____ that plot proceeds from character.

9. The students went to Fort Lauderdale for a week of _____.

10. The journalist was sued for _____ a police officer in his article.

Sense or Nonsense

Indicate whether each sentence makes good sense or not.
Put S (SENSE) if it does, and put N (NONSENSE) if it does not.

1. The unscrupulous newspaper regularly defames public figures to boost circulation. _____

2. The candidate was elected governor on a platform of moral purity and debauchery. _____

3. The company's credo is "The buyer is king." _____

4. No one called the boxer craven after he asked the referee to stop the bout; he had been knocked down six times and was bleeding profusely. _____

5. A trial should be conducted with decorum. _____

UNIT 20

default / dɪˈfɔːlt / *v.* to fail to act 未履行，拖欠；欺诈，欺骗

Economists have pointed out the danger of using government money to help banks in danger of *defaulting* on a loan: such help might encourage banks to take excessive risks on the future, knowing they will be "bailed out" by the government. 运用政府资金来帮助那些可能因被拖欠贷款而陷入困境的银行，经济学家认为这是有风险的，因为这种帮助会鼓励银行今后在放贷上过度冒险，因为他们知道到时有政府"纾困"。

deference / ˈdefərəns / *n.* respect; regard for another's wish 依从，顺从；尊重

There was a movement to condemn slavery among some of the writers of the Declaration of Independence, but despite many misgivings, the proposal was dropped in *deference* to the objections of a number of people. 《独立宣言》的部分起草者发起了谴责奴隶制的运动，尽管不少人心存疑虑，但鉴于对一些成员反对意见的尊重，大家便不再讨论此事。

【派】**defer** *v.* to submit to the wishes of another due to respect or recognition of the person's authority or knowledge 依从，顺从；尊重

The young lawyer *deferred* to the view of the senior partner in the law firm. 律师事务所里的这位年轻律师很尊重老律师的意见。

defunct / dɪˈfʌŋkt / *adj.* no longer existing 不复存在的

Skeptics have been prognosticating that Moore's Law, which says computer processing power doubles every 18 months, will soon become *defunct*, but the ingenuity of engineers, coupled with commercial incentives, has so far succeeded in preventing the law from being invalidated. 摩尔定律认为计算机处理能力每18个月会翻一番，怀疑论者总是预言这一定律很快就会失效，但是工程师的精巧设计加上商业刺激因素使得该定律目前仍旧有效。

delineate / dɪˈlɪnieɪt / *v.* to represent or depict 描写；描绘，勾画

Quantum theory led to the formulation of the uncertainty principle, which was *delineated* in 1937 by Werner Heisenberg. 量子理论引发了测不准原理的形成，该原理由维尔纳·海森堡于1937年提出。

● 常见学科术语 ●
---

uncertainty principle: the statement in quantum mechanics stating that it is impossible to measure accurately two properties of a quantum object, such as its position and momentum
测不准原理：量子力学理论中的一则原理，它提出观察者不可能同时准确地测出量子物体的两个特性，如位置和动量。

demographic / ˌdeməˈɡræfɪk / *adj.* related to the study of human population 人口统计的

Demographic trends in many European countries indicate that in the next generation there will be relatively fewer working people to support retired people. 许多欧洲国家的人口统计趋向显示下一代将会有相对较少的劳动人口来赡养退休人口。

【派1】**demography** *n.* the study of human population 人口统计学

Demography makes use of the knowledge of other fields such as geography and statistics. 人口统计学会运用其他领域的知识，比如地理学和统计学。

【派2】demographer *n.* one who studies human population 人口统计学家

If, beginning in the mid-twentieth century, many governments in the world had not taken steps to promote birth control among their citizens, causing a diminution in the birth rate, *demographers* say the world would now have a much greater population than it does. 人口统计学家说, 如果不是多国政府从20世纪中期开始有步骤地推行计划生育, 降低人口出生率, 那么世界人口会比现在多得多。

demotic / dɪˈmɑːtɪk / *adj.* pertaining to people 民众的

Walt Whitman is considered by many to be a quintessentially American poet, a poet who celebrated the glory of the ordinary person; one critic praised him as a poet who was able to "make the *demotic* sing." 许多人将颂扬着普通人荣耀的沃尔特·惠特曼视为美国诗人的典型, 一位评论家赞扬他是"可以让所有人歌唱"的诗人。

demur / dɪˈmɜːr / *v.* to express doubt 提出异议, 反对

The Supreme Court's decision was not unanimous; one justice *demurred*, saying that the majority decision used specious reasoning. 最高法院所做出的裁决并未获得全体一致通过。 一位法官表示反对, 说大多数决议都是基于似是而非的推理得出的。

denigrate / ˈdenɪɡreɪt / *v.* to slur someone's reputation 诽谤, 诋毁, 毁誉; 贬低

According to a recent biography of Napoleon Bonaparte, the famous leader felt a need to *denigrate* women. 最近的一部拿破仑传记提到, 这位著名的领袖觉得有必要贬低一下女性。

denizen / ˈdenɪzn / *n.* ① inhabitant 居民 ② a regular visitor 常客, 老主顾

The U.S. Census Bureau has the responsibility of collecting information about the *denizens* of the United States. 美国人口普查局负责收集美国居民的有关信息。

denouement / ˌdeɪnuːˈmɑː / *n.* outcome; the final resolution of the plot of a play or work of literature 结局; 结果

The book tells the story of what was for Europe a rather embarrassing *denouement* to the Crusades. 这本书讲述了十字军东征的故事, 其结局让欧洲读者觉得很尴尬。

REVIEW 20

Matching

Match each word with its definition:

1. default
2. deference
3. defunct
4. delineate
5. demographic
6. demotic
7. demur
8. denigrate
9. denizen
10. denouement

a. to express doubt
b. respect; regard for another's wish
c. inhabitant
d. relating to the study of human population
e. to slur someone's reputation
f. to fail to act
g. to represent or depict
h. outcome
i. pertaining to people
j. no longer existing

Fill-ins

Choose the best word to fill in the blank in each sentence.

default	deference	defunct	delineated	demographic
demotic	demurred	denigrated	denizens	denouement

1. The _____ of a novel by crime writer Mickey Spillane is generally very violent.
2. Data gathered in the census provides planners with important _____ information.
3. On his first scuba dive, Kenny was happy to find that the _____ of the sea did not appear to be hostile.
4. Solid-state electronic equipment has made vacuum tube equipment _____ in most areas other than very specialized applications.
5. The political science professor _____ a plan to reorganize the United Nations to make it better reflect the realities of the contemporary world.
6. The chairperson asked for a vote on the proposal; since no one _____, it passed unanimously.
7. The professor never watches movies, which he calls "_____ entertainment for the semiliterate."
8. Rather than _____ on her car loan payments after losing her job, Ruth worked out an agreement that allowed her to make lower monthly payments.
9. In Victorian times servants were expected to show great _____ to their employers.
10. In many societies women have been _____ as inferior to men.

Sense or Nonsense

Indicate whether each sentence makes good sense or not.
Put S (SENSE) if it does, and put N (NONSENSE) if it does not.

1. The denouement at the beginning of the story really caught my interest. _____
2. The book delineates the characters clearly. _____
3. The demotic king was deposed in the popular uprising. _____
4. Demographic trends in Japan show that the proportion of old people to young people is increasing. _____
5. Since Singapore became an independent country in 1965, its denizens have become among the wealthiest in the world. _____

UNIT 21

deride / dɪˈraɪd / *v.* to mock 嘲笑，嘲弄；讥讽

Innovation often requires challenges to orthodox thinking; for example, in the late 1960s, scientists from the U.S. Department of Defense's Advanced Research Projects Agency presented their idea of a vast network of computers to leading scientists from IBM and AT&T—companies with innumerable research breakthroughs to their credit—and were *derided* as impractical visionaries. 创新经常需要挑战正统思想，例如，20世纪60年代后期，美国国防部高级研究计划局的科学家们向国际商业机器公司和美国电话电报公司的主要科学家介绍了他们对大型计算机网络的构想，这两家公司已无数次在科研上取得了重大突破，但国防部的科学家们的想法被耻笑为不切实际的幻想。

derivative / dɪˈrɪvətɪv / *n.* something derived 衍生物；派生词 *adj.* 衍生的；无创意的

The drug morphine—considered by doctors to be one of the most effective analgesics—is the principal *derivative* of opium, which is the juice in the unripe seed pods of the opium poppy. 被医生视为一种最有效的止痛药的吗啡是鸦片的主要衍生物，是从未成熟的罂粟蒴果中提取的液汁制品。// The critic dismissed the new novel as dull and *derivative*. 评论家谴责这部新小说沉闷乏味且毫无创意。

【派】**derive** *v.* to obtain from another source 从…得来，得到；推导出

One of the attempts to create a lingua franca resulted in Esperanto, a synthetic language whose vocabulary is created by adding various affixes to individual roots and is *derived* from Latin and Greek, as well as Germanic and Romance languages. 人们为创造通用语而不断尝试，成果之一就是世界语。世界语是一种合成语言，其词汇都是通过给独立词根添加词缀而创造出的，并与拉丁语、希腊语以及日耳曼语和罗曼语有渊源。

● **常见学科术语** ●
---

lingua franca: a language used as a medium of communication between peoples of different languages

通用语：使用不同语言的人交流时共同使用的语言。

affix: word elements that are affixed to the beginning（prefix）or the end（suffix）of words to refine the meaning or change the word's grammatical form

词缀：词素，添加在词首（即"前缀"）或词尾（即"后缀"）细化单词含义或改变其语法结构。

Romance languages: the Romance languages, or Indo-European languages that descended from Vulgar Latin, include Italian, Romanian, Spanish, Portuguese, French, their many dialects, and the pidgins and creoles （mixed languages）that developed from them. The term "Romance" is from Vulgar Latin romanice loqui（vulgar languages derived from Latin）.

罗曼语：也称为印欧语，源于通俗拉丁语，包括意大利语、罗马尼亚语、西班牙语、葡萄牙语、法语、上述这些语言的各种方言以及由这些语言发展而来的洋泾浜和克里奥尔语（混杂语）。Romance一词来自通俗拉丁语中的romanice loqui（意思是"从拉丁语演变来的俗语"）。

desiccate / ˈdesɪkeɪt / *v.* to dry completely 完全变干；使干枯，使枯竭

The dry desert air caused the bodies of the dead animals to *desiccate* quickly. 沙漠干燥的空气使得动物尸体很快干枯了。

desuetude / dɪˈsuːətuːd / *n.* a state of disuse 废弃，废止

NASA is considering a plan to refurbish booster rockets from the Apollo Program that have fallen into *desuetude*. 美国航空航天局正打算重新改造阿波罗计划中已废弃的助推火箭。

desultory / ˈdesəltɔːri / *adj.* random; disconnected; rambling 随意的；散乱的，不连贯的

The jury had difficulty following the witnesses' *desultory* testimony. 证人的证词杂乱无章，陪审团很难跟上他的思路。

deterrent / dɪˈtɜːrənt / *n.* something that discourages or hinders 震慑物，制止物；遏制力

During the Cold War, the United States maintained a large number of nuclear weapons as a *deterrent* to aggression by the Soviet Union and its allies. 冷战期间美国持有大量核武器，以此威慑苏联及其盟国。

detraction / dɪˈtrækʃn / *n.* ① the act of taking away 转移 ② derogatory comment on a person's character 诽谤，毁誉

The writer responded in a letter to the critic's long list of *detractions* about his book. 该作者写信回应对他的书做出长篇毁誉的评论家。

diaphanous / daɪˈæfənəs / *adj.* ① transparent 透明的 ② fine-textured 精致的 ③ insubstantial; vague 幻想的，不切实际的；模糊的

In World War II, many soldiers went to war with *diaphanous* dreams of glory, but found instead horror and death. 二战时，许多士兵抱着对荣誉的幻想去参战，但却体验到恐惧与死亡。

diatribe / ˈdaɪətraɪb / *n.* bitter verbal attack 谩骂；谴责

The speaker launched into a *diatribe* against what he called "the evils of technology." 演讲者对他所谓的"技术邪恶"进行谴责。

dichotomy / daɪˈkɑːtəmi / *n.* division into two usually contradictory parts 两分；二分法

The philosopher is a dualist who argues that there is a *dichotomy* between the mind and physical phenomena. 这位哲学家是一个认为精神与物质是截然对立的二元论者。

● 常见学科术语 ●
---

dualist: one who believes in dualism, the theory that two basic entities constitute reality（such as mind and matter or good and evil）

二元论者：持二元论者。二元论认为世界由两种基本实体构成，如精神与物质、善与恶等。

REVIEW 21

Matching

Match each word with its definition:

1. deride
2. derivative
3. desiccate
4. desuetude
5. desultory
6. deterrent
7. detraction

a. something that discourages
b. bitter verbal attack
c. to dry completely
d. random; disconnected
e. the act of taking away
f. something derived
g. division into two contradictory parts

8. diaphanous   h. a state of disuse

9. diatribe   i. transparent; fine-textured

10. dichotomy   j. to mock

Fill-ins

Choose the best word to fill in the blank in each sentence.

derided	derivative	desiccated	desuetude	desultory
deterrent	detraction	diaphanous	diatribe	dichotomy

1. In his book *Supernature* the British biologist Lyell Watson argues that the _____ between nature and the supernatural exists more in the human mind than in reality.

2. The two areas of the room are separated only by a _____ curtain.

3. Scientists are studying the _____ bones to see if they are the remains of a person.

4. Some studies suggest that capital punishment is a _____ against murder.

5. The critics _____ the movie as "a waste of $100 million dollars."

6. The poet describes his work as _____ because it draws on the work of many other poets.

7. The two men walked along the beach, engaged in _____ conversation.

8. The rise of Irish nationalism has probably helped bring the Irish language back from the _____ it was falling into in the nineteenth century.

9. The prime minister's _____ against foreign influence in the country lasted three hours.

10. The only _____ from the excellence of the climate is the rainy winter.

Sense or Nonsense

Indicate whether each sentence makes good sense or not.
Put S (SENSE) if it does, and put N (NONSENSE) if it does not.

1. In many traditional societies women wear diaphanous clothing to hide their bodies. _____

2. Early attempts to communicate by the use of electromagnetic waves were derided by many people as ridiculous. _____

3. The book is a long, desultory narrative recounting its author's life. _____

4. The senator's speech was a diatribe against the increasing influence of government in everyday life. _____

5. The country maintains a large military force as a deterrent against aggression. _____

UNIT 22

diffidence / ˈdɪfɪdəns / *n.* shyness; lack of confidence 羞怯，胆怯；缺乏自信

As a result of the strength of his opposition to the Vietnam War Senator Eugene McCarthy overcame his *diffidence* and ran against President Lyndon Johnson for the Democratic nomination for President. 由于强烈反对越战，参议员尤金·麦卡锡克服了自己的胆怯，与林登·约翰逊总统角逐民主党的总统提名。

diffuse *v.* / dɪˈfjuːz / to spread out（使）传播，扩散 *adj.* / dɪˈfjuːs / wordy; rambling; spread out 冗长的，啰嗦的

The idea of equality and liberty *diffused* through society after the French Revolution. 法国大革命后，平等和自由的思想在社会上广为传播。// This essay is so *diffuse* it is difficult to follow its central argument. 这篇论文极其啰嗦，让人抓不住它的中心论点。

digression / daɪˈɡreʃn / *n.* ① the act of straying from the main point 偏离主题 ② an instance of digressing 离题话

The novel *Zen and the Art of Motorcycle Maintenance* by Robert M. Pirsig contains many fascinating *digressions* from the main story that discuss topics such as Platonic philosophy. 罗伯特·M·皮尔西格的小说《禅与摩托车维修艺术》里有许多有趣的离题话，讨论的主题包括柏拉图哲学等内容。

> —— • 常见学科术语 • ——
>
> **Platonic:** refers to the philosophy of Plato, an ancient Greek philosopher who held that both actual things and ideas such as beauty and truth are copies of transcendent ideas
> 柏拉图的：与柏拉图的哲学有关的。柏拉图是古希腊哲学家，他认为实体和诸如美、真理等理念都是超验理念的复制品。形容词platonic小写p时指 "纯精神的，超越肉欲的，纯理论上的"（英文释义为spiritual, without sensual desire, theoretical）

dirge / dɜːrdʒ / *n.* funeral hymn 哀乐；挽歌

The music critic described the movement of the symphony portraying the hero's last days as "*dirge.*" 那位音乐评论家描述说交响乐中表现英雄最后那段日子的乐章好像"哀乐"。

disabuse / ˌdɪsəˈbjuːz / *v.* to free from a misconception 解惑，消除错误观点；使省悟

The chairman of the Federal Reserve used his testimony before Congress to *disabuse* his audience of the idea that the business cycle had been eliminated by the unprecedented period of prosperity. 美国联邦储备委员会主席利用其在国会的证词消除了公众的一种误解。该误解认为史无前例的繁荣期消除了经济周期。

discerning / dɪˈsɜːrnɪŋ / *adj.* perceptive; exhibiting keen insight and good judgment 有识别力的，有眼力的

Discerning movie critics have praised the work of producer Stanley Kubrick, who produced such excellent films as *2001, Dr. Strangelove, A Clockwork Orange,* and *Lolita.* 不少颇具欣赏眼光的影评家都对制作了《2001太空漫游》、《奇爱博士》、《发条橙》和《洛丽塔》等优秀影片的制片人斯坦利·库勃里克称赞不已。

【派】 discern *v.* to perceive something obscure 辨别，识别；觉察出

Superficially, expressionism can appear to be unrealistic because of its extreme distortion of reality, but upon closer examination, an inner psychological reality can often be *discerned*. 表面上看，表现主义因其对现实的极度扭曲而显得脱离实际，但通过进一步观察，常常能够觉察出其内在的心理现实。

● 常见学科术语 ●

expressionism: an artistic style in which the artist expresses emotional experience as opposed to his or her view of the external world. Expressionists often use distortion and exaggeration. El Greco, Van Gogh, and Edward Munch are examples of expressionist artists.

表现主义： 艺术家用来表达其情感体验的一种艺术风格，其忽视对外部世界的描摹。表现主义艺术家通常运用扭曲或夸张的手法，其代表人物有埃尔·格列柯、梵高和爱德华·蒙克。

---

discomfit / dɪsˈkʌmfɪt / *v.* to make uneasy; disconcert 使困窘；使惊慌

The young man was *discomfited* being the only male in the play. 那个年轻人因自己是剧中唯一的男性而感到很别扭。

discordant / dɪsˈkɔːrdənt / *adj.* not in tune (声音)不协调的，不悦耳的

In a pluralistic society there exists a cacophony of *discordant* voices, each shouting to be heard. 多元的社会中总是存在着许多不和谐的声音，每一种声音都奋声疾呼渴望被听到。

discredit / dɪsˈkredɪt / *v.* to dishonor; disgrace; cause to be doubted 破坏名誉，使丢脸，诽谤；使被怀疑

The candidate's attempt to *discredit* his opponent by spreading damaging rumors about him failed. 候选者通过散布谣言来诋毁竞争对手的企图落空了。

discrepancy / dɪsˈkrepənsi / *n.* difference 差异；矛盾；不符合之处

The book studies the *discrepancy* in values and outlook between men who fought in the war, whether voluntarily or not, and those who remained civilians. 这本书比较研究了两种人的价值观和态度：一种在战场上打过仗，不论其自愿与否；另一种则是普通平民。

REVIEW 22

Matching

Match each word with its definition:

1. diffidence		a.	to free from a misconception
2. diffuse		b.	to spread out
3. digression		c.	to make uneasy
4. dirge		d.	the act of straying from the main point
5. disabuse		e.	difference
6. discerning		f.	shyness
7. discomfit		g.	not in tune
8. discordant		h.	funeral hymn
9. discredit		i.	to dishonor; disgrace
10. discrepancy		j.	exhibiting keen insight and good judgment

Fill-ins

Choose the best word to fill in the blank in each sentence.

diffidence	diffuse	digressions	dirge	disabuse
discerning	discomfited	discordant	discredited	discrepancy

1. One year of medical school was enough to _____ Steve of the idea that medical school is a "piece of cake."

2. Auditors are investigating the _____ between the company's stated earnings and its projected earnings based on sales.

3. The band played a _____ at the soldier's funeral.

4. Some readers are annoyed by the long _____ on geology and other scientific subjects in Kim Stanley Robinson's *Mars* trilogy; other readers, however, find them fascinating, illuminating and beautifully written.

5. Historians of science study theories that have become accepted by modern science as well as those that have been _____.

6. One of the aims of the English literature course is to help students become _____ readers.

7. The study suggests that women do not find _____ in men to be an attractive quality.

8. The intravenous drug will _____ through the patient's body in about 20 minutes.

9. Many people are _____ by the idea of their own death.

10. The governor traveled around the state listening to the _____ views on the controversial issue.

Sense or Nonsense

Indicate whether each sentence makes good sense or not.
Put S (SENSE) if it does, and put N (NONSENSE) if it does not.

1. A woman of discerning taste in literature, Jane mainly reads works by William Shakespeare, William Blake, Henry James, and Willa Cather. _____

2. There is a great discrepancy between the performance of the best student in the class and the worst student. _____

3. Good writers often use digression to help keep their discussion on the main topic. _____

4. The opposition party tried to discredit the leadership of the ruling party by charging it with corruption. _____

5. A week doing the house cleaner's chores disabused Cindy of the idea that the house cleaner was an easy job. _____

UNIT 23

discrete / dɪˈskriːt / *adj.* constituting a separate thing; distinct 分离的，个别的；不相关联的

Like the physicist, the abstract artist strives to identify the *discrete* elements of reality and to understand how they interact. 抽象派艺术家同物理学家一样，力求确认现实中各种不相关的元素并弄清它们是如何相互作用的。

discretion / dɪˈskreʃn / *n.* ① quality of showing self-restraint in speech or actions; circumspection 谨慎，周详 ② freedom to act on one's own 选择的自由

In nineteenth-century Britain gentlemen were expected to behave with *discretion*. 19世纪的英国绅士的言谈举止应该谨慎。

disingenuous / ˌdɪsɪnˈdʒenjuəs / *adj.* not candid; crafty 不真诚的，不坦率的；狡猾的

When a person starts a sentence, "I don't mean to appear *disingenuous*," one might be tempted to suspect that the person is being just that. 如果一个人张口就说"我并非有意表现得不诚恳"，那么我们就要怀疑他实际上就是不诚恳。

disinterested / dɪsˈɪntrəstɪd / *adj.* unprejudiced; objective 公正的，无偏见的；客观的

The newspaper reporter looked for *disinterested* witnesses to the events so that she could get an objective account of what had happened. 报社记者寻找能公正描述整个事件的目击者，这样她就能对到底发生了什么有客观的了解。

disjointed / dɪsˈdʒɔɪntɪd / *adj.* lacking order or coherence; dislocated 不连贯的，杂乱无章的

The technique of telling a story through a *disjointed* narrative is a technique best left to masters of the modern novel such as James Joyce and William Faulkner. 通过支离破碎的叙述来讲故事是詹姆斯·乔伊斯和威廉·福克纳这样的现代小说大师才能驾驭的技巧。

dismiss / dɪsˈmɪs / *v.* to put away from consideration; reject 不予考虑，拒绝接受；不承认；抛弃

Investigators *dismissed* the man's account of a visit to another planet aboard an alien spacecraft as the product of an overactive imagination. 那人描述说他曾经乘坐一艘外星宇宙飞船到了另一颗行星，调查者认为这是胡思乱想的产物，所以不予理会。

disparage / dɪˈspærɪdʒ / *v.* to belittle 贬低；轻视

Though sometimes *disparaged* as merely an intellectual game, philosophy provides us with a method for inquiring systematically into problems that arise in areas such as medicine, science, and technology. 尽管哲学有时被贬低为只是单纯的智力游戏，它还是给我们提供了一种方法，以系统地研究医学、科学以及技术等领域出现的问题。

disparate / ˈdɪspərət / *adj.* dissimilar 全然不同的，不同的

Many technological projects are interdisciplinary, requiring a knowledge of fields as *disparate* as physics and biology. 许多技术工程都是跨学科的，需要掌握跨度极大的学科知识，比如物理学和生物学。

【派】**disparity** *n.* the condition of being unequal or unlike 不同，差异；差距

The huge income *disparity* in the world is clearly illustrated by the fact that the assets of the world's 200 richest people exceed the combined income of 41% of the world's population. 世界前200位富人的资产超过全球人口总收入的41%，这一事实清楚地表明人们收入的差距极为悬殊。

dissemble / dɪ'sembl / *v.* to pretend; disguise one's motives 掩饰，隐藏(动机)

"Miss," the prosecutor said, "I believe you are *dissembling*. I want you to tell me the whole truth about what happened that night." 检察官说："小姐，我认为你是在掩饰。我要你老老实实地告诉我那晚到底发生了什么事情。"

disseminate / dɪ'semɪneɪt / *v.* to spread; scatter; disperse 传播，散布；扩散

While belief in reincarnation appeared as doctrine first in India and was *disseminated* throughout Asia by Buddhism, it is interesting that it was accepted by the most influential philosophy of the West, Platonism, and by some important early Christian thinkers, such as the theologian Origen. 当转世轮回说作为教义最先出现在印度，并通过佛教在整个亚洲传播时，在西方出现了一个有趣的现象，它得到了西方最有影响力的哲学——柏拉图主义以及一些重要的早期基督思想家，如神学家奥利金的认同。

• 常见学科术语 •

Platonism: the philosophy of Plato, which holds that both actual things and ideas such as beauty and truth are copies of transcendent ideas

柏拉图主义：柏拉图的哲学思想，其认为实体和诸如美、真理等理念都是超验理念的复制品。

REVIEW 23

Matching

Match each word with its definition:

1. discrete	a. lacking order or coherence
2. discretion	b. unprejudiced; objective
3. disingenuous	c. dissimilar
4. disinterested	d. to belittle
5. disjointed	e. to spread; disperse
6. dismiss	f. circumspection
7. disparage	g. to pretend
8. disparate	h. not candid; crafty
9. dissemble	i. constituting a separate thing; distinct
10. disseminate	j. to reject

Fill-ins

Choose the best word to fill in the blank in each sentence.

discrete	**discretion**	**disingenuous**	**disinterested**	**disjointed**
dismissed	**disparaged**	**disparate**	**dissembled**	**disseminated**

1. The historian tries to take a _____ view of how the United States got involved in the Vietnam War.

2. The great increase in travel in modern times makes it difficult to determine how and where a disease originated, as well as how it was _____, so that measures can be taken to mitigate its effects.

3. The novel's narrative is so _____ that many readers have trouble following it.

4. Scientific laws identify a common fundamental element in seemingly _____ phenomena.

5. The historian describes her method as "not so much the study of _____ events but rather the study of relationships between those events."

6. The judge _____ the evidence as not relevant to the case at hand.

7. The school lets its teachers use considerable _____ in designing lessons for students.

8. The investigating committee ruled that the governor "had been _____" in not providing important information to them.

9. The noted director Stanley Kubrick, who turned down the chance to go to college when he was 17, _____ formal education, saying, "I never learned anything at all at school."

10. The girl _____ when her date asked if she had ever been kissed.

Sense or Nonsense

Indicate whether each sentence makes good sense or not.
Put S (SENSE) if it does, and put N (NONSENSE) if it does not.

1. The technician dissembled the computer to find out what was wrong with it. _____

2. The battalion's commander told his men to use their own discretion in selecting enemy targets. _____

3. Diplomats must be discrete to do their job effectively. _____

4. The disingenuous student must work harder than other students to make up for his lack of ability. _____

5. The writer was proud to have her work disparaged by leading critics. _____

UNIT 24

dissident / ˈdɪsɪdənt / n. a person who disagrees about beliefs, etc. 持异议者；持不同政见者

Some of the most notorious concentration camps in history were the Gulag camps used by the Soviet Union to control *dissidents*. 历史上最臭名昭著的集中营包括了前苏联政府为镇压持不同政见者而设的古拉格集中营。

─────────── • 常见学科术语 • ───────────

Gulag: forced-labor prison camps in the Soviet Union. Established in the 1920s, the Gulag system had 476 camps throughout the country used to imprison people considered a threat to the state.

古拉格： 前苏联劳改集中营。建于20世纪20年代的古拉格集中营系统在全国共有476个集中营，用来监禁被认为会对国家构成威胁的人。

dissolution / ˌdɪsəˈluːʃn / *n.* disintegration; debauchery 瓦解，解体；放荡

Some philosophers maintain that the *dissolution* of the body does not mean the destruction of the mind. 一些哲学家坚称肉体的消亡不代表精神的解体。

dissonance / ˈdɪsənəns / *n.* discord; lack of harmony 不一致，不和谐，不协调

In psychology, the term "cognitive *dissonance*" refers to a conflict resulting from inconsistency between one's beliefs and one's actions. For example, a soldier who believes that all killing is immoral but is forced to kill by his superiors might experience cognitive *dissonance*. 在心理学上，"认知失调"这一术语指由人的信仰与行为之间的矛盾而引发的冲突。比如，一名坚信所有的杀戮都是罪恶的士兵却不得不听从上级的命令而去杀人，他就可能会经历认知失调。

distend / dɪˈstend / *v.* to expand; swell out 扩展；膨胀

People in an advanced stage of starvation often have *distended* bellies. 人在极度饥饿时会腹胀如鼓。

distill / dɪˈstɪl / *v.* to extract the essential elements 蒸馏；精炼，提取

In his book *Men of Ideas: Some Creators of Contemporary Philosophy*, Bryan Magee manages to *distill* the essence of leading thinkers such as W. V. Quine, John Searle, Iris Murdoch, and Noam Chomsky. 在《思想家：当代哲学的创造者们》一书中，布赖恩·马吉萃取著名思想家W. V. 奎因、约翰·瑟尔、伊丽丝·默多克、诺姆·乔姆斯基等人的思想精髓。

distrait / dɪsˈtreɪ / *adj.* inattentive; preoccupied 心神不定的，心烦意乱的

The chairperson became *distrait* because his secretary was not sitting in her usual position on his right. 主席感到心神不宁，因为秘书没有像往常那样坐在他的右边。

diverge / daɪˈvɜːrdʒ / *v.* to vary; go in different directions from the same point 分歧，相异；分开，岔开

A famous line in American poetry is from Robert Frost's "The Road Not Taken":

Two roads *diverge*d in a wood, and I—

I took the one less traveled by...

下面这句美国诗歌中的名句出自罗伯特·弗罗斯特的《未选择的路》：

"一片森林里两条路分岔，

而我选择了人迹更少的一条……"

【派】divergence *n.* 背离；分离

Psychological tests show that there is a wide *divergence* between citizens of different countries in how much importance they place on the virtue of justice, on the one hand, and the virtue of mercy, on the other hand. 心理学测验结果表明，对于是坚守正义还是慈悲为怀，不同国家公民的侧重点存在很大的差异。

divest / daɪˈvest / *v.* to strip; deprive; rid 剥夺；脱去，摆脱

The candidate for secretary of defense pledged to *divest* himself of the shares he held in defense-related companies. 竞选国防部长的候选人发誓他将放弃他在国防公司持有的股份。

divulge / dəˈvʌldʒ / *v.* to make known something that is secret 泄露，暴露

Under the Geneva Conventions, prisoners of war cannot be tortured and forced to *divulge* information. 《日内瓦公约》规定，不许虐待战俘并强迫其透漏机密信息。

doctrinaire / ˌdɑːktrəˈner / *adj.* relating to a person who cannot compromise about points of a theory or doctrine; dogmatic; unyielding 教条主义的，空谈理论的；武断的

The old man was a *doctrinaire* communist. 那个老人是一名教条主义的共产主义者。

REVIEW 24

Matching

Match each word with its definition:

1. dissident		a.	unyielding; dogmatic
2. dissolution		b.	to extract the essential elements
3. dissonance		c.	disintegration
4. distend		d.	to strip; deprive
5. distill		e.	to expand; swell out
6. distrait		f.	to go in different directions from the same point
7. diverge		g.	inattentive; preoccupied
8. divest		h.	to make known something secret
9. divulge		i.	a person who disagrees about beliefs
10. doctrinaire		j.	lack of harmony

Fill-ins

Choose the best word to fill in the blank in each sentence.

dissidents	**dissolution**	**dissonance**	**distended**	**distill**
distrait	**diverged**	**divested**	**divulge**	**doctrinaire**

1. How the poet John Keats was able to _____ so much beauty and wisdom into his poetry remains a mystery.

2. The members' vote of no confidence in the ruling government led to the _____ of parliament.

3. The man who ate more than 50 hot dogs to win the hot dog eating competition gained 7 pounds and had a _____ belly for a few days.

4. According to the child psychologist, _____ between family and school is normal.

5. The psychologist's patient _____ himself of the secrets he had been carrying within for 30 years.

6. During World War I many people in the United States considered conscientious objectors to be radical _____.

7. Pam's life _____ from Bob's after they graduated from college in 1971; he was drafted and sent to fight in Vietnam and she went to Paris to do a Ph.D. in French literature.

8. The guest seemed to be melancholy and _____, so I asked him what was troubling him.

9. Companies that are not publicly listed and have no major debt normally do not need to _____ much about their sales and other matters to financial markets.

10. "If the world is lucky enough to enjoy peace, it may even one day make the discovery, to the horror of _____ free-enterprisers and doctrinaire planners alike, that what is called capitalism and what is called socialism are both capable of working quite well."

(J. K. Galbraith, American economist)

Sense or Nonsense

Indicate whether each sentence makes good sense or not.

Put S (SENSE) if it does, and put N (NONSENSE) if it does not.

1. Peter and Paul disagree on most political issues, but their views diverge on religion. _____

2. During the off-season the hotel distends its opening hours to accommodate customers. _____

3. The *Bhagavad-Gita*, one of the holy books of the Hindus, is a long poem that distills much of the teachings of Hinduism. _____

4. The foreign government gave dissidents in the country support in the hope of destabilizing the country. _____

5. The reporter was distrait so he couldn't concentrate on his report. _____

UNIT 25

document / ˈdɑːkjument / *v.* to provide with written evidence to support 提供证明；证明

The insurance company asked Debbie to *document* her claim with letters from the doctors who treated her for her condition. 保险公司要求黛比出具给她治疗的医生的信件，为她的索赔提供文件证明。

doggerel / ˈdɔːgərəl / *n.* poor verse 蹩脚的诗，打油诗

In his book *Poetic Meter and Poetic Form*, the literary citric Paul Fussell quotes this bit of *doggerel* from a U.S. Army latrine during World War II:

Soldiers who wish to be a hero

Are practically zero.

But those who wish to be civilians

Jesus, they run into millions.

在《诗歌的韵律和形式》一书中，文学评论家保罗·富塞尔引用了二战时期美国军队厕所里的一首打油诗：

想当英雄的士兵，

实际上一个都没有（译者注：双关，zero字面上可理解为"什么也不是"，暗指"死去"）。

想当百姓的士兵，

老天，那是成千上万（译者注：双关，run into millions字面可理解为"会升官发财"，暗指"活下来"）。

dogmatic / dɔːgˈmætɪk / *adj.* stating opinions without proof 教条的；固执己见的，武断的

Since every case is unique, jurists must not be *dogmatic* in applying precedents to make their decision, but instead must base their decision on a combination of such precedents and the facts of the case at hand. 鉴于每个案件都是独特的，法学家切忌教条般地援引先例作为判案的依据。相反，他们必须将此类先例与手头案件的实际情况结合起来，综合考量后再作判决。

【派】**dogma** *n.* a belief asserted on authority without evidence 教条，教义

Religions whose *dogma* specifies a time of the creation of the world have found difficulty in reconciling their view of creation with that of modern science. 有些宗教的教义明确说明世界是在某一特定时间创造出来的，这些创世观很难和现代科学的创世观统一起来。

The original meaning of **dogma** was "that which seems good." In Christian theology it came to mean truths known by divine revelation and taught by the Church.

dogma 最初是指"看起来不错的事物"。在基督教神学中指通过神谕和教堂传授而为人所知的真理。

dormant / ˈdɔːrmənt / *adj.* inactive 不活跃的；蛰伏的，休眠的

There is a considerable body of evidence showing that many diseases, such as ulcers, asthma, and hypertension have a large psychological component; the working hypothesis is that they represent manifestations of *dormant* emotional disturbances. 有大量证据表明溃疡、哮喘、高血压等疾病都存在很大的心理因素，运作假设认为这些实际上是潜在情绪波动的外在表现。

dross / drɔːs / *n.* ① waste; worthless matter 垃圾，废物 ② trivial matter 微不足道的东西

One of the ways the *dross* among blogs on the Internet are filtered out from the worthwhile ones is through links good blogs provide to other good blogs. 想在因特网上过滤出有价值的博客并且摒弃垃圾博客的方法之一就是通过好博客上提供的链接找到其他的好博客。

blog: short for weblog, an on-line journal
博客：网络博客的缩写，即在线日记。

dupe / duːp / *v.* to deceive; trick 欺骗，哄骗

"In friendship, as well as in love, the mind is often *duped* by the heart." (Philip Dormer Stanhope) "在友情和爱情中，我们的思想经常被心灵所欺骗。"（菲利普·多默·斯坦诺普）

ebullient / ɪˈbʊliənt / *adj.* exhilarated; enthusiastic 兴高采烈的；充满热情的

The *ebullient* candidate for President appeared before his supporters to announce that he had won in a landslide. 这位总统候选人神采飞扬地对自己的支持者宣布他已获得了压倒性的胜利。

eclectic / ɪˈklektɪk / *adj.* selecting from various sources 选择的；博采众长的，兼容并蓄的

Neo-Platonism—an *eclectic* third-century synthesis of Platonic, Pythagorean, Aristotelian, Stoic, and Jewish philosophy—was an essentially mystical belief that a person can achieve spiritual emancipation through union of the soul with the ultimate source of existence. 形成于公元三世纪的新柏拉图主义是融合了多种思想的综合产物，其中包括柏拉图哲学、毕达哥拉斯主义、亚里士多德哲学、斯多葛主义以及犹太哲学的观点，其从根本上说是一种神秘主义信仰，认为人能通过灵魂与终极存在的融合而获得精神解放。

Platonic: refers to the philosophy of Plato, an ancient Greek philosopher who held that both actual things and ideas such as beauty and truth are copies of transcendent ideas

柏拉图式的：与柏拉图哲学相关的。柏拉图是古希腊哲学家，他认为实体和诸如美、真理等理念都是超验理念的复制品。

Pythagorean: refers to the philosophy of Pythagoras, a sixth-century B.C. philosopher and mathematician. Pythagoras described reality in terms of arithmetical relationships.

毕达哥拉斯的：与毕达哥拉斯相关的哲学。毕达哥拉斯是公元前6世纪的古希腊哲学家、数学家。他以数的法则描述现实世界。

Aristotelian: refers to the philosophy of Aristotle, an ancient Greek scientist and philosopher whose teaching had a great influence on Western thought, especially in the areas of logic, metaphysics, and science

亚里士多德的：与亚里士多德哲学相关的。亚里士多德是古希腊科学家、哲学家，其教学对西方思想产生了巨大影响，尤其是在逻辑学、形而上学以及科学等领域。

Stoic: refers to Stoicism, a philosophy of ancient Greece that taught that the highest good is virtue, which is based on knowledge. The Stoics believed that the wise live in harmony with Divine Reason that governs nature and are indifferent to suffering and the changing fortunes of life.

斯多葛学派的：与斯多葛主义相关的。斯多葛主义认为德行为上善，而德行基于知识。斯多葛派学者认为智者与主宰自然的神圣理性和谐共处，对人生的苦难和时运变迁泰然处之。

mystical: related to mysticism, the practice of putting oneself into direct relation with God, the absolute, or any unifying principle of life

神秘主义的：和神秘主义相关的。神秘主义把个人直接和上帝、绝对或者任何统一的人生原则相联系。

---

effervescence / ˌefər'vesns / *n.* ① a state of high spirits or liveliness 活泼，活跃 ② the process of bubbling as gas escapes 冒泡，泡腾

Effervescence occurs when hydrochloric acid is added to a block of limestone. 向石灰岩中注入盐酸时会产生气泡。

【派】**effervescent** *adj.* 兴奋的，活跃的；冒泡的

A person who believes himself to be physically unattractive might develop an *effervescent* personality as a compensation for his perceived deficiency. 一个人如果觉得自己外貌平平，就可能形成活泼的个性以弥补他感知到的缺陷。

effete / ɪ'fiːt / *adj.* ① depleted of vitality 枯竭的，缺乏生气的 ② overrefined 过于娇柔的，软弱的 ③ decadent 颓废的；堕落的

In 1969, U.S. Vice President Spiro T. Agnew denounced people protesting against the Vietnam War: "A spirit of national masochism prevails, encouraged by an *effete* corps of impudent snobs who characterize themselves as intellectuals." 在1969年，美国副总统斯皮罗·T·阿格纽在指责反越战的民众时说："现在全国上下一片受虐狂似的风气，都是那一小撮自诩为知识分子，实际上却鲁莽、自以为是且软弱无能的人唆使的。"

REVIEW 25

Matching

Match each word with its definition:

1. document
2. doggerel
3. dogmatic

a. to deceive
b. poor verse
c. to provide with written evidence to support

4. dormant   d. a state of high spirits

5. dross   e. selecting from various sources

6. dupe   f. stating opinions without proof

7. ebullient   g. exhilarated

8. eclectic   h. inactive

9. effervescence   i. depleted of vitality

10. effete   j. worthless matter

Fill-ins

Choose the best word to fill in the blank in each sentence.

documented	doggerel	dogmatic	dormant	dross
duped	ebullient	eclectic	effervescent	effete

1. Clinical psychologists provide treatment for psychological disorders, and today can choose from an array of psychotherapies; often they are _____, choosing elements of therapies best suited to each particular case.

2. Police investigators _____ the case with photographs and recorded interviews.

3. The country's leaders _____ the people into thinking it was necessary to declare war.

4. Even the _____ of a great poet like John Milton is interesting.

5. It is interesting to observe how some traditions remain strong, while others gradually become _____.

6. The philosopher Bertrand Russell once observed that people are often most _____ about things that it is least possible to be certain about.

7. Julia's _____ personality makes her one of the college's most popular students.

8. The doctor suspected that the patient had once contracted malaria, but that the disease was now _____.

9. One of the traditional functions of literary critics is to help separate the _____ from the worthwhile among the many books published every year.

10. Oregon State baseball fans were _____ after their team captured the College World Series in June 2006.

Sense or Nonsense

Indicate whether each sentence makes good sense or not.
Put S (SENSE) if it does, and put N (NONSENSE) if it does not.

1. The poet's sonnets are superb, but it is his doggerel that has made him immortal. _____

2. The student duped the teacher into thinking she had written the paper herself. _____

3. The historian was happy to find several sources documenting the same event. _____

4. The bride and groom looked ebullient after the priest pronounced them man and wife. _____

5. The dogmatic philosopher has a well-deserved reputation for being open-minded. _____

UNIT 26

efficacy / ˈefɪkəsi / *n.* efficiency; effectiveness 功效，效力

A cardinal rule of medicine is that the *efficacy* of a treatment should be measured against the seriousness of its side effects. 药品生产过程中，必须遵循的至高准则是对该药物的疗效及其副作用的严重性进行权衡。

【派】**efficacious** *adj.* 有效的，奏效的

In a situation where some subjects are benefiting while others are not, a researcher is likely to have ambivalent feelings, since he or she is in a "no-win" situation. In such a situation, the experimenter must choose between, on the one hand, getting more conclusive results by continuing the experiment and, on the other hand, stopping it and administering the drug that has proven *efficacious* to those who have not received it. 当药物对一些实验对象有效，而对另一些则无效时，研究人员会感到左右为难，因为成功和失败各占了一半。在这种情况下，实验者必须做出决定，是继续实验，以获得更为确凿的结果，还是停止眼下的实验，而将被证明确实有效的药物用于一些未接受实验的人群。

effrontery / ɪˈfrʌntəri / *n.* shameless boldness; presumptuousness 厚颜无耻；自以为是，狂妄的样子

In her essay the student had the *effrontery* to argue that school is largely a waste of time. 这个学生在她的文章中狂妄地论辩上学在很大程度上是浪费时间。

egoism / ˈiːɡoʊɪzəm / *n.* the tendency to see things in relation to oneself; self-centeredness 自我主义，利己主义

The beginning of philosophy has been described as a moving away from *egoism* to an understanding of the larger world. 人们把哲学的发轫描述为人类脱离利己主义，转向理解大千世界。

egotistical / ˌiːɡəˈtɪstɪkl / *adj.* excessively self-centered; conceited 极端自我的；任性的

The critics accused the writer of being *egotistical* since she wrote only about herself. 评论家谴责那个作家过于自我，因为她只写与她自己相关的事。

elegy / ˈelədʒi / *n.* a poem or song expressing lamentation 哀歌，挽歌

Adonais is a pastoral *elegy* written by Percy Bysshe Shelley in the spring of 1821 after he learned of the death of his friend and fellow poet John Keats. 《阿多尼》是一首牧歌式的挽歌，是珀西·比希·雪莱于1821年春天在得知他的朋友和同辈诗人约翰·济慈的死讯后创作的。

elicit / iˈlɪsɪt / *v.* to provoke; draw out 引出，诱出；得出

The Socratic method is designed to *elicit* responses that guide the student toward understanding. 苏格拉底问答法旨在诱导学生给出答案，从而引导其实现对事物的理解。

● 常见学科术语 ●

Socratic method: a method of seeking the truth about a subject through systematic questioning. Often it results in the questioning of assumptions. The Socratic method is attributed to the ancient Greek philosopher Socrates.

苏格拉底问答法： 通过系统的提问探求真理的方法。一般都会引发对假设的质疑。该方法源自古希腊哲学家苏格拉底。

elixir / ɪˈlɪksər / *n.* a substance believed to have the power to cure ills 灵丹妙药

The doctor said that her prescription would help to alleviate my condition but that I could not expect it to be an *elixir*. 医生说她的处方可以缓解我的症状，但我可不能指望它是灵丹妙药。

Elysian / ɪˈliːʒən / *adj.* blissful; delightful 极乐世界的，乐土的；幸福的

In Book VI of Virgil's *Aeneid*, the hero Aeneas descends to the Underworld where he meets the soul of his dead father, Anchises, in the *Elysian* fields and learns from him the future of the Roman race. 维吉尔在《埃涅阿斯纪》第六卷中写道，英雄埃涅阿斯下到冥界，在极乐世界里遇见他已故父亲安喀塞斯的鬼魂，从他那里得知了罗马人未来的命运。

• 常见学科术语 •

Elysian fields/Elysium: in Greek and Roman mythology this refers to an otherworld where the spirits of the virtuous and heroic dwell after being transported there without experiencing death.

Elysium is described in Homer's *Odyssey* as a place of eternal spring where the souls of heroes and others who are blessed by the gods wander blissfully. Homer placed Elysium at the western edge of the Earth near the stream of Oceanus, while other ancient Greek poets, such as Hesiod and Pindar, placed it in the Isles of the Blessed, or the Fortunate Islands, of the Western Ocean. Later, in the *Aeneid*, Virgil describes it as being located in the realms of the dead under the Earth.

极乐世界： 在希腊和罗马神话中，极乐世界指的是圣贤和英雄们的灵魂生活的地方，他们无需经历死亡即被带到此处。

根据荷马的《奥德赛》中的描述，极乐世界有着永恒的春天，英雄和其他神佑之人的灵魂在那里自由快乐地徜徉。在荷马的笔下，极乐世界处于地球的西边，靠近海洋之神奥希娜斯化身的河流。而希赛德和品达等古希腊诗人认为极乐世界在大西洋中的赐福岛（也叫幸运岛）。后来，维吉尔《埃涅阿斯纪》里把极乐世界描写成位于地下的死者国度内。

---

emaciated / ɪˈmeɪsieɪtɪd / *adj.* thin and wasted 消瘦的；憔悴的；衰弱的

The prisoner was *emaciated* after being fed only bread and water for three months. 过了三个月只有面包和水的生活，犯人变得很瘦弱。

embellish / ɪmˈbelɪʃ / *v.* to adorn; decorate; make more attractive by adding details 美化，装饰，修饰；对…加以渲染

The story he had been told was so powerful that the writer felt no need to *embellish* it. 作家觉得自己听到的故事很有感染力，无需再进行加工了。

REVIEW 26

Matching

Match each word with its definition:

1. efficacy		a.	blissful; delightful
2. effrontery		b.	a song expressing lamentation
3. egoism		c.	a substance that cures ills
4. egotistical		d.	seeing things in relation to oneself

5. elegy	e. shameless boldness
6. elicit	f. excessively self-centered
7. elixir	g. thin and wasted
8. Elysian	h. to provoke; draw out
9. emaciated	i. efficiency
10. embellish	j. to adorn; decorate

Fill-ins

Choose the best word to fill in the blank in each sentence.

efficacious	**effrontery**	**egoism**	**egotistical**	**elegy**
elicit	**elixirs**	**Elysian**	**emaciated**	**embellish**

1. In the nineteenth century, snake oil salesmen traveled around America selling _____ to gullible people.

2. One theory of child development is that the infant moves from _____ to an increased ability to understand the viewpoint of other people.

3. Nothing the teacher could say was able to _____ a response from the bored students.

4. The aid program provides emergency food to feed the _____ people of the drought-stricken country.

5. Some critics consider the artist _____ because he does only self-portraits.

6. It seems to be almost a natural human trait to _____ a good story to make it an even better story.

7. The politician has found a grassroots approach to garnering support to be most _____.

8. The teachers were shocked when the student council had the _____ to pass a motion stating that teachers were using outdated methods of instruction.

9. The novel portrays an _____ world in which suffering and death have been eliminated.

10. The poet wrote an _____ for the soldiers who had given their lives for their country.

Sense or Nonsense

Indicate whether each sentence makes good sense or not.
Put S (SENSE) if it does, and put N (NONSENSE) if it does not.

1. No one could solve the efficacious math problem. _____

2. In her second account of events, the witness emaciated her story. _____

3. Some people are considered egotistical simply because they are not conceited. _____

4. The poem contains an allusion to an elixir that was believed to make a person immortal. _____

5. The scientist embellished the results of his experiment with data that had not been subjected to rigorous testing. _____

UNIT 27

emollient / ɪˈmɑːlɪənt / *adj.* soothing; mollifying 软化的；缓和的，安抚的 *n.* an agent that soothes or makes more acceptable 润肤剂；缓和剂

The politician's speech is filled with *emollient* phrases to make his message more palatable. 该政客演说时使用了很多充满安抚性的话语，以使听众更易于接受他的想法。

empirical / ɪmˈpɪrɪkl / *adj.* derived from observation or experiment 以经验为依据的，经验主义的

Some people erroneously cite the theory of relativity as support for ethical relativism, whereas in reality the former is a scientific theory, while the latter is a moral issue, and thus by its nature is not subject to *empirical* verification. 一些人错误地引用相对论来支持伦理相对论，然而事实上前者是一个科学理论，后者则是道德问题，在本质上不能由经验证实。

【派】**empiricism** *n.* ① the view that experience is the only source of knowledge 经验主义 ② the employment of empirical methods, as in science 经验方法的运用

● 常见学科术语 ●

theory of relativity: the theory of the relative as opposed to the absolute character of motion and mass, and the interdependence of matter, space, and time

相对论：相对于物质的绝对特征——运动和质量而提出的理论，研究物质、空间以及时间的相互依赖关系。

---

emulate / ˈemjuleɪt / *v.* to imitate; copy 模仿；模拟；效仿

Bionics uses technology to *emulate* nature, but sometimes a similar process occurs in reverse, in which scientists use technology as a heuristic tool to better understand natural processes. 仿生学通过技术模拟自然，但有时类似过程会发生逆转，在这种情况下科学家把技术视为启发性工具，以便更好地理解自然进程。

● 常见学科术语 ●

bionics: the application of biological principles to the design of electrical or engineering systems

仿生学：应用生物学原理来设计电子和工程系统。

heuristic[1]: relating to a speculative formulation guiding the investigation or solution of a problem

探试性的：与指引人们调查和解决问题的推测性构想相关的

heuristic[2]: of or relating to an educational method in which students learn from their own investigations

启发式的：学生通过自己的调查而获得知识的一种教育方法的

---

encomium / enˈkoʊmɪəm / *n.* a formal expression of praise 赞美，称赞；颂词

The Prime Minister asked her speechwriter to compose an *encomium* for the retiring general. 首相让她的演讲稿撰写人为即将退休的将军写一篇颂词。

endemic / ɪnˈdemɪk / *adj.* inherent; belonging to an area 固有的；地方性的

Malaria, once *endemic* to the area, has now been largely eradicated. 疟疾曾经是这个地方的地区病，不过现在已经基本根除。

enervate / ˈenərveɪt / *v.* to weaken 削弱

During the war, the commanders counted on the bitter cold to *enervate* German soldiers invading their country. 在战争期间，军官们依靠酷寒削弱了入侵的德军力量。

engender / ɪnˈdʒendər / *v.* to cause; produce 造成，引起；产生

Freudians believe that the traumatic events of infancy often *engender* repression that creates neuroses. 弗洛伊德学者认为幼年时期的创伤性经历往往会造成情感的压抑，进而引起神经官能症。

───── • 常见学科术语 • ─────

Freudian: the follower of Sigmund Freud, the nineteenth-century physician who pioneered the study of the unconscious mind. Some central ideas of Freudian psychology are given below.
弗洛伊德学者：西格蒙德·弗洛伊德的追随者，19世纪的弗洛伊德医生是无意识研究的创始人。下面列出弗洛伊德心理学中的一些重要概念：

repression: a psychological process by which desires and impulses are kept out of the conscious mind and kept in the subconscious mind
压抑：人把自己的欲望和冲动从意识中去除并隐藏在潜意识里的心理过程。

neurosis: a mental disease that causes distress but does not interfere with a person's ability to function in everyday life. In Freudian psychology, a neurosis results from an ineffectual strategy adopted by the *Ego to resolve conflict between the *Id and the *Superego.
神经官能症：一种精神疾病，会引起忧虑或紧张，但不影响人的日常生活。弗洛伊德认为，"自我"在寻求解决"本我"和"超我"之间冲突的方案时，会采用无效的策略，此时就导致了神经官能症。

*Ego: in Freudian psychology, the part of the mind that tries to match the desires of the Id with what is required by reality
自我：在弗洛伊德理论中，自我是意识中平衡本我欲望和现实需要的部分。

*Id: in Freudian psychology, the part of the mind that is the source of instinctual drives and needs
本我：在弗洛伊德理论中，本我是意识中产生本能冲动和需求的根源。

*Superego: in Freudian psychology, the part of the mind that opposes the desires of the Id. It is based on the childhood process by which a person makes the values of society part of his or her personality.
超我：在弗洛伊德理论中，超我是与本我欲望相抵触的那部分意识。它基于个体的童年经历，在此期间个体把社会道德标准变成自己人格的一部分。

enhance / ɪnˈhæns / *v.* to increase; improve 提高，改善

Although it is widely believed that the primary objective of the researchers developing the Internet was to secure the American nuclear missile system, in fact their main goal was to foster science by *enhancing* the ability of technology to disseminate information among scientists. 虽然人们普遍认为研究者发展互联网的初衷是为了保护美国的核导弹系统，但实际上他们的主要目的是通过加强技术在科学家之间传播信息的能力来促进科学的发展。

entomology / ˌentəˈmɑːlədʒi / *n.* the scientific study of insects 昆虫学

Considering that there are approximately 925,000 species of insects（more than all other species combined）, *entomology* is a vast field of study. 世界上大约有92.5万种昆虫（比其他所有物种加起来的数目都要大），因此昆虫学是一个巨大的研究领域。

【派】**entomologist** *n.* 昆虫学家

enunciate / ɪˈnʌnsieɪt / *v.* to pronounce clearly 发音；（清楚地）表达

In everyday speech the sounds of many words are not *enunciated* clearly. 在日常言语中很多词的发音都不是很清晰。

REVIEW 27

Matching

Match each word with its definition:

1.	emollient	a.	to increase; improve
2.	empirical	b.	inherent; belonging to an area
3.	emulate	c.	an agent that soothes or makes more acceptable
4.	encomium	d.	the scientific study of insects
5.	endemic	e.	derived from observation or experiment
6.	enervate	f.	to cause; produce
7.	engender	g.	to pronounce clearly
8.	enhance	h.	to weaken
9.	entomology	i.	to imitate; copy
10.	enunciate	j.	a formal expression of praise

Fill-ins

Choose the best word to fill in the blank in each sentence.

emollient	**empirical**	**emulated**	**encomiums**	**endemic**
enervating	**engendered**	**enhance**	**entomologist**	**enunciate**

1. As technology developed at a prodigious rate in the nineteenth and twentieth centuries, technologists increasingly _____ the professionalization and methodology of science by establishing, for example, professional associations and publications that published peer-reviewed articles.

2. The dream of many Internet users is the building of a network connected entirely by optical cable, which would greatly _____ the ability of the system to cope with the vast amount of data that it carries.

3. It has been said that Charles Darwin, virtually single-handedly, emancipated science from the ideologies of philosophy and religion by being fiercely independent in his thinking, rejecting all prevailing dogmas as to the immutability of species, and relying solely on _____ evidence.

4. Many people who travel to tropical countries find the heat _____.

5. There is a tendency in casual conversation for speakers to not _____ each word clearly.

6. Faced with _____ high unemployment, the government lowered taxes on foreign investment to encourage economic growth.

7. Much of the tragedy of the Holocaust can be attributed to the fanatical racism _____ by the Nazis.

8. _____ to Pope Paul II began to be published in newspapers around the world shortly after his death in 2005.

9. The veteran mediator is famous for his _____ approach that rarely fails to find a way to bring opposing sides together.

10. The eminent Harvard biologist Edward O. Wilson is an _____ specializing in ants.

Sense or Nonsense

Indicate whether each sentence makes good sense or not.
Put S (SENSE) if it does, and put N (NONSENSE) if it does not.

1. Knowing the entomology of a difficult word can help you remember it. _____

2. Carrying the 50-pound pack in the 95° Fahrenheit heat enervated the infantryman. _____

3. The Supreme Court ruling has engendered new debate on the controversial issue. _____

4. When learning to speak a new language, it is a good idea to enunciate words clearly. _____

5. It is advisable to see a doctor before traveling to countries in which malaria or other infectious diseases are endemic. _____

UNIT 28

ephemeral / ɪˈfemərəl / *adj.* short-lived; fleeting 短暂的，转瞬即逝的

Impressionist painters such as Claude Monet share with the Romantics an affinity for nature, but the Impressionists took a more scientific interest in it, attempting to accurately depict *ephemeral* phenomena such as the play of light on water. 克洛德·莫奈等印象派画家和浪漫派画家一样亲近自然，但是印象派画家对自然的兴趣更具有科学性，他们试图精确描绘出转瞬即逝的自然现象，如水面上波光的变幻。

────────── • 常见学科术语 • ──────────

impressionist: refers to Impressionism, a movement in art that began in France in the late nineteenth century. Impressionism seeks to portray the visual effects of light reflected on subjects. Claude Monet is one of the most famous Impressionist painters. The term can also be used to refer to literature that tries to convey a general impression of a subject rather than a detailed one and to musical compositions that create impressions and moods.

印象派：印象主义者。印象主义是19世纪末始于法国的一场艺术运动。印象主义试图描绘物体反射的光线所造成的视觉效果。克洛德·莫奈是该派最著名的代表画家之一。该词也可用来表示那些试图表现一种整体印象而非再现具体细节的文学作品，或者能让人产生深刻印象并唤起情绪的音乐作品。

epistemology / ɪˌpɪstəˈmɑːlədʒi / *n.* a branch of philosophy that examines the nature of knowledge【哲】认识论

A major question in *epistemology* is whether the mind can ever gain objective knowledge, limited as it is by its narrow range of sense experience. 认识论的一个主要问题是：受制于有限的感官体验，人类意识能否客观认识事物。

equable / ˈekwəbl / *adj.* steady; unvarying; serene 稳定的，不变的；镇定的，安静的

Throughout the crisis the president remained *equable*. 在整个危机中，总裁始终保持镇定。

【区】**equitable** *adj.* fair; just; impartial 公平的；公正的

Much of modern economic history can be seen as a dialectic between advocates of laissez-faire policies, who want to leave the market free to create wealth untrammeled by restrictions（believing it will "trickle down" to all members of the society），and exponents of redistribution of wealth, who want to ensure that the fruits of capitalism are shared *equitably*. 现代经济史的很大一部分可以看作是鼓吹自由放任论者和主张财产重新分配者之间的对立。前者希望放任市场不受限制地自由创造财富，并认为财富会"缓缓流向"社会的所有成员，后者则想要确保资本主义果实被公平分享。

● **常见学科术语** ●

dialectic: in this context, dialectic refers to the action of opposing forces in society
辩证： 在例句中指社会中对立力量的斗争。

laissez-faire: in economics and politics, doctrine that an economic system functions best when there is no interference by government. It is based on the belief that the natural economic order tends, when undisturbed by artificial stimulus or regulation, to secure the maximum well-being for the individual and therefore for the community as a whole.
自由放任主义： 政治学和经济学中的一个学说，认为在没有政府干预的情况下，经济体制运行效果最佳。其理论基础是，在不受人为刺激因素和调控干扰的情况下，自然经济秩序倾向于保证个人的最大福利，因此也就保障了整个社会的最大利益。

equanimity / ˌekwəˈnɪməti / *n.* composure; calmness 平静；镇定，镇静

Emergency room doctors and nurses are trained to maintain their *equanimity* when treating patients. 急诊室的医生和护士要通过训练，从而在治疗病人时保持镇定。

equivocate / ɪˈkwɪvəkeɪt / *v.* to intentionally use vague language 支吾，含糊其辞；推诿

The businessperson has earned a reputation as someone who never *equivocates* and can be trusted to do exactly what he promises. 这个商人因从不含糊其辞而声名远播，因此可以相信他会言出必行。

【派】**equivocation** *n.* 模棱两可的话，含糊的话

The saying "It's a matter of semantics" is often used to indicate that the real meaning of something is being lost in verbiage, often with the implication that there is obfuscation or *equivocation*. "这是一个语义学问题"这个说法经常被用来指真正的含义迷失在冗词赘语中，并暗示着其语言费解难懂、含义模糊。

errant / ˈerənt / *adj.* mistaken; straying from the proper course 错误的；脱离正轨的，误入歧途的

The pitcher's *errant* fastball struck the batter on the shoulder. 棒球投手的快球脱离了正轨，击中了击球手的肩膀。

erudite / ˈerudaɪt / *adj.* learned; scholarly 博学的，学识渊博的

Frederick Copleston, author of the nine-volume *History of Philosophy*, was undoubtedly one of the most *erudite* people who ever lived. 九卷本《科普勒斯顿哲学史》的作者弗雷德里克·科普勒斯顿，无疑是有史以来最博学的人士之一。

【派】**erudition** *n.* 博学，学识渊博

Great *erudition* does not necessarily mean that a person is sagacious. 一个人学识渊博并不意味着他就有远见卓识。

esoteric / ˌesəˈterɪk / *adj.* ① hard to understand 深奥的 ② known only to a few 只有小部分人懂的，秘传的

Epidemiologists, using *esoteric* statistical analyses, field investigations, and complex laboratory techniques, investigate the cause of a disease, its distribution （geographic, ecological, and ethnic）, method of spread, and measures for preventing or controlling it. 流行病学家利用非常专业的数据分析、实地考察以及复杂的实验技术来研究疾病的成因、分布(包括地理、生态以及种族上的分布情况)、传播方式以及预防和控制措施。

━━━━━━━━ • 常见学科术语 • ━━━━━━━━

epidemiologist: an expert in the branch of medicine that deals with the study of the causes, distribution, and control of disease in populations

流行病学家: 医学的一个分支——流行病学方面的专家，该学科主要研究发生于人群中的疾病的起因、分布和控制。

essay / eˈseɪ / *v.* to make an attempt; subject to a test 试图，企图；试验

The composer began work on a sonata, a form she had not previously *essayed*. 该作曲家开始创作奏鸣曲，这是她以前从未尝试过的一种音乐形式。

estimable / ˈestɪməbl / *adj.* ① admirable 值得尊敬的 ② possible to estimate 可估计的

Alistair Cooke's book *Six Men* contains character studies of *estimable* modern figures including H. L. Mencken, Humphrey Bogart, and Adlai Stevenson. 阿利斯泰尔·库克在其《六个人》一书中对H.L. 门肯、汉弗莱·博加特、阿德莱·史蒂文森等值得尊敬的现代人物进行了性格分析。

REVIEW 28

Matching

Match each word with its definition:

1. ephemeral

2. epistemology

a. admirable

b. a branch of philosophy that examines the nature of knowledge

3. equable   c. hard to understand
4. equanimity   d. steady; unvarying; serene
5. equivocate   e. to intentionally use vague language
6. errant   f. mistaken
7. erudite   g. to make an attempt
8. esoteric   h. short-lived; fleeting
9. essay   i. learned
10. estimable   j. composure; calmness

Fill-ins

Choose the best word to fill in the blank in each sentence.

ephemeral	epistemology	equable	equanimity	equivocate
errant	erudition	esoteric	essayed	estimable

1. Much slang originates in a specific group as a sort of argot that allows that group to share something _____.
2. Although most slang is _____, there are many examples of slang that endures and even comes to be accepted as legitimate.
3. Swami Vivekananda, the founder of the Ramakrishna Math, an Indian order of monks, counseled that one should try to maintain one's _____, even in trying circumstances.
4. The _____ missile had to be destroyed after it veered off course.
5. Members of the Society of Jesus (often called Jesuits), are famous for their _____, which they believe should be used in the service of God.
6. The cognitive sciences are providing _____ with new insights into how the mind acquires knowledge.
7. "Don't _____; tell me if you want to marry me or not," Ruth said to Seth.
8. The infant _____ walking up a stairs for the first time in her life.
9. Perth, Australia is often cited as a pleasant place to live because of its _____ climate.
10. Chris Evert was an _____ tennis player who won three Wimbledon titles.

Sense or Nonsense

Indicate whether each sentence makes good sense or not.
Put S (SENSE) if it does, and put N (NONSENSE) if it does not.

1. One of the important disciplines that a doctor must master to become a brain surgeon is epistemology. _____
2. The young history Ph.D. candidate is not as erudite as his supervising professor, who appears to know just about everything that happened in history. _____
3. The literary critic essayed the new novel in her review. _____
4. In view of the fact that journalism is so often ephemeral, the reporter was pleased when some of her work was published in book form. _____
5. The logic of the argument is so errant we cannot help but agree with it. _____

UNIT 29

ethnocentric / ˌeθnoʊˈsentrɪk / *adj.* based on the attitude that one's group is superior 民族（或种族）优越感的，民族（或种族）中心主义的

The words "primitive" and "savage" reflect an *ethnocentric* bias in Western culture that regards societies that do not have Western science and technology as inferior because they have not achieved as much material success as Western societies. "落后的"及"未开化的"这一类词反映了西方文化中的民族中心主义偏见，即那些不具备西方科学技术的社会都是劣等的，因为它们没有获得像西方社会一样丰富的物质财富。

【派】ethnocentrism *n.* 民族（或种族）优越感，民族（或种族）中心主义

During certain periods of this country's history, foreigners were considered to be "barbarians"; perhaps this *ethnocentrism* made it difficult for the people to accept innovations from other countries. 在该国历史上的某些时期，外国人被称为"蛮夷"，也许正是这种民族优越感使得其人民很难接受外国的创新。

etiology / ˌiːtiˈɑːlədʒi / *n.* causes or origins 原因；起源

The *etiology* of mental illness is complex because of the diversity of factors—social, biological, genetic, and psychological—that contribute to many disorders. 精神疾病的病因很复杂，因为社会、生物、遗传、心理等各方面的因素都会导致身心机能的失调。

etymology / ˌetɪˈmɑːlədʒi / *n.* origin and history of a word 词源

The origin of the word "barbarian" reflects the ethnocentrism of the ancient Greeks; its *etymology* is that it comes（through Latin and French words）from the Greek word barbaros, meaning non-Greek, foreign. barbarian（野蛮人）一词的起源反映出古希腊人的民族优越感。此词来源于希腊语barbaros，表示"非希腊人，异族"，后经拉丁语和法语演变而来。

eugenics / juːˈdʒenɪks / *n.* study of factors that influence the hereditary qualities of the human race and ways to improve these qualities 优生学

The science fiction novel describes a military *eugenics* program designed to create a race of "super-soldiers" possessing intelligence, strength, and other qualities far in advance of the ordinary person. 这部科幻小说描述了一项军人人种改良计划，该计划旨在创造出在智慧、力量和其他方面都远远优于常人的"超级战士"。

eulogy / ˈjuːlədʒi / *n.* high praise, especially of a person who has recently died 颂词；颂扬；悼词

After the death of Abraham Lincoln, many *eulogies* of him appeared in newspapers throughout America. 亚伯拉罕·林肯死后，全美各大报纸刊登了许多关于他的悼词。

euphemism / ˈjuːfəmɪzəm / *n.* use of agreeable or inoffensive language in place of unpleasant or offensive language 委婉语；婉言

An illustration of the tendency toward *euphemism* is the change （reflecting the political concerns of the day）in the accepted appellation of poor countries from the unambiguous poor, to undeveloped, to underdeveloped, to less developed, to developing. 委婉语演变趋势可以用对贫困国家的公认称谓的改变（反映了当时的政治焦点）这一例子来说明，从语义明确的"贫穷"，到"不发达"，到"欠发达"，再到"不够发达"，最后变成"发展中"。

euphoria / juːˈfɔːriə / *n.* a feeling of extreme happiness 狂喜，兴高采烈；极度愉快的心情

There was *euphoria* in the professor's house after it was learned that she had received the Nobel Prize for Chemistry. 教授得知自己获得了诺贝尔化学奖，她的屋里充溢着极度喜悦的气氛。

euthanasia / ˌjuːθəˈneɪʒə / *n.* mercy killing 安乐死

Modern medicine's ability to prolong life has raised ethical questions, such as "Is *euthanasia* ever morally justifiable?" 现代医学延长寿命的功能已经引发了道德问题，比如：从道义上讲，安乐死是否正当合理？

evince / ɪˈvɪns / *v.* to show plainly; be an indication of 表示，表明

The student's response to the teacher's question *evinced* his ignorance of the subject. 该学生对老师提问的回答表明他对该学科一无所知。

evocative / ɪˈvɑːkətɪv / *adj.* tending to call to mind or produce a reaction 唤起的，引起的

Somerset Maugham's short stories are often *evocative* of exotic places such as Pago-Pago and Gibraltar. 萨默塞特·毛姆的短篇小说总能唤起人们对异国的向往，诸如帕果帕果和直布罗陀。

【派1】**evocation** *n.* 唤起，召唤；再现

Some literary critics believe that Charles Dickens's use of caricature makes his characters one-dimensional, but others see these characters as *evocations* of universal human types that resonate powerfully with readers' experiences of real people. 一些文学评论家认为查尔斯·狄更斯的漫画手法导致他所塑造的角色缺乏深度，但也有人认为这些人物是普通人的再现，读者同真人打交道时的经历会使他们对这些角色产生强烈的共鸣。

【派2】**evoke** *v.* 唤起，引起；再现

The terms "loaded language" and "charged language" are used to specify language that has so many connotations for most readers that it is difficult for a writer to use it without *evoking* myriad associations, which will distract attention from the topic under discussion. "意味深长的语言"和"感情强烈的语言"特指对大多数读者而言具有言外之意的语言，因此作者在使用该语言时很难不引起读者种种联想，尽管这些联想会分散读者的注意力，使其不能集中于话题本身。

● 常见学科术语 ●

one-dimensional: relating to a portrayal of a character that lacks depth
一维的： 对人物的塑造缺少深度。

REVIEW 29

Matching

Match each word with its definition:

1. ethnocentric
2. etiology
3. etymology
4. eugenics
5. eulogy
6. euphemism

a. origins
b. high praise
c. based on attitude that a person or group is superior
d. a feeling of extreme happiness
e. tending to produce a reaction
f. use of inoffensive language in place of offensive language

7. euphoria
8. euthanasia
9. evince
10. evocative

g. origin and history of a word
h. mercy killing
i. study of factors that influence hereditary qualities
j. to show plainly

Fill-ins

Choose the best word to fill in the blank in each sentence.

| ethnocentrism | etiology | etymology | eugenics | eulogy |
| euphemisms | euphoria | euthanasia | evinces | evocative |

1. "Folk _____ " is the term used by linguists to refer to popular theories of how words originated or changed their meaning.
2. The book describes the _____ among Allied soldiers after Japan surrendered in 1945.
3. *The Oxford Dictionary of the English Language* _____ the scholarship of a large team of dedicated scholars.
4. The diversity of factors involved in triggering cancers makes it difficult to be certain of the _____ of a particular case of cancer.
5. Alexander Graham Bell advocated a form of _____; from his research, he concluded that deafness was hereditary and in 1881 he recommended that deaf people be prohibited from getting married.
6. The novel includes many descriptions _____ of New England in winter.
7. The captain's _____ of the dead soldier described his bravery in battle.
8. In order to discourage _____ the college requires students to take three courses dealing with other cultures.
9. Advances in medical technology have made the question of whether _____ is morally justifiable an important issue in many countries.
10. Modern warfare has produced _____ such as antipersonnel mines for mines that rip soldiers' bodies into shreds with bits of metal and collateral damage for noncombatants killed as a result of war.

Sense or Nonsense

Indicate whether each sentence makes good sense or not.
Put S (SENSE) if it does, and put N (NONSENSE) if it does not.

1. The phrase "domestic helper" can be considered a euphemism for "maid." _____
2. The patient was given euthanasia before undergoing major surgery. _____
3. The euphoria in the stadium rose to a fever pitch as the seconds ticked down on the college football team's 12th straight victory. _____
4. The eulogy talked only about the many flaws in the dead man's character. _____
5. The ethnocentric villagers have no interest in anything outside their own little world. _____

UNIT 30

exacerbate / ɪgˈzæsərbeɪt / *v.* to aggravate; make worse 使加剧；使恶化

The release of carbon dioxide from the burning of fossil fuels has increased the amount of this gas in the atmosphere, *exacerbating* the naturally occurring "greenhouse effect" that has predominated in Earth's recent past. 化石燃料在燃烧过程中释放的二氧化碳使得大气中该气体的含量增加，从而导致原本自然发生、而近年在地球上占主导地位的"温室效应"日益加剧。

> **● 常见学科术语 ●**
>
> **greenhouse effect:** the process by which a planet's atmosphere warms the planet
> **温室效应**：行星的大气层使行星变暖的过程。

exact / ɪgˈzækt / *v.* to force the payment of; demand and obtain by authority 索取，勒索；要求，强求

The conquering rulers *exacted* a tax of 10% from every adult male in the country. 战胜的统治者向这个国家的每个成年男性强征10%的人头税。

【派】**exacting** *adj.* extremely demanding 极度苛求的

Early in his career the English writer Aldous Huxley made this comment: "What occupation is pleasanter, what less *exacting*, than the absorption of curious literary information?" 在其写作生涯初期，英国作家奥尔德斯·赫胥黎作出过这样的评论："还有什么职业比遨游在奇妙的文学信息的海洋中能获得更多的轻松和快乐呢？"

exculpate / ˈekskʌlpeɪt / *v.* to clear of blame; vindicate 开脱，辩白；辩护

The report *exculpated* the FBI of any wrongdoing in its handling of the investigation. 这则报道为美国联邦调查局调查中所犯的所有过错开脱。

execrable / ˈeksɪkrəbl / *adj.* detestable; abhorrent 糟糕的，拙劣的；可憎的

When folk artists such as Bob Dylan began to use rock instruments, many folk music traditionalists considered it an *execrable* travesty. 当像鲍勃·迪伦这样的民间艺术家开始用摇滚乐器的时候，很多传统民乐艺术家认为这是拙劣的效仿。

exhort / ɪgˈzɔːrt / *v.* to urge by strong appeals 劝告，劝说；勉励

In 1943 U.S. General George S. Patton *exhorted* American troops about to attack Hitler's Europe, saying that victory was assured because American soldiers were more virile and courageous than their German counterparts. 1943年要进攻希特勒统治下的欧洲时，美国的乔治·S·巴顿将军勉励美国军队，他声称胜利必然属于美国，因为美国的士兵要比德国的士兵更刚强、更勇敢。

exigency / ˈeksɪdʒənsi / *n.* crisis; urgent requirements 紧急事件；迫切要求

Astronauts must be prepared for *exigencies* such as damage to their spacecraft's life support system. 宇航员必须为诸如宇宙飞船的生命保障系统受到破坏等突发事件做好准备。

existential / ˌegzɪˈstenʃəl / *adj.* ① having to do with existence 关于存在的 ② based on experience 基于经验的 ③ having to do with the philosophy of existentialism【哲】存在主义的

Existential writers such as Jean-Paul Sartre have argued that human beings are free, but that this freedom entails a burden of responsibility that makes them anxious. 让·保罗·萨特等存在主义作家曾提出，人类是自由的，但这种自由带来的难以回避的责任重负会使他们焦虑。

• 常见学科术语 •

existentialism: a philosophical movement that stresses individual experience in relation to the world. Existential thought is very varied, but often concerns itself with the ideas of freedom, responsibility, and the isolation of the individual self.

存在主义：强调个人存在与世界关系的哲学运动。存在主义思想包罗万象，但通常关注自由意志、责任以及个体的孤独。

---

exorcise / ˈeksərsaɪz / v. ① to expel evil spirits 驱除恶魔，驱邪 ② to free from bad influences 摆脱不好的影响

A modern parallel to the shaman is the psychiatrist, who helps the patient *exorcise* personal demons and guides him toward mental wholeness. 萨满的现代对应者是精神病医生，他们能帮助病人驱除内心恶魔，并引导病人走向完善的精神世界。

• 常见学科术语 •

shaman: a tribal healer who is believed to be able to enter the world of good and evil spirits. Shamans often enter a trance and practice divination.

萨满：一种能够进入好精灵和恶精灵灵魂世界的部落医生。萨满能够进入一种恍惚状态，进行占卜。

---

expatiate / ɪkˈspeɪʃieɪt / v. to speak or write at length 细说；详述

Every year the book club invites a famous author to come to *expatiate* on the art of writing. 每年读书俱乐部都会邀请一位著名作家来详述写作艺术。

expatriate / ˌeksˈpeɪtriət / v. to send into exile 使移居国外；流放 n. a person living outside his or her own land 移居国外者 adj. 被流放的；移居国外的

People seeking asylum in another country are sometimes *expatriated*. 在国外寻求政治避难的人有时是被驱逐的。

REVIEW 30

Matching

Match each word with its definition:

1.	exacerbate	a.	crisis; urgent requirements
2.	exact	b.	to clear of blame
3.	exculpate	c.	relating to existence
4.	execrable	d.	to make worse
5.	exhort	e.	to speak or write at length
6.	exigency	f.	to urge by strong appeals
7.	existential	g.	to force the payment of
8.	exorcise	h.	to send into exile
9.	expatiate	i.	to free from bad influences
10.	expatriate	j.	detestable

Fill-ins

Choose the best word to fill in the blank in each sentence.

exacerbating	exacting	exculpated	execrable	exhorted
exigency	existential	exorcises	expatiate	expatriate

1. The Boy Scouts motto, "Be Prepared." is a concise reminder to be ready for any _____.

2. In E. M. Forster's *A Passage to India*, Miss Quested, one of the novel's important characters, _____ what she calls her psychological "bothers" by coming to terms with their underlying cause.

3. In India, small farmers are increasingly abandoning their farms to live in urban centers, _____ the problems faced by already overcrowded cities with insufficient infrastructure and services.

4. Amateur radio equipment generally is not built to the _____ standards that professional and military radio equipment is.

5. The eminent poet T. S. Eliot was born in the United States in 1888 and lived in England as an _____ from 1914 until 1927, when he became a British subject.

6. The principal _____ the students to study hard for the final exams.

7. The literature student was amazed that the professor could _____ for an hour on a poem containing only 12 words.

8. The people living in the slums of Mexico City live in _____ conditions.

9. _____ writers such as Albert Camus and Jean-Paul Sartre tend to focus on the individual human condition as opposed to human social interaction.

10. The defendant's attorney brought forward new evidence that _____ her of the crime.

Sense or Nonsense

Indicate whether each sentence makes good sense or not.
Put S (SENSE) if it does, and put N (NONSENSE) if it does not.

1. The builder exculpated the ground to build a foundation for the house. _____

2. The football fans exhorted their team's defense to keep the opposition from scoring a touchdown. _____

3. The expedition to Antarctica brought equipment to help deal with any exigency. _____

4. The philosopher's existential approach stresses an objective, rational approach to seeking truth. _____

5. The expatriate loves her country so much that she has never set foot on foreign soil. _____

UNIT 31

expiate / ˈekspieɪt / *v.* to atone for 补偿；使悔过

The pilgrims undertook their long journey to *expiate* their sins. 朝圣者们开始了他们漫长的赎罪征途。

【派】expiation *n.* 补偿；赎罪

explicate / ˈeksplɪkeɪt / *v.* to explain; interpret; clarify 解释；说明；阐明

The literature exam requires students to *explicate* three poems they studied in class and one they have not studied. 文学考试要求学生们阐释三首在课上学过的诗歌及一首尚未学过的诗歌。

【派】explication *n.* 阐明；说明

expository / ɪkˈspɑːzətɔːri / *adj.* explanatory 说明的；解释的

There is no one model of *expository* prose that a student can emulate, since each piece of good writing is unique. 就写说明文而言，没有现成的模板可供学生们模仿，因为每一篇好的作品都是独一无二的。

extant / ekˈstænt / *adj.* in existence; not lost 现存的；无遗失的

Unfortunately for Bible scholars, there are no *extant* writings of Jesus Christ. 遗憾的是对于《圣经》学者而言，现在不存在任何耶稣本人的著作。

extemporaneous / ekˌstempəˈreɪniəs / *adj.* unrehearsed 即兴的，无准备的

I enjoyed the speaker's *extemporaneous* remarks more than her prepared speech, because they gave me insight into her personality that helped me understand the decisions she made during her time as a federal judge. 相对于她有所准备的演说，我更欣赏这位演讲家的即兴评论，因为这能让我深入了解她的个性，从而帮助我理解她在担任联邦法官期间所作的决策。

extirpate / ˈekstərpeɪt / *v.* to root up; destroy totally 根除；灭绝

The new federal prosecutor promised voters that he would *extirpate* corruption in the state. 新上任的联邦检察官向选民保证他将根除国内的腐败现象。

extraneous / ɪkˈstreɪniəs / *adj.* not essential 无关的，不相干的

The encyclopedia editors worked hard to cut out *extraneous* material so that readers could find information easily on a given subject. 百科全书的编辑们辛勤地删除了与已给话题不相关的内容，以便于读者能轻松地找到某一给定主题的相关信息。

extrapolation / ɪkˌstræpəˈleɪʃn / *n.* the act of estimation by projecting known information 推断；推定

The economist's *extrapolation* suggests that the economy will grow by 4% next year. 经济学家预测明年经济将会增长4%。

【派】extrapolate *v.* 推断

Strict determinists believe that it is possible, at least theoretically, to *extrapolate* the future movement of every atom in the universe based on present conditions. 严格的决定论者认为，根据目前状况来推算宇宙中每个原子在未来的运动，至少从理论上是可能的。

> **determinist:** the follower of the belief that all events are determined by causes external to the will
> **决定论者:** 决定论的追随者,认为所有事物都取决于意志以外的原因。

extrinsic / eks'trınsık / *adj.* not inherent or essential 外在的;非本质的

The experiment is designed to exclude factors that are *extrinsic* to the phenomenon. 本实验的目的在于排除现象产生的外在因素。

facetious / fə'si:ʃəs / *adj.* humorous 滑稽的;诙谐的

The comedian's *facetious* comments about prominent politicians kept the audience amused. 喜剧演员对政要的诙谐评论让观众觉得很好笑。

REVIEW 31

Matching

Match each word with its definition:

1. expiate
2. explicate
3. expository
4. extant
5. extemporaneous
6. extirpate
7. extraneous
8. extrapolation
9. extrinsic
10. facetious

a. unrehearsed
b. the act of estimation by projecting known information
c. to root up; destroy totally
d. in existence; not lost
e. humorous
f. to explain; interpret
g. not inherent or essential
h. explanatory
i. to atone for
j. not essential

Fill-ins

Choose the best word to fill in the blank in each sentence.

expiate	explication	expository	extant	extemporaneous
extirpate	extraneous	extrapolating	extrinsic	facetious

1. Joan's comments are so subtle some of us have trouble telling whether she is being _____ or not.

2. If you would like to read a profound _____ of English Romantic poetry, a good book to read is Harold Bloom's *The Visionary Company*.

3. To solve the mystery of who had committed the crime, the detective systematically eliminated _____ evidence.

4. Three modern masters of _____ writing are Bertrand Russell, C. S. Lewis, and Lewis Thomas.

5. The book contains all the _____ writings of Edgar Allan Poe.

6. The students were assigned to give a/an _____ talk on a subject of their choice.

7. Many of the comic book heroes of the 1950s pledged to _____ evil wherever they found it.

8. Being born to a wealthy family can be considered a/an _____ advantage to a person.

9. The priest advised the man to perform penance to _____ his sins.

10. _____ from present trends, scientists predict that the star will explode 100 million years from now.

Sense or Nonsense

Indicate whether each sentence makes good sense or not.
Put S (SENSE) if it does, and put N (NONSENSE) if it does not.

1. Upon investigation, we found that the extant of the problem was not as great as we had feared. _____

2. The two events that occurred in 1969 were extemporaneous. _____

3. Using complex mathematical extrapolations, astronomers predict that the asteroid will pass by the Earth at a distance of 400,000 miles. _____

4. The book contains clear explications of 20 difficult poems. _____

5. The new ruler made it a priority to extirpate gangs of criminals. _____

UNIT 32

facilitate / fəˈsɪlɪteɪt / *v.* to make less difficult 使容易；使便利

The Internet—together with the availability of relatively inexpensive personal computers—has greatly *facilitated* the ability of ordinary people to conveniently exchange information with one another and with large computer systems. 网络以及相对便宜的个人电脑的普及，极大地增强了人与人，以及与大型计算机系统间进行信息交换的能力。

factotum / fækˈtoʊtəm / *n.* a person who does all sorts of work; a handyman 家务总管；杂务工

In Shakespeare's play *Twelfth Night*, the character Malvolio aspires to become more than merely a *factotum* in the house of Lady Olivia. 在莎士比亚的戏剧《第十二夜》中，马尔瓦里奥并不甘心只在奥利维亚小姐家中做个杂役。

fallacious / fəˈleɪʃəs / *adj.* based on a false idea or fact; misleading 谬误的；靠不住的

The belief of the Nazis that they could create a "master race" was based on the *fallacious* premise that some races are inherently superior to others. 纳粹分子认为他们可以创造出"优等民族"，这个观念是建立在一个荒谬的前提下的，即有些民族生来就优于其他民族。

【派】**fallacy** *n.* an incorrect idea 谬论，谬误

Critics of the "strong" anthropic principle argue that its proponents are guilty of a logical *fallacy*: on the basis of one known case of intelligent life, they extrapolate the existence of a multitude of such cases. 强人择原理的批评家认为该原理的支持者犯了这样一个逻辑错误，即他们认为先有一种智慧生命的存在，进而推断出其他类似智慧生命的大量存在。

> **anthropic principle:** the theory that only a limited number of possible universes are favorable to the creation of life and that of these only some have intelligent observers. Since humankind exists, it follows that the universe is suited to the evolution of intelligence.
>
> **人择原理：** 该原理认为有利于生命诞生的空间是有限的，并且仅有一小部分空间上面才有智慧的观察者。正是因为人类的存在，宇宙才适合智慧生命的进化。

fallow / ˈfæloʊ / *adj.* plowed but not sowed; uncultivated 休耕的；未经耕作的

At the beginning of each school year the teacher looks out at the new students and thinks of a *fallow* field, ready to be cultivated. 每个学年伊始，老师都会把新学生们看作是有待耕作的未开垦之地。

fatuous / ˈfætʃuəs / *adj.* foolishly self-satisfied 愚昧的，愚蠢的；昏庸的

The student could not understand why no one took seriously his *fatuous* comments. 这个学生无法理解为什么没人严肃地对待他愚蠢的评论。

fauna / ˈfɔːnə / *n.* animals of a period or region 动物区系；动物群

When humans introduce *fauna* from one habitat into another habitat, the ecological balance is upset. 当人们把某一动物群从一个栖息地引入另一个栖息地时，生态平衡就会遭到破坏。

fawning / ˈfɔːnɪŋ / *adj.* seeking favor by flattering 乞怜的，奉承的

The boss has a reputation for hiring *fawning* employees. 这个老板以好雇用拍马屁的职员而出名。

felicitous / fəˈlɪsɪtəs / *adj.* suitably expressed; appropriate; well-chosen（措辞等）恰当的，贴切的；合适的

The Gettysburg Address is full of *felicitous* phrases such as "government of the people, by the people, and for the people." 葛底斯堡演说通篇措辞恰当，例如其所提到的"民有、民治、民享的政府"。

feral / ˈfɪrəl / *adj.* existing in a wild or untamed state 野生的；未驯服的

Feral dogs returning to an untamed state after domestication sometimes form packs, becoming a threat to humans. 驯养过的野狗一旦回归到野生状态，有时甚至会成群结队，对人类构成威胁。

fervor / ˈfɜːrvər / *n.* warmth and intensity of emotion 炙热；热情；热诚

American soldiers were welcomed back to the United States with *fervor* after the end of World War II. "二战"结束后，美国士兵回到祖国，受到了热烈的欢迎。

【派】**fervent** *adj.* full of strong emotion, or impassioned 热情的；强烈的

The *fervent* libertarian believed that government is a necessary evil that should be constrained from excessive interference in the affairs of individuals. 狂热的自由主义者认为，政府是个必要之恶，应该对它进行约束，以防过度干涉个人私事。

REVIEW 32

Matching

Match each word with its definition:

1. facilitate
2. factotum
3. fallacious

a. foolishly self-satisfied
b. existing in a wild state
c. to make less difficult

4. fallow   d. suitably expressed

5. fatuous   e. based on a false idea or fact

6. fauna   f. plowed but not sowed

7. fawning   g. a person who does all sorts of work

8. felicitous   h. seeking favor by flattering

9. feral   i. animals of a period or region

10. fervor   j. warmth and intensity of emotion

Fill-ins

Choose the best word to fill in the blank in each sentence.

facilitate	factotum	fallacious	fallow	fatuous
fauna	fawning	felicitous	feral	fervor

1. The _____ of Australia includes quite a number of species introduced from Europe.

2. The bishop's secretary tries to be respectful of his superior's office without being _____.

3. _____ dogs have become a problem in the more rural areas of the city, where many people buy dogs as pets only to later abandon them.

4. The general's aide-de-camp functions as the general's _____.

5. President John F. Kennedy expressed the idea of duty to the country in these _____ words: "Ask not what your country can do for you; ask what you can do for your country."

6. Carbon-14 dating is predicated on the assumption that the amount of carbon-14 in the atmosphere remains constant, but recently this has been proved _____.

7. The football team's leading running back blocks and runs with equal _____.

8. The teacher was becoming tired of her students' _____ response to literature.

9. The black box on commercial airliners, which records flight and engineering data, is usually painted a bright color to _____ finding it after a crash.

10. The farmer could not afford to let any of his fields lie _____.

Sense or Nonsense

Indicate whether each sentence makes good sense or not.
Put S (SENSE) if it does, and put N (NONSENSE) if it does not.

1. The chairperson of the investigative committee announced, "I will not make a decision until all the factotums in the case have been discovered. _____

2. Vegetarians eat only fauna. _____

3. The President's chief speechwriter is admired for his felicitous style. _____

4. The statement "George Washington was the first President of the United States" is fallacious. _____

5. The farmer let his field lie fallow for three years. _____

UNIT 33

fetid / ˈfetɪd / *adj.* having a bad smell 有臭味的；恶臭的

Many people find the smell of Limburger cheese *fetid*. 许多人认为林堡干酪气味难闻。

fetter / ˈfetər / *v.* to bind; confine 束缚；限制 *n.* something that restricts or restrains 束缚；羁绊

The poet William Blake believed that each person creates "mind-forged manacles," *fettering* his or her natural instincts and spirit. 诗人威廉·布莱克认为每个人都给自己创造出一副"心智镣铐"，束缚了其自然本能与情绪的展现。

【派】**fettered** *adj.* bound or confined 束缚的，受限制的

fiat / ˈfiːæt / *n.* arbitrary order; authorization 专横的命令；批准，授权

The dictator rules almost entirely by *fiat*. 独裁者几乎完全凭其专横的命令实施统治。

fidelity / fɪˈdeləti / *n.* ① loyalty 忠诚 ② exact correspondence 保真；准确

Monks joining the Franciscan Order pledge *fidelity* to the ideals and rules of the Order. 加入圣方济各会的修士宣誓要遵循教规和教义。

filibuster / ˈfɪlɪbʌstər / *n.* the use of obstructive tactics in a legislature to block passage of a law （在立法过程中通过冗长演说等手段）阻挠议案等通过

The senator threatened that his *filibuster* would include a full reading of his eight-volume autobiography. 那位参议员威胁说他将在会上朗读其长达八卷的自传来阻挠议案的通过。

finesse / fɪˈnes / *v.* ① to handle with a deceptive or evasive strategy 耍诡计 ② to use finesse, that is, refinement in performance 巧妙地做，以技巧做

Engineers decided that the problem could be *finessed* by using lighter materials. 工程师们发现，那个问题可以通过使用较轻的材料来巧妙处理。

fissure / ˈfɪʃər / *n.* crevice 裂缝；裂口

Geologists measure the width of the *fissure* regularly to monitor movement of the Earth's plates in the area. 地质学家通过定期测量裂缝的宽度来监测这个地区地球板块的运动情况。

flag / flæg / *v.* to droop; grow weak 消沉，低落；变弱

Noticing that the students' attention was *flagging*, the professor gave them a short break. 教授注意到学生们精力都不集中了，便让他们休息一小会儿。

fledgling / ˈfledʒlɪŋ / *n.* beginner; novice 新手；初学者 *adj.* immature; inexperienced 不成熟的；无经验的

The coach said that some of the team's *fledglings* would play in Saturday's game. 教练说这个队里一些新手将要参加周六的比赛。

flora / ˈflɔːrə / *n.* plants of a region or era 植物区系；植物群

Singapore's Botanical Gardens contain an extensive collection of the *flora* of Southeast Asia. 新加坡植物园里生长着大量东南亚的植物。

REVIEW 33

Matching

Match each word with its definition:

1. fetid	a. use of obstructive tactics in a legislature to block passage of a law
2. fetter	b. crevice
3. fiat	c. arbitrary order
4. fidelity	d. to droop; grow weak
5. filibuster	e. loyalty
6. finesse	f. to bind; confine
7. fissure	g. plants of a region or era
8. flag	h. to handle with deceptive strategy
9. fledgling	i. having a bad smell
10. flora	j. beginner; novice

Fill-ins

Choose the best word to fill in the blank in each sentence.

fetid	**fettered**	**fiat**	**fidelity**	**filibuster**
finesse	**fissures**	**flag**	**fledgling**	**flora**

1. In the U.S. Senate, a two-thirds vote is required to break a _____ .
2. Mosquitoes are breeding in the _____ pond.
3. _____ to one's spouse is one of the most important requirements for a successful marriage.
4. The country's prime minister reflected how much easier it would be to rule by _____ than by seeking consensus.
5. The marathon runner began to _____ about two miles from the finish line.
6. The _____ reporter was assigned to cover mundane events such as school board meetings.
7. Botanists at the university have carried out a comprehensive survey of the _____ of the region.
8. He refused to be _____ by the conventions of society.
9. The boxer is known for relying more on _____ than strength.
10. The appearance of _____ in the rock suggested to geologists a movement in the Earth's crust.

Sense or Nonsense

Indicate whether each sentence makes good sense or not.
Put S (SENSE) if it does, and put N (NONSENSE) if it does not.

1. We all enjoyed the fetid smell of the meal being cooked. _____

2. Members of the minority party in the Senate were so much against the legislation that they threatened to filibuster. _____

3. The libertarian believes that modern democratic governments place unacceptable fetters on individual liberty. _____

4. The President gave a speech to rally flagging public support for the war. _____

5. The fledgling soldiers gradually became accustomed to army life. _____

UNIT 34

florid / ˈflɔːrɪd / *adj.* ① ruddy; reddish 红润的；微红的 ② flowery 辞藻华丽的

As he grew older, the novelist eschewed the *florid*, ostentatious style of his youth in favor of a more direct and sparse style. 随着年龄的增长，该小说家的写作风格由年轻时的华丽浮夸转为直接简明。

flourish / ˈflɜːrɪʃ / *n.* an embellishment or ornamentation 华丽辞藻；装饰物 *v.* to grow vigorously; thrive 茂盛；兴旺

The sophists often gave interminable speeches full of rhetorical *flourishes*. 诡辩家总是做些冗长而充满华丽辞藻的演说。// Capitalism *flourished* in the eighteenth century in Europe and the United States as the industrial revolution created a prodigious amount of wealth that, for the first time in history, was in the hands of landowners. 工业革命创造了惊人的财富，并且在历史上这些财富首次由土地所有者拥有，从而促使资本主义在18世纪的欧洲和美国兴盛起来。

● 常见学科术语 ●

sophist: fifth-century B.C. Greek philosopher who speculated on theology, science, and metaphysics. Many people came to dislike the Sophists, accusing them of dishonest reasoning. The word sophistry means reasoning that is subtle and seemingly true but is actually incorrect.

诡辩家： 公元前五世纪在神学、科学和形而上学等方面以诡辩出名的古希腊哲学家。很多人不喜欢诡辩派，认为他们的推理是骗人的。sophistry 指看似精辟、正确但其实是错误的推理。

---

flout / flaʊt / *v.* to treat scornfully 轻蔑，鄙视，低估

In his book *Poetic Meter and Poetic Form* the distinguished literary critic Paul Fussel discusses the dangers poets face when they *flout* poetic conventions. 著名文学批评家保罗·富塞尔在其著作《诗歌的格律与形式》中论述了诗人轻视诗歌传统时面临的危险。

flux / flʌks / *n.* flowing; a continuous moving 流动；变迁

In some cultures time is conceptualized as a *flux* moving in one direction. 在一些文化中，时间被视为流水般一去不返。

foment / foʊˈment / *v.* to incite; arouse 煽动；挑起

The government accused the newspaper of *fomenting* unrest in the country. 政府谴责这家报社挑起国家动乱。

forbearance / fɔːrˈberəns / *n.* patience 克制；忍耐

The President warned that great courage and *forbearance* would be required to see the war through to a successful conclusion. 总统告诫大家赢得战争需要极大的忍耐和无比的勇气。

forestall / fɔːrˈstɔːl / *v.* to prevent; delay 预先阻止

The government took steps to *forestall* an economic downturn by increasing government spending. 政府通过采取扩大财政支出的措施来防止经济衰退。

formidable / fərˈmɪdəbl / *adj.* menacing; threatening 令人敬畏的；难以应付的

By the middle of the nineteenth century the United States had become a *formidable* economic and military power. 到19世纪中叶，美国已成为一个令人生畏的经济和军事大国。

forswear / fɔːrˈswer / *v.* to renounce; repudiate 发誓抛弃；拒绝

When she became a U.S. citizen, Julia *forswore* allegiance to all other countries and pledged to defend the United States if called upon to do so. 成为美国公民时，朱莉娅发誓不再效忠其他任何国家，并起誓如果需要会为保卫美国而战。

founder / ˈfaʊndər / *v.* to sink; fail; collapse 沉没；失败；倒塌

Most attempts to create advanced new technology by government fiat *founder*, probably because of the difficulty in anticipating changes in the fluid world of high technology. 政府大多数关于发展高新技术的尝试都以失败告终，很可能是因为很难对日新月异的高新技术产业进行预测。

REVIEW 34

Matching

Match each word with its definition:

1.	florid	a.	an embellishment or ornamentation
2.	flourish	b.	menacing; threatening
3.	flout	c.	patience
4.	flux	d.	a continuous moving
5.	foment	e.	to fail; collapse
6.	forbearance	f.	to treat scornfully
7.	forestall	g.	to renounce; repudiate
8.	formidable	h.	to prevent; delay
9.	forswear	i.	ruddy; reddish
10.	founder	j.	to incite; arouse

Fill-ins

Choose the best word to fill in the blank in each sentence.

florid	**flourishes**	**flouts**	**flux**	**foment**
forbearance	**forestall**	**formidable**	**forswear**	**foundered**

1. Rhetorical _____ are generally frowned upon under the canons of modern English.
2. The negotiations _____ when agreement could not be reached on the central issue.

3. The head football coach and his staff spent the week devising a way to break down the _____ defense of the next week's opponent.

4. Peace activists are working to get governments to _____ the use of nuclear weapons.

5. The education system is in a state of _____, as administrators struggle to keep up with changes in society.

6. Negotiators worked frantically to _____ the outbreak of hostilities.

7. The country accused the neighboring country of employing agents to _____ revolution.

8. The student's essay _____ the rules of written English.

9. The governor urged the people of the state to show _____ during the crisis.

10. A _____ style is generally best avoided when one is writing a business letter or report.

Sense or Nonsense

Indicate whether each sentence makes good sense or not.
Put S (SENSE) if it does, and put N (NONSENSE) if it does not.

1. Good Scottish whiskey must be fomented for at least 12 years. _____

2. The company was foundered by a Scot who came to America in 1828. _____

3. "If you insist on flouting the law," the warden told the prisoner, "you'll be spending a lot more time behind bars." _____

4. The U.S. Navy's Seventh Fleet, with its more than 50 ships and 350 aircraft, possesses a formidable amount of firepower. _____

5. The teacher took steps on the first day of school to forestall discipline problems in the class. _____

UNIT 35

fracas / ˈfreɪkəs / *n.* a loud quarrel; brawl 争吵；打架
> The police were called in to break up a *fracas* that had erupted in the bar. 警察被叫来制止一场发生在酒吧里的打架事件。

fractious / ˈfrækʃəs / *adj.* quarrelsome; unruly; rebellious 爱争吵的；难驾驭的；难控制的
> In an effort to unify their divided party, its leaders decided to first placate the party's most *fractious* elements. 为了统一一已经分裂的政党，领袖们决定先安抚住那些难以控制的党派分子。

fresco / ˈfreskoʊ / *n.* a painting done on plaster 湿壁画
> The Italian Renaissance was the greatest period of *fresco* painting, as seen in the work of artists such as Michelangelo, Raphael, and Giotto. 湿壁画在意大利文艺复兴时期最为盛行，从米开朗基罗、拉斐尔及乔托等人的作品中可见一斑。

frieze / friːz / *n.* ornamental band on a wall 带状装饰；浮雕
> One of the best-known *friezes*, on the outer wall of the Parthenon in Athens, is a 525-foot depiction of the Panathenaic procession honoring Athena. 雅典帕特农神庙外墙上的浮雕带是世界上最知名的浮雕作品之一，它长525英尺，描绘了为向雅典娜致敬而举行的帕那太耐节的游行庆祝活动。

• 常见学科术语 •

Parthenon: the chief temple of the goddess Athena on the Acropolis in Athens

帕特农神庙： 雅典卫城中女神雅典娜的最主要的神庙。

Panathenaic: relating to the Panathenaea, an Athenian festival held in honor of the Greek goddess Athena, the patron goddess of Athens

帕那太耐节的： 与泛雅典娜节有关的，泛雅典娜节是雅典人为了纪念希腊女神雅典娜，即雅典的守护神而举办的节日。

froward / ˈfrouwərd / adj. stubbornly contrary; obstinately disobedient 顽固的；刚愎的；难驾驭的

The teacher had no choice but to send the *froward* child to the vice-principal for disciplining. 老师只得将这个不听话的孩子送到副校长那里接受管教。

frugality / fruˈgæləti / n. thrift 节约，节俭

In these days of credit card and installment plan buying, *frugality* seems to have become a rarely practiced virtue. 在充斥着信用卡和分期付款的时代，节俭好像成为了一种稀有的美德。

fulminate / ˈfʌlmɪneɪt / v. to attack loudly; denounce 大声而有力地斥责；谴责

The senator *fulminated* against what he termed "foreign meddling in America's business." 这位议员强烈谴责了他称之为"别国干预美国事务"的说法。

fulsome / ˈfʌlsəm / adj. so excessive as to be disgusting 令人厌恶的，令人作呕的

The actor was embarrassed by the *fulsome* praise he received after winning the Academy Award for best actor. 这位演员在赢得奥斯卡最佳男演员奖后，因别人过分的夸赞而感到非常尴尬。

fusion / ˈfjuːʒn / adj. union; synthesis 熔解；聚变

A hydrogen bomb requires tremendous heat to trigger the *fusion* reaction, which is provided by the detonation of a fission bomb. 氢弹需要巨大的热量以触发聚变反应，而这种热量是由裂变弹的爆炸提供的。

• 常见学科术语 •

fusion: In physics, nuclear fusion is the process by which multiple nuclei join together to form a heavier nucleus, resulting in the release of energy.

聚变： 在物理学上，核聚变是指大量原子核结合成一个相对较重的原子核，从而释放出热量的过程。

fission: splitting into two parts. In physics, nuclear fission is a process where a large nucleus is split into two smaller nuclei. In biology, binary fission refers to the process whereby a prokaryote （a single-celled organism lacking a membrane-bound nucleus）reproduces by cell division.

裂变： 分成两部分。在物理学上，核裂变指的是一个原子核裂变成两个较小的原子核的过程。在生物学上，二分裂是指一个原生物核(即一个缺少原核细胞膜的单细胞组织)利用细胞分裂进行繁殖的过程。

futile / ˈfjuːtl / adj. ineffective; useless; fruitless 无用的；无效的；徒劳的

To some non-philosophers, the discipline seems frivolous and *futile* because it produces no tangible benefits. 对于一些非哲学家来说，哲学是一门无聊且无用的学科，因为不会产生有形的利益。

REVIEW 35

Matching

Match each word with its definition:

1. fracas
2. fractious
3. fresco
4. frieze
5. froward
6. frugality
7. fulminate
8. fulsome
9. fusion
10. futile

a. a painting done on plaster
b. so excessive as to be disgusting
c. stubbornly contrary
d. useless
e. quarrelsome; unruly
f. ornamental band on a wall
g. to denounce
h. synthesis
i. a loud quarrel
j. thrift

Fill-ins

Choose the best word to fill in the blank in each sentence.

fracas	fractious	fresco	frieze	froward
frugality	fulminated	fulsome	fusion	futile

1. The philosopher's conclusion is that it is _____ to try to understand the ultimate meaning of existence.
2. The genesis of the computer revolution lay, to a large extent, in a _____ of science and technology.
3. A _____ broke out on the field after the pitcher hit a third batter in a row.
4. Many people find _____ a difficult virtue to practice.
5. The _____ horse resisted every effort of its rider to make it follow the path.
6. Archaeologists are studying the _____, which they hope will give them a better understanding of life in ancient Greece.
7. The guest of honor at the banquet warned her hosts that she would leave if speakers began to heap _____ praise on her for her work for the poor.
8. _____ elements within the party have prevented a consensus from being reached on the issue.
9. The reformer _____ against a society in which wealth is distributed so unequally.
10. The earliest form of _____ in history was Egyptian wall paintings in tombs.

Sense or Nonsense

Indicate whether each sentence makes good sense or not.
Put S (SENSE) if it does, and put N (NONSENSE) if it does not.

1. The development of modern frieze allows us to enjoy foods from all over the world. _____

2. We had to fulminate the house to kill the insects that had infested it. _____
3. The froward child refuses to go to bed when he's told to. _____
4. The country's leader urged citizens to practice frugality to help reduce private debt. _____
5. There were quite a few futile attempts at manned flight before the Wright brothers. _____

UNIT 36

gainsay / ˌɡeɪnˈseɪ / *v.* to deny; dispute; oppose 反驳；反对；否定
No one can *gainsay* the fact that she put great effort into the project. 没有人能否定她在这个项目中付出的巨大努力。

gambol / ˈɡæmbl / *v.* to frolic; leap playfully 雀跃；嬉戏 *n.* frolicking about 嬉戏；嬉闹
The children *gamboled* on the lawn while their parents ate lunch. 父母吃午饭时，孩子们在草坪上嬉戏。

garrulous / ˈɡærələs / *adj.* very talkative; wordy 唠叨的，喋喋不休的
The *garrulous* houseguest made it difficult for us to get much work done on the project. 留宿客人喋喋不休，使我们很难进行项目工作。

gauche / ɡoʊʃ / *adj.* coarse and uncouth; clumsy 粗鲁的，粗野的；笨拙的
What is considered *gauche* in one culture might not be considered *gauche* in another culture; for example, burping is considered rude in America but is acceptable in some other countries. 有些行为在一种文化中被认为不雅，但在另一种文化中却不是，例如，打嗝在美国被视为是粗鲁的，但在其他一些国家却是可接受的。

geniality / ˌdʒiːniˈæləti / *n.* cheerfulness; kindliness; sociability 亲切；温和；友好
Hosts of television talk shows are generally people who possess a great deal of *geniality*. 电视访谈节目的主持人通常是极具亲和力的人。
【派】genial *adj.* having a pleasant or friendly disposition 友好的；亲切的

gerrymander / ˈdʒerimændər / *v.* to divide an area into voting districts in a way that favors a political party 为政党利益改划选区
An argument against the practice of *gerrymandering* is that it tends to make it difficult for the party that is out of power to regain power. 一些人反对实行改划选区以谋取利益的做法，因为这会使在野党很难重获权力。

glib / ɡlɪb / *adj.* fluent in an insincere way; offhand 能说会道的；油嘴滑舌的
Sharon's parents were not satisfied by her *glib* explanation of why she had not been able to study for the exam. 莎伦为自己不好好复习考试进行狡辩，让她的父母很不满意。

goad / ɡoʊd / *v.* to prod; urge on 刺激；激励；激怒
Goaded by his friends into trying out for the football team as a walk-on, Jeff went on to become an all-American linebacker. 在朋友的激励下，杰夫去参加了橄榄球队临时队员的选拔，却一发不可收拾，成了一名全美中后卫球员。

gossamer / ˈgɑːsəmər / *adj.* sheer; light and delicate, like cobwebs 轻薄的，如丝的

Some experts in NASA believe that what they call a gigantic "*gossamer* spacecraft" could be constructed in space using extremely lightweight materials. 美国航空航天局的一些专家认为他们可以用极轻的材料在太空中建造"蝉翼航天器"。

gouge / gaʊdʒ / *v.* to tear out; scoop out; overcharge 敲竹杠，诈骗

The store is able to *gouge* its customers because it is the only store in the area that carries that particular line of merchandise. 这家商店之所以敢抬高物价是因为它是特许店在这个地区唯一的一家分店。

REVIEW 36

Matching

Match each word with its definition:

1. gainsay		a.	to tear out; overcharge
2. gambol		b.	to prod; urge on
3. garrulous		c.	to deny; dispute
4. gauche		d.	very talkative
5. geniality		e.	sheer; light and delicate, like cobwebs
6. gerrymander		f.	to frolic; leap playfully
7. glib		g.	fluent in an insincere way
8. goad		h.	cheerfulness; kindliness
9. gossamer		i.	coarse and uncouth
10. gouge		j.	to divide into voting districts so that a political party is favored

Fill-ins

Choose the best word to fill in the blank in each sentence.

gainsay	**gambol**	**garrulous**	**gauche**	**geniality**
gouged	**glib**	**goaded**	**gossamer**	**gerrymandering**

1. The _____ witness keeps digressing from his account of the incident to tell amusing anecdotes.

2. Semi-tame deer _____ in the lush green field.

3. The host's _____ impressed everyone at the party.

4. The suspect's explanation sounded suspiciously _____ to the detective.

5. The political scientist suggested that _____ be prohibited so that political districts would remain the same over the years.

6. Jim's friends _____ him into joining the Marines.

7. The pilot assured me that the glider's _____ wings would support the aircraft just fine, but I still had my doubts.

8. The protagonist of the novel is a shy woman who becomes flustered and _____ in formal social situations.

9. Engineers _____ a new channel for the stream to follow.

10. No one can _____ the fact that China has made great progress in improving the lives of its people over the past half century.

Sense or Nonsense

Indicate whether each sentence makes good sense or not.
Put S (SENSE) if it does, and put N (NONSENSE) if it does not.

1. Ted gamboled away his savings in Atlantic City. _____
2. The river gerrymanders through Ocean County. _____
3. After goading on the problem for several days, the mathematician hit on a solution. _____
4. The garrulous baseball announcer told a record 26 anecdotes in the course of a single game. _____
5. The dean applauded the students for their gauche, decorous behavior. _____

UNIT 37

grandiloquent / grænˈdɪləkwənt / *adj.* pompous; bombastic 浮夸的；言过其实的
The orator abandoned *grandiloquent* phrases and instead uses simple and direct language. 演说者舍弃了浮夸辞藻，而使用简单直白的语言。

gregarious / grɪˈgeriəs / *adj.* sociable 合群的；爱交友的；友好的
A recent anthropological theory is that human beings are *gregarious* creatures that are comfortable living in groups of around 150 individuals. 最新人类学理论表明，人类是好交际的生物，要住在约有150人的生活圈中才感觉舒服。

grouse / graʊs / *v.* to complain 抱怨，发牢骚，诉苦 *n.* 怨言
Instead of *grousing* about the policy, do something about it: write to your congressional representative. 与其抱怨政策不好，不如做点实事：写信给你们州的国会代表。 // The lieutenant told his men "If you have any *grouses*, take them to the captain." 中尉对手下士兵说："如果你们有不满，就去跟上尉说。"

guileless / ˈgaɪlləs / *adj.* free of cunning or deceit; artless 诚实的；厚道的
One of the charms of the novel is that the *guileless* hero manages to defeat the scheming villain. 这部小说的一个吸引人之处就是诚实厚道的主人公成功地打败了狡猾奸诈的恶棍。
【派】*guile* *n.* deception or trickery 欺骗；诡计
Playing poker well requires *guile* as well as skill. 要想玩好扑克牌，既要有技巧，又要有谋略。

guise / gaɪz / *n.* ① outward appearance 外观，外表 ② false appearance; pretense 假象；假装
In Greek mythology, the god Zeus often appeared to mortal women to whom he was attracted in strange *guises*: as a swan, he made love to Leda of Sparta, with other women he took on the form of a shower of gold, or a bull, or thunder and lightning. 在希腊神话中，天神宙斯经常以奇怪的外表出现在吸引他的凡间美女面前：他变成天鹅向斯巴达王后勒达示爱，在其他女人面前又变成一阵金雨、一头公牛或电闪雷鸣。

Zeus, known to the Romans as Jupiter, was the head of the Olympian pantheon and the god of weather. An amorous god, his liaisons with goddesses, nymphs, and mortal women produced many offspring, including Perseus, Heracles, Hermes, Ares, the Fates, and the Muses.

宙斯，在罗马神话中的名字是朱庇特，是奥林匹亚十二山的众神之首，也是天气之神。他是一个多情的天神，他与许多女神、仙女、凡间美女相爱并孕育儿女，他的后代有珀尔修斯、赫拉克勒斯、赫尔墨斯、阿瑞斯、命运女神和缪斯。

Leda was the wife of King Tyndareus of Sparta. Her union with Zeus produced Helen and Polydeuces.

勒达是斯巴达国王延达瑞俄斯的妻子，她与宙斯生下海伦和波吕杜克斯。

gullible / ˈgʌləbl / *adj.* easily deceived 轻信的；易受骗的

Gullible members of the audience believed the young performer's claim that he had composed "Hey, Jude." 这个年轻演奏者声称《嘿，裘德》这首歌是他作曲的，一些轻信的观众相信了他的话。

gustatory / ˈgʌstəˌtɔːri / *adj.* affecting the sense of taste 品尝的；味觉的

According to scientists, our *gustatory* sense depends to a large extent on our olfactory sense. 据有关科学家说，人类的味觉在很大程度上依赖于嗅觉。

halcyon / ˈhælsiən / *adj.* ① calm and peaceful; happy 平静的；幸福的 ② golden; prosperous 繁荣的 *n.* a genus of kingfisher 翠鸟

The movie evokes the *halcyon* years immediately after World War II when America was at peace and the economy was booming. 这部电影让人想起"二战"后不久美国的太平年代，生活安定，经济繁荣。

In folklore the **halcyon** (kingfisher) is a bird that brings peace and calm to the ocean waves for several days around the time of winter solstice, when it builds its nest on the sea and lays its eggs there, and symbolizes life and renewal. The expressions halcyon days and halcyon years describes periods of time that are tranquil and happy.

The origins of the halcyon myth can be traced back to ancient Greece and the story of the queen Alcyone (Halcyone) who threw herself into the sea when she saw the dead body of her husband Ceyx, the King of Thessaly, who had drowned in a shipwreck. Pitying Alcyone, the gods transformed both her and Ceyx into kingfishers, and they remained in the sea where they mated and had young. While Alcyone laid her eggs and brooded over the nest on the sea, Aeolus, keeper of the sea winds, restrained these winds so that the ocean surface would remain calm and peaceful.

在民间传说中halcyon是一种翠鸟，大约冬至时，它会在海上做巢、产蛋，给波涛汹涌的大海带来平静，其象征着生命和重生。halcyon days 和halcyon years 指安定、和平、幸福的日子。

翠鸟的神话可以追溯到古希腊亚克安娜（金牛座）王后。故事中，当她看到漂浮在海上的丈夫西宇克斯（萨塞利的国王，他在船只失事时被淹死）的尸体时，也投身入海。神同情亚克安娜，把她和她丈夫都变成了翠鸟，他们就永远地在海上相伴、繁衍。当亚克安娜在海上产卵和孵蛋时，风神埃俄罗斯就控制风力，使海平面保持平静。

hallowed / ˈhæloʊd / *adj.* holy; sacred 神圣的

The questioning of scientific and religious orthodoxy by scientists such as Charles Lyell and Charles Darwin led to stupendous advances in both geology and biology, as these fields freed themselves from the fetters of *hallowed*, but fallacious, assumptions about the age and development of the Earth and life. 查尔斯·赖尔和查尔斯·达尔文等科学家对科学和宗教正统说法的质疑，使得地质和生物这两个领域挣脱了神圣却又荒谬的关于地球和生命的寿命及其发展的假说，并取得长足进步。

【派】**hallow** *v.* 使神圣

harangue / həˈræŋ / *n.* a long, pompous speech; tirade 长篇大论；高谈阔论

The football team sat silently listening to their coach's half-time *harangue* about poor tackling, dropped passes, and lost opportunities to score. 中场休息时，球员们安静地坐着，听教练慷慨激昂地评论他们抱球传球失误，还错失进球良机。

REVIEW 37

Matching

Match each word with its definition:

1. grandiloquent		a.	free of deceit
2. gregarious		b.	affecting the sense of taste
3. grouse		c.	a long, pompous speech
4. guileless		d.	easily deceived
5. guise		e.	calm and peaceful
6. gullible		f.	pompous; bombastic
7. gustatory		g.	outward appearance
8. halcyon		h.	to complain
9. hallowed		i.	holy; sacred
10. harangue		j.	sociable

Fill-ins

Choose the best word to fill in the blank in each sentence.

grandiloquent	**gregarious**	**grouse**	**guileless**	**guises**
gullible	**gustatory**	**halcyon**	**hallowed**	**harangue**

1. "Anyone with a _____ about my marking can see me in my office after class," the law professor told her class.

2. Researchers have found that many primates—such as chimpanzees and humans, for example— are _____, while others, like the orangutan, live largely solitary lives.

3. The field in France is _____ by the graves of the brave soldiers who fought and died for their country.

4. Abraham Lincoln's famous adage—"You can fool some of the people all the time, and all of the people some of the time, but you cannot fool all of the people all the time."—can be paraphrased: "There are a lot of _____ people in the electorate, but there are also some people who insist on knowing the truth."

5. The President governs with the adage " _____ phrases don't house the homeless" always in mind.

6. The restaurant critic called the dish "a _____ triumph."

7. According to Hindu belief, God appears throughout history in many _____.

8. In Somerset Maugham's story "The Facts of Life" a _____ young man triumphs over a crafty, worldly-wise young woman who tries to steal his money.

9. In retrospect, the prosperous 1950s seem like _____ years to many Americans.

10. The professor finished his _____ about student tardiness with the words, "The next time any of you are late, don't bother coming to my class."

Sense or Nonsense

Indicate whether each sentence makes good sense or not.

Put S (SENSE) if it does, and put N (NONSENSE) if it does not.

1. Gustatory winds made it difficult to sail the yacht back to port. _____

2. The con man is always on the lookout for guileless individuals. _____

3. The poem harkens back to an imagined halcyon Golden Age. _____

4. Many of America's greatest thinkers and leaders have passed through the hallowed halls of Harvard University. _____

5. The computer dating service helps people too gregarious to mingle with others at social functions to find a partner. _____

UNIT 38

harrowing / ˈhærouɪŋ / *adj.* extremely distressing; terrifying 十分痛苦的；令人害怕的

The journey "inward" to explore the unconscious mind has been described as more *harrowing* than the most dangerous voyage to explore the Earth. 对潜意识进行探索的"内心之旅"被描述成比最危险的探索世界之旅更为惊险。

herbivorous / hɜːrˈbɪvərəs / *adj.* relating to a herbivore, an animal that feeds mainly on plants 食草的

Most researchers now believe that the common ancestor of apes and humans was a strongly *herbivorous* animal. 现在大多数研究人员都认为人类和类人猿的共同祖先是一种食草性倾向非常明显的动物。

hermetic / hɜːrˈmetɪk / *adj.* ① tightly sealed 密封的 ② magical 与秘术相关的；神秘的

Scholars have traced many of the *hermetic* traditions of ancient Greece to Egypt. 学者们发现古希腊很多秘术传统可以追溯到古埃及。

heterodox / ˈhetərədɑːks / *adj.* unorthodox; not widely accepted 非正统的；异端的；不被广泛接受的

The orthodox view among scientists is that the ancestors of the great apes and humans evolved solely in Africa; however, recently a competing, *heterodox* view has arisen theorizing that they also may have evolved in Euroasia. 科学家所持的正统观点认为类人猿和人类的祖先仅生活在非洲，然而最近一个具有挑战性的异端观点认为它们也很有可能在欧亚地区完成进化。

hieroglyphics / ˌhaɪərəˈɡlɪfɪks / *n.* ① a system of writing in which pictorial symbols represent meaning or sounds 象形文字书写体系（用图示符号表示意思或声音的书写体系）；象形文字 ② writing or symbols that are difficult to decipher 难以理解的书写或符号 ③ the symbols used in advanced mathematics 高等数学中的符号

The deciphering of *hieroglyphics* on the Rosetta Stone in 1822 was a great step forward in understanding *hieroglyphics*. 1822年对罗塞塔石碑上象形文字的破译是象形文字研究中的一大进步。

> ——— ● 常见学科术语 ● ———
>
> **Rosetta Stone:** a granite stone inscribed with the same passage of writing in two Egyptian languages and one in classical Greek. Comparative translation helped scholars to gain a much better understanding of hieroglyphics.
>
> 罗塞塔石碑：该花岗岩石碑上刻有描述相同内容的两种古埃及语言及古典希腊语。三种语言的对照译文有助于学者们更好地了解象形文字。

hirsute / ˈhɜːrsuːt / *adj.* covered with hair 多毛的

One of the most obvious differences between humans and closely related species such as chimpanzees is that the latter are *hirsute*, while the former have relatively little hair. 将人与黑猩猩等近亲物种相比，会发现最显著的区别之一就是后者毛发浓密，而前者毛发相对较少。

histrionic / ˌhɪstriˈɑːnɪk / *adj.* relating to exaggerated emotional behavior calculated for effect; theatrical arts or performances 戏剧性的；戏剧的

Whenever the star of the movie does not get her way on the set, she flies into a *histrionic* fit. 一旦这位电影演员不能在片场为所欲为，她就开始装腔作势起来。

【派】**histrionics** *n.* emotional behavior done for effect 装腔作势

"Cut the *histrionics* and tell me how you really feel," the woman said to her angry husband. "别再给我演戏了，告诉我你到底是怎么想的"，女人对愤怒的丈夫说道。

homeostasis / ˌhoʊmiəˈsteɪsɪs / *n.* automatic maintenance by an organism of normal temperature, chemical balance, etc. within itself 动态静止；体内平衡

An example of *homeostasis* in mammals is the regulation of glucose levels in the blood, which is done mainly by the liver and insulin secreted by the pancreas. 有关哺乳动物体内平衡的一个例子就是对血液中葡萄糖含量的调节，这主要由肝脏和胰腺分泌的胰岛素完成。

【派】**homeostatic** *adj.* 自我平衡的

homily / ˈhɑːməli / *n.* sermon; a tedious moralizing lecture; platitude 布道；讲道；说教

The pastor's *homilies* have been published in an anthology. 牧师的布道文刊登在了一本文学作品集上。

homogeneous / ˌhoʊməˈdʒiːniəs / *adj.* composed of identical parts; uniform in composition 同类的；均匀的

Pluralists in America argue that the country's institutions can withstand great diversity, and even be strengthened by it, while those who argue for a more *homogeneous* society believe that such a situation results in unhealthy contention and animosity between groups. 在美国，多元论者认为国家体系能够承受多元化的冲击，而且还能因此得以加强；然而支持一个同质社会的人则认为这种多元化的社会状况会引起群体间有害的争端和仇恨。

• 常见学科术语 •

pluralist: the follower of pluralism, the belief that it is beneficial to have a variety of distinct ethnic and cultural groups in society

多元论者：多元论的追随者，他们认为多种不同的种族和文化群体的共存对社会大有裨益。

REVIEW 38

Matching

Match each word with its definition:

1.	harrowing	a.	unorthodox
2.	herbivorous	b.	extremely distressing
3.	hermetic	c.	relating to exaggerated emotional behavior calculated for effect
4.	heterodox	d.	composed of identical parts
5.	hieroglyphics	e.	tightly sealed; magical
6.	hirsute	f.	covered with hair
7.	histrionic	g.	sermon
8.	homeostasis	h.	automatic maintenance by an organism
9.	homily	i.	relating to a herbivore, an animal that feeds mainly on plants
10.	homogeneous	j.	a system of writing in which pictorial symbols represent meaning or sounds

Fill-ins

Choose the best word to fill in the blank in each sentence.

harrowing	herbivorous	hermetic	heterodox	hieroglyphics
hirsute	histrionic	homeostatic	homily	homogeneous

1. This Sunday's _____ deals with the parable of the Good Samaritan.
2. The "_____ tradition" refers to a number of interrelated subjects such as alchemy, magic, and astrology.
3. The theologian's _____ conclusions were censured by the Church.
4. Many primatologists believe that early human beings were _____, living on fruit, seeds, and nuts.

5. J. R. R. Tolkien's story *The Lord of the Rings* recounts Frodo Baggin's _____ journey to carry the One Ring from Rivendell to the Crack of Doom and destroy it before the evil Sauron could get his hands on it.

6. Some educators believe it is best to group students according to their ability, while others prefer _____ grouping.

7. Anthropologists believe that early human beings were _____.

8. The removal of waste products by excretory organs such as the lungs and kidneys is an important _____ process in mammals.

9. The UFO researcher claims to have found writings inscribed on the side of an alien craft that resemble _____.

10. Most mothers are astute at judging whether their child's tears are genuine or merely _____.

Sense or Nonsense

Indicate whether each sentence makes good sense or not.
Put S (SENSE) if it does, and put N (NONSENSE) if it does not.

1. Stan's herbivorous diet consists mainly of hamburgers and steaks. _____

2. In the seventeenth century, a voyage by ship from London to New York was a harrowing experience. _____

3. Many patients are turning to homeostasis as an alternative to traditional medicine. _____

4. The heterodox pastor teaches only doctrines approved by his church. _____

5. Hieroglyphics on the Egyptian pot indicate it was used to store records of the pharaoh's accounts. _____

UNIT 39

hyperbole / haɪˈpɜːrbəli / *n.* purposeful exaggeration for effect 夸张

The American tradition of the tall tale uses *hyperbole* to depict a world in which the inhabitants and their deeds are larger than life. 传统的美式荒诞故事用夸张的手法刻画出一个世界，那里面人物的言行举止都是夸大的。

iconoclastic / aɪˌkɑːnəˈklæstɪk / *adj.* attacking cherished traditions 打破旧习的

The linguist and political commentator Noam Chomsky has been described as gleefully *iconoclastic* because of the zeal with which he attacks many of the central beliefs of American society. 语言学家和时政评论员诺姆·乔姆斯基被认为是一名乐此不疲的反传统者，因为他总是满腔热情地攻击美国社会的诸多主流信仰。

【派】**icon** *n.* an image or representation 肖像；代表；象征

The internal combustion engine is a ubiquitous feature of modern industrial society, helping the automobile to become an *icon* of the twentieth century, loved by many people but loathed by environmentalists. 内燃机是现代工业社会无处不在的标志，它使汽车成为20世纪的象征；虽然有很多人喜欢它，却遭到了环保主义者的痛恨。

The **icons** of the Eastern Orthodox Church are usually portraits of holy men and women that worshipers use as a help to focus their prayers. A person who smashes such an object is an iconoclast, which comes from the Greek word eikonoklastes meaning "breaking of an image." Iconoclastic has come to be used more generally to refer to an attack on any cherished belief.

通常，东正教堂的圣像是圣人的画像，这类画像用来帮助信徒集中注意力祈祷。而一个毁坏此类事物的人就被称为iconoclast(偶像破坏者)，该词源于希腊语eikonoklaste，意为"损坏画像"。iconoclastic(打破旧习的)则常用于指对任何受推崇的信仰进行攻击的行为。

idolatry / aɪˈdɑːlətri / *n.* idol worship; blind or excessive devotion 偶像崇拜；盲目崇拜

During the Protestant Reformation images in churches were felt to be a form of *idolatry* and were banned and destroyed. 新教改革时期，教堂里的画像被视为盲目崇拜的一种形式，因而遭到取缔和摧毁。

igneous / ˈɪɡniəs / *adj.* produced by fire; volcanic 火的，似火的；火山的

The presence of *igneous* rocks on the beach suggests that there was a volcanic eruption in the area millions of years ago. 海滩上的火成岩表明，数百万年前这里曾有过火山爆发。

imbroglio / ɪmˈbrouliou / *n.* complicated situation; an entanglement 纷乱，纷扰；纠缠

The plot of many of Somerset Maugham's stories consists of an unraveling of an *imbroglio* in which the main character finds himself. 萨默塞特·毛姆的大部分作品中都会有主人公置身于纠葛中并发现自我的情节。

immutable / ɪˈmjuːtəbl / *adj.* unchangeable 不变的

If humanity colonizes Mars, it will become a tabula rasa on which we will inscribe our *immutable* values and beliefs in a new environment. 如果人类开拓火星，它就会成为一块白板，我们可以在这个全新的环境中镌刻下我们永恒不变的价值观和信仰。

【派】**immutability** *n.* 不变；永恒性

The dogma of creation and the *immutability* of species was endorsed virtually unanimously by the leading anatomists, botanists, and zoologists of Charles Darwin's day. 在查尔斯·达尔文时期，几乎所有主流解剖学家、植物学家和动物学家都一致认可造物法则和物种的不可变性。

tabula rasa: something that is new and not marked by external influence. Tabula rasa is from Latin, meaning "scraped tablet" (a tablet from which the writing has been erased).

白板：全新的、没有受到过任何外界影响的东西。tabula rasa 一词源于拉丁文，原意为"被刮干净了的板或碑"(一块被刮干净字迹的板或碑)。

impair / ɪmˈper / *v.* to damage; injure 损害

Alcohol has been shown to seriously *impair* the functioning of the brain. 研究表明，酒精会严重损害大脑运行。

impassive / ɪmˈpæsɪv / *adj.* showing no emotion 冷漠的

The judge sat, *impassive*, listening to the man's emotional account of the crime. 法官面无表情地坐着，听那个男人情绪激动地讲述自己的罪行。

impecunious / ˌɪmpɪˈkjuːniəs / *adj.* poor; having no money 贫穷的；没有钱的

The businessman's biography tells how he went from being an *impecunious* student in the 1980s to one of the richest people in America. 这位商人的传记告诉我们他是如何从20世纪80年代的一个穷学生变成美国最富有的人之一的。

impede / ɪmˈpiːd / *v.* to hinder; block 阻碍；限制

The development of the western region of China has been *impeded* by a lack of trained workers. 由于缺乏大批熟练技术工人，中国西部的发展进程受到了制约。

REVIEW 39

Matching

Match each word with its definition:

1.	hyperbole	a.	complicated situation
2.	iconoclastic	b.	to damage
3.	idolatry	c.	purposeful exaggeration for effect
4.	igneous	d.	worshipping idols
5.	imbroglio	e.	to hinder
6.	immutable	f.	unchangeable
7.	impair	g.	attacking cherished traditions
8.	impassive	h.	poor
9.	impecunious	i.	volcanic
10.	impede	j.	showing no emotion

Fill-ins

Choose the best word to fill in the blank in each sentence.

hyperbole	iconoclastic	idolatry	igneous	imbroglio
immutable	impaired	impassive	impecunious	impeded

1. It would be _____ to say that scientists have gained a perfect understanding of the process of human evolution; however, it is fair to say that over the last century and a half a reasonably clear idea of it has emerged.

2. The _____ artist is applying for a grant so that she can continue painting full-time.

3. Anthropologists, mindful of the danger of ethnocentrism, avoid the use of emotionally charged words such as " _____."

4. The President warned Congress that the United States should not become involved in the diplomatic _____.

5. This week's essay topic is "War has _____ human progress."

6. The philosopher searches for _____ truths, striving to gain a comprehensive view of reality.

7. _____ rocks are formed when molten rock cools and solidifies.

8. The _____ book debunks the belief that all of America's Founding Fathers believed fervently in democracy.

9. The judge sat _____ through the entire murder trial, carefully considering the evidence presented.

10. A recent study found that the ability of many high school students to concentrate on their studies is _____ by a lack of sleep.

Sense or Nonsense

Indicate whether each sentence makes good sense or not.

Put S (SENSE) if it does, and put N (NONSENSE) if it does not.

1. Politicians often use hyperbole to embellish their achievement so that the electorate will vote for them. _____

2. Modern biologists regard evolution to be an immutable law of nature. _____

3. Gorillas are an igneous species in which a single male usually dominates a family unit. _____

4. The doctor warned her patient that alcohol would impede the action of the antibiotics that she had prescribed. _____

5. Since he regularly questioned conventional wisdom, the philosopher Socrates can be described as an iconoclast. _____

UNIT 40

impermeable / ɪmˈpɜːrmiəbl / *adj*. impossible to penetrate 不可渗透的

The virus protection software is said to be *impermeable* to attacks by malicious software sent over the Internet. 据说那款病毒防护软件可阻止网络上散布的恶意软件的攻击。

imperturbable / ˌɪmpərˈtɜːrbəbl / *adj*. not easily disturbed 泰然自若的

Buddha counseled that one should try to remain *imperturbable* through life's vicissitudes. 佛劝告人们要从容面对人世浮沉。

impervious / ɪmˈpɜːrviəs / *adj*. ① impossible to penetrate 不能渗透的 ② incapable of being affected 不受影响的

We were amazed how Laura could sit at the noisy party studying organic chemistry, *impervious* to the noise around her. 看到劳拉竟然能在喧闹的派对上潜心学习有机化学，对身边的一切充耳不闻，这让我们大为吃惊。

impinge / ɪmˈpɪndʒ / *v*. to strike; encroach 撞击；侵犯

Scientists have found chimpanzees to be a territorial species; individuals that are not members of a group *impinging* on the territory of that group are normally met with aggression. 科学家发现黑猩猩是一种具有领地意识的物种，一群落成员如果侵占另一群落的领地则会遭到迎头痛击。

implacable / ɪmˈplækəbl / *adj*. inflexible; incapable of being pleased 难以和解的；难以取悦的

Sacrifice, patience, understanding and *implacable* purpose may be our lots for years to come. 接下来的几年，我们需要有牺牲、耐心、理解和不达目的誓不罢休的决心。

implausible / ɪmˈplɔːzəbl / *adj.* unlikely; unbelievable 不可能的；难以置信的

To say that Napoleon Bonaparte achieved what he did merely because he was compensating for his shortness is simplistic, reductionistic, and *implausible*. 把拿破仑·波拿巴的成就仅仅归因于他弥补自己身高不足的努力，显然是过于简单化了，难以令人信服。

> ───── • 常见学科术语 • ─────
>
> **reductionistic:** attempting to explain complex phenomena by simple principles
> 简化主义的：试图用简单的原则解释复杂现象的。

implicit / ɪmˈplɪsɪt / *adj.* implied; understood but not stated 暗合的，暗示的；含蓄的

Implicit in the review is the idea that the writing of serious literature is a moral undertaking. 这篇评论的言外之意就是严肃文学是一项道德事业。

【派】**implication** *n.* 含义；暗示

The guiding principle of common law is that decisions of previous courts should be followed unless there are compelling reasons for ruling differently, which by *implication* would invalidate the earlier rulings. 普通法的指导原则应以之前在法庭上所作出的判决为准，除非有不得不改判的原因，而一旦改判就意味着之前的判决失效。

implode / ɪmˈploʊd / *v.* to collapse inward violently 内爆

The building was *imploded* in order to make way for the construction of a new apartment complex. 为了腾出空地建设新公寓大楼，这座楼被引爆了。

【派】**implosion** *n.* 向内破裂

imprecation / ˌɪmprɪˈkeɪʃn / *n.* curse 诅咒

The convicted man was taken away by court officers, uttering *imprecations* against the jury that had found him guilty. 罪犯被法庭工作人员带走了，嘴里还咒骂着判他有罪的陪审团。

impute / ɪmˈpjuːt / *v.* ① to relate to a particular cause or source; attribute the fault to 归咎于；归因于；归罪于 ② to attribute 归于，归功于

Primatologists generally *impute* relatively high intelligence to chimpanzees based on, among other things, the ability of chimpanzees to recognize themselves in a mirror. 灵长类动物学家通常认为黑猩猩具有较高的智商首先是因为它们能在镜子中辨认自己。

REVIEW 40

Matching

Match each word with its definition:

1. impermeable
2. imperturbable
3. impervious
4. impinge
5. implacable
6. implausible
7. implicit
8. implode

a. unlikely
b. to encroach
c. curse
d. to collapse inward violently
e. implied
f. impossible to penetrate
g. to attribute the fault to
h. incapable of being affected

9. imprecation
10. impute

i. inflexible
j. not easily disturbed

Fill-ins

Choose the best word to fill in the blank in each sentence.

| impermeable | imperturbable | impervious | impinging | implacable |
| implausible | implicit | implosions | imprecations | impute |

1. It seems _____ to some people that a complex organ such as the human eye developed purely as a result of the process of evolution through natural selection.

2. Sometimes seen as _____ foes of science, many theologians are working to reconcile divergent views of science and religion.

3. _____ in the idea of democracy is the notion of individual liberty.

4. Submarines are pressurized to prevent catastrophic _____ due to the pressure of water on the hull.

5. When you look at a star that is 50 light-years away, the light that is _____ on your retina forms an image of the star as it was 50 years in the past.

6. The plastic coating on the table's surface makes it _____ to water.

7. Joe, _____ to reason, insisted on trying to swim to the island alone.

8. An important attribute of a leader is the ability to remain_____ in a crisis.

9. People often _____ great cleverness to cats.

10. Frustrated by his inability to gain revenge on his enemies, all George could do was hurl _____ at them.

Sense or Nonsense

Indicate whether each sentence makes good sense or not.
Put S (SENSE) if it does, and put N (NONSENSE) if it does not.

1. The young soldiers were amazed how their captain sat, imperturbable, through the heavy enemy bombardment, chatting and playing cards. _____

2. Cornered by the police, the fleeing suspect began to utter imprecations. _____

3. Before the development of radio, the idea that people could speak to each other over thousands of miles was generally regarded as implausible. _____

4. Everyone in the class likes Professor Wilson because of her fair, flexible, and implacable marking. _____

5. The first mate warned the captain of the submarine that implosion was imminent. _____

UNIT 41

音频

inadvertently / ˌɪnədˈvɜːrtəntli / *adv.* carelessly; unintentionally 无意地；随意地

The songwriter says that it is easy to **inadvertently** use the melody of another song when composing. 那位作曲家说在创作过程中很容易不经意就用到其他歌曲的旋律。

incarnate / ɪnˈkɑːrnət / *adj.* having bodily form 人体化的；化身的

Christians believe that Jesus Christ was God **incarnate**. 基督教徒们认为耶稣基督是上帝的化身。

inchoate / ɪnˈkoʊət / *adj.* imperfectly formed or formulated 未成熟的；不完善的

In his book *Chronicles*, Bob Dylan describes the process of how some of his songs went from an **inchoate** state to finished, well-produced songs. 鲍勃·迪伦在其自传《像一块滚石》中讲述了他的歌曲是如何从最初的生涩不堪变得完美动听。

incongruity / ˌɪnkɑːnˈɡruːəti / *n.* a state of not fitting 不协调；不合适

There is an **incongruity** between the poem's solemn tone and its light-hearted theme. 这首诗的主题欢快愉悦，但基调严肃庄重，二者极不协调。

【派】**incongruous** *adj.* 不协调的；不一致的

The assumptions underlying Jonathan Swift's definition of literary style—"The proper words in the proper order"—recognize that there are many effective styles, but that the effectiveness of each is dependent on the context within which it is found: for example, the rambling, exuberant style of Walt Whitman's poem "Song of Myself" would be **incongruous** in Alexander Pope's *The Rape of the Lock*, with its dependence on sustained wit and irony. 乔纳森·斯威夫特给"文体"下的定义是："用适当的方式讲适当的话"。这句话背后的含义是：给人印象深刻的文体有多种，但一种文体恰当与否取决于其所在的语境。举例来说，沃尔特·惠特曼的诗作《自我之歌》，其文体风格散漫晦涩而又热情洋溢，但这种文体若用到亚历山大·蒲柏诙谐幽默、讽刺意味浓厚的《夺发记》一书中，则极不相称。

● 常见学科术语 ●

Jonathan Swift: Anglo-Irish writer（1667–1745），known today mainly for his prose satires such as *Gulliver's Travels*

乔纳森·斯威夫特：英裔爱尔兰作家（1667–1745），以讽刺文见长，代表作为《格列佛游记》。

Walt Whitman: American poet（1819–1892），widely regarded as one of the nation's greatest writers. His most famous work is *Leaves of Grass*

沃尔特·惠特曼：美国诗人（1819–1892），被誉为美国最伟大的诗人之一，其最著名的作品是《草叶集》。

Alexander Pope: English poet（1688–1744），known today mainly for his satirical poetry, most notably *The Rape of the Lock*

亚历山大·蒲柏：英国诗人（1688–1744），以讽刺诗见长，最著名的作品为《夺发记》。

inconsequential / ˌɪnˌkɑːnsɪˈkwenʃl / *adj.* insignificant; unimportant 不重要的

The meeting of the two women seemed *inconsequential* at the time, but in retrospect it led to one of literature's great collaborations. 两位女士的会面在当时看来似乎不甚重要，但现在回想起来，它竟促成了文学史上的一次伟大合作。

incorporate / ɪnˈkɔːrpəreɪt / *v.* to introduce something into another thing already in existence; combine 吸收；纳入，并入

According to Bob Dylan in his autobiography, *Chronicles*, he systematically tried to *incorporate* what he learned about life and music into the songs he wrote. 鲍勃·迪伦在其自传《像一块滚石》中，提到自己曾一直致力于将对生活和音乐的感悟融入到所写的歌曲中。

incursion / ɪnˈkɜːrʒn / *n.* sudden invasion 突然入侵

At first, the Native Americans were not too concerned about the *incursions* of European settlers, but their anxiety grew with the relentless flow of people, until, finally, calamitous wars were fought between the two sides. 起初，美洲印第安人对欧洲移民的侵入并不是很担忧，然而随着移民源源不断地涌入，他们的担忧与日俱增，最终爆发了一场恶战。

indeterminate / ˌɪndɪˈtɜːrmɪnət / *adj.* uncertain; indefinite 不明确的；不确定的

The novel describes the main character as "being of an *indeterminate* age, somewhere between 50 and 60". 这本小说的主人公"年龄不明，大约五六十岁吧"。

indigence / ˈɪndɪdʒəns / *n.* poverty 贫穷；困顿

Most economists believe that the best way to prevent *indigence* is to expand employment opportunities. 大多数经济学家都认为预防贫穷的最好办法就是增加就业机会。

【派】**indigent** *adj.* 贫困的；贫穷的

For approximately 20% of the world's population, nearly all of whom are *indigent*, malnutrition is the main impediment to achieving good health. 对于约百分之二十的世界人口（几乎都是贫困人口）来说，营养不良是他们拥有健康体魄的主要障碍。

indolent / ˈɪndələnt / *adj.* habitually lazy; idle 懒散的；怠惰的

An argument against welfare is that it encourages people to be *indolent*. 福利制度反对者的一个论点是它容易助长人的惰性。

REVIEW 41

Matching

Match each word with its definition:

1. inadvertently	a. imperfectly formed
2. incarnate	b. to introduce something into another thing already in existence; combine
3. inchoate	c. insignificant; unimportant
4. incongruity	d. sudden invasion
5. inconsequential	e. habitually lazy; idle
6. incorporate	f. carelessly; unintentionally
7. incursion	g. poverty

8. indeterminate
9. indigence
10. indolent

h. having bodily form
i. uncertain; indefinite
j. a state of not fitting

Fill-ins

Choose the best word to fill in the blank in each sentence.

inadvertently	incarnate	inchoate	incongruous	inconsequential
incorporates	incursions	indeterminate	indigent	indolent

1. In view of the fact that in most elections fewer than half the eligible voters cast their ballot, it would appear that many citizens consider their vote to be _____ .
2. In societies that place a high value on hard work, people who spend most of the day sitting around chatting are often considered to be _____ .
3. During an ice age, the polar ice caps make _____ into regions that are temperate at other times.
4. The study of human evolution _____ the latest research from primatology, anthropology, and related fields.
5. The writer is approaching that _____ age at which one cannot accurately be described either as young or middle-aged.
6. In retrospect, it seems _____ that a country founded on the principle of liberty condoned slavery.
7. Astronomers believe that the solar system formed out of an _____ mass of dust and gas.
8. The typesetter _____ omitted a line from the poem.
9. Many people consider Adolf Hitler to have been evil _____ .
10. The new welfare program is targeted to help the truly _____ in the population.

Sense or Nonsense

Indicate whether each sentence makes good sense or not.
Put S (SENSE) if it does, and put N (NONSENSE) if it does not.

1. "The method you use to memorize the information is inconsequential," the teacher told her class, "as long as it works." _____
2. The book *The Historical Jesus* by John Dominic Crossan incorporates the methodology of and insights of a number of fields, including anthropology, history, and theology. _____
3. Military intelligence indicates that the enemy has been making incursions into our territory. _____
4. The President hailed the unprecedented economic growth as "ushering in a new era of industry and indigence." _____
5. The poem is the writer's attempt to articulate an inchoate vision of the future that was beginning to form in her mind. _____

UNIT 42

ineluctable / ˌɪnɪˈlʌktəbl / *adj.* not to be avoided or escaped; inevitable 不可避免的

No one can escape the *ineluctable* truth that every creature that is born will one day die. 没有人可以摆脱生老病死这个无法逃避的现实。

inert / ɪˈnɜːrt / *adj.* unable to move; sluggish 无活力的；惰性的

The teacher was frustrated by his inability to get an answer to his question from his *inert* class. 这个老师的课堂气氛很不活跃，他无法让学生回答他的提问，这让他很有挫败感。

【派】**inertia** *n.* disinclination to action or change 惰性；迟钝

The fact that industrialization occurred in Europe hundreds of years before it did in China, which had reached a similar level of technology, is perhaps attributable to cultural factors such as bureaucratic *inertia* in China and a culture that placed a high value on the status quo. 欧洲工业化进程比拥有相似技术水平的中国早了几百年，这可能要归因于文化因素，如中国僵化的官僚体系以及过度重视维持现状的文化。

> ● 常见学科术语 ●
>
> **status quo:** the existing state of affairs（Latin, state in which）
> 现状：事物存在的状态（源自拉丁文）

ingenuous / ɪnˈdʒenjuəs / *adj.* naive and trusting; lacking sophistication 天真的；朴实的

The con man could not bring himself to take advantage of the *ingenuous* boy. 这个骗子不忍心欺骗那个天真无邪的小男孩。

inherent / ɪnˈhɪrənt / *adj.* firmly established by nature or habit 天性的；固有的

Some studies of random numbers generated by computers suggest that an *inherent* order exists in nature, since certain patterns appear that one would not expect in a random system, but skeptics dismiss such patterns as either artifacts of imperfectly designed experiments, or as the attempt of the human mind to impose a pattern where there is no intrinsic order. 对一些由电脑随机生成的数字的研究表明，自然界中存在某种固有的次序，因为随机系统不会生成这样的模式。但是，怀疑论者认为这些模式只是设计不完善的实验的人工产物，或是人类意志强加给没有固有顺序事物的一种模式。

innocuous / ɪˈnɑːkjuəs / *adj.* harmless 无害的

The bodyguard looked *innocuous* enough, but under his jacket were several weapons that could kill an attacker in seconds. 那个保镖看上去并不令人生畏，但是，他的夹克里藏着几件武器，足以在几秒内杀死攻击者。

insensible / ɪnˈsensəbl / *adj.* unconscious; unresponsive 无意识的；无知觉的

The gas is intended to render enemy soldiers *insensible*. 使用毒气的目的在于让敌军失去意识。

insinuate / ɪnˈsɪnjueɪt / *v.* to suggest; say indirectly; imply 暗示

If you read his speech carefully you will see that the senator is *insinuating* that his party has taken the wrong path. 如果你认真阅读他的演讲稿，就会发现该议员是在暗示他所属的党派已走上歧路。

insipid / ɪnˈsɪpɪd / *adj.* lacking in flavor; dull 乏味的；无趣的

Ironically, the book about how to write lively, engaging prose is an *insipid* piece of writing. 具有讽刺意味的是，这本关于如何写出生动有趣的文章的书籍，本身却非常枯燥无趣。

insouciant / ɪnˈsuːsɪənt / *adj.* indifferent; lacking concern or care 漠不关心的

Considering the gravity of the situation, Nancy's colleagues could not understand her *insouciant* attitude. 考虑到事态的严重性，南希的同事们难以理解她置身事外的态度。

【派】**insouciance** *n.* 漠然；冷漠

insularity / ˌɪnsəˈlærəti / *n.* narrow-mindedness; isolation 思想狭隘；与外界隔绝

The *insularity* of many tribes in New Guinea allows anthropologists to study cultures that have been relatively uninfluenced by the modern world. 新几内亚的许多部落与外界隔绝，从而有助于人类学家研究那里几乎未受现代世界影响的文化。

【派】**insular** *adj.* 岛屿的；孤立的

REVIEW 42

Matching

Match each word with its definition:

1. ineluctable
2. inert
3. ingenuous
4. inherent
5. innocuous
6. insensible
7. insinuate
8. insipid
9. insouciant
10. insularity

a. to suggest; say indirectly
b. indifferent; lacking concern
c. unable to move
d. unconscious; unresponsive
e. lacking in flavor; dull
f. not to be avoided or escaped
g. firmly established by nature or habit
h. narrow-mindedness; isolation
i. naive and trusting
j. harmless

Fill-ins

Choose the best word to fill in the blank in each sentence.

ineluctable	inert	ingenuous	inherent	innocuous
insensible	insinuating	insipid	insouciance	insularity

1. The referee stopped the bout after one boxer was rendered _____.

2. The country's _____ makes it difficult for its people to accept ideas from different cultures.

3. Indonesians who travel to America sometimes find the food so _____ that they add chili to it.

4. The Internet "scam" relies on _____ people to sign up and spend money for which they get essentially nothing in return.

5. Scientists are still studying the question of how life arose from _____ matter.

6. The lawyer apologized to the judge for _____ that she was biased.

7. The "cool" look that many fashion models affect seems meant to convey a look of _____.

8. The judicious doctor knows that sometimes the best therapy is not physical but emotional, reassuring the patient that the illness will run its course as a result of the body's _____ powers of self-healing.

9. We cannot escape the _____ truth that someone in the group has betrayed our cause.

10. The toxic chemical is present in the drug in such minute amounts that it is _____.

Sense or Nonsense

Indicate whether each sentence makes good sense or not.

Put S (SENSE) if it does, and put N (NONSENSE) if it does not.

1. The mathematician has devised an ingenuous solution to the problem. _____

2. Innocuous weapons such as the hydrogen bomb are capable of killing millions of people in an instant. _____

3. The professor's comment on the student's essay read, "An insensible and incoherent piece of writing." _____

4. Spicy, insipid dishes are popular throughout Southeast Asia. _____

5. In today's interconnected world, countries that remain insular face the risk of falling behind technologically. _____

UNIT 43

insuperable / ɪnˈsuːpərəbl / *adj.* insurmountable; unconquerable 不可逾越的；无法克制的

Attempts by the United States to develop an antiballistic missile system have met with limited success because of the almost *insuperable* difficulties presented by the speed of the approaching warhead that must be intercepted. 由于在拦截高速行进的弹头上存在几乎无法克服的困难，美国人开发反弹道导弹系统的努力成果很有限。

intangible / ɪnˈtændʒəbl / *adj.* not material 无形的

When considering what occupation to pursue it is prudent to consider *intangible* rewards as well as financial ones. 当考虑应该从事什么职业时，谨慎的做法是在考虑经济回报的同时，还应考虑无形回报。

interdict / ˈɪntərdɪkt / *v.* to forbid; prohibit; confront and halt the activities, advance, or entry of 禁止；阻止

Under U.S. law, *interdicted* goods can be seized by customs officials. 依据美国法律，海关官员有权扣押违禁物品。

internecine / ˌɪntərˈnesɪn / *adj.* deadly to both sides 两败俱伤的

The U.S. Civil War (1861–1865) was an *internecine* conflict that lead to the deaths of 620,000 soldiers out of the 2.4 million who fought in the war. 美国内战(1861–1865)是一场两败俱伤的战争，它导致240万参战士兵中62万人战死。

interpolate / ɪnˈtɜːrpəleɪt / v. ① to insert 插入 ② to change by adding new words or material 篡改

The book *The Five Gospels* was produced by having leading Bible scholars vote on which sayings of Jesus they believe to be authentic and which they believe to have been *interpolated* by other writers. 研究《圣经》的学者们就书中哪些是耶稣真实说过的、哪些是其他作者添加的箴言进行了投票，投票的结果就促生了《五福音》一书。

interregnum / ˌɪntəˈreɡnəm / n. interval between reigns; gap in continuity 中断；空位期；过渡期

Those who believe that Western culture represents the culmination of history are not disheartened by considering the fall of previous dominant civilizations, believing that these were merely *interregnums* in the march of humanity from the cave to a united world founded on Western principles. 一些人坚信西方文化代表人类历史的最高点，他们并没有因先前主流文明的没落而灰心，因为他们坚信那只是人类从洞穴文化发展为一个建立在西方法则之上的团结世界过程中的过渡期。

intimate adj. / ˈɪntɪmət / marked by close acquaintance 亲密的；密切的 v. / ˈɪntɪmeɪt / to make known subtly and indirectly 暗示

During the 1990s Bob Dylan and Jerry Garcia became good, though not *intimate*, friends. 20世纪90年代，鲍勃·迪伦和杰里·加西亚成了好朋友，不过并不亲密。// The editor *intimated* that substantial changes would have to be made in the book. 编辑暗示这本书的改动会相当大。

【派】**intimacy** n. 亲密

The American artist Grandma Moses, although considered by art experts to be deficient in technique, achieved an admirable *intimacy* with her subject matter. 一些艺术专家认为美国艺术家摩西奶奶在技术上虽有不足之处，但她在题材选择上却具有令人赞叹的亲和力。

intractable / ɪnˈtræktəbl / adj. not easily managed 不易处理的

General practitioners are equipped to deal with most psychosomatic disorders, but in *intractable* cases a psychiatrist is consulted. 全科医生可以处理大多数心身失调病症，但遇到一些棘手的病例时，则会咨询精神病专家。

● 常见学科术语 ●
---

psychosomatic disorder: a disease with physical symptoms believed to be caused by emotional or psychological factors
身心失调：一种有生理症状、但是由情感或精神因素引发的疾病。

intransigence / ɪnˈtrænzɪdʒəns / n. stubbornness; refusal to compromise 固执；不妥协

Each side in the negotiations accused the other of *intransigence*, so talks broke down. 谈判双方都认为对方固执己见，因此谈判破裂。

introspective / ˌɪntrəˈspektɪv / adj. contemplating one's own thoughts and feelings 内省的，自省的，反省的

In many ways William Wordsworth's great poem *The Prelude* is an *introspective* work, retrospectively exploring his thoughts and feelings as he matured. 从许多方面来看，威廉·华兹华斯的著名诗篇《序曲》是一部内省作品，回顾式地探索了作者在成熟过程中经历的思想和情感变化。

REVIEW 43

Matching
Match each word with its definition:

1.	insuperable	a.	stubbornness
2.	intangible	b.	insurmountable
3.	interdict	c.	not easily managed
4.	internecine	d.	not material
5.	interpolate	e.	deadly to both sides
6.	interregnum	f.	marked by close acquaintance
7.	intimate	g.	interval between reigns
8.	intractable	h.	contemplating one's own thoughts and feelings
9.	intransigence	i.	to forbid
10.	introspective	j.	to insert

Fill-ins
Choose the best word to fill in the blank in each sentence.

insuperable	intangible	interdicting	internecine	interpolated
interregnum	intimate	intractable	intransigence	introspection

1. The _____ of both sides means that there will be no progress in the peace talks.
2. Over the years the boss and her assistant have become _____ friends as well as colleagues.
3. Since, according to the theory of relativity, an object traveling at the speed of light would have infinite mass, astronauts traveling at that speed would, presumably, face _____ difficulties.
4. Military intelligence officers played a major role in _____ spies attempting to pass top-secret intelligence to the enemy.
5. In addition to providing a salary, a job often provides _____ benefits such as camaraderie with colleagues.
6. Scholars disagree on whether the text is entirely the work of the original author or contains passages _____ by later writers.
7. The book analyzes the _____ struggles within Christianity throughout its history.
8. The injunction "Know Thy Self," which was inscribed over the sanctuary of Apollo at Delphi, suggests that for spiritual advancement it is necessary to engage in _____.
9. The _____ between the two empires was a period of near anarchy.
10. Although the majority of Americans are members of what has been called the "affluent society," poverty remains an _____ problem, with a sizable minority of people living below what is considered to be an acceptable standard of living.

Sense or Nonsense

Indicate whether each sentence makes good sense or not.
Put S (SENSE) if it does, and put N (NONSENSE) if it does not.

1. The king's interregnum lasted 22 years, during which time he presided over a happy and peaceful kingdom. _____

2. Greater intransigence on the part of both sides will increase the chance of an agreement. _____

3. The problem seemed intractable at first, but after we analyzed it as being the result of a number of smaller problems, we were able to solve it. _____

4. The old text contains a number of interpolations by a rival group seeking to justify their views. _____

5. Many African countries are beset by internecine conflict between rival tribes. _____

UNIT 44

inundate / ˈɪnʌndeɪt / *v.* to cover with water; overwhelm 淹没

【派】**inundation** *n.* 淹没；洪水

Farmers in the arid areas called for the government to build a dam to provide water to irrigate their crops and provide hydroelectric power; however, this plan was opposed by environmentalists, who dislike *inundation* of land because it would have an adverse effect on wildlife. 干旱地区的农民呼吁政府建设大坝以灌溉谷物和水力发电；然而，该提议却遭到环保主义者反对，因为他们不想土地被淹没，那会对该地区的野生动植物产生负面影响。

inure / ɪˈnjʊr / *v.* to accustom 使习惯于

After 20 years in the army, the chaplain had not become *inured* to the sight of men dying in the battlefield. 尽管已在军队中待了20年，牧师还是没能习惯目睹士兵战死沙场的情景。

invective / ɪnˈvektɪv / *n.* verbal abuse 辱骂

The debate judge cautioned participants not to engage in *invective*, but rather in reasoned and decorous discourse. 辩论裁判告诫双方不能出言不逊，用词要有理、得体。

inveigh / ɪnˈveɪ / *v.* to disapprove; protest vehemently 不赞同；猛烈抨击

The conservative writer *inveighed* against the school board's decision to exclude moral education from the curriculum. 对学校董事会从课程表中删除道德教育的决定，这位保守的作家表示强烈反对。

inveigle / ɪnˈveɪgl / *v.* to win over by flattery or coaxing 哄骗；诱使

The students *inveigled* their professor into postponing the test for a week. 学生们哄骗教授将考试推迟了一周。

inveterate / ɪnˈvetərət / *adj.* confirmed; long-standing; deeply rooted 牢固的；长期形成的；根深蒂固的

The columnist is an *inveterate* iconoclast who continually questions conventional wisdom. 这位专栏作家骨子里就是一个提倡打破旧习的人，他总是不断质疑传统智慧。

invidious / ɪnˈvɪdiəs / *adj.* likely to provoke ill will; offensive 讨厌的；引起反感的；招致不满的

Most publications in the United States prohibit their writers from making *invidious* comparisons between racial groups. 在美国，大多数出版物都禁止作家针对不同种族作易招致不满的比较。

irascible / ɪˈræsəbl / *adj.* easily angered 易怒的

The *irascible* old man complains every time someone makes a little noise. 这个老人脾气暴躁，每次有人弄出一点声响，他都会抱怨一番。

irresolute / ɪˈrezəluːt / *adj.* unsure of how to act; weak 犹豫不决的，优柔寡断的

The President admonished Congress, saying that although it faced difficult choices it must not be *irresolute*. 总统告诫国会，即使面临艰难的抉择，也不能犹豫不决。

itinerant / aɪˈtɪnərənt / *adj.* wandering from place to place; unsettled 巡回的；流动的

According to state law, companies hiring *itinerant* workers must provide adequate housing for them. 依据州法，雇用流动工人的公司必须为其提供足够的住所。

REVIEW 44

Matching

Match each word with its definition:

1.	inundate	a.	to disapprove; protest vehemently
2.	inure	b.	to accustom
3.	invective	c.	wandering from place to place
4.	inveigh	d.	to overwhelm
5.	inveigle	e.	verbal abuse
6.	inveterate	f.	confirmed; long-standing
7.	invidious	g.	unsure of how to act; weak
8.	irascible	h.	likely to provoke ill will
9.	irresolute	i.	easily angered
10.	itinerant	j.	to win over by flattery

Fill-ins

Choose the best word to fill in the blank in each sentence.

inundated	**inured**	**invective**	**inveigh**	**inveigle**
inveterate	**invidious**	**irascible**	**irresolute**	**itinerant**

1. The talk show host uses _____ to anger his guests so that they say things they ordinarily would not.

2. The _____ young man gets into a fight practically every weekend.

3. The book makes _____ comparisons between French and American culture.

4. The writer spent his years as a/an _____ salesperson traveling throughout the Midwest.

5. The country's leaders regularly _____ against "the corrupting influence of Western decadence."

6. Some developing countries argue that they lack the capacity to compete in a completely free world market, and that in such a situation their domestic market would be _____ with foreign goods to the detriment of local manufacturers.

7. An _____ gambler, every year Tom offers his family a choice of two vacation destinations—Las Vegas, Nevada, or Atlantic City, New Jersey.

8. War has raged for so long in the country that people have become _____ to violence.

9. The President warned the nation that we must not be _____ in our determination to prevent terrorism.

10. I was amazed how Charlie, Doris, and Marcia managed to _____ Fred into playing bridge, a game he finds completely boring.

Sense or Nonsense

Indicate whether each sentence makes good sense or not.
Put S (SENSE) if it does, and put N (NONSENSE) if it does not.

1. Sam inured himself for one million dollars before going on the dangerous expedition. _____

2. Every summer, the apple orchard hires itinerant workers to pick the apples. _____

3. The educators are concerned that students are being inundated with so much information that they have trouble making sense of it. _____

4. Medical researchers are working on a cure for various types of invective. _____

5. The pastor warned his congregation that they must not be irresolute in facing evil. _____

UNIT 45

itinerary / aɪˈtɪnəreri / *n.* a route of a traveler's journey 旅行日程
We planned our *itinerary* to be flexible, so that if we especially enjoyed a particular place we could stay there longer. 我们制定了灵活的旅行日程，以便能在特别喜欢的地方多逗留一段时间。

jaundiced / ˈdʒɔːndɪst / *adj.* ① having a yellowish discoloration of the skin 患黄疸病的 ② affected by envy, resentment, or hostility 狭隘的；有偏见的
Norman's experience as an infantryman during the war has given him a *jaundiced* view of human nature. 诺曼在战争期间当步兵的经历使他对人性产生了偏见。
【派】**jaundice** *n.* a medical condition often due to liver disease and characterized by yellowness of the skin 黄疸病（由肝脏病变引起的疾病，表现特征是皮肤呈黄色）

jibe / dʒaɪb / *v.* to be in agreement 与…一致
The auditor checked the company's account books to make sure that they *jibed* with the tax return it filed. 审计员审查了公司的账簿，以确认它们和公司提交的纳税申报单的记录一致。

jocose / dʒəˈkoʊs / *adj.* fond of joking; jocular; playful 开玩笑的；诙谐的；好玩的
【派】**jocosity** *n.* 诙谐

juggernaut / ˈdʒʌɡərnɔːt / n. huge force destroying everything in its path 不可抗拒的强大力量

Some people in Britain regard American English as a *juggernaut* sweeping through the British Isles, destroying British English. 在英国，一些人认为美式英语作为一股强大的力量正在席卷不列颠群岛，摧毁着英式英语。

junta / ˈhʊntə / n. a group of people united in political intrigue 执政团

The country's ruling *junta* consists of a general, an admiral, and the mayor of the capital city. 这个国家当权的政府由一名陆军上将、一名海军上将及首都的市长构成。

juxtapose / ˌdʒʌkstəˈpoʊz / v. to place side by side 并列；并置

To illustrate their case, opponents of functionalism *juxtapose* the products of modern architecture and those of classical architecture, such as the Parthenon, or those of medieval architecture, such as the Cathedral of Notre-Dame. 为了阐明自己的观点，功能主义的反对者把现代建筑与帕特农神庙等古典建筑或中世纪建筑，如巴黎圣母院，放在一起进行对比。

【派】juxtaposition *n.* a side-by-side placement 并置

kudos / ˈkuːdɑːs / n. fame; glory; honor 名誉；光荣；荣誉

Kudos won by Bob Dylan include an honorary doctorate in music from Princeton University. 鲍勃·迪伦所赢得的荣誉包括普林斯顿大学的荣誉音乐博士学位。

labile / ˈleɪbl / adj. likely to change 易变的

Blood pressure in human beings is, to varying degrees, *labile*. 人的血压会有不同程度的变化。

laconic / ləˈkɑːnɪk / adj. using few words 简洁的

The *laconic* actor seemed to be a good choice to play the strong, silent hero in the western. 那个演员寡言少语，似乎是那部西部片中强悍又沉默的主角的不错人选。

REVIEW 45

Matching

Match each word with its definition:

1. itinerary
2. jaundiced
3. jibe
4. jocose
5. juggernaut
6. junta
7. juxtapose
8. kudos
9. labile
10. laconic

a. to be in agreement
b. to place side by side
c. fond of joking; jocular
d. likely to change
e. having a yellowish discoloration of the skin
f. fame; glory
g. a group of people united in political intrigue
h. a route of a traveler's journey
i. using few words
j. huge force destroying everything in its path

Fill-ins

Choose the best word to fill in the blank in each sentence.

itinerary	jaundiced	jibe	jocose	juggernaut
junta	juxtaposed	kudos	labile	laconic

1. During the first several years of World War II, the German army was a/an _____, easily defeating any force that tried to stop it.
2. A military _____ seized power in the country in 1988.
3. Dr. Taylor's considerable _____ manner made him the obvious choice to play Santa Claus in the faculty Christmas play.
4. The _____ for our visit to Edinburgh, Scotland included a visit to Edinburgh University and Edinburgh Castle.
5. The psychologist's diagnosis was that Eric was emotionally _____.
6. The textual scholar _____ the two translations in order to compare them.
7. Infectious hepatitis is a viral form of hepatitis that causes fever and makes a person's skin _____.
8. Most scientists regard the Noble Prize as the highest _____ they can receive.
9. It is difficult for a person who tends to be _____ to learn how to speak a new language.
10. Listening to the witness' testimony, the judge discovered that it did not _____ with the account of the incident he had given to the police.

Sense or Nonsense

Indicate whether each sentence makes good sense or not.
Put S (SENSE) if it does, and put N (NONSENSE) if it does not.

1. The young jazz trumpeter decided he should learn to "talk the jibe." _____

2. The juggernauts performed amazing feats of legerdemain that had the children laughing all afternoon. _____

3. In a healthy individual body temperature is not labile. _____

4. The host has decided to seat people at the formal dinner so that people who tend to be laconic sit next to individuals that are more garrulous. _____

5. Thirty years on the police force has given Captain Lucas a jaundiced view of life. _____

UNIT 46

lambaste / læm'bæst / *v.* to thrash verbally or physically 抨击；痛打

The critic *lambasted* the movie in her column, calling it "the most insipid, jejune film made in our generation." 这位评论家在她的专栏里猛烈抨击那部电影，称之为"当代最为苍白空洞、枯燥无聊的作品"。

lascivious / lə'sɪviəs / *adj.* lustful 淫荡的；好色的

The court ruled that the movie could be censored because its sole aim was to promote *lascivious* thoughts. 法院裁定这部电影应当接受审查并删减，因为它的唯一目标就是传播色情思想。

lassitude / 'læsɪtuːd / *n.* lethargy; sluggishness 疲乏倦怠；无精打采

After the death of his wife, Steven suffered a three-month period of *lassitude* and depression. 自妻子过世后整整三个月，史蒂文一直很颓唐，郁郁寡欢。

latent / 'leɪtnt / *adj.* present but hidden; potential 潜在的；隐藏的

Some experts in human psychology believe that we are just beginning to explore the *latent* powers of the human mind. 有些人类心理学家认为，我们在探索人类思想的潜能方面才刚刚起步。

laud / lɔːd / *v.* to praise 称赞，赞扬

The literary critic *lauded* Jane Austen's *Pride and Prejudice*, calling it a novel that "explores the tension between a person's life as a social being and his or her individual consciousness." 那位文学评论家称赞简·奥斯汀的小说《傲慢与偏见》是一部好作品，称其"探索了人的生活作为一个社会存在与个体意识之间的紧张关系"。

lethargic / le'θɑːrdʒɪk / *adj.* inactive 无精打采的

After the 18-hour flight from New York to Singapore, the passengers were *lethargic*. 从纽约到新加坡整整飞行了18个小时，乘客们都感到十分疲惫。

levee / 'levi / *n.* an embankment that prevents a river from overflowing 防洪堤

An extensive system of *levees* is the only way to prevent the river from flooding the area during periods of heavy rain. 要保证这个地区在雨季不受洪水侵袭，唯一的办法就是修筑大规模的防洪堤系统。

levity / 'levəti / *n.* light manner or attitude 轻佻，轻浮；不严肃

The comedian has a gift for finding an element of *levity* in the most serious of subjects. 这位喜剧演员很有天分，能从最严肃的题材中挖掘出轻松有趣的元素。

liberal / ˈlɪbərəl / *adj.* tolerant; broad-minded; generous; lavish 宽容的；开明的；慷慨的

Bankruptcy laws should not be too stringent, or not enough people will venture their capital; on the other hand, they should not be too *liberal*, or entrepreneurs will take unreasonable risks and waste capital. 破产法不宜太过严格，否则会导致只有少数人敢于进行风险投资；另一方面，破产法也不宜太过宽松，否则会使创业者们盲目冒险，浪费资金。

libertine / ˈlɪbərtiːn / *n.* one without moral restraint 放荡不羁的人

Don Juan is a legendary, archetypal *libertine* whose story has been told by many poets, such as Lord Byron. 唐璜是一个传奇式的、放荡不羁的典型人物形象，其故事已有许多诗人讲述过，比如说拜伦勋爵。

REVIEW 46

Matching

Match each word with its definition:

1. lambaste	a. an embankment that prevents a river from overflowing
2. lascivious	b. to thrash verbally or physically
3. lassitude	c. to praise
4. latent	d. lustful
5. laud	e. inactive
6. lethargic	f. tolerant
7. levee	g. present but hidden; potential
8. levity	h. light manner or attitude
9. liberal	i. a person without moral restraint
10. libertine	j. lethargy; sluggishness

Fill-ins

Choose the best word to fill in the blank in each sentence.

lambasted	lascivious	lassitude	latent	lauded
lethargic	levee	levity	liberal	libertine

1. Engineers worked to reinforce the _____ after the prediction of an unprecedented amount of rain.

2. To everyone's surprise, the 14-point underdog _____ the reigning champions 42-0.

3. Suddenly overcome by _____ in the afternoon, Jill decided to take a nap.

4. The former President was _____ for his indefatigable efforts to bring peace to the war-torn area.

5. In the view of some commentators, a paradox of modern _____ democracy is that although people have more freedom than ever, they often are unable to use this freedom to find meaningful values and goals.

6. The goal of the course is to help people develop their _____ abilities.

7. After the long winter layoff, many of the baseball players were _____ at the first day of spring training.

8. The bikini-clad young woman attracted _____ stares from a group of men.

9. The speaker decided to tell a joke to introduce some _____ into the solemn occasion.

10. James Boswell, the eighteenth-century Scottish writer best remembered for his biography of the eminent literary figure Samuel Johnson, was a heavy drinker and a _____.

Sense or Nonsense

Indicate whether each sentence makes good sense or not.
Put S (SENSE) if it does, and put N (NONSENSE) if it does not.

1. The captain lauded his troops into battle. _____

2. The psychologist suggested that the patient take life less seriously and try to introduce some levity into her life every day. _____

3. The picnickers were overcome by lassitude after eating a heavy lunch. _____

4. Carol discovered late in life that she had a latent ability for mathematics. _____

5. The women's rights group condemned the swimsuit part of the Miss Galaxy contest "designed solely to appeal to men's lascivious impulses." _____

UNIT 47

libido / lɪˈbiːdoʊ / *n.* sexual desire 性欲，性冲动
According to psychologists, the *libido* of human males peaks at around the age of 18. 心理学家们认为，男性在18岁左右性冲动达到顶峰。

lilliputian / ˌlɪlɪˈpjuːʃn / *adj.* extremely small 微小的
Microbiologists study *lilliputian* organisms. 微生物学家们研究微小生物。

limn / lɪm / *v.* to draw; describe 绘画；描绘
The artist based his painting on a sketch he had *limned* several years earlier. 这位艺术家以自己几年前画的一幅素描为原型进行油画创作。

limpid / ˈlɪmpɪd / *adj.* clear; transparent 清晰的；透明的
At the bottom of the *limpid* pond we could see hundreds of fish swimming. 我们看到数百条鱼儿在清澈的池水中游来游去。

linguistic / lɪŋˈgwɪstɪk / *adj.* pertaining to language 语言（方面）的
Humans are at the acme of their *linguistic* proficiency in the first several years of life, during which they master thousands of complex grammatical operations. 人类的语言习得能力在幼年时期处于最高水平，在这一阶段他们可以掌握上千种复杂的语法结构。
【派1】**linguistics** *n.* the scientific study of language 语言学
【派2】**linguist** *n.* someone who studies language 语言学家
Linguists such as Noam Chomsky believe that what people come to know and believe depends on experiences that evoke a part of the cognitive system that is latent in the mind. 诺姆·乔姆斯基等语言学家认为，人们知道或相信什么取决于某些经验，而这些经验则能唤起潜伏在大脑中的一部分认知系统。

litany / ˈlɪtəni / *n.* lengthy recitation; repetitive chant 冗长的讲述；喋喋不休

The student listened intently to his teacher's *litany* of the grammatical errors committed by the class. 那个学生专注地聆听老师一遍又一遍指出并纠正同学们犯的语法错误。

literati / ˌlɪtəˈrɑːti / *n.* scholarly or learned persons 文人学士

"Any test that turns on what is offensive to the community's standards is too loose, too capricious, too destructive of freedom of expression to be squared with the First Amendment. Under that test, juries can censor, suppress, and punish what they don't like, provided the matter relates to 'sexual impurity' or has a tendency 'to excite lustful thoughts.' This is community censorship in one of its worst forms. It creates a regime where in the battle between the *literati* and the Philistines, the Philistines are certain to win."

—U.S. Supreme Court Justice William O. Douglas,
dissenting in the case of Roth v. United States, 1957

"任何一项关于是否触犯了社会标准的检查都过于松散，缺乏稳定性，严重违背宪法第一修正案赋予的言论自由。在这种检查中，只要是与'淫秽'或'引发色情思想'相关的案件，陪审团就可以根据他们的喜好进行审查删减、压制和惩罚。这是大众审查制度最糟糕的形式之一，它导致了一种体制，这种体制下，文人学士与市侩庸人之间进行斗争，必然会以文人的失败而告终。"

—美国最高法院法官威廉·O·道格拉斯对1957年美国罗斯案的异议

● **常见学科术语** ●

First Amendment: a part of the United States Bill of Rights prohibiting the federal legislature from making laws that establish a state religion or prefer a certain religion, prevent free exercise of religion, infringe the freedom of speech; infringe the freedom of the press; limit the right to assemble peaceably; limit the right to petition the government for a redress of grievances

美国宪法第一修正案： 美国《权利法案》的一部分，内容是禁止联邦立法制定关于下列事项的法律：建立国教或倾向于某一特定宗教，限制宗教信仰自由；剥夺言论自由、出版自由；限制人民和平集会的自由和向政府请愿伸冤的权利。

Philistine: people considered to be ignorant of the value of cultures and smug and conventional in their thinking

市侩： 不懂文化价值的、自以为是且墨守成规的人

---

litigation / ˌlɪtɪˈɡeɪʃn / *n.* legal proceedings 诉讼；起诉

The radio amateur's neighbor resorted to *litigation* in an attempt to have her neighbor dismantle his 100-foot-high antenna tower. 那位业余无线电爱好者的邻居付诸法律手段，希望能令他拆除他那100英尺高的天线塔。

log / lɔːɡ / *n.* a record of a voyage; a record of daily activities（旅行、航海等的）日志；记录 *v.* to put information in a record 记录

Although no longer required to do so by the Federal Communications Commission, many amateur radio operators nevertheless keep a meticulous record of stations they communicate with, *logging* the details of each contact. 尽管美国联邦通信委员会已不再要求，但许多业余无线电爱好者仍旧一丝不苟地记录下与他们通讯的站点，并坚持对每次联络做详细的记录。

loquacious / ləˈkweɪʃəs / *adj.* talkative 多话的；滔滔不绝的

Eighty meters is a portion of the radio spectrum where a shortwave listener can often hear *loquacious* "hams" chatting ("chewing the rag" in amateur radio parlance) for hours. 在80米的无线电频谱内，短波听众常常可以连续几小时听到无线电通讯爱好者们七嘴八舌聊天的声音（他们的行话叫"唠嗑"）。

REVIEW 47

Matching

Match each word with its definition:

1. libido		a.	transparent
2. lilliputian		b.	sexual desire
3. limn		c.	legal proceedings
4. limpid		d.	to draw; describe
5. linguistic		e.	talkative
6. litany		f.	extremely small
7. literati		g.	lengthy recitation
8. litigation		h.	scholarly or learned persons
9. log		i.	a record of a voyage
10. loquacious		j.	a pertaining to language

Fill-ins

Choose the best word to fill in the blank in each sentence.

libido	**lilliputian**	**limning**	**limpid**	**linguistics**
litany	**literati**	**litigation**	**logs**	**loquacious**

1. The study's hypothesis is that the low birthrate is a result of a reduction in many people's
   _____.

2. According to the historian Richard J. Hofstadter, there has been a strong feeling of suspicion of
   the _____ throughout American history.

3. The _____ of the eighteenth-century ships' captains provide an interesting perspective
   on that time.

4. The judge warned the _____ attorney to stop digressing and "cut to the chase."

5. The critic praised the novel for its _____ prose and original characters.

6. The United Nations Human Rights Commission outlined a _____ of the rights
   regularly being abused in the country.

7. The threat of _____ was enough to induce the company to settle the claim against it.

8. The writer Somerset Maugham had a gift for _____ a character perfectly in a few
   paragraphs.

9. Applied _____ takes the findings of theoretical linguistics and applies them to such
   areas as language learning.

10. After his experiences in the war, the problems Howard encountered in civilian life seemed
    positively _____.

Sense or Nonsense

Indicate whether each sentence makes good sense or not.
Put S (SENSE) if it does, and put N (NONSENSE) if it does not.

1. If ants can perceive human beings, we must appear lilliputian to them. _____

2. Exhaustive litigation has proven that gravity exists throughout the universe. _____

3. To the unaided eye the liquid appears limpid, but in reality it contains millions of microscopic organisms. _____

4. Magazines read regularly by most members of the New York literati include *The New Yorker* and the *New York Review of Books*. _____

5. The judge warned the witness not to use the occasion to give a litany of his personal grievances. _____

UNIT 48

lucid / ˈluːsɪd / *adj.* bright; clear; intelligible 清楚的；易懂的

The eminent surgeon Dr. Christian Barnard, who performed the first human heart-transplant operation in 1967, made his views on euthanasia clear in this *lucid* injunction: "The prime goal is to alleviate suffering, and not to prolong life. And if your treatment does not alleviate suffering, but only prolongs life, that treatment should be stopped." 杰出的外科医生克里斯琴·巴纳德于1967年成功地完成了第一例心脏移植手术。他用几句简单的话表明了自己对于安乐死的看法：“安乐死的主要目的在于减轻痛苦而不是延长生命。如果治疗仅能延长病人的生命而不能减轻其痛苦，这种治疗就应该终止。”

lucre / ˈluːkər / *n.* money or profits 钱财；收益

Many religions regard the pursuit of *lucre* for what it can do to help others as laudable. 很多宗教认为，如果追求财富的目的是为了帮助他人，那么这种行为就值得称赞。

luminous / ˈluːmɪnəs / *adj.* bright; brilliant; glowing 发光发亮的；鲜亮的

The Moon is the most *luminous* object in the night sky. 月亮是夜空中最明亮的物体。

【派】**luminosity** *n.* 光度；光明；光辉

A supernova can suddenly increase its *luminosity* to as much as a billion times its normal brightness. 超新星能够突然变亮，这种亮度是原来正常亮度的10亿倍之多。

> ● 常见学科术语 ●
>
> **supernova:** a rare astronomical event in which most of the material in a star explodes, resulting in the emission of vast amounts of energy for a short period of time
> 超新星：一种罕见的天文现象，恒星内部的大部分物质爆炸，在短时间里释放出大量的能量。

lustrous / ˈlʌstrəs / *adj.* shining 闪亮的

On the clear night we gazed up in awe at the *lustrous* stars. 我们满怀敬意地凝视晴朗夜空中闪耀的群星。

Machiavellian / ˌmækiəˈveliən / *adj.* crafty; double-dealing 不择手段的，耍诡计的

One theory of the evolution of high intelligence in primates is that it evolved largely as a result of *Machiavellian* calculations on the part of apes. 一种关于灵长类动物的高等智慧的进化理论是：它在很大程度上是由猿类身上好耍诡计的一面进化而来。

• 常见学科术语 •

Machiavelli: Niccolo Machiavelli（1469–1527）was an Italian philosopher known for his writings on how a ruler should govern, notably by favoring expediency over principles.

马基雅弗利：全名尼科洛·马基雅弗利（1469–1527），意大利哲学家，他撰写了一系列关于统治者该如何进行统治的文章，强调要利用权益而不是一味地注重原则。

machination / ˌmækəˈneɪʃn / *n.* plot; scheme 阴谋；谋划

The mayor resorted to behind-the-scenes *machinations* to try to win his party's nomination for governor. 市长企图依靠幕后操作来赢取其所在党的州长提名。

maelstrom / ˈmeɪlstrɑːm / *n.* whirlpool; turmoil 混乱；大漩涡

Nearly everyone in Europe was caught up in the *maelstrom* that was World War II. 欧洲几乎所有的人都被卷入了"二战"的大漩涡中。

magnanimity / ˌmæɡnəˈnɪməti / *n.* generosity; nobility 宽宏大度；高贵

The senator showed his *magnanimity* when he conceded defeat to his opponent in the disputed election, saying that further uncertainty would be harmful to public confidence in the political system. 在有争议的选举中，那位参议员在向竞选对手认输时表现出了不凡的气度，他表示，政局的持续不稳将会导致民众对政体失去信心。

malign / məˈlaɪn / *v.* to speak evil of 中伤；诽谤

Lawyers are sometimes *maligned* as greedy and dishonest. 律师有时候会受到诽谤，被说成是贪婪、不诚实的人。

malinger / məˈlɪŋɡər / *v.* to feign illness to escape duty 装病以逃避责任

In order to discourage *malingering*, the company decided to require employees taking sick leave to produce a doctor's certification of their illness. 为减少员工装病逃避工作的现象，公司决定要求每一位请病假的员工出示医生开具的证明。

REVIEW 48

Matching

Match each word with its definition:

1. lucid
2. lucre
3. luminous
4. lustrous
5. Machiavellian
6. machination
7. maelstrom
8. magnanimity
9. malign
10. malinger

a. bright; brilliant; glowing
b. money or profits
c. generosity; nobility
d. plot; scheme
e. to feign illness to escape duty
f. whirlpool; turmoil
g. clear; intelligible
h. to speak evil of
i. crafty; double-dealing
j. shining

Fill-ins

Choose the best word to fill in the blank in each sentence.

lucid	**lucre**	**luminous**	**lustrous**	**Machiavellian**
machinations	**maelstrom**	**magnanimity**	**maligned**	**malingering**

1. The magazine *Scientific American* can be relied on to provide _____ discussions of complex scientific topics.
2. We could only imagine the _____ maneuvering that allowed Stan to replace his boss as the company's manager.
3. The Sun is by far the most _____ object in the daytime sky.
4. Tired of being _____ as a coach who "can't win the big games," Coach Butler resolved that his team would be ready for the Super Bowl.
5. The lure of _____ draws many people to speculate in the stock market.
6. Harriet Beecher Stowe described saintliness as "a certain quality of _____ and greatness of soul that brings life within the circle of the heroic."
7. The soldiers marched toward battle under the _____ Moon.
8. The book tells the story of a young British soldier thrust into the _____ of the Napoleonic Wars.
9. One of a military commander's most difficult tasks is to separate soldiers who are seriously battle-stressed from those who are merely _____.
10. No one outside a few powerful party leaders could say by what _____ they had managed to have their crony nominated to run for governor.

Sense or Nonsense

Indicate whether each sentence makes good sense or not.
Put S (SENSE) if it does, and put N (NONSENSE) if it does not.

1. Several of us malingered late at the party, discussing politics. _____
2. The dual pursuits of lucre and adventure have been the motivation of many explorers throughout history. _____
3. The mechanic maligned my tires, so I took my car to another mechanic. _____
4. Most offices seem to have at least one Machiavellian schemer, ready to do almost anything to get ahead. _____
5. Eric proposed to Wendy, calling her eyes "as lustrous as this diamond that will soon be on your finger." _____

UNIT 49

malleable / ˈmæliəbl / *adj.* capable of being shaped by pounding; impressionable 可塑的；易受影响的

Behaviorists such as B. F. Skinner believe that human nature is *malleable*, and that people's behavior can be changed by changing their environment. B. F. 斯金纳等行为主义者认为人性是可塑的，可通过改变人的外部环境来改变人的行为。

> ──● 常见学科术语 ●──
>
> **behaviorist:** the follower of behaviorism, the school of psychology that seeks to explain behavior entirely in terms of observable responses to environmental stimuli
>
> **行为主义者：** 行为主义的追随者。行为主义是心理学的一个流派，试图完全通过可观察到的人类对环境刺激做出的反应来解释其行为。

maverick / ˈmævərɪk / *n.* dissenter 持异议者；特立独行者

Bernie Sanders of Vermont has a reputation as a *maverick*; he is one of only two members of the United States Congress who is independent (that is, not a member of the Republican or Democratic Party). 佛蒙特州的伯尼·桑德斯以其特立独行闻名。他是美国国会中仅有的两位独立人士(既不隶属于共和党也不隶属于民主党)之一。

megalomania / ˌmegələˈmeɪniə / *n.* delusions of power or importance 妄自尊大

In his farewell speech the retiring trial judge warned his colleagues to beware of *megalomania* as they exercise their power in the courtroom. 在告别演说中，即将退休的初审法官告诫同事们，在法庭上行使权力时要谨防狂妄自大。

menagerie / məˈnædʒəri / *n.* a variety of animals kept together 动物群，兽群

Linda seems to take home every abandoned pet in the town; she now has an incredible *menagerie* of dogs, cats, turtles, rabbits, and other animals. 琳达好像把镇上所有的流浪动物都带回家了。她现在有一大群狗、猫、乌龟、兔子和其他各种动物。

mendacious / menˈdeɪʃəs / *adj.* dishonest 不真实的；捏造的

The judge ruled the testimony inadmissible because he considered it *mendacious*. 法官认为这份证据是捏造的，故而不予采纳。

mendicant / ˈmendɪkənt / *n.* beggar 行乞者；化缘者

In Thailand it is traditional for young men to become monks for a year, a period during which they become *mendicants*. 泰国历来有一种传统：年轻男子要做一年的和尚，在此期间行乞化缘。

meretricious / ˌmerəˈtrɪʃəs / *adj.* gaudy; plausible but false; specious 华而不实的，徒有其表的

One of the allures of jargon is that it can make a poor idea appear worthwhile, or something *meretricious* easier to accept because it is dressed in fancy language. 行话有一种魔力，它可以让一个拙劣的想法变得有价值，或让事物因为华丽的语言包装而变得光鲜，更易为人们所接受。

mesmerize / ˈmezməraɪz / *v.* to hypnotize 迷住；使进入催眠状态

The audience sat, *mesmerized*, listening to the retired soldier's account of hand-to-hand combat against the Japanese in New Guinea during World War II. 听众们静静地坐着，被这位退伍老兵讲述的二战期间在新几内亚与日本兵进行肉搏战的故事吸引了。

metamorphosis / ˌmetəˈmɔːrfəsɪs / *n.* change; transformation 变形；转变

In recent years, many areas of China have been undergoing a *metamorphosis*, transforming themselves from predominantly agricultural areas to industrial ones. 近年来，中国大部分地区都经历了从农业主导区向工业主导区转变的过程。

【派】**metamorphose** *v.* 变形；转变

metaphysics / ˌmetəˈfɪzɪks / *n.* a branch of philosophy that investigates the ultimate nature of reality 玄学，形而上学

To skeptics, *metaphysics* is an arbitrary search for a chimerical truth. 对怀疑论者来说，形而上学只是武断地寻找一个荒唐的真理罢了。

【派1】**metaphysical** *adj.* pertaining to metaphysics 玄学的，形而上学的

Some critics of evolution object to its implication that human thought is reduced to a peripheral phenomenon; they find it implausible that the ability to conceptualize—to write a sonnet, a symphony, a *metaphysical* treatise—would have evolved in early hominids solely as a secondary effect. 一些进化论的批评者反对该学说把人类思想仅仅视为一种非本质的现象。进化论把人类构思的能力——如写十四行诗、创作交响乐、写玄学专著——仅仅视为人类进化为早期智人的一种伴随结果，这对他们来说也是无法接受的。

【派2】**metaphysician** *n.* a person who is an expert in metaphysics 玄学家，形而上学者

Whether we are aware of it or not, we are all *metaphysicians* in the sense that we all have beliefs about what things are the most real; for example, a person who believes in God may believe that God is the "ultimate reality." 不管我们有没有意识到，我们其实都是形而上学者，因为我们都坚信有完全真实的事物，比如，一个信仰上帝的人会坚信上帝就是"终极存在"。

REVIEW 49

Matching

Match each word with its definition:

1. malleable
2. maverick
3. megalomania
4. menagerie
5. mendacious
6. mendicant

7. meretricious
8. mesmerize
9. metamorphosis
10. metaphysics

a. dissenter
b. variety of animals kept together
c. transformation
d. beggar
e. delusions of power
f. a branch of philosophy that examines the nature of reality
g. to hypnotize
h. impressionable
i. gaudy
j. dishonest

Fill-ins

Choose the best word to fill in the blank in each sentence.

malleable	**mavericks**	**megalomania**	**menagerie**	**mendacious**
mendicant	**meretricious**	**mesmerized**	**metamorphosed**	**metaphysical**

1. Realist novelists such as Charles Dickens seem to have had little interest in _____ questions; rather, they seem to have been interested mainly in analyzing social and psychological reality.

2. We were amazed when we saw Lionel after ten years; he had _____ from a lazy, carefree young man into a hard-working and responsible member of the community.

3. Tom spent one year as a _____ before becoming a priest.

4. It is hard to escape the feeling that it requires at least a touch of _____ to run for the office of President of the United States.

5. For many years the prevailing view among social scientists was that human nature is essentially _____; however, recent thinking in the field has placed more emphasis on the part played by genes in human nature.

6. The World Wide Web has made it easier for _____ to have their views on controversial issues heard.

7. The judge ruled that the defendant's argument was rejected as disingenuous and _____.

8. The students, _____ by the professor's fascinating lecture, did not realize the class had run overtime.

9. The writer's biographer could not escape the conclusion that her subject had given _____ testimony on various occasions.

10. The local SPCA shelter has a _____ of animals—parrots, cats, dogs, and many others.

Sense or Nonsense

Indicate whether each sentence makes good sense or not.
Put S (SENSE) if it does, and put N (NONSENSE) if it does not.

1. One thing that no one disputes is that metaphysics does more than any other area of human pursuit to put food on the table. _____

2. Many people consider it unfair that approximately 200 super-wealthy mendicants control 60% of the country's wealth _____

3. In four years, Leonard Rice has metamorphosed from a gangling 140-pound freshman third-string football player into a 210-pound All-State tailback. _____

4. The party leader can always count on the vote of a group of loyal party mavericks. _____

5. The teacher regards her students as malleable clay that she can mold into fine, intelligent young people. _____

UNIT 50

meteorological / ˌmiːtiə'rɑːlədʒɪkl / *adj.* concerned with the weather 气象的

Some experts believe that reports of UFOs are attributable to natural astronomical or *meteorological* phenomena. 一些专家认为关于不明飞行物的报告可归因于某些天文或气象现象。

【派1】**meteorology** *n.* a science that deals with weather and atmospheric phenomena 气象学(研究天气和大气现象的科学)

【派2】**meteorologist** *n.* those who study meteorology or forecast weather conditions 气象学家（研究气象学和进行天气状况预测的人）

The term "butterfly effect" to refer to the process driving chaotic systems was first used in 1979 by *meteorologist* E. M. Lorenz In an address entitled, "Predictability: Does the Flap of a Butterfly's Wings in Brazil Set Off a Tornado in Texas?" "蝴蝶效应"这个表示引起系统混乱过程的术语首次出现于1979年，由气象学家E. M. 洛伦兹在一次题为《可预报性：一只蝴蝶在巴西扇动下翅膀会引发得克萨斯的一场龙卷风吗？》的演讲中提出。

meticulous / mə'tɪkjələs / *adj.* very careful; fastidious 小心谨慎的

Science is an empirical field of study based on the belief that the laws of nature can best be discovered by *meticulous* observation and experimentation. 科学是一种经验主义的研究，它建立在"一丝不苟的观察和实验才能最好地揭示出自然的规律"这一信念之上。

mettle / 'metl / *n.* courage; endurance 勇气；忍耐力

In many cultures, young men are expected to test their *mettle* by performing difficult and dangerous tasks. 在许多文化中，年轻男子都要通过完成一些艰巨而危险的任务来证明他们的勇气。

mettlesome / 'metlsəm / *adj.* full of courage and fortitude; spirited 勇敢的；精神饱满的

The *mettlesome* young officer was well regarded by all the senior officers. 这位英勇的年轻军官在所有高级军官中口碑极佳。

【区】**meddlesome** *adj.* inclined to interfere 好干涉的，爱管闲事的

microcosm / 'maɪkroʊkɑːzəm / *n.* ① a small system having analogies to a larger system 缩影 ② a small world 微观宇宙；微观世界

For many years the atom was seen as a sort of *microcosm* of the universe, with electrons—analogous to the planets of a solar system—orbiting the nucleus, or "sun." 多年来，原子被视为是无限宇宙的一个缩影，而电子就像是太阳系的行星，绕着原子核，即"太阳"旋转。

militate / 'mɪlɪteɪt / *v.* to work against 反对

The manager asked all of his employees to think of any factors that might *militate* against the project's success. 经理让所有员工考虑任何可能影响项目完成的因素。

minatory / 'mɪnətɔːri / *adj.* threatening; menacing 恐吓的；威胁的

Intelligence information suggests *minatory* troop concentrations on the border. 谍报显示，对我们构成威胁的敌军集结于边境处。

minuscule / ˈmɪnəskjuːl / *adj.* very small 极小的

Ancient geological processes are beyond the scope of carbon-14 dating （which is at most 120,000 years） because the amount of carbon-14 in material from such processes that has not decayed is *minuscule*. 远古的地质进程无法用碳14元素进行测年（此方法测试的最长年份只有12万年），因为在这个进程中，物质中未腐败的碳14元素数量微乎其微。

minutiae / mɪˈnuːʃiː / *n.* petty details 细节

President Ronald Reagan said that a President should concentrate on the formulation and execution of broad policy and leave the *minutiae* of running the country to subordinates. 罗纳德·里根总统曾说，总统应该关注的是国家大政方针的制定和执行，而应把治理国家的细节问题留给下属。

misanthrope / ˈmɪsənθroʊp / *n.* one who hates humanity 厌恶人类者；厌世者

One of the most famous *misanthropes* in literature is the protagonist of the seventeenth century French writer Moliere's play Le *Misanthrope*（The *Misanthrope*）. 在文学作品中最著名的厌恶人类者是17世纪法国作家莫里哀的知名剧作《厌世者》当中的主人公。

【派】**misanthropic** *adj.* 厌恶人类的

REVIEW 50

Matching

Match each word with its definition:

1. meteorological		a.	courage; endurance
2. meticulous		b.	very small
3. mettle		c.	very careful; fastidious
4. mettlesome		d.	to work against
5. microcosm		e.	one who hates humanity
6. militate		f.	a small system having analogies to a larger system
7. minatory		g.	full of courage and fortitude; spirited
8. minuscule		h.	concerned with the weather
9. minutiae		i.	threatening
10. misanthrope		j.	petty details

Fill-ins

Choose the best word to fill in the blank in each sentence.

meteorological	meticulous	mettle	mettlesome	microcosm
militates	minatory	minuscule	minutiae	misanthropic

1. After a month of inter-squad scrimmage, the members of the football team were eager to test their _____ against another team.

2. _____ data collected from around the world helps scientists to get an accurate picture of the world's weather patterns.

3. In many of Arthur Conan Doyle's Sherlock Holmes stories the detective reveals quite strong _____ tendencies.

4. The student's laziness _____ strongly against the likelihood of his success.

5. In the retired general's memoirs, he says that most of the battles he fought were won through a combination of courage on the part of soldiers, _____ planning, and luck.

6. The student stood silent as the teacher scolded him, her hand making _____ gestures.

7. Political pollsters keep a close watch on the town because they view it as a representative _____ of American society.

8. The _____ horse can only be controlled by a very skillful rider.

9. Engineers decided that the anomaly was so _____ that it could safely be ignored.

10. The general's factotum deals with the _____ of everyday life, leaving him free to do his job as commander of the Third Division.

Sense or Nonsense

Indicate whether each sentence makes good sense or not.
Put S (SENSE) if it does, and put N (NONSENSE) if it does not.

1. The poison is so powerful that even minuscule amounts of it can cause harm. _____

2. The diary contains a meticulous record of the events of the poet's life when she traveled to France in 1888. _____

3. "Stop being mettlesome and mind your own business," we told the busybody. _____

4. "Not only do I not like human beings in the abstract, I don't like even one individual member of the human race," the misanthrope declared. _____

5. The scientist's meteorological record deals exclusively with meteors and comets in orbit around the Sun. _____

UNIT 51

miscellany / ˈmɪsəleɪni / *n.* a mixture of writings on various subjects 杂录，杂集
   The book is a fascinating *miscellany* collected from the writer's life work. 这本文集收录了这位作家毕生作品之精华，内容非常引人入胜。

miscreant / ˈmɪskriənt / *n.* villain; criminal 恶棍，罪大恶极之人；罪犯
   The public execution of *miscreants* was common in Great Britain in the eighteenth century. 在18世纪的英国，对罪犯进行公开处决是家常便饭。

misogynist / mɪˈsɑːdʒɪnɪst / *n.* one who hates women 厌恶女人的人 *adj.* 厌恶女人的
   Some people have called the philosopher Friedrich Nietzsche a *misogynist* because of the numerous negative comments he made about women. 有人说哲学家弗里德里希·尼采是一个厌恶女人的人，因为他发表了很多关于女人的消极评论。

mitigate / ˈmɪtɪɡeɪt / *v.* to cause to become less harsh, severe, or painful; alleviate 缓和；减轻

Although the Supreme Court under the leadership of Chief Justice Warren Burger did not rescind any of the fundamental rulings of the Warren Court that preceded it, its decisions did *mitigate* the effects of some of the rulings of the Warren Court. 尽管联邦首席法官沃伦·伯格领导的最高法院没有撤回上届沃伦法院作出的任何重大裁决，但伯格法院的判决确实缓和了沃伦法院所作出的一些裁决的力度。

【派】**mitigation** *n.* the act of reducing the severity or painfulness of something 减轻；缓和；平静

Before sentencing the woman, the judge asked if she had anything to say in *mitigation*. 在判决这个女人之前，法官问她是否还有可以为自己减轻刑罚的陈词。

● 常见学科术语 ●

Warren Court: Earl Warren was named Chief Justice of the Supreme Court in 1953, and served on the Court until 1969. Under his leadership the Supreme Court tended to interpret the Constitution boldly, frequently with the result that disadvantaged people were helped.

沃伦法院：厄尔·沃伦在1953年被任命为美国最高法院的首席法官，其任期一直持续到1969年。在他的领导下，最高法院趋于对宪法进行大胆的解释，并常常因此帮助了社会底层的人。

---

mnemonic / nɪˈmɑːnɪk / *adj.* related to memory; assisting memory 跟记忆有关的；帮助记忆的

In the introduction to a collection of poetry, *By Heart*, the British poet Ted Hughes says that "the more absurd, exaggerated, grotesque" the images used as a *mnemonic* device to help remember a poem, the easier it will be to recall. 在诗集《由心》(编者注：译者翻译的，目前未有权威的中文译名)的序言中，英国诗人特德·休斯说，越是荒诞不经、夸张可笑的意象，越能帮助人记忆诗歌。

【派】**mnemonics** *n.* a system that develops and improves the memory 记忆术；记忆法

Symbolic languages—the second generation of computer languages — were developed in the early 1950s, making use of *mnemonics* such as "M" for "multiply," which are translated into machine language by a computer program. 符号语言——第二代计算机语言——发展于20世纪50年代早期，它采用了英文缩写记忆法，如用字母M代表单词multiply，然后再由计算机程序翻译成机器语言。

modicum / ˈmɑːdɪkəm / *n.* limited quantity 少量

The scientist Carl Sagan wrote about astronomy and other scientific subjects in a way that enabled a reader with even a *modicum* of knowledge of science to understand what he was saying. 科学家卡尔·萨根所写的有关天文学和其他科学的作品非常浅显易懂，即使科学知识有限的读者也能理解。

mollify / ˈmɑːlɪfaɪ / *v.* to soothe 使平静；使缓和

The prime minister tried to *mollify* people protesting the tax increase with a promise that she would order a study of other means to raise revenue. 首相竭力安抚那些对提高税收表示抗议的人们，承诺她会另想办法提高财政收入。

monolithic / ˌmɑːnəˈlɪθɪk / *adj.* solid and uniform; constituting a single, unified whole 庞大的；统一的；整体的

In the fifteenth century, there was a significant movement to revitalize the Church from within; however, it had become so *monolithic* over the centuries and contained so many vested interests that piecemeal reform was difficult and ineffective. 15世纪，一场声势浩大的运动希望通过教会自内而外的改革使其重新焕发生机。然而，几个世纪以来，教会已变得坚不可摧，加之其拥有众多的既得利益，使得对其作微小的改革也举步维艰、见效甚微。

morose / məˈroʊs / *adj.* ill-humored; sullen 郁闷的；孤僻的

The assessment of some skeptical critics of existentialism is that it is generally a view of life created by a group of thinkers whose distinguishing characteristic is that they are *morose*. 持怀疑论的批评家是这样评价存在主义的：大体上而言，存在主义是被一群性格明显郁郁寡欢的思想家创造出来的人生观。

motley / ˈmɑːtli / *adj.* many colored; made up of many parts 五颜六色的；混杂的

The new political party is made up of a *motley* group of people who are unhappy with the existing parties. 新政党是由一群对现存政党不满的各色人等组成的。

REVIEW 51

Matching

Match each word with its definition:

1.	miscellany	a.	solid and uniform
2.	miscreant	b.	villain
3.	misogynist	c.	limited quantity
4.	mitigate	d.	ill-humored; sullen
5.	mnemonic	e.	a mixture of writings on various subjects
6.	modicum	f.	one who hates women
7.	mollify	g.	related to memory
8.	monolithic	h.	many colored; made up of many parts
9.	morose	i.	to alleviate
10.	motley	j.	to soothe

Fill-ins

Choose the best word to fill in the blank in each sentence.

miscellany	**miscreant**	**misogynist**	**mitigate**	**mnemonic**
modicum	**mollify**	**monolithic**	**morose**	**motley**

1. The writer was able to offer constructive criticism of the feminist movement without being called a _____.

2. To _____ war "hawks," the President ordered a one-week bombing campaign against the country.

3. Socialists tend to view big business as _____; however, many large corporations are in direct competition with one another, and thus collusion is usually not to their advantage.

4. Many people find it useful to use _____ devices to memorize information.

5. The volume contains a _____ of the writings of Walt Whitman.

6. Mr. Samuels was _____ for over a month following the death of his beloved wife.

7. In the nineteenth century, accurate prognosis based on the history of disease began to be possible, but it was not until the twentieth century that doctors were able to actually cure a number of diseases rather than merely _____ their effects.

8. "I'm not looking for adulation, just a _____ of respect," the angry teacher told his class.

9. The judge said she had no alternative but to sentence the _____ to 20 years imprisonment.

10. The protest began with a _____ group of people from virtually all occupations.

Sense or Nonsense

Indicate whether each sentence makes good sense or not.
Put S (SENSE) if it does, and put N (NONSENSE) if it does not.

1. Mnemonic devices currently supply nearly 20% of the country's electric power. _____

2. Anyone with even a modicum of common sense could see that the plan had little chance of success. _____

3. Hindus believe that one should not be morose as one approaches death, since physical death means only the death of the body and not the soul. _____

4. The speaker's misogynist comments drew the ire of several women's rights groups. _____

5. The President ordered the creation of a commission to study ways to mitigate the effects of unemployment on the poor. _____

UNIT 52

multifarious / ˌmʌltɪˈferɪəs / *adj.* diverse 多样的

Modern technology is so complex and *multifarious* that it requires thousands of specialists to devise and operate; thus, even a brilliant engineer could not by himself fabricate a sophisticated radio or computer without the help of existing black boxes and expertise. 现代技术如此复杂多样，以至于需要由成千上万的专家共同设计与操作。因而，即便是一名出色的工程师，若没有现存的未知框和专业知识，也无法独自创造出一台复杂的录音机或电脑。

mundane / mʌnˈdeɪn / *adj.* worldly as opposed to spiritual; concerned with the ordinary 世俗的；平凡的

Fundamentalists contend that the Bible's account of the creation is literally true, while others believe that it is the retelling of a powerful myth current in the Middle East that sought to explain the *mundane* in spiritual language. 原教旨主义者认为，《圣经》中对创世的描述从字面上看是真实的，而其他人认为它是在复述中东一个神秘有力的趋势，这种趋势试图以一种神灵的语言解释世俗世界。

• 常见学科术语 •
---

fundamentalist: the one who stresses adherence to a set of basic beliefs, especially in religion. Specifically, fundamentalism refers to the movement in Protestantism stressing a literal interpretation of the Bible.

原教旨主义者： 强调坚持基本信仰的人，尤其是在宗教意义上。具体来说，原教旨主义指一场新教运动，强调按字面理解去阐释《圣经》。

necromancy / ˈnekroʊmænsi / *n.* black magic 巫术

Television might seem like *necromancy* to a time traveler from the fifteenth century. 对一个来自于15世纪的时空旅行者来说，电视可能看起来就像是神奇的巫术。

negate / nɪˈgeɪt / *v.* to cancel out; nullify 否定；使无效

The soldiers' poor treatment of the prisoners *negated* the goodwill they had built up among the population. 士兵们虐待战俘的行为使得他们在大众心中树立的良好形象化为乌有。

neologism / niˈɑːlədʒɪzəm / *n.* a new word or expression 新词；新用法

The word "anesthesia" was the *neologism* of the American physician and poet Oliver Wendell Holmes, who used it in 1846 in a letter to Dr. William Morton, who had recently demonstrated the use of ether; the word is derived from the Latin word anaisthesia, meaning "lack of sensation." "anesthesia（麻醉）" 是美国医生、诗人奥利弗·温德尔·霍尔姆斯创造的新词，他在1846年给威廉·莫顿医生的信中首次用到该词，而后者在此之前刚刚展示了乙醚的使用方法。这个词来自拉丁语 "anaisthesia"，意思是 "失去感觉"。

neophyte / ˈniːəfaɪt / *n.* novice; beginner 新手，初学者

The school provides extensive support and guidance for *neophyte* teachers. 学校为新教师提供多种支持和指导。

nexus / ˈneksəs / *n.* ① a means of connection; a connected group or series 连结；关系；② center 中心，核心

Wall Street is the *nexus* of America's financial system. 华尔街是美国金融体系的枢纽。

nonplus / ˌnɑːnˈplʌs / *v.* to bewilder 使困惑

The members of the football team were *nonplussed* by the presence of a female reporter in the locker room. 球队更衣室里出现了一名女记者，这让橄榄球队员们很困惑。

【派】**nonplussed** *adj.* 困惑的

nostalgia / nɑːˈstældʒə / *n.* sentimental longing for a past time 乡愁；怀旧之情

The product's marketing is centered on *nostalgia* for the 1950s. 这个产品的市场营销策略是迎合人们对20世纪50年代的怀旧情结。

【派】**nostalgic** *adj.* 怀旧的；乡愁的

The idea of an extended family existing in nineteenth-century America consisting of loving uncles and doting aunts has been shown to be largely a product of a *nostalgic* and romanticized view of the past. 看起来19世纪的美国大家庭——即包括有慈爱的叔伯、姑婶的家庭——很大程度上不过是人们缅怀过去并将其浪漫化的一个产物。

nostrum / ˈnɑːstrəm / *n.* medicine or remedy of doubtful effectiveness; supposed cure 秘方；偏方

Although there are many *nostrums* urged on obese consumers, the only effective remedy for this condition is prosaic but nonetheless valid: eat less and exercise more. 尽管有许多给肥胖病人的秘方，但唯一有效的疗法虽是老生常谈但却十分有效，即少吃多锻炼。

REVIEW 52

Matching

Match each word with its definition:

1. multifarious		a.	to cancel out
2. mundane		b.	novice
3. necromancy		c.	black magic
4. negate		d.	diverse
5. neologism		e.	sentimental longing for a past time
6. neophyte		f.	a new word or expression
7. nexus		g.	to bewilder
8. nonplus		h.	remedy of doubtful effectiveness
9. nostalgia		i.	a connected group or series
10. nostrum		j.	worldly as opposed to spiritual

Fill-ins

Choose the best word to fill in the blank in each sentence.

multifarious	**mundane**	**necromancy**	**negated**	**neologisms**
neophyte	**nexus**	**nonplussed**	**nostalgia**	**nostrums**

1. A number of commentators have argued that the benefits offered by television are _____ by its narcotic effect on viewers.

2. Some theologians regard attempts to prove God's existence logically valuable largely as pointers toward God, helping to turn a person's attention from the _____ to the spiritual.

3. Even the normally unflappable police officer was _____ when confronted by the armed suspect.

4. Many _____ for "correcting" English to make it more consistent and "rational" have been proposed, but the language is robust and has survived such attempts.

5. Although intelligence agents have identified parts of the terrorist organization around the world, they are still working to locate its _____.

6. Dr. Robert Burchfield, Chief Editor of the *Oxford English Dictionary*, has estimated that approximately 90% of English _____ originate in the United States.

7. The head football coach at a Division I college has _____ duties, such as supervising the coaching staff, recruiting players, and talking to the media.

8. The advertisement is based on _____ for an America that probably never existed.

9. The _____ novelist was fortunate to have the advice of an established older writer.

10. A colorful term used to belittle something regarded as nonsense is "voodoo"; another one is " _____."

Sense or Nonsense

Indicate whether each sentence makes good sense or not.

Put S (SENSE) if it does, and put N (NONSENSE) if it does not.

1. Mrs. Morrison was nonplussed when she discovered that her husband was a humanoid creature from the planet Varga, a small planet in a nearby galaxy. _____

2. After suffering through ten losing football seasons in a row, the president of the college's alumni association suggested—somewhat sarcastically, no doubt—hiring a necromancer to replace the current head coach. _____

3. It is generally advisable to avoid neologisms such as "like" and "and" when writing. _____

4. After running the giant corporation for 30 years, the retiring CEO found himself looking forward to a simple life doing mundane tasks around his house. _____

5. The speaker mounted the nostrum to give the keynote speech of the convention. _____

UNIT 53

nugatory / ˈnuːgətɔːri / *adj.* trifling; invalid 琐碎的；无效的

The historian has a knack for focusing on information that appears *nugatory* but that, upon examination, illuminates the central issue. 那位历史学家有种本领：他会关注那些看似琐碎无用的信息，但这些信息经过仔细研究，会揭示核心问题。

obdurate / ˈɑːbdərət / *adj.* stubborn 顽固的

Coach Knight is *obdurate* about one thing: the offensive line is the heart of his football team. 奈特教练始终坚持一点，那就是对方的防线是他的橄榄球队攻击的中心。

obsequious / əbˈsiːkwiəs / *adj.* overly submissive 谄媚的；顺从的；曲意逢迎的

【派】obsequiousness *n.* 谄媚；顺从

Tom's tendency to submit meekly to any bullying authority is so great that his wife suggested he overcome this *obsequiousness* by taking an assertiveness training course. 汤姆倾向于对任何强势的权威人士都卑躬屈膝，于是他的妻子建议他参加相关培训，锻炼决断力，克服过分顺从的毛病。

obsequy / ˈɑːbsəkwi / *n.* funeral ceremony 葬礼（常用复数形式obsequies）

Solemn *obsequies* were held for President John F. Kennedy following his assassination on November 22, 1963. 美国为在1963年11月22号遇刺身亡的约翰·F·肯尼迪总统举行了庄重的葬礼。

obviate / ˈɑːbvieɪt / *v.* to make unnecessary; anticipate and prevent 排除；避免；消除

An experienced physician can often discern if a patient's symptoms are psychosomatic, thus *obviating* the need for expensive medical tests. 经验丰富的医生通常能甄别病人的症状是否是由心理负担导致的，这样病人就不必去做昂贵的检查了。

occlude / əˈkluːd / *v.* to shut; block 关上；挡住

One of the primary uses of solar cells is in spacecraft to provide electric power; this is because space is an environment uniquely suited to these devices since it has no weather to *occlude* the Sun and it is not susceptible to interruptions in sunlight caused by the rotation of the Earth. 太阳能电池的主要用途之一是为宇宙飞船提供电力，这是因为太空的环境特别适合这些设备：那里没有天气变化阻挡阳光，并且不易受地球自转所造成的阳光中断所影响。

occult / ə'kʌlt / *adj.* re lating to supernatural phenomena 超自然的；神秘的 *n.* practices connected with supernatural phenomena 神秘学

In his book *Supernature* the biologist Lyall Watson explores what he regards as phenomena on the border between natural and *occult* phenomena. 生物学家莱尔·沃森在其著作《超自然现象》中探索了他认为介于自然和超自然之间的现象。

odyssey / 'ɑːdəsi / *n.* a long, adventurous voyage; quest 冒险旅行；探索

Steve's quest for enlightenment took him on a spiritual *odyssey* that helped him to gain an understanding of many philosophers and religions. 史蒂夫对思想启迪的追求使他踏上了精神旅程，深入认识了很多哲学家和宗教。

officious / ə'fɪʃəs / *adj.* too helpful; meddlesome 过于殷勤的；爱管闲事的

Some of us on the tour found the guide *officious*, but others thought she was helpful and courteous. 我们旅行团里有些人觉得导游过分殷勤，但另一些人则认为她乐于助人且彬彬有礼。

olfactory / oʊl'fæktəri / *adj.* concerning the sense of smell 嗅觉的

Wine connoisseurs say that the *olfactory* senses play as important a part in appreciating good wine as the sense of taste. 葡萄酒鉴赏家说，在品鉴美酒时嗅觉和味觉一样重要。

REVIEW 53

Matching

Match each word with its definition:

1. nugatory		a.	too helpful
2. obdurate		b.	overly submissive
3. obsequious		c.	stubborn
4. obsequy		d.	a long voyage
5. obviate		e.	to shut; block
6. occlude		f.	funeral ceremony
7. occult		g.	trifling; invalid
8. odyssey		h.	practices connected with supernatural phenomena
9. officious		i.	concerning the sense of smell
10. olfactory		j.	to make unnecessary

Fill-ins

Choose the best word to fill in the blank in each sentence.

nugatory	**obdurate**	**obsequious**	**obsequies**	**obviated**
occludes	**occult**	**odyssey**	**officious**	**olfactory**

1. The assertiveness-training course helped Jeremy go from being _____ to being assertive and confident.

2. Nuclear power has _____ the needs for submarines to refuel frequently, allowing long undersea voyages.

3. Sometimes a/an _____ stimulus can trigger a memory associated with that particular smell.

4. The director of the government agency encouraged workers to provide efficient service without being _____.

5. The _____ has been described as what does not fit into a rationalistic view of the world.

6. Astronomers welcome an eclipse of the Sun because when the Moon _____ the light of the Sun, observation of that body becomes easier.

7. The President is _____ about the issue; he will not negotiate with terrorists.

8. In the television show *Star Trek: The Next Generation*, the Enterprise embarks on a/an _____ to explore the Universe.

9. After the judge ruled the evidence he had presented to the court to be _____, the lawyer muttered jocularly to his partner, "Negatory."

10. Solemn _____ were held for Pope John Paul II after his death in 2005.

Sense or Nonsense

Indicate whether each sentence makes good sense or not.

Put S (SENSE) if it does, and put N (NONSENSE) if it does not.

1. Modern refinement in olfactory processes have made it possible to mass-produce complex electronic circuits. _____

2. Since the Sun was occluded by clouds, the sailor could not use it to determine his position. _____

3. After the couple retired they went on an odyssey around the world. _____

4. Science is concerned primarily with the study of occult phenomena. _____

5. The obdurate student refused to study despite repeated warnings that he would fail if he did not start to work in the course. _____

UNIT 54

oligarchy / ˈɑːləgɑːrki / *n.* form of government in which power belongs to only a few leaders 寡头统治政府

In 411 B.C., democratic government was overthrown in Athens and a conservative *oligarchy* called the Four Hundred came to power. 公元前411年，雅典的民主政府被推翻，相对保守的寡头执政集团"四百人议事会"开始掌权。

onerous / ˈɑːnərəs / *adj.* burdensome 繁重的，麻烦的；艰巨的

The duty the judge considers most *onerous* is sentencing convicted criminals. 法官认为最艰巨的职责就是判决被定罪的犯人。

onomatopoeia / ˌɑːnəˌmætəˈpiːə / *n.* formation or use of words that imitate sounds of the actions they refer to 拟声

One theory of the origin of language is that it began as a sort of *onomatopoeia* as early humans imitated sounds they heard. 一个关于语言起源的理论认为，起初语言只是原始人类对听到声音的模仿。

opprobrium / əˈproʊbriəm / *n.* disgrace; contempt 耻辱；责骂

It is difficult to imagine the *opprobrium* heaped on a person who is a traitor to his or her group. 当一个人背叛其所处的团体时，落到他头上的耻辱是难以想象的。

ornithologist / ˌɔːrnɪˈθɑːlədʒɪst / *n.* a scientist who studies birds 鸟类学家

Ornithologists believe that there currently exist only about 20 individuals of a bird called the Balinese sparrow. 鸟类学家认为，目前世上仅存大约20只巴厘麻雀。

oscillate / ˈɑːsɪleɪt / *v.* to move back and forth 摆动；犹豫

The teacher *oscillates* between a student-centered approach to teaching and a subject-centered approach. 这名老师在以学生为中心的教学方法还是以学科为中心的教学方法上举棋不定。

ostentatious / ˌɑːstenˈteɪʃəs / *adj.* showy; trying to attract attention; pretentious 卖弄的；想惹人注目的；自命不凡的

A member of the bourgeoisie might purchase a vacation home on Maui or Cape Cod that some would regard as an *ostentatious* display of wealth, but that the person regards as simply a pleasant place to go on vacation. 一名中产阶级可能会在毛伊岛或科德角买一套度假别墅，这在别人看来是炫耀财富，但其本人却只把它当成一个度假的好去处。

overweening / ˌoʊvərˈwiːnɪŋ / *adj.* presumptuous; arrogant; overbearing 自负的；过于自信的

The ancient Greeks believed that *overweening* pride—what they called hubris—would be punished, eventually, by the gods. 古希腊人认为，过于骄傲，也就是他们所说的"狂妄"，终会受到神的惩罚。

paean / ˈpiːən / *n.* a song of joy or triumph; a fervent expression of joy 赞美歌；欢乐歌

Fundamentally, the poem is a *paean* of joy, celebrating the coming of democracy to the country. 从根本上说，这首诗是一首庆祝国家即将到来的民主的欢乐赞美歌。

paleontology / ˌpeɪliɑːnˈtɑːlədʒi / *n.* study of past geological eras through fossil remains 古生物学

Primatology, together with anthropology, *paleontology*, and several other fields, has given scientists a fairly accurate picture of the evolution of homo sapiens. 灵长类动物学和人类学、古生物学以及其他几个领域已经向科学家们展示了一幅相当精确的人类演化的画卷。

【派】**paleontologist** *n.* an expert in the field of paleontology 古生物学家

The attempts of the Jesuit priest and *paleontologist* Teilhard de Chardin to reconcile evolution and the Catholic dogma of original sin were regarded by Church authorities as nearly heretical, and he had to abandon his position in 1926. 耶稣会牧师、古生物学家德日进尝试调和进化论与天主教教义中的原罪思想之间的矛盾，但是他的努力被教会权威视为近乎异端邪说，以至于他不得不在1926年放弃了其主张。

• 常见学科术语 •

primatology: the branch of zoology that deals with the study of primates, that is, mammals belonging to any of the suborders of primates: Anthropoids（great apes, and several others）, Prosimii（lemurs and several others）, and Tarsiidea. Primates are characterized by a high level of social interaction, flexible behavior, and use of hands.

REVIEW 54

Matching

Match each word with its definition:

1.	oligarchy	a.	disgrace; contempt
2.	onerous	b.	showy
3.	onomatopoeia	c.	burdensome
4.	opprobrium	d.	a song of joy or triumph
5.	ornithologist	e.	government by a few leaders
6.	oscillate	f.	to move back and forth
7.	ostentatious	g.	presumptuous; arrogant
8.	overweening	h.	a scientist who studies birds
9.	paean	i.	study of past geological eras through fossil remains
10.	paleontology	j.	formation of words that imitate sounds of actions they refer to

Fill-ins

Choose the best word to fill in the blank in each sentence.

oligarchy	onerous	onomatopoeia	opprobrium	ornithologists
oscillating	ostentatious	overweening	paeans	paleontologists

1. After the end of the war, churches across the country rang out _____ of joy.
2. The country is ruled by an _____ consisting of senior military officers.
3. Over the last few days, the weather has been _____ between sunny and cloudy.
4. _____ are studying a bird that can fly without stopping from Scotland to Africa.
5. The physician faced the _____ task of telling the patient that the disease was terminal.
6. The system of gathering, identifying, dating, and categorizing fossils allows _____ to place newly discovered fossils in their proper place, making their picture of the past progressively more accurate.
7. An argument for the wearing of school uniforms is that it discourages _____ displays of wealth through the wearing of expensive jewelry and clothing.
8. The manager's _____ ambition led her to do something she regretted for the rest of her life: she told a lie about a vice president to help her get the job.
9. The country incurred global _____ for its poor treatment of prisoners of war.
10. The word "ping-pong" arose from _____; the sound of the words is similar to the sound of a table tennis ball hitting first one paddle and then another.

Sense or Nonsense

Indicate whether each sentence makes good sense or not.

Put S (SENSE) if it does, and put N (NONSENSE) if it does not.

1. Onomatopoeia helps scientists to understand the nature of the atom. _____
2. The paeans live a basic existence, subsisting mostly on rice and vegetables. _____
3. Ornithologists are concerned that Canadian geese migrating south no longer have enough places to rest and feed along the way. _____
4. Geologists called in a paleontologist to examine fossils they had uncovered. _____
5. When it was discovered that the scientist had published a paper based on data he knew was falsified, he received the opprobrium of the scientific community. _____

UNIT 55

pallid / ˈpælɪd / *adj.* lacking color or liveliness 苍白的；暗淡的；无生气的

Archeological evidence indicates that women have been using makeup to give color to a *pallid* face for millennia. 考古学证据表明，女人们通过化妆来给苍白的面容添色已有千年历史。

panegyric / ˌpænəˈdʒɪrɪk / *n.* elaborate praise; formal hymn of praise 赞美，称颂；颂词

Many *panegyrics* were written to Abraham Lincoln in the years after his death, and he has become one of the most revered figures in American history. 亚伯拉罕·林肯辞世后，人们写下很多赞美他的诗篇，他也成为美国历史上最受人爱戴的伟人之一。

paragon / ˈpærəgɑːn / *n.* model of excellence or perfection 模范，典范

The epic poet Homer was regarded by the ancient Greeks as a *paragon* of literary excellence. 史诗巨匠荷马被古希腊人视为高深文学造诣的典范。

partisan / ˈpɑːrtəzn / *adj.* one-sided; committed to a party, group, or cause; prejudiced 片面的；党派的；偏袒的

Supporters of constitutional monarchy believe that while in this system, as it is generally practiced today, virtually all power is vested in popularly elected assemblies, the institution of the monarchy continues to serve a purpose as a focus of national unity above the furor of *partisan* politics. 君主立宪制的拥护者们相信，在这一体制中，正如如今所广泛践行的那样，几乎所有的权利都属于普遍选举产生的议会，而君主制度则超越了党派纷争，继续发挥着维护国家统一的功能。

pathological / ˌpæθəˈlɑːdʒɪkl / *adj.* departing from normal condition 病态的；病理学的

People sometimes confound psychology and psychiatry: the former is the science that studies cognitive and affective functions, both normal and *pathological*, in human beings and other animals, whereas the latter is a branch of medicine that deals with mental disorders. 人们有时将心理学和神经病学混为一谈，但前者是研究人类和其他动物的认知和情感功能的，包括正常的和病态的两方面，而后者却是医学的一个分支，研究精神失常。

【派1】**pathology** *n.* 病理学；病理，病状

Some of the most spectacular examples of spin-off in the twentieth century are the advances that have been made in medicine as an unforeseen result of pure biological research; an example of this is diagnostic testing for defective genes that predispose a person to certain *pathologies*. 20世纪最令人瞩目的副产品包括人类在医学上取得的进展，这些进展都是单纯生物学研究产生的一些意料之外的成果，其中一个例子就是能检查出致人患某些病的缺陷基因的诊断性检测。

【派2】**pathos** *n.* a quality that causes a feeling of pity or sorrow 同情；痛苦

patois / ˈpætwɑː / *n.* a regional dialect; nonstandard speech; jargon 方言；行话

In Singapore the lingua franca is increasingly becoming Singapore English, widely regarded as a *patois*. 新加坡式英语已经逐渐成为当地的通用语，并且被广泛地视为一种英语方言。

paucity / ˈpɔːsəti / *n.* scarcity 少量；缺乏，不足

An argument sometimes advanced for euthanasia is that the amount of money spent on prolonging a person's life for several months is exorbitant in relation to the *paucity* of funds available for preventive health programs and child health, both of which are highly cost-effective. 为支持安乐死而提出的一个论点认为，延续一个人几个月寿命的费用太高昂了，与之相比，用在预防保健项目和儿童健康方面的资金却少得可怜，而这两项才是高性价比投资。

pedantic / pɪˈdæntɪk / *adj.* showing off learning 卖弄学问的；学究式的；迂腐的

The Sophists have acquired a reputation as being learned but rather *pedantic* entertainers who gave didactic talks on every subject under the Sun; the truth, however, is that some of the Sophist philosophers （notably Protagoras） were very able thinkers. 诡辩家们对天底下的任何事都能给出学究式的说辞，因此被人们视作虽博学但只是迂腐的书呆子，然而事实上有些诡辩家(特别是普罗塔哥拉)是非常优秀的思想家。

【派】**pedant** *n.* an uninspired, boring academic 书呆子，学究

pellucid / pəˈluːsɪd / *adj.* transparent; translucent; easily understood 透明的，清澈的；易懂的

Two writers often mentioned as having an admirably *pellucid* style are Bertrand Russell and George Orwell. 有两个作家常常因清新的写作风格而被人提起，一个是伯特兰·罗素，另一个则是乔治·奥威尔。

penchant / ˈpentʃənt / *n.* inclination 爱好，嗜好

Sue has a *penchant* for science, while her brother is more interested in the arts. 苏喜欢科学，可是她的哥哥更喜欢艺术。

REVIEW 55

Matching

Match each word with its definition:

1. pallid
2. panegyric
3. paragon
4. partisan
5. pathological
6. patois
7. paucity
8. pedantic
9. pellucid
10. penchant

a. a regional dialect; nonstandard speech
b. one-sided
c. showing off learning
d. departing from normal condition
e. inclination
f. transparent; easily understood
g. model of excellence
h. lacking color or liveliness
i. scarcity
j. elaborate praise

Fill-ins

Choose the best word to fill in the blank in each sentence.

pallid	**panegyric**	**paragons**	**partisan**	**pathology**
patois	**paucity**	**pedantic**	**pellucid**	**penchant**

1. Subtle differences in symptoms between one patient and another one with a similar condition allow a competent doctor to diagnose the nature of the underlying _____.

2. The textbook was so well written and edited that students describe it as "wonderfully _____."

3. Academic writing should be erudite without being _____.

4. The job of political scientists is the objective study of government and politics; thus they are expected to be aloof from _____ politics.

5. The people of the area speak a _____ based on English, Spanish, and French.

6. According to archeologists, Roman tiles were not the _____ objects we see today; rather, they were painted a variety of vivid colors.

7. In his later years Lewis was able to indulge the _____ for performing music that he had as a young man.

8. The business professor assigned her students to select the three firms they would consider _____ for other companies to imitate.

9. No funeral _____ for the slain general was as eloquent as the looks of grief on the faces of the mourners at his funeral.

10. The historian is unable to reach a definite conclusion about when the battle began because of a _____ of evidence.

Sense or Nonsense

Indicate whether each sentence makes good sense or not.
Put S (SENSE) if it does, and put N (NONSENSE) if it does not.

1. Every weekend the Scott family has a gathering on the patois. _____

2. The museum has an exhibition of elaborately carved penchants. _____

3. There is a paucity of specialist doctors in many rural areas of the United States. _____

4. The class became bored listening to the pedantic, long-winded professor. _____

5. Steve's penchant for collecting things when he was a child led his mother to speculate that he might become a museum curator. _____

UNIT 56

penury / ˈpenjəri / *n.* extreme poverty 贫穷；贫困

The autobiography tells the story of the billionaire's journey from *penury* to riches beyond his imagining. 这本自传讲述了一位亿万富翁从一贫如洗到富得超乎其本人想象的历程。

peregrination / ˌperəgrɪˈneɪʃn / *n.* a wandering from place to place 旅行；游历

Swami Vivekananda's *peregrinations* took him all over India. 斯瓦米·维韦卡南达(法号"辨喜")足迹遍布印度各角落。

peremptory / pəˈremptəri / *adj.* imperative; leaving no choice 断然的，专制的；绝对的

The general's words were spoken in the *peremptory* tone of a man who is used to having his commands obeyed without question. 将军讲话的口气很强硬，全然一派习惯了别人无条件服从的口吻。

perennial / pəˈreniəl / *adj.* present throughout the years; persistent 长期的；持久的；反复的

Perennial warfare has left most of the people of the country in poverty. 长年的战火使得那个国家的多数人民处于贫困之中。

perfidious / pərˈfɪdiəs / *adj.* faithless; disloyal; untrustworthy 不忠的；背信弃义的

The novel tells the story of the hero's *perfidious* lover. 这本小说讲述了男主人公遭情人背叛的故事。

perfunctory / pərˈfʌŋktəri / *adj.* superficial; not thorough; performed really as a duty 敷衍的；马虎的；例行公事的

The *perfunctory* inspection of the airplane failed to reveal structural faults in the wing. 例行公事般的航检没能检查出飞机机翼结构上的缺陷。

perigee / ˈperɪdʒiː / *n.* the point in an orbit that is closest to the Earth (月球等轨道的)近地点

The Earth observation satellite reaches a *perigee* of 320 miles above the Earth's surface. 地球观测卫星飞抵了距地球表面320英里的近地点。

permeable / ˈpɜːrmiəbl / *adj.* penetrable 能透过的；具有渗透性的

Wetsuits, used by divers in cold water, are *permeable* to water but designed to retain body heat. 潜水员在冷水潜水时所穿的潜水服虽然会渗水，但是具有防寒作用。

perturb / pərˈtɜːrb / *v.* to disturb greatly; make uneasy or anxious; cause a body to deviate from its regular orbit 使烦恼；使不安；扰乱

The findings that violence is increasing in schools greatly *perturbed* government officials. 日见增多的校园暴力使得政府官员忧心忡忡。

【派】**perturbation** *n.* disturbance 骚动；不安；【物理】微扰

Scientists believe that the Earth has undergone alternating periods of relatively cooler and warmer climate, and that this is due largely to fluctuations in the intensity of the greenhouse effect and *perturbations* in the Earth's orbit around the Sun. 科学家们认为地球经历了相对较冷和较暖的交替时期，这在很大程度上是由温室气体浓度的起伏变化和地球绕太阳公转的轨道发生微扰造成的。

pervasive / pərˈveɪsɪv / *adj.* spread throughout every part 普遍的；弥漫的

It is a plausible hypothesis that the atheistic and materialistic philosophy of Marxism was readily accepted in China because of its similarities with Confucian views on spiritual matters, which had a *pervasive* influence in China for more than two thousand years. 这样的推断或许可信，即马克思主义中的无神论和唯物论之所以能在中国被广泛接受，是因为它们与在中国盛行了两千多年的孔子思想中涉及精神方面的内容有诸多相似之处。

【派1】**pervasiveness** *n.* 普遍性；广泛性；无处不在

An indicator of the *pervasiveness* of psychotropic drugs in American society is the fact that approximately 50% of adults have used tranquilizers at some time in their lives. 事实表明在美国50%左右的成年人都在他们生命中的某个时期使用过镇静剂，这说明了精神治疗药物在美国使用之广。

【派2】**pervade** *v.* 遍及；弥漫

REVIEW 56

Matching

Match each word with its definition:

1. penury		a.	penetrable
2. peregrination		b.	superficial
3. peremptory		c.	the point in an orbit closest to body being orbited
4. perennial		d.	present throughout the years
5. perfidious		e.	to disturb greatly
6. perfunctory		f.	extreme poverty
7. perigee		g.	imperative
8. permeable		h.	spread throughout every part
9. perturb		i.	a wandering from place to place
10. pervasive		j.	faithless; disloyal

Fill-ins

Choose the best word to fill in the blank in each sentence.

penury	**peregrinations**	**peremptory**	**perennial**	**perfidious**
perfunctory	**perigee**	**permeable**	**perturbed**	**pervasive**

1. Scientists calculate that the satellite will have a _____ of 120 miles from Earth.

2. Our well draws water from a _____ rock layer （an aquifer） in which the water is under pressure, so we generally do not have to use a pump.

3. Caricature is _____ in the work of the English novelist Charles Dickens.

4. Once again, Congress debated the _____ problem of the budget deficit.

5. While its diplomats were negotiating a peace settlement with the enemy, its _____ leaders were planning a full-scale invasion.

6. The great expense of his continual legal battles has practically reduced the man to _____.

7. A proverb says that time heals everything; it might be commented, however, that its healing is rarely complete and is often _____.

8. The rock band's _____ have taken it to over 50 cities around the world.

9. Military leaders were _____ by the report that important classified information had fallen into enemy hands.

10. The boss dismissed her employee's suggestion with a _____ laugh.

Sense or Nonsense

Indicate whether each sentence makes good sense or not.

Put S (SENSE) if it does, and put N (NONSENSE) if it does not.

1. The consumer group accused the bank of using penury to amass vast profits. _____

2. The poet laureate wrote a perigee condemning the nation's king as an incompetent ruler. _____

3. Astronomers believe that the distant star's orbit is being perturbed by some unknown body. _____

4. The dictator was used to having his peremptory commands obeyed. _____

5. Typhoons are a perennial problem in the coastal areas of Southeast China during the late summer and early autumn. _____

UNIT 57

petulant / ˈpetʃələnt / *adj.* rude; peevish 易怒的，爱发脾气的；耍性子的
The boy's father worried that his disobedient and *petulant* child would grow up to be a bitter and annoying man. 男孩的父亲担心他那不听话又爱耍性子的孩子将来会是一个爱抱怨而令人反感的人。

phlegmatic / flegˈmætɪk / *adj.* calm in temperament; sluggish 冷漠的；镇定的；迟钝的
"*Phlegmatic* natures can be inspired to enthusiasm only by being made into fanatics." (Friedrich Nietzsche) "要激发冷漠的人的热情，那么只有把他变成狂热分子。"（弗里德里希·尼采）

phoenix / ˈfiːnɪks / *n.* ① a mythical, immortal bird that lives for 500 years, burns itself to death, and rises from its ashes 凤凰（神话中的不死鸟，活了500年后焚身而死，然后从焚灰中重生）② anything that is restored after suffering great destruction 任何毁灭之后重生的事物
The captain believed the battalion had been destroyed by the enemy and was amazed to see it arise, *phoenix*-like, its men still fighting valiantly. 营长本以为他的军队被敌人打垮了，然而令他吃惊的是他的队伍又站了起来，凤凰涅槃一般，继续英勇作战。

physiognomy / ˌfɪziˈɑːnəmi / *n.* ① art of judging character from facial features 观相术，相面术 ② facial features 相貌
The art teacher assigned her students to make drawings of people with a wide variety of *physiognomy*. 美术老师给学生们布置作业，让他们给各种长相的人画像。

piety / ˈpaɪəti / *n.* devoutness 虔诚
Saint Bernard of Clairvaux was a medieval French monk revered for his *piety*. 圣伯纳德是中世纪的一位法国僧侣，以其虔诚而受人尊敬。

piquant / ˈpiːkənt / *adj.* ① appealingly stimulating 刺激的；振奋的 ② pleasantly pungent 辛辣的；开胃的 ③ attractive 有趣的；迷人的

Many of the guests enjoyed the *piquant* barbecue sauce, but others found it too spicy for their taste. 很多客人都喜欢烤肉辣酱，但是其他人都觉得太辣了。

pique / piːk / *n.* a fleeting feeling of hurt pride 伤自尊 *v.* to provoke or arouse 唤起，激起

Sally left the restaurant in a fit of *pique* after her date called to say he couldn't come because he was working late. 萨利黯然离开餐馆，因为她的约会对象打电话说要工作到很晚所以无法赴约。// The geologist's curiosity was *piqued* by the unusual appearance of the rock formation. 不同寻常的岩层构造激发了这位地质学家的兴趣。

placate / ˈpleɪkeɪt / *v.* to lessen another's anger; pacify 安抚；抚慰；使平静

After his team's third consecutive winless season, the Big State football coach opened his address to the irate alumni with a barrage of clichés and euphemisms to try to *placate* them: "Gentlemen, it is not my intention today to pull the wool over your eyes. Heaven only knows I have given my all. I have truly made the old college try. Unfortunately, however, by any reasonable criteria we have been less than completely successful in our endeavors, but I assure you that hope springs eternal in the human breast and next year we will rise to the occasion, put our noses to the grindstone and emerge triumphant in the face of adversity. I certainly admit that we have had a run of bad luck but that is nothing that can't be cured by true grit and determination." 在连续三个赛季毫无建树之后，大洲足球教练开始了他那充斥着大量陈词滥调和委婉语的演说，企图安抚那些愤怒的校友："各位，我今天并不想蒙骗大家。只有老天知道我已经竭尽所能，我真的已经尽力了。然而不幸的是，不论以何种标准评判，较之我们所付出的艰辛，我们所取得的成果都不尽人意，可我向各位保证，希望永远会在我们胸中激荡，来年我们会直面困难，奋发图强，不畏艰险，勇夺桂冠。当然我得承认我们一直时运不济，但是只要我们拿出铁杵成针的毅力和决心，我们就会无往不前。"

placid / ˈplæsɪd / *adj.* calm 平静的

We were amazed how the monk was able to remain *placid* despite the fire that was raging through the building. 那个和尚火烧房梁都能处乱不惊，让我们都很吃惊。

plaintive / ˈpleɪntɪv / *adj.* melancholy; mournful 忧郁的；哀伤的

After the battle all that could be heard was the *plaintive* cries of women who had lost their husbands. 战后所能听到的尽是丧夫的妇人的哭喊。

REVIEW 57

Matching

Match each word with its definition:

1. petulant
2. phlegmatic
3. phoenix
4. physiognomy
5. piety
6. piquant
7. pique

a. calm

b. calm in temperament; sluggish

c. rude; peevish

d. art of judging character from facial features

e. mournful

f. a mythical, immortal bird

g. a fleeting feeling of hurt pride

8. placate   h. pleasantly pungent

9. placid   i. to pacify

10. plaintive   j. devoutness

Fill-ins

Choose the best word to fill in the blank in each sentence.

petulant	**phlegmatic**	**phoenix**	**physiognomy**	**piety**
piquant	**piqued**	**placated**	**placid**	**plaintive**

1. Rebecca is a quiet person, but beneath a _____ exterior lies a continual ferment of emotion.

2. The monk is admired for his _____ .

3. The only sound after the battle was the _____ cry of a soldier who had been disemboweled.

4. The teacher _____ the students' interest in geology by taking them on a field trip to look at the rock formation.

5. Studies show that a person's _____ has an effect on his or her life; for example, people considered to have attractive features are more likely to be successful than those considered to be unattractive.

6. The _____ child will not stop complaining that he does not like the present he has been given.

7. Japan rose like a _____ from the destruction of World War II to become one of the world's leading industrial nations.

8. The restaurant manager apologized for the poor service and _____ the customer by saying that the meal was on the house.

9. The chef is known throughout Texas for his wonderfully _____ sauces.

10. The emergency room doctor trained herself to be _____ despite the great suffering she witnessed every day.

Sense or Nonsense

Indicate whether each sentence makes good sense or not.
Put S (SENSE) if it does, and put N (NONSENSE) if it does not.

1. The chef has prepared a range of plaintive desserts for our enjoyment. _____

2. People stare at the man because of his unusual physiognomy. _____

3. After being destroyed by an atomic bomb in 1945, the Japanese city of Hiroshima rose like a phoenix to become once again one of Japan's major cities. _____

4. Tom, with his phlegmatic and excitable personality, is not the person I would like to see in charge during a crisis. _____

5. The pastor urged the members of his congregation to show their piety by attending church every week. _____

UNIT 58

plasticity / plæˈstɪsəti / *n*. condition of being able to be shaped or formed; pliability 可塑性

The sociologist is continually amazed by the *plasticity* of social institutions. 社会习俗的可塑性总是令社会学家吃惊不已。

platitude / ˈplætɪtuːd / *n*. stale, overused expression 陈词滥调

Though Sarah's marriage didn't seem to be going well, she took comfort in the *platitude* that the first six months of a marriage were always the most difficult. 虽然莎拉的婚姻看似不合她意，但常言道：婚后半年最难熬，她就用这话宽慰自己。

platonic / pləˈtɑːnɪk / *adj*. spiritual; without sensual desire; theoretical 柏拉图式的；纯精神的；理论的

Gradually what had been a *platonic* relationship between Tim and Kyoko became a romantic one. 渐渐地，蒂姆和京子之间的柏拉图式关系变得很浪漫。

plethora / ˈpleθərə / *n*. excess; overabundance 过多；过于丰富

Because it deals with death and grieving, the funeral business has produced a *plethora* of euphemisms such as "slumber room" for the place where the corpse is placed for viewing. 由于处理与死亡和哀悼相关的业务，殡葬行业催生了过多的委婉语，例如用"灵堂"来表示停放尸体以供瞻仰之地。

plumb / plʌm / *v*. ① to determine the depth 测量深度 ② to examine deeply 探索，探究

A recurrent theme of mystical experience is "the dark night of the soul," in which a person *plumbs* the depths of despair before finding a transcendent reality that brings the person closer to what he or she regards as God. 神秘历程中反复出现的一个主题是"灵魂的暗夜"——人在发现那个能带他接近他所认为的上帝的超现实前，总是会陷入绝望的无底深渊。

【区】**plume** / pluːm / *v*. to congratulate oneself in a self-satisfied way 自豪，沾沾自喜

John *plumed* himself on his ability to read both Sanskrit and Greek. 约翰颇为自己既懂梵语又懂希腊语而自豪。

plummet / ˈplʌmɪt / *v*. to fall; plunge 坠落；垂直落下；骤然落下

The fighter jet, struck by an enemy missile, *plummeted* to earth. 那架喷气式战斗机被敌方导弹击中而坠落到地面。

plutocracy / pluːˈtɑːkrəsi / *n*. society ruled by the wealthy 富豪统治，财阀统治

It has been argued that modern democracies are *plutocracies* to the extent that wealth allows certain people to have a disproportionately large influence on political decision-making. 有人认为，就财富可以令某些人过分地影响政治决策这点来说，当代民主社会从很大程度上说是一个富豪统治社会。

porous / ˈpɔːrəs / *adj*. full of holes; permeable to liquids 多孔的；能渗透的

If you go camping, make sure to spend enough money to buy a tent with a roof that is not *porous*. 如果你要去野营，一定要花足够的钱购买一顶顶部不会渗水的帐篷。

poseur / poʊˈzɜːr / *n.* a person who affects an attitude or identity to impress others 装腔作势的人；装模作样的人

The critic labeled the writer a *poseur* who was more interested in getting the public's attention than in writing good books. 批评家称这位作家为装腔作势的人，他更关注的是吸引公众的注意，而不在于写出好书。

pragmatic / præɡˈmætɪk / *adj.* practical 实用的；实际的

The cult of romantic love was a major factor in making a marriage for love, rather than for more *pragmatic* reasons, a ubiquitous phenomenon in the West by the nineteenth century. 对浪漫之爱的推崇是使人为爱情而不是为实用原因结婚的主要因素，这在19世纪的西方是非常普遍的现象。

【派1】**pragmatism** *n.* a practical way of approaching situations or solving problems 实用主义

Pragmatism is similar to Positivism in rejecting lofty metaphysical conceptions and in asserting that the main role of philosophy is to help clarify phenomena experienced. 实用主义与实证主义在以下两个方面是相似的：排斥高调的形而上学观念以及坚持哲学的主要作用是帮助人们阐明所目睹的现象。

【派2】**pragmatist** *n.* someone who approaches situations in a practical way 实用主义者

The word "*pragmatist*" often used to refer to someone who is willing to sacrifice his principles to expediency. "实用主义者"通常指那些常常甘愿牺牲原则以获得实利的人。

REVIEW 58

Matching

Match each word with its definition:

1. plasticity	a. overused expression
2. platitude	b. full of holes; permeable to liquids
3. platonic	c. practical
4. plethora	d. excess
5. plumb	e. to fall; plunge
6. plummet	f. spiritual; without sensual desire
7. plutocracy	g. pliability
8. porous	h. society ruled by the wealthy
9. poseur	i. to examine deeply
10. pragmatic	j. a person who affects an identity to impress others

Fill-ins

Choose the best word to fill in the blank in each sentence.

plasticity	**platitudes**	**platonic**	**plethora**	**plumbed**
plummet	**plutocracy**	**porous**	**poseur**	**pragmatic**

1. The _____ of excellent rock bands makes it difficult for new bands to gain an audience.

2. The _____ clay allows the track to dry quickly.

3. Scholars are not certain whether Socrates' relation with his student Plato was only _____.

4. The poet William Wordsworth _____ his own psyche in his masterpiece, *The Prelude*, or *Growth of a Poet's Mind*.

5. The motivational speaker is full of _____ , such as "Nothing succeeds like success."

6. The members of the stage club finally realized that Anthony was a _____ who enjoyed acting like an actor more than doing all the work necessary to be a real actor.

7. Some commentators have likened the United States more to a _____ than a democracy because of the great power held by the rich.

8. A _____ leader is not constrained by ideological preconceptions and continually adjusts his plans to conform to reality.

9. A compelling body of evidence has been built up by scientists suggesting that the _____ of human nature is more limited than was generally believed by social scientists for much of the twentieth century.

10. Scientists predict that the satellite will decay over the next few days and it will _____ to Earth.

Sense or Nonsense

Indicate whether each sentence makes good sense or not.
Put S (SENSE) if it does, and put N (NONSENSE) if it does not.

1. Anthropologists and sociologists tend to stress the plasticity of human nature, whereas biologists emphasize the role of genes. _____

2. State law forbids platonic relationships between members of the same family. _____

3. The tennis court is designed to be porous enough to dry thoroughly in a few hours. _____

4. The coach told the press, "It might be a platitude, but I really mean it: We're taking the season one game at a time." _____

5. Some of his friends consider Morris to be a bit of a poseur: he loves to hang out at the café, sipping an espresso and acting as if he were America's most famous writer. _____

UNIT 59

prate / preɪt / *v.* to talk idly; chatter 闲聊；瞎扯

The "talk radio" program allows people to call in and ***prate*** about their pet peeves. 谈话类广播节目允许听众打进电话来聊一聊自己的小烦恼。

prattle / ˈprætl / *n.* meaningless, foolish talk 无聊话；闲聊

The sociologist theorizes that what may seem like ***prattle*** often has an important social function: what might be labeled "gossip" is an important means for people to communicate valuable information about themselves and others. 社会学家提出这样的理论，那些看似无聊的闲扯其实有着很重要的社会功用。那些通常被视为"八卦"的闲聊，其实是人们用来交流有关自己或他人的重要信息的重要渠道。

preamble / priˈæmbl / *n.* preliminary statement 序言，前言，导言

Along with the opening words of the Declaration of Independence and the Gettysburg Address, the *preamble* to the Constitution of the United States contains some of the most memorable language in American history: "We the People of the United States, in order to form a more perfect Union, establish justice, insure domestic tranquility, provide for the common defense, promote the general welfare, and secure the blessings of liberty, to ourselves and our posterity, do ordain and establish this Constitution for the United States of America." 同《独立宣言》和《葛底斯堡演说》的开场白一样，美国宪法的序文部分也包含了美国历史上最脍炙人口的话语："我们美利坚合众国的人民，为了构建一个更完善的联邦，树立正义，保障国内安宁，建立共同防御，增进全民福祉，并确保我们自己及我们子孙得享自由带来的幸福，乃为美利坚合众国制定和确立此宪法。"

precarious / priˈkeriəs / *adj.* uncertain 不确定的；不稳定的；危险的

The prime minister's *precarious* hold on power ended when she lost a vote of confidence in Parliament. 当首相失去了议会中一张信任票后，她本就不稳固的执政也随之结束了。

precept / ˈpriːsept / *n.* principle; law 准则，规范

A good *precept* to follow in writing is to avoid redundancies such as "track record" (unless the record was set on a racecourse), "revert back," "free gift," and "general consensus." 写作中应遵循的一条重要准则就是避免冗赘。例如，不要说"人生轨道记录"(在赛道上创下纪录除外〔译者注：track一词含义较丰富，可指人生轨迹也可指跑道，在这里是利用了该词的多义〕)、"归还回去"、"免费的赠品"和"普遍的共识"。

precipitate *v.* / priˈsipiteit / ① to cause to happen 引发 ② to throw down from a height 猛抛
adj. / priˈsipitət / rash; hasty; sudden 鲁莽的；草率的；仓促的

Full-scale American entry into World War II remained unpopular with the vast majority of Americans until a declaration of war was *precipitated* by the Japanese attack on the naval base at Pearl Harbor, a day that President Roosevelt predicted, in a memorable phrase, would "live in infamy." 全面介入第二次世界大战的想法在美国人中并不受欢迎，直到日本偷袭美国海军基地珍珠港，美国才向日本宣战。这就是美国总统罗斯福所说的让人记忆深刻的 "耻辱的一天"。// The secretary of state advised the President not to take *precipitate* action. 国务卿建议总统不要草率行事。

【派1】**precipitous** *adj.* hasty; quickly with too little caution. 轻率的；草率的

【派2】**precipitation** *n.* water droplets or ice particles from atmospheric water vapor that falls to Earth 降水

It would be helpful if the atmosphere could be induced to deposit its *precipitation* more evenly over the Earth's surface, so that some land areas are not inundated while others remain arid. 要是能引导大气使其降水均匀分布在地球上会大有裨益，这样就不会有些地方发生洪涝，而另一些地方却出现干旱了。

precursor / priˈkɜːrsər / *n.* forerunner; predecessor 先驱；前辈；前导

The *precursor* to the theory of plate tectonics was the theory of continental drift. 板块构造学说的前身是大陆漂移说。

● 常见学科术语 ●
---

plate tectonics: geological theory stating that the outer part of the Earth's interior is composed of two layers, one of which "floats" on the other. According to this theory, which is widely accepted by scientists, ten major plates move in relation to one another, creating such phenomena as earthquakes and mountain building along the boundaries of the plates.

> **板块构造学说**：地质学理论。该学说认为地球内部的外围部分由两层组成，其中一层漂浮在另一层上面。根据这个目前已被科学家广泛接受的理论，十大主要板块相互作用，在板块边缘处就会产生地震、造山运动等现象。
>
> **continental drift:** the theory that the continents shift their positions over time
> **大陆漂移说**：该假说认为陆地的位置会随着时间的变化而发生位移。

preempt / prɪˈempt / v. ① to supersede 取代，代替 ② to appropriate for oneself 先发制人

The movie was *preempted* for the President's emergency address to the nation. 这部电影要先声夺人，替总统的全国紧急讲话造势。

prehensile / prɪˈhensaɪl / adj. capable of grasping 可盘卷的

Many more animals in South America have *prehensile* tails than those in Southeast Asia and Africa, possibly because the greater density of the forest there favored this adaptation over the ability to glide through the trees. 与东南亚和非洲的动物相比，南美的许多动物都长着可盘卷的尾巴，这很可能是因为南美的森林相对而言更加茂密，而这样的尾巴则利于在林间穿梭。

REVIEW 59

Matching

Match each word with its definition:

1. prate		a.	capable of grasping
2. prattle		b.	to talk idly
3. preamble		c.	preliminary statement
4. precarious		d.	to cause to happen
5. precept		e.	meaningless talk
6. precipitate (*adj.*)		f.	to supersede
7. precursor		g.	principle; law
8. preempt		h.	rash; hasty
9. prehensile		i.	uncertain
10. precipitate (*v.*)		j.	forerunner

Fill-ins

Choose the best word to fill in the blank in each sentence.

prated	**prattle**	**preamble**	**precarious**	**precepts**
precipitate	**precursor**	**preempted**	**prehensile**	**precipitated**

1. Thomas Edison's famous laboratory in Menlo Park, New Jersey, was a _____ to the great laboratories later created by corporations such as AT&T and IBM, out of which have poured a torrent of new techniques and devices.

2. Moral _____ vary from society to society, but all societies have sanctions against certain acts, such as murder.

3. _____ tails help many arboreal animals to find and eat food as they move through the trees.

4. Steve earns a _____ living as a part-time waiter.

5. Tired of the gossip's _____, Alicia said she was late for an appointment so she could end the conversation.

6. The _____ to the bill describes the background of the legislation and explains how it relates to existing laws.

7. The increased tariffs in the 1930s _____ a collapse in world trade, exacerbating the Great Depression.

8. All TV and radio broadcasts have been _____ by an emergency announcement by the President.

9. The commander said he would not be pressured into making a _____ decision.

10. The retired couple _____ all evening about their latest trip to Europe, oblivious to the fact that no one had the slightest interest in what they were talking about.

Sense or Nonsense

Indicate whether each sentence makes good sense or not.
Put S (SENSE) if it does, and put N (NONSENSE) if it does not.

1. Scientists have shown that the precursor to birds was a flying dinosaur. _____

2. The Democrats have a precarious majority in the state senate. _____

3. The audience of distinguished scientists listened intently as the Nobel Prize-winning physicist prated eloquently about her latest discovery. _____

4. The man studied the religion's precepts so that he could be accepted as a convert. _____

5. A preamble to the official report describes its rationale and how the commission gathered its information. _____

UNIT 60

premonition / ˌpremə'nɪʃn / *n.* forewarning; presentiment 前兆；预感
　　Shortly after his reelection in 1864, President Abraham Lincoln had a *premonition* of his impending death, and on April 14, 1865, he was shot and died the next day. 1864年再次当选总统后不久，亚伯拉罕·林肯就预感到死神的临近，1865年4月14日他遇刺并于次日身亡。

presage / prɪ'seɪdʒ / *v.* to foretell; indicate in advance 预言；预示
　　The English poet William Blake believed his work *presaged* a new age in which people would achieve political, social, psychological, and spiritual freedom. 英国诗人威廉·布莱克坚信，他的作品预示了一个新时代的到来，一个人们能够获得政治、社会、心理及精神自由的时代。

presumptuous / prɪ'zʌmptʃuəs / *adj.* rude; improperly bold 专横的；冒失的
　　The new employee did not offer her advice to her boss because she was afraid he might consider it *presumptuous* for a recent graduate to make a suggestion to someone with 30 years experience in the field. 这名新职员没有向她的老板提出她的建议，因为她担心老板会觉得她很冒失：一名刚毕业的大学生居然向一位已在业内奋斗了30年的人提建议！

【派1】**presume** *v.* 假定；推测

Proponents of the view *presume* that there exist only two antithetical positions, with no middle ground between their opponent's view and their own (eminently more reasonable) position. 这种观点的支持者认为只存在两种对立的立场，在他们自己（合理得多）的观点和反对者的观点之间不存在任何中间立场。

【派2】**presumption** *n.* 放肆，傲慢；推测

Anti-Semitism originated in the *presumption* that Jews were responsible for Jesus' crucifixion, and was responsible for periodic persecutions such as the expulsion of Jews from Spain in 1492. 反犹太主义观点源于这样一种设想，即犹太人要对耶稣的受难负责。该观点要为周期性的迫害犹太人的行为负责，如1492年西班牙驱逐犹太人出境。

preternatural / ˌpriːtərˈnætʃrəl / *adj.* beyond the normal course of nature; supernatural 超自然的；异常的，奇特的

Most scientists believe that putative *preternatural* phenomena are outside the scope of scientific inquiry. 大多数科学家都认为一般认定的超自然现象都不在科学研究的范围之内。

prevaricate / prɪˈværɪkeɪt / *v.* to quibble; evade the truth 支吾其辞

Journalists accused government leaders of *prevaricating* about the progress of the war. 记者指责政府领导人对战争进展情况支吾其辞。

primordial / praɪˈmɔːrdiəl / *adj.* original; existing from the beginning 原始的；原生的

Scholars are divided as to whether polytheism represents a degeneration from a *primordial* monotheism, or was a precursor to a more sophisticated view, monotheism. 多神论是原始一神论的退化，还是一种更高级的一神论的先驱，学者们对此各执己见。

> ● **常见学科术语** ●
>
> **polytheism:** belief in the existence of more than one god
> **多神论：**信仰多种神灵
>
> **monotheism:** belief in the existence of one god
> **一神论：**信仰唯一神灵

pristine / ˈprɪstiːn / *adj.* untouched; uncorrupted 未触及的；原始的；纯朴的

The bank's hermetically sealed vault has kept the manuscript in *pristine* condition for 50 years. 这份手稿在银行密闭的地下室中原封不动地保存了50年。

probity / ˈproʊbəti / *n.* honesty; high-mindedness 正直；诚实

No one questioned the *probity* of the judge being considered for elevation to the U.S. Supreme Court; what was at issue was his controversial views on several important issues. 正被考虑调入美国最高法院的法官，其正直无人质疑；但问题的关键在于他对几个重要问题的看法引发了争议。

problematic / ˌprɑːbləˈmætɪk / *adj.* posing a problem; doubtful; unsettled 有疑问的；成问题的；怀疑的；未知的

The idea of the universe originating at a certain point in time seems *problematic* to many scientists. 宇宙源于时间上的某一点的说法在许多科学家看来是有问题的。

prodigal / ˈprɑːdɪgl / *adj.* wasteful; extravagant; lavish 浪费的；奢侈的；挥霍的

Betty warned her husband that he must stop his *prodigal* spending on sports cars and expensive clothing. 贝蒂告诫她的丈夫必须停止挥霍金钱去买跑车和昂贵的衣服。

REVIEW 60

Matching
Match each word with its definition:

1. premonition
2. presage
3. presumptuous
4. preternatural
5. prevaricate
6. primordial
7. pristine
8. probity
9. problematic
10. prodigal

a. rude
b. doubtful
c. beyond the normal course of nature
d. existing from the beginning
e. forewarning
f. honesty
g. to foretell
h. wasteful
i. to quibble
j. untouched

Fill-ins
Choose the best word to fill in the blank in each sentence.

premonition	**presage**	**presumptuous**	**preternatural**	**prevaricating**
primordial	**pristine**	**probity**	**problematic**	**prodigal**

1. Scientists are investigating Edna's claim to having a _____ ability to predict the future.
2. Air strikes against military bases _____ a full-scale invasion.
3. Ruth's dream contained a _____ that war would break out.
4. The museum exhibition allows visitors to experience what a _____ forest was like.
5. The President told the senator to stop _____ on the issue and give him her decision by Monday on whether she had his support.
6. Tom keeps his pride and joy, a 1966 Triumph, in _____ condition in his temperature-controlled garage.
7. One of the considerations that makes a return to a military draft _____ is that gender equality would almost certainly require the equal participation of males and females.
8. Bruce's _____ spending on luxuries left him nearly bankrupt.
9. The math student decided that it would be _____ of her to correct the error in the eminent mathematics professor's calculations.
10. The senator's unquestioned _____ and incisive intelligence made her a unanimous choice to lead the sub-committee investigating official misconduct.

Sense or Nonsense

Indicate whether each sentence makes good sense or not.
Put S (SENSE) if it does, and put N (NONSENSE) if it does not.

1. A primordial number is an integer divisible only by itself or one. _____
2. The premonition to the play introduces us to the main characters and the setting. _____
3. Some people believe that prevaricating helps to develop character because it encourages a person to make up his or her mind quickly. _____
4. The chairperson of the finance committee warned that the state's prodigal spending would have to stop. _____
5. The brain researcher believes that what may appear to be preternatural occurrences are actually the result of the activation of certain areas of the brain. _____

UNIT 61

profound / prəˈfaʊnd / *adj.* deep; not superficial 深刻的；意义深远的

There is an adage in philosophy that everyone is born either a Platonist or an Aristotelian, meaning that everyone has a predisposition to believing either that reality is completely "here and now," or that there exists a more *profound*, hidden reality. 哲学中有一句格言：每个人生来不是柏拉图主义者就是亚里士多德主义者，就是说每个人要么认为现实完全是指"此时此刻"，要么相信存在一个更深刻、更隐蔽的现实。

【派】**profundity** *n.* the quality of being profound 深刻；深度

———————————— • 常见学科术语 • ————————————

Aristotle was Plato's student; In contrast to Plato, he believed that there exist no entities separate from matter.
亚里士多德是柏拉图的学生。与柏拉图相反，他认为实体离不开物质。

prohibitive / prəˈhɪbətɪv / *adj.* so high as to prevent the purchase or use of; preventing; forbidding 令人望而却步的；禁止的；阻碍的

Most people in poor countries are unable to purchase a computer because of its *prohibitive* price. 贫穷国家的大多数人都买不起电脑，他们觉得电脑的价格高得惊人。

【派】**prohibition** *n.* 禁止；禁令

The word taboo was taken from Polynesia (tabu in Tongan) and broadened to mean any culture's *prohibition* of a particular object or activity. "taboo"一词源于波利尼西亚(即汤加语中的tabu)，后泛指任何文化中对某种特别的事物或活动的禁忌。

proliferate / prəˈlɪfəreɪt / *v.* to increase rapidly 激增

With the pervasive influence of American culture, "fast-food" restaurants are *proliferating* in many countries. 受美国文化的广泛影响，许多国家快餐店数量激增。

【派】**proliferation** *n.* 激增

A problem with the *proliferation* of jargon is that it impedes communication between different fields of knowledge. 大量使用行话造成的一个问题是，它阻碍了不同知识领域间的交流。

propensity / prə'pensəti / *n.* inclination; tendency 倾向；趋势

There is a natural *propensity* to stress the importance of what one is saying by exaggerating it. 通过夸大自己所说的内容来增强其重要性，是人与生俱来的倾向。

propitiate / prə'pɪʃieɪt / *v.* to appease 抚慰，劝慰，使息怒

M.E.W. Sherwood, an author alive at the time of the U.S. Civil War, eloquently expressed the sacrifice made by soldiers on both sides of that great conflict: "But for four years there was a contagion of nobility in the land, and the best blood of North and South poured itself out a libation to *propitiate* the deities of Truth and Justice. The great sin of slavery was washed out, but at what a cost！" 美国内战时期的作家 M.E.W.舍伍德以极富文采的笔触，描述了双方士兵在这场巨大冲突中做出的牺牲：“内战的四年间，一种崇高的精神到处蔓延，南北方最宝贵的热血泼洒在告慰真理和正义之神的祭坛上。奴隶制的罪孽终被洗刷，但付出的代价是多么惨重啊！”

propriety / prə'praɪəti / *n.* correct conduct; fitness 得体；妥当；适合

Judges are expected to conduct themselves with *propriety*, especially in the courtroom. 法官的言行举止要得体，尤其是在法庭上。

proscribe / proʊ'skraɪb / *v.* to condemn; forbid; outlaw 谴责；禁止；排斥

The expert in English believes that since the tendency to use hyperbole is natural and often enriches the language, it should not be *proscribed*. 英语专家认为，既然运用夸张手法是人类本能的倾向，而且又能丰富语义，那就不应该禁止。

【派】**proscriptive** *adj.* relating to prohibition 禁止的；排斥的

Proponents of the view that dictionaries should be *proscriptive*, dictating what correct usage is, believe that without such guides the standard of language will decline; however, advocates of descriptive dictionaries argue that dictionary makers have no mandate to dictate usage and therefore should merely record language as it is used. 一些人认为词典应该规定语言使用的禁忌，规定正确的用法，他们认为如果没有这些指导，语言的水准就会降低；而描述性词典的拥护者却认为编撰者没有资格规定语言的用法，因此他们只应该如实地记录语言。

provident / 'prɑːvɪdənt / *adj.* providing for future needs; frugal 有先见之明的；深谋远虑的

Most people have heard the story of the prodigal grasshopper and the *provident* ant that spends the summer saving food for the winter. 多数人都听过挥霍无度的螳螂和深谋远虑的蚂蚁的故事。蚂蚁极有远见，夏天就储藏过冬的粮食。

puissant / 'pjuːɪsənt / *adj.* powerful 强大的；有权力的

The article analyzes the similarities and differences between the Roman Empire and the British Empire when each was at its most *puissant*. 这篇文章分析了罗马帝国和大英帝国在各自极盛时期的异同。

【派】**puissance** *n.* 权力；权势；影响

punctilious / pʌŋk'tɪliəs / *adj.* careful in observing rules of behavior or ceremony 谨小慎微的；一丝不苟的

The prime minister reminded his staff that they must be *punctilious* in following protocol during the visit by the foreign head of state. 首相提醒他的幕僚，在外国元首来访期间，一定要一丝不苟地遵循礼仪。

Matching

Match each word with its definition:

1. profound		a.	correct conduct
2. prohibitive		b.	powerful
3. proliferate		c.	preventing; forbidding
4. propensity		d.	to condemn
5. propitiate		e.	not superficial
6. propriety		f.	frugal
7. proscribe		g.	inclination; tendency
8. provident		h.	careful in observing rules of behavior
9. puissant		i.	to win over
10. punctilious		j.	to increase rapidly

Fill-ins

Choose the best word to fill in the blank in each sentence.

profound	prohibitive	proliferating	propensity	propitiated
propriety	proscribes	provident	puissant	punctilious

1. In 1972, the United States Supreme Court voided all state and federal laws specifying the death penalty on the basis that they are unconstitutional, since they violated the Eighth Amendment of the Constitution, which _____ "cruel and unusual punishment."

2. As Russ grew older, he found his intellectual interests _____ rather than narrowing, as he had expected.

3. Sharon is _____ in doing her homework; every evening she reviews all of the day's classes and carefully completes the written tasks.

4. American cultural influence in the world has been described as a force more _____ than any army.

5. _____ in that country demands that young single women be accompanied in public by an adult female.

6. Defenders of philosophy say that, far from being a superfluous and self-indulgent activity, it is one of the most _____ of human enterprises, having given humankind such useful fields of thought as science, and conceived of such noble ideas as freedom, democracy, and human rights.

7. In her article the anthropologist suggests that homo sapiens is a species with an innate _____ for violence.

8. A belief in angry gods who must be _____ to prevent them from venting their wrath on human beings is pervasive in human cultures.

9. According to some scientists, the technology exists for establishing a base on Mars, but the cost of doing so would be _____.

10. The _____ housekeeper insists on buying everything when it is on sale.

Sense or Nonsense

Indicate whether each sentence makes good sense or not.

Put S (SENSE) if it does, and put N (NONSENSE) if it does not.

1. The letter argues that the city council must take measures to control the proliferation of wild dogs. _____

2. No one could blame the passengers on the jetliner for being a bit puissant after a UFO was sighted flying off their plane's wing. _____

3. Throughout the priest's writings is a profound regard for the dignity and sanctity of human life. _____

4. The chief of protocol planned every official function so that propriety was strictly observed. _____

5. The prohibitive cost of many modern medical therapies makes them unsuitable for patients in poor countries. _____

UNIT 62

pungent / ˈpʌndʒənt / *adj.* ① strong or sharp in smell or taste 刺鼻的 ② penetrating; caustic 尖刻的，挖苦的；腐蚀性的 ③ to the point 中肯的

Slang frequently expresses an idea succinctly and *pungently*. 俚语常常能简洁而中肯地表达观点。

purport / pərˈpɔːrt / *v.* to profess; suppose; claim 声称；表明 *n.* meaning intended or implied 意义；含义

In the United States religion plays a large role, since nearly everyone *purports* to believe in God and many people are members of churches. 宗教在美国占据着重要位置，因为几乎所有美国人都声称自己信仰上帝，而且很多人都是教会成员。

pusillanimous / ˌpjuːsɪˈlænɪməs / *adj.* cowardly 懦弱的；优柔寡断的

Traditionally, a ship captain is considered *pusillanimous* if he abandons his ship before everyone else has. 传统观点认为，先于其他人弃船而逃的船长是懦夫。

【派】**pusillanimity** *n.* cowardice 懦弱

quagmire / ˈkwæɡmaɪər / *n.* marsh; a difficult situation 沼泽地；困境

The federal government's antitrust suit in the 1990s against Microsoft created a legal *quagmire*. 联邦政府在20世纪90年代针对微软采取的反托拉斯诉讼引起了一个法律困境。

quail / kweɪl / *v.* to cower; lose heart 退缩；胆怯

The defendant *quailed* when the judge entered the room to announce the sentence. 当法官走进法庭准备宣判时，被告变得胆怯。

qualified / ˈkwɑːlɪfaɪd / *adj.* limited; restricted 有限的；限定性的

In Indian philosophy a position between monism at one extreme and dualism at the other is *qualified* nondualism, a philosophy in which reality is considered to have attributes of both dualism and monism. 在印度哲学体系中，居于一元论和二元论这两个极端之间的是有限非二元论，它认为现实兼具一元论和二元论的特点。

【派1】**qualification** *n.* limitation or restriction 限制；限定条件

So many *qualifications* had been added to the agreement that Sue was now reluctant to sign it. 协议附加了那么多限定条件，苏现在都有点不愿意签约了。

【派2】**qualify** *v.* to modify or limit 限制，限定

● 常见学科术语 ●

monism: the belief that reality is a unified whole consisting of one fundamental principle
一元论：认为现实是一个整体，只包含一种基本原则。

dualism: the theory that two basic entities constitute reality（e.g. mind and matter or good and evil）
二元论：认为现实由两个基本实体构成，比如物质与意识、善与恶。

---

qualm / kwɑːm / *n.* ① a sudden feeling of faintness or nausea 恶心，不适 ② an uneasy feeling about the rightness of actions 疑虑；担心

The judge had no *qualms* about sentencing the thief to five years imprisonment. 法官没有因判处窃贼五年徒刑而感到不安。

query / ˈkwɪri / *v.* to question 询问 *n.* a question 疑问；质问

Until widespread industrialization caused massive pollution in the nineteenth and twentieth centuries, the ability of the biosphere to dissipate and assimilate waste created by human activity was not *queried*. 直到19、20世纪大规模的工业化进程造成严重的环境污染，人们才开始质疑生物圈吸收并消化人类活动所制造的垃圾的能力。// The history professor answered the student's interesting *query* about the influence of Arabic thought on Western civilization. 历史老师回答了学生"阿拉伯式思维对西方文明的影响"这一颇具趣味性的问题。

quibble / ˈkwɪbl / *v.* to argue over insignificant and irrelevant details 吹毛求疵 *n.* 牵强之词；遁词

The lawyers spent so much time *quibbling* over details that they made little progress in reaching an agreement on the central issue. 律师们花费了太多时间争论无关紧要的细节，至于在核心问题上达成一致，他们倒没取得什么进展。

quiescent / kwiˈesnt / *adj.* inactive; still 不活动的；静止的

Although malignant tumors may remain *quiescent* for a period of time, they never become benign. 尽管恶性肿瘤在一段时间内可能不会扩散，但它们绝不可能转为良性的。

【派】**quiescence** *n.* 静止；沉默

REVIEW 62

Matching

Match each word with its definition:

1. pungent
2. purport
3. pusillanimous
4. quagmire
5. quail
6. qualified

a. a difficult situation
b. to argue over insignificant details
c. to profess; suppose
d. inactive
e. strong or sharp in smell or taste
f. limited

7. qualm   g. cowardly

8. query   h. to question

9. quibble   i. to lose heart

10. quiescent   j. an uneasy feeling

Fill-ins

Choose the best word to fill in the blank in each sentence.

pungent	purported	pusillanimous	quagmire	quailed
qualified	qualms	query	quibble	quiescent

1. The Nissan Patrol sank halfway into the _____.

2. The _____ alien craft turned out to be an experimental aircraft performing unusual maneuvers.

3. During our tennis match we smelled the _____ odor of lamb curry being cooked.

4. The bank teller _____ as the masked robber threatened her with a gun.

5. The soldier said he has no _____ about killing the enemy since it was his duty.

6. The fortune-teller answered her customer's _____ with an ambiguous "It will come about if Fate wills it."

7. The student's essay asserts that "Humanity made great progress in the twentieth century"; however, when her teacher asked her what she meant by "progress" she _____ her statement by specifying that she meant that humanity made great economic and scientific progress.

8. The senator argued that it would be _____ for Congress to simply rubber-stamp every bill proposed by the President.

9. When asked by reporters which of the starting pitchers he thought was better, the manager replied, "I'm not going to _____ about which is better. They're both superb."

10. The patient's emotional disturbance appeared to be _____, but the psychologist feared that it would manifest itself again soon.

Sense or Nonsense

Indicate whether each sentence makes good sense or not.
Put S (SENSE) if it does, and put N (NONSENSE) if it does not.

1. The discovery was purported to be the most important technological breakthrough of the modern age. _____

2. The head football coach called spring practice a qualified success because the conditioning program had gone well but there had been only limited progress in other areas. _____

3. The quiescent volcano is spewing out lava that is threatening to destroy the nearby town. _____

4. "Let's accept the report's conclusion and not quibble over inconsequential details," the manager told his workers. _____

5. U.S. military leaders are leery of becoming involved in a quagmire that would drain resources and limit their forces' effectiveness in other theatres. _____

UNIT 63

quorum / ˈkwɔːrəm / *n.* number of members necessary to conduct a meeting (会议)法定人数

The U.S. Senate's majority leader asked three members of his party to be available to help form a *quorum*. 美国参议院的多数党领袖要求自己的政党指派三人以达到会议法定人数的要求。

raconteur / ˌrækɑːnˈtɜːr / *n.* a witty, skillful storyteller 机智、健谈的人

Former President Bill Clinton is known as an accomplished *raconteur* who can entertain guests with amusing anecdotes about politics all evening. 美国前总统比尔·克林顿是一个善于交际的健谈者，会见宾客时，一整晚他都能讲些有趣的政治轶事以飨宾客。

rail / reɪl / *v.* to scold with bitter or abusive language 责备；辱骂；抱怨

The critic of globalization *railed* against its effect on the poor people of the world. 评论家怒斥全球化对全球贫困者的影响。

raiment / ˈreɪmənt / *n.* clothing 衣饰，服装

It took two hours for the princess' handmaidens to help her put on her splendid *raiment* for her coronation as queen. 侍女们花了两小时才帮公主穿上加冕女王典礼时需要穿的华丽服饰。

ramification / ˌræmɪfɪˈkeɪʃn / *n.* implication; outgrowth; consequence 后果；影响

The full *ramification* of the invention of the laser did not become apparent for many years; now it is used in a great variety of applications, from DVD players to surgery. 激光被发明后很长一段时间内，其效用都未得到充分关注，但现在它已广泛应用于DVD播放机及外科手术等各领域。

rarefied / ˈrerəfaɪd / *adj.* refined 精制的，良好的；纯化的，纯净的

Many scholars flourish in the *rarefied* intellectual atmosphere of the Institute for Advanced Studies in Princeton, New Jersey. 位于新泽西州的普林斯顿高等研究院具有良好的学术氛围，许多学术人才在此取得不凡成就。

【派】**rarefy** *v.* to make thinner, purer, or more refined 使纯化，提纯；精炼

rationale / ˌræʃəˈnæl / *n.* fundamental reason 根本原因

The philosophy of "enlightened self-interest" justifies acting in one's own interest by asserting that this is not selfish or motivated by a "beggar thy neighbor" *rationale*, but is simply the best way to ensure the welfare of the entire community. "启蒙性的利己主义"哲学为人们的利己行为进行辩护，声称这并非出于自私或"以邻为壑"的心理，仅仅因为这是确保整个社会福祉的最好方式。

rebus / ˈriːbəs / *n.* a puzzle in which pictures or symbols represent words 谜；画谜

Egyptian writing uses the principle of the *rebus*, substituting pictures for words. 埃及的书写运用了以画代字的原则，用图片代替文字。

recalcitrant / rɪˈkælsɪtrənt / *adj.* resisting authority or control 反抗权威的；拒不服从的

The officer had no choice but to recommend that the *recalcitrant* soldier be court-martialed. 军官别无选择，只能建议把那个不服管的士兵送交军事法庭审判。

recant / rɪˈkænt / *v.* to retract a statement or opinion 取消；撤除

The bishop told the theologian that he must *recant* his heretical teaching or risk excommunication. 主教告诫神学家必须放弃异端学说，否则就要把他逐出教会。

REVIEW 63

Matching

Match each word with its definition:

1. quorum	a.	fundamental reason
2. raconteur	b.	implication
3. rail	c.	refined
4. raiment	d.	clothing
5. ramification	e.	a witty, skillful storyteller
6. rarefied	f.	resisting authority or control
7. rationale	g.	to retract a statement or opinion
8. rebus	h.	to scold with bitter or abusive language
9. recalcitrant	i.	a puzzle in which pictures or symbols represent words
10. recant	j.	number of members necessary to conduct a meeting

Fill-ins

Choose the best word to fill in the blank in each sentence.

quorum	raconteur	rails	raiment	ramifications
rarefied	rationale	rebus	recalcitrant	recant

1. A counselor was called in to talk to the _____ student.

2. Carl Sagan's novel *Contact* explores the _____ for humanity of contact with an advanced alien civilization.

3. The _____ offered for invading the country was that it posed a threat to peace in the region.

4. As a girl Sheila dreamed of being dressed in the golden _____ of a princess.

5. Every week the newspaper columnist _____ against what he calls the "unprecedented stupidity of our age."

6. Unable to obtain a _____, leaders of the majority party had no choice but to postpone the vote on the legislation.

7. The _____ was the life of the party, telling hilarious jokes long into the evening.

8. Saint Thomas Aquinas combined an acute, practical intellect and the most _____ spirituality.

9. The fourth-grade class project was to design a _____ incorporating pictures of animals.

10. The company said it would drop its lawsuit for defamation if the journalist agreed to publicly _____ his false statement about its products.

Sense or Nonsense

Indicate whether each sentence makes good sense or not.

Put S (SENSE) if it does, and put N (NONSENSE) if it does not.

1. The witch cast a raiment on the man, turning him into a tree. _____

2. Scientists had to destroy the rebus because they were afraid it would break out of the lab and infect the population of the city. _____

3. The speaker railed against profligate government spending. _____

4. The raconteur has a repertoire of over 300 jokes, all of which he can tell with perfect timing. _____

5. Some fans questioned the rationale for the coach's decision to attempt the risk of a two-point conversion after the touchdown rather than the nearly certain one-point conversion. _____

UNIT 64

recluse / rɪˈkluːs / *n.* a person who lives in seclusion and often in solitude 隐士

The monk spent three years of his life as a *recluse*, praying and meditating. 那位僧侣隐居了三年，整日祈祷和冥想。

【派】**reclusive** *adj.* 隐遁的，隐居的

John is a *reclusive* person who enjoys reading more than anything else. 约翰离群索居，最喜欢阅读。

recondite / ˈrekəndaɪt / *adj.* abstruse; profound 晦涩的；深奥的

Many classical and biblical references known to educated nineteenth-century readers are now considered *recondite* by most readers. 19世纪受过教育的读者所熟知的很多经典著作和圣经故事，对现在大多数读者来说都显得晦涩难懂。

redoubtable / rɪˈdaʊtəbl / *adj.* formidable; arousing fear; worthy of respect 可怕的；值得敬畏的

As a result of winning 95% of her cases, the prosecutor has earned a reputation as a *redoubtable* attorney. 经她辩护的案件有95%都获胜了，因此这位公诉人着实是一位令人敬畏的律师。

refractory / rɪˈfræktəri / *adj.* stubborn; unmanageable; resisting ordinary methods of treatment 执拗的；难治的

The general practitioner called in specialists to help determine the cause of the patient's *refractory* illness. 全科医生请来专科医生，帮助诊断病人得此顽疾的原因。

【派】**refract** *v.* to deflect sound or light 挡光；隔声

Intermittently the ionosphere *refracts* radio waves of certain frequencies, allowing transmissions between distant points on the Earth. 电离层能够间歇性地阻挡一定频率的无线电波，使地球上相距甚远的两点之间得以传播声音。

refulgent / rɪˈfʌldʒənt / *adj.* brightly shining; resplendent 辉煌的；灿烂的

On the queen's neck was a necklace of jewels, in the middle of which was a large, *refulgent* diamond. 女王戴了一条珠宝项链，中间有一颗璀璨夺目的大钻石。

refute / rɪˈfjuːt / *v.* to contradict; disprove 反驳；驳倒

The eighteenth-century English author Samuel Johnson claimed to have *refuted* the philosophy of idealism by kicking a large stone. 18 世纪的英国作家塞缪尔·约翰逊宣称自己通过踢大石头驳倒了唯心主义哲学。

【派】**refutation** *n.* 反驳；驳斥

Fundamentalism arose in Protestantism as a *refutation* of the liberal theology of the early twentieth century, which interpreted Christianity in terms of contemporary scientific theories. 20世纪早期，人们试图用现代科学理论来诠释基督教，而作为对这种自由主义神学的驳斥，基督新教中随之产生了原教旨主义。

● 常见学科术语 ●

idealism: the belief that everything that exists is fundamentally mental in nature
唯心主义：认为万物的本性皆为意识。

---

regale / rɪˈgeɪl / *v.* to entertain 使高兴

Former U.S. Presidents Lyndon Johnson, Ronald Reagan, and Bill Clinton often *regaled* visitors with amusing political anecdotes. 美国前总统林登·约翰逊、罗纳德·里根和比尔·克林顿经常讲些有趣的政坛轶事来博取嘉宾一笑。

relegate / ˈrelɪgeɪt / *v.* to consign to an inferior position 贬谪；放逐

Idealist philosophers are a common target of satire; however, instead of *relegating* them all to the garbage can, one should reflect that thinkers such as Plato and Kant have given humanity some of its most profound ideas. 唯心主义哲学家经常是人们的嘲讽对象，但我们不应将他们全部贬得一文不值，而应该认识到，像柏拉图和康德这样的哲学家确实对人性提出了不少极为深刻的见地。

● 常见学科术语 ●

idealist: refers to the followers of idealism
唯心主义者：唯心主义的拥护者

Immanuel Kant(1724–1804): the German philosopher who held that the mind shapes the world as it perceives it and that this world takes the form of space and time
伊曼纽尔·康德（1724–1804）：德国哲学家，主张意识在感知世界时塑造了世界，世界表现为时间和空间两种形式。

---

remonstrate / rɪˈmɑːnstreɪt / *v.* to object or protest 反对；抗议

Minority members of the committee *remonstrated* with the majority members, saying that the proposal was unjust; nevertheless, it was approved. 虽然少数委员反对多数委员的意见，声称该提议不公平，但它还是通过了。

renege / rɪˈneɪg / *v.* to go back on one's word 食言，背信；违约

Generally, if one party to an agreement *reneges* on its contractual obligations, it must provide appropriate compensation to the other party. 一般来说，如果协议一方未能履行合同规定的责任，该方则必须对另一方进行赔偿。

REVIEW 64

Matching

Match each word with its definition:

1.	recluse	a.	brightly shining
2.	recondite	b.	to entertain
3.	redoubtable	c.	abstruse; profound
4.	refractory	d.	to object or protest
5.	refulgent	e.	to contradict; disprove
6.	refute	f.	a person who lives in seclusion
7.	regale	g.	stubborn; unmanageable
8.	relegate	h.	to go back on one's word
9.	remonstrate	i.	arousing fear
10.	renege	j.	to consign to an inferior position

Fill-ins

Choose the best word to fill in the blank in each sentence.

recluse	recondite	redoubtable	refractory	refulgent
refute	regaled	relegated	remonstrated	reneged

1. The guest speaker _____ the audience with hilarious anecdotes from her childhood.
2. The school has announced plans to deal with the _____ students.
3. Students of religion have discerned a pattern in many religions in which some gods gradually attain prominence and others are _____ to an inferior status.
4. Tim _____ on his bet with Harry, claiming it had just been a joke.
5. Astronomers are studying the _____ object that suddenly appeared in the sky.
6. Edith's friends are concerned that she is becoming a _____; she does not go out with them anymore and rarely leaves her house.
7. The book *God and the New Physics* by the Australian physicist Paul Davies succeeds in making _____ areas of physics more comprehensible to the general public.
8. The prospect of being interviewed for admission by the _____ dean of the law school was a daunting one.
9. The conservative and liberal _____ with each other over the issue long into the night.
10. One way to _____ an argument is to show that one or more of the premises on which it is based is false.

Sense or Nonsense

Indicate whether each sentence makes good sense or not.
Put S (SENSE) if it does, and put N (NONSENSE) if it does not.

1. When learning a new subject, it is wise to start with straightforward, recondite topics first.

_____

2. The retired football coach regaled the young coaches with stories from his playing days with the Green Bay Packers in the 1950s. _____

3. In the English professional soccer league, a team can be relegated from the "premier" division to a lower division because of poor performance. _____

4. The debate coach reminded his team to refute every argument made by the opposing team. _____

5. The recluse has many friends at his house every night. _____

UNIT 65

reparation / ˌrepəˈreɪʃn / n. amends; compensation 赔偿；补偿

The judge said she would not sentence the man to jail on the condition that he pay full *reparation* to the family hurt by his crime. 法官表示，如果肇事者能够对被害家庭做出全部赔偿，她可以不判处他监禁。

repine / rɪˈpaɪn / v. to fret; complain 抱怨

The President told the congressional representative he should stop *repining* over the lost opportunity and join the majority in exploring new ones. 总统告诉那个国会代表不要为错失一次机会而不断抱怨，应该和大家一起寻找新的机会。

reprise / rɪˈpriːz / v. to repeat 重奏 n. repetition, especially of a piece of music 重奏

The standing ovation at the end of the set meant that the band had little choice but to *reprise* a few of their most popular tunes. 演出结束时，观众长时间起立鼓掌，因此乐队别无选择，只能重奏他们的一些经典曲目。

reproach / rɪˈprəʊtʃ / v. to find fault with; blame 指责 n. a mild rebuke or criticism 批评，指责

The speaker in Andrew Marvell's poem "To His Coy Mistress" *reproaches* his beloved for ignoring the passing of time and for not being willing to physically express her love for him. 安德鲁·马韦尔《致羞怯的情人》一诗的主人公指责他爱的人既无视时光的流逝，又不愿用行动表达对他的爱。

reprobate / ˈreprəbeɪt / n. a morally unprincipled person 堕落者；品行不端之人

The social worker refused to give up hope of reforming the criminal who was generally regarded as a *reprobate*. 尽管该罪犯被公认为道德败坏，可社会工作者坚持不放弃对他的改造。

repudiate / rɪˈpjuːdieɪt / v. to reject as having no authority 否认，驳斥

In the 1960s, many black leaders such as Malcolm X and Stokely Carmichael *repudiated* integration and nonviolence in favor of black separatism and passive resistance in the fight for civil rights. 20世纪60年代，许多黑人领袖如马尔科姆·X、斯托克利·卡迈克尔都反对黑人与白人融合和非暴力运动，而主张黑人分离主义和为争取民权进行消极抵制。

rescind / rɪˈsɪnd / v. to cancel 废除；取消

The salesperson said he would *rescind* his offer to sell the goods at a 10% discount unless he received full payment within 24 hours. 销售人员说如果他未在24小时内收到全额付款，就会取消货品打九折的优惠。

resolution / ˌrezəˈluːʃn / *n.* determination; resolve 决意；坚定

Fred's *resolution* to succeed is unshaken despite the many setbacks he has suffered. 尽管屡遭挫败，但弗雷德成功的决心未曾动摇。

resolve / rɪˈzɑːlv / *n.* determination; firmness of purpose 决心；坚定 *v.* to decide 决定；坚决

President Abraham Lincoln displayed remarkable *resolve* in preventing the Confederate States from seceding. 亚伯拉罕·林肯总统为防止南方联盟分离出去，表现出了非凡的决心。

reticent / ˈretɪsnt / *adj.* not speaking freely; reserved; reluctant 谨慎的；有所保留的；勉强的

Many people in the West are *reticent* to criticize science, which in the view of many has become a sacred cow. 多数西方人在批判科学时总是非常谨慎，科学在很多人眼中是神圣不可侵犯的。

● 常见学科术语 ●

sacred cow: something that is so greatly respected that it is beyond question, e.g. "The virtue of free trade is a sacred cow of modern economic theory."

神圣不可侵犯的人或物：因为广受推崇而不容置疑的事物，例如：自由贸易在现代经济理论中的地位神圣不可侵犯。

REVIEW 65

Matching

Match each word with its definition:

1. reparation		a.	to blame
2. repine		b.	to fret
3. reprise		c.	determination
4. reproach		d.	firmness of purpose
5. reprobate		e.	to reject as having no authority
6. repudiate		f.	a morally unprincipled person
7. rescind		g.	amends
8. resolution		h.	reserved
9. resolve		i.	repetition
10. reticent		j.	to cancel

Fill-ins

Choose the best word to fill in the blank in each sentence.

reparations	**repine**	**reprise**	**reproached**	**reprobate**
repudiated	**rescinded**	**resolution**	**resolved**	**reticent**

1. Janet _____ her friend for being lazy.
2. John _____ to study hard so he would get an "A" in chemistry.
3. The gangster _____ all his past associations with criminals in the city.
4. The company _____ its job offer when it was found that the candidate had provided falsified documents.
5. Every year Joanne makes a firm _____ to work harder.

6. The court ordered the convicted woman to make _____ to the family that she had done so much harm to.

7. The counselor was finally able to get the _____ boy to talk about the problems in his family.

8. The employee did not _____ at being assigned to do the arduous task, but rather, accepted it as a challenge.

9. The judge warned the convicted man that he was beginning to consider him a hopeless _____ who should be kept in prison away from innocent people.

10. The New Year's Eve revelers demanded a _____ of "Auld Lang Syne."

Sense or Nonsense

Indicate whether each sentence makes good sense or not.
Put S (SENSE) if it does, and put N (NONSENSE) if it does not.

1. The burden of war reparations plunged the country into a financial crisis. _____

2. The counselor is encouraging the reticent patient to talk about his feelings. _____

3. The teacher reproached the student for her sloppy work. _____

4. The gangster pledged to start a new life and repudiate his past involvement with criminals. _____

5. The couple's grandchildren decided to reprise them with a 30th anniversary party. _____

UNIT 66

reverent / ˈrevərənt / *adj.* expressing deep respect; worshipful 虔诚的；崇拜的

The biologist Loren Eiseley had what could be described as a *reverent* attitude toward nature. 生物学家罗伦·埃斯利对自然的态度可称得上是虔诚。

【派】revere *v.* 敬畏；尊敬

riposte / rɪˈpoʊst / *n.* a retaliatory action or retort 报复性行动或反驳

The commander decided that the enemy attack must be countered with a quick *riposte*. 指挥官决定对敌方的攻击要立即予以还击。

rococo / rəˈkoʊkoʊ / *adj.* excessively ornate; highly decorated 过分精巧繁杂的；过度修饰的
n. a style of architecture in eighteenth-century Europe 洛可可式

In music, the *Rococo* period （1730–1780）comes between the preceding Baroque period and the subsequent Classical period. The highly ornamented style of the *Rococo* period created new forms of dissonance that to listeners in previous eras would have sounded cacophonous. 在音乐方面，洛可可时期(1730–1780)上承巴洛克时期，下接古典时期。洛可可时期极度华丽的风格创造出一种新的不和协音，对之前各时期的听众来说，这种声音听起来简直刺耳不堪。// The noted authors Lawrence Durrell and Vladimir Nabokov often wrote in a rich, almost *rococo* style. 著名作家劳伦斯·达雷尔和弗拉迪米尔·纳博科夫的写作风格通常极为华丽，几乎称得上是洛可可风格。

Rococo: a style of architecture that made use of elaborate curved forms. Examples of the Rococo in architecture are the extremely ornate court and opera buildings of Mannheim and Stuttgart in Germany.

洛可可：一种大量使用精致曲线的建筑风格。位于德国的曼海姆和斯图加特的那些极其华丽堂皇的宫廷及剧院建筑，都属洛可可风格。

rubric / ˈruːbrɪk / n. ① title; heading 标题，题目 ② category 类别 ③ established mode of procedure or conduct; protocol 成规；习俗

The data from the experiment was so diverse that the scientist decided to design a new *rubric* to organize it. 实验得出的数据种类繁多，科学家决定建立一个新的标题类别来管理它们。

rue / ruː / v. to regret 后悔

The judge told the convicted man that he would come to *rue* his decision to commit the crime. 法官告诉被告，他终将为自己犯下的罪行感到后悔。

ruse / ruːz / n. trick; crafty stratagem; subterfuge 把戏，诡计；计策，谋略

In July, 1999, a group of Christians from the United Kingdom traveled to various countries in which Crusaders had massacred people to apologize; however, some people spurned this overture, believing it to be another Crusade in the form of a *ruse*. 1999年7月，一群英国基督教徒到当年十字军进行屠杀的国家旅行，并表达自己的歉意；但有人对此举不以为然，认为这不过是他们耍了个诡计，来发动又一次十字军东征罢了。

sage / seɪdʒ / adj. wise 贤明的 n. a wise older person 圣贤的老人

Samuel Johnson gave this *sage*, albeit hard, advice to writers wishing to improve their style: "Read over your compositions, and whenever you meet with a passage that you think is particularly fine, strike it out." 塞缪尔·约翰逊曾给希望提高写作水平的作者提过这样的建议，这是条难以做到却很明智的建议："通读你的文章，把你认为尤其出色的段落删掉。"

salacious / səˈleɪʃəs / adj. lascivious; lustful 好色的；贪欲的

The school board decided that the book is too *salacious* to be in the school library. 校董事会认为那本书过于淫秽，不适合放在学校图书馆。

salubrious / səˈluːbriəs / adj. healthful 有益健康的

The *salubrious* effects of exercise on both physical and mental health have been well documented. 文献充分证明，锻炼有益身心健康。

salutary / ˈsæljəteri / adj. expecting an improvement; favorable to health 有益的；有益健康的

The system of universal education is in our age the most prominent and *salutary* feature of the spirit of enlightenment...

—President Benjamin Harrison, 1892

当今时代，全民教育是文明开化最显著且最有益的特征……

——本杰明·哈里森总统，1892年

REVIEW 66

Matching
Match each word with its definition:

1. reverent
2. riposte
3. rococo
4. rubric
5. rue
6. ruse
7. sage
8. salacious
9. salubrious
10. salutary

a. crafty stratagem
b. lustful
c. a wise older person
d. excessively ornate
e. expecting an improvement
f. expressing deep respect
g. to regret
h. retaliatory action
i. favorable to health
j. title; heading

Fill-ins
Choose the best word to fill in the blank in each sentence.

revere	riposte	rococo	rubric	rue
ruse	sage	salacious	salubrious	salutary

1. In Chinese culture children are expected to _____ their parents.
2. The talk show host is always ready with a clever _____ to the barbs of her guests.
3. The defendant told the members of the jury that they would _____ the day they had convicted him.
4. As a _____, the President's press secretary opened the news conference with the statement that the government would guarantee everyone in America a minimum salary of $100,000 per year.
5. The ancient Greek philosopher Socrates was a _____ who believed that everyone must engage in his or her own search for truth.
6. The movie was given an "R" rating because of its _____ content.
7. Many people from the Midwest retire to Arizona because of the _____ climate.
8. Advocates of Prohibition believed that it would have a _____ effect on people who enjoyed drinking alcoholic beverages.
9. The author decided to discuss forced sterilization under the _____ of eugenics.
10. The _____ furniture seems out of place in the ultramodern building.

Sense or Nonsense
Indicate whether each sentence makes good sense or not.
Put S (SENSE) if it does, and put N (NONSENSE) if it does not.

1. The debater prepared clever ripostes for the arguments she expected her opponent to make.
   _____

2. Some readers find the writer's straightforward, rococo style boring. _____
3. Confucius was a Chinese sage revered for his wisdom. _____
4. The fraternity brother who came up with the best ruse was told he would get a date with the homecoming queen. _____
5. To have your article published in the chemistry journal, you must carefully follow the rubric provided by its editor. _____

UNIT 67

sanction / ˈsæŋkʃn / *v.* ① to approve; ratify; permit 认可；批准；许可 ② to penalize 处罚；制裁 *n.* ① approval; ratification; permission 认可；批准；许可 ② penalization 处罚；制裁

The establishment of the state of Israel from Palestinian territory in 1948 was the realization of a hallowed dream for Zionists, but for many Palestinians it meant the *sanctioning* of continued domination of their land by Europeans. 对很多犹太复国主义者来说，1948年以色列从巴勒斯坦脱离并建立一个国家，意味着一个神圣梦想的实现。但对于多数巴勒斯坦人来说，这就意味着允许欧洲人继续占据他们的土地。// In the West, the institution of marriage is traditionally given formal *sanction* by both the Church and the State, which has the social function of reinforcing its importance and the seriousness of the duties it entails. 根据传统，西方的婚姻需得到教会和国家正式认可，这就起到了强调其重要性和它所承载的责任的严肃性的社会功效。// The United Nations has the power to compel obedience to international law by *sanctions* or even war, but there must be unanimity for such action among the five permanent members of the Security Council. 联合国有权通过制裁甚至战争迫使会员国服从国际法，但这种行为必须得到联合国安理会五个常任理事国的一致通过。

sardonic / sɑːrˈdɑːnɪk / *adj.* cynical; scornfully mocking 讽刺的；嘲笑的

Satire that is too *sardonic* often loses its effectiveness. 讽刺文若过于讥讽，通常会失去效果。

sartorial / sɑːrˈtɔːriəl / *adj.* pertaining to tailors 裁缝的，缝纫的

Off-screen, the glamorous actress' *sartorial* style runs more to jeans and T-shirts than to elaborate gowns. 在荧屏外，这位富有魅力的女演员的着装风格更偏向于牛仔裤和T恤衫，而不是精致的礼服。

satiate / ˈseɪʃieɪt / *v.* to satisfy 满足

The bully *satiated* his fury by pummeling the helpless little boy. 那个小霸王对那个无助的小男孩一顿暴揍，以此来宣泄他的愤怒。

saturate / ˈsætʃəreɪt / *v.* to soak thoroughly; imbue throughout 使浸透；使饱和

The writer's recollection of her childhood is *saturated* with sunshine and laughter. 那位作家回忆中的童年充满了充满阳光和欢声笑语。

saturnine / ˈsætərnaɪn / *adj.* gloomy 阴郁的

When the long list of casualties from the battle were announced, the mood in the room was *saturnine*. 当长长的阵亡人员名单被宣布时，整个房间的氛围都变得阴郁。

satyr / ˈseɪtər / *n.* ① a creature that is half-man, half-beast with the horns and legs of a goat 半人半兽的森林之神 ② lecher 好色之徒

One of the best-known *satyrs* is Pan, the god of the woods in Greek mythology. 半兽人中最有名的一个是潘，希腊神话中的森林之神。

savor / ˈseɪvər / *v.* ① to enjoy 享受；品位 ② to have a distinctive flavor or smell 有···的滋味

The coach gave his team a day off practice to *savor* their big victory. 教练给全队放了一天假，让大家尽情品尝完胜的滋味。

schematic / skiːˈmætɪk / *adj.* relating to or in the form of an outline or diagram 概要的；图解的

The engineer outlined the workings of the factory in *schematic* form. 工程师用示意图描画了工厂的运行方式。

secrete / sɪˈkriːt / *v.* to produce and release substance into organism 分泌

The pancreas gland *secretes* a fluid that helps fat, carbohydrates, and protein to be digested in the small intestine. 胰腺分泌出一种液体，帮助消化小肠中的脂肪、碳水化合物和蛋白质。

REVIEW 67

Matching

Match each word with its definition:

1. sanction		a.	pertaining to tailors
2. sardonic		b.	a creature that is half-man, half-beast
3. sartorial		c.	relating to a diagram
4. satiate		d.	to approve; ratify
5. saturate		e.	to produce and release substance into organism
6. saturnine		f.	to satisfy
7. satyr		g.	cynical
8. savor		h.	gloomy
9. schematic		i.	to enjoy
10. secrete		j.	to soak thoroughly

Fill-ins

Choose the best word to fill in the blank in each sentence.

sanctions	sardonic	sartorial	satiate	saturated
saturnine	satyr	savored	schematic	secrete

1. Celebrating the end of her diet, Tina _____ every mouthful of the ice cream sundae.

2. A fried chicken dinner should be enough to _____ the hungry student's appetite.

3. June is one of those people whose mood can suddenly become _____ and then just as quickly become sunny and cheerful.

4. The company decided to try to sell another product because the market for personal computers had become _____.

5. Economic _____ against the country have made life difficult for its people; even everyday necessities are becoming scarce.

6. The book claims to give advice that solves men's _____ problems easily and cheaply.

7. Hugh has a reputation as a bit of a _____ among the women in the office.

8. The electrical engineer made a _____ diagram of the circuit.

9. Cells in the mucous membrane of the stomach _____ hydrochloric acid to help in the digestion of food.

10. The satirist's unremittingly _____ tone left the reviewer feeling that here was a man of great talent who had, sadly, retreated to a bitterly cynical, even misanthropic attitude toward the world.

Sense or Nonsense

Indicate whether each sentence makes good sense or not.
Put S（SENSE）if it does, and put N（NONSENSE）if it does not.

1. The novel is a satyr on human nature. _____

2. We satiated our appetite for science fiction novels by reading 20 of them on summer vacation. _____

3. Not everyone appreciates the comedian's sardonic commentary on modern life. _____

4. Twelve hours of heavy rain left the field saturated. _____

5. I suggest you savor the food, not just gobble it down. _____

UNIT 68

sedition / sɪˈdɪʃn / *n.* behavior-prompting rebellion 煽动；暴动

The federal prosecutor argued that the journalist's article could be interpreted as an act of *sedition* since it strongly suggested that the government should be overturned. 联邦检察官认为，那个记者的文章可看作是一种煽动行为，因为其强烈建议推翻政府。

sedulous / ˈsedʒələs / *adj.* diligent 勤勉的

The Nobel Prize-winning scientist attributed his success to what he termed "curiosity, a modicum of intelligence, and *sedulous* application." 那位获得诺贝尔奖的科学家把自己的成功归于他提出的"好奇心强，稍有头脑，孜孜不倦，学以致用"。

seismic / ˈsaɪzmɪk / *adj.* relating to earthquakes; earthshaking 地震的；震撼全球的

The study of *seismic* waves enables scientists to learn about the Earth's structure. 对地震波的研究使科学家们了解到了地球的内部构造。

sensual / ˈsenʃuəl / *adj.* ① relating to the senses 感觉的；感官的 ② gratifying the physical senses, especially sexual appetites 肉欲的

The yogi teaches his students that attachment to *sensual* pleasure is one of the great hindrances to spiritual advancement. 瑜伽师告诉他的学生，耽于感官享受是妨碍实现精神飞跃的桎梏之一。

sensuous / ˈsenʃuəs / *adj.* relating to the senses; operating through the senses 感觉上的；依感官的

The American painter Georgia O'Keeffe is known especially for her *sensuous* paintings of plants and flowers and for her landscapes. 美国画家乔治娅·欧姬芙尤以其极具美感的植物花草画和风景画闻名于世。

sentient / ˈsentiənt / *adj.* aware; conscious; able to perceive 有感觉的；意识到的；察觉到的

Charles Darwin regarded many animals as being *sentient* and as having intelligence. 查尔斯·达尔文认为很多动物既有知觉又有智力。

【派】**sentience** *n.* 知觉

An analgesic relieves pain but unlike an anesthetic, does not cause loss of sensation or *sentience*. 与麻醉剂不同，止痛剂能减轻疼痛，但不会使人失去感觉或知觉。

servile / ˈsɜːrvaɪl / *adj.* submissive; obedient 服从的；顺从的

None of the dictator's *servile* citizens dared question his decree. 受独裁者奴役的顺民都敢质疑独裁者的政令。

sextant / ˈsekstənt / *n.* a navigational tool that determines latitude and longitude 六分仪（用于测量经纬度的航海仪器）

Because it enabled precise determination of position, the *sextant* quickly became an essential tool in navigation after its invention in 1731. 由于能精确定位，六分仪在1731年问世之后迅速成为航海必备工具。

shard / ʃɑːrd / *n.* a piece of broken glass or pottery 玻璃碎片；陶器碎片

Archeologists were able to reconstruct the drinking vessel from *shards* found around the ancient campsite. 考古学家能够根据古遗址附近发现的碎片重塑当时的酒器。

sidereal / saɪˈdɪriəl / *adj.* relating to the stars 恒星的；根据恒星测定的

A *sidereal* year is longer than a solar year by 20 minutes and 23 seconds. 一个恒星年比一个太阳年长20分23秒。

REVIEW 68

Matching

Match each word with its definition:

1. sedition	a.	operating through the senses
2. sedulous	b.	a navigational tool
3. seismic	c.	behavior-prompting rebellion
4. sensual	d.	a piece of broken glass or pottery
5. sensuous	e.	gratifying the physical senses
6. sentient	f.	aware
7. servile	g.	diligent
8. sextant	h.	relating to the stars
9. shard	i.	submissive
10. sidereal	j.	relating to earthquakes

Fill-ins

Choose the best word to fill in the blank in each sentence.

sedition	sedulous	seismic	sensual	sensuous
sentient	servile	sextant	shards	sidereal

1. Most of the population of the occupied country behaved in a _____ manner toward the foreign soldiers.
2. _____ is treated so seriously because it is a threat to the very existence of the state.
3. The detective was _____ in collecting evidence to prove his client's innocence.
4. According to geologists, in its early history the Earth was continually shaken by massive _____ disturbances.
5. _____ found at the site suggest that there was human habitation in the area 5,000 years ago.
6. Because it is not dependent on electricity for power, the _____ is still used as a backup navigational tool on many ships.
7. The science fiction novel describes a _____ adventure.
8. The book explores the question of how _____ beings that evolved differently from humans would regard the world.
9. The book describes a society almost entirely dedicated to _____ delight.
10. The philosopher Plato believed that a process of reason, independent of _____ information, could help a man arrive at the true nature of reality.

Sense or Nonsense

Indicate whether each sentence makes good sense or not.
Put S (SENSE) if it does, and put N (NONSENSE) if it does not.

1. The French Revolution was a momentous event that sent seismic shocks through Western civilization. _____
2. Sidereal surveillance of the suspect provided police with enough evidence to make an arrest. _____
3. One of the goals of artificial intelligence is to produce a machine that an unbiased observer judges to be sentient. _____
4. The police captain warned the protesters that they were in danger of crossing the line between lawful public protest and sedition. _____
5. The invention of the magnetic compass and the sextant were two of the major developments in

UNIT 69

simian / ˈsɪmiən / *adj.* apelike; relating to apes 类人猿的；像猿的

Many people in the nineteenth century denied the evolutionary significance of the *simian* characteristics of human beings. 在19世纪，很多人否认人类身上与猿相近的特征所含有的进化论意义。

simile / ˈsɪməli / *n.* comparison of one thing with another using "like" or "as" 明喻

In his autobiographical book *Chronicles*, Volume 1, Bob Dylan uses two *similes* in succession to try to convey the experience of writing a song: "A song is like a dream, and you try to make it come true. They're like strange countries you have to enter." 鲍勃·迪伦在其自传《像一块滚石》第一卷中连续用了两个明喻来描述写歌的经历："歌犹如梦想，你努力去实现它。它们好比你必须进入的陌生国度。"

sinecure / ˈsɪnɪkjʊr / *n.* a well-paying job or office that requires little or no work 闲职；挂名差事

The company established the high-paying position of senior advisor as a *sinecure* for the man who had been instrumental in the company's success for so many years. 该公司专门为多年来帮助公司走向成功的功臣设置了高级顾问这种高薪挂名职位。

singular / ˈsɪŋɡjələr / *adj.* unique; extraordinary; odd 唯一的，非凡的；奇怪的；单数的

The defendant's *singular* appearance made it easy for the witness to identify him as the person at the scene of the crime. 被告的相貌很特别，目击证人很容易就认出在犯罪现场的就是他。

sinuous / ˈsɪnjuəs / *adj.* winding; intricate; complex 弯曲的，蜿蜒的；错综复杂的

The students had trouble following the philosopher's *sinuous* line of reasoning. 学生们难以跟上哲学家那错综复杂的推理过程。

skeptic / ˈskeptɪk / *n.* one who doubts 怀疑论者

Like the nihilist, a comprehensive philosophic *skeptic* can be a difficult person to debate: if you tell him you know you exist, he is likely to ask you to prove it—and that can be harder than it first appears. 像虚无主义者一样，领悟力强且富有哲思的怀疑论者也很难被驳倒：如果你告诉他说你确信自己的存在，他很可能就会让你证明自己的存在——这可比乍看上去难多了。

【派】**skeptical** *adj.* 怀疑的

A good scientist is *skeptical* about inferences made from data; however, he must not be dogmatic about the possible implications the data might have. 优秀的科学家总会对由数据得出的推论持怀疑态度；但他判断数据可能蕴含的意义时也不能太教条主义。

───── ● 常见学科术语 ● ─────

nihilist: one who believes that existence and all traditional values are meaningless
虚无主义者：他们认为存在甚至所有传统价值观都毫无意义。

sobriety / səˈbraɪəti / *n.* seriousness 冷静；严肃

The student approaches her studies with commendable *sobriety*. 这个女生以令人称道的严肃态度推进研究。

sodden / ˈsɑːdn / *adj.* thoroughly soaked; saturated 浸透的；渗透的

The *sodden* field makes it difficult for the soccer players to move effectively. 湿漉漉的场地使得足球运动员难以快速跑动。

solicitous / səˈlɪsɪtəs / *adj.* concerned; attentive; eager 挂念的；热心的；热切的

The nurse is extremely *solicitous* of the health of every patient in the ward. 护士非常关切病房里每个病人的健康状况。

soliloquy / səˈlɪləkwi / *n.* literary or dramatic speech by one character, not addressed to others 独白

The nineteenth-century English poet Robert Browning used the dramatic monologue—which is essentially a *soliloquy* in a poem—successfully in many of his poems. 19世纪的英国诗人罗伯特·布朗宁成功地在其很多诗歌作品中运用了戏剧独白——从根本上说是诗歌中的独白。

REVIEW 69

Matching

Match each word with its definition:

1. simian
2. simile
3. sinecure

4. singular
5. sinuous
6. skeptic
7. sobriety
8. sodden
9. solicitous
10. soliloquy

a. a well-paying job requiring little work
b. seriousness
c. comparison of one thing with another using "like" or "as"
d. thoroughly soaked
e. unique
f. one who doubts
g. dramatic speech by one character
h. concerned
i. apelike
j. winding

Fill-ins

Choose the best word to fill in the blank in each sentence.

simian	similes	sinecure	singular	sinuous
skeptic	sobriety	sodden	solicitous	soliloquy

1. The judge recommended her law clerk for the position in the law firm as "a young person of probity and _____."

2. "Money is a _____ thing. It ranks with love as man's greatest source of joy. And with death as his greatest source of sorrow.

—John Kenneth Galbraith

3. Mary complains that when they were young her husband was very _____ of her, but now he practically ignores her.

4. The _____ argued that the purported exhibition of occult powers was created by the use of conjurer's tricks.

5. We often use _____ in expressions like "as old as the hills" and "as sharp as a tack" without being consciously aware that they are similes.

6. The governor awarded his advisor with a _____ as a reward for 20 years of service to the party and the state.

7. The _____ road curves along the mountainside.

8. In Act III of *Hamlet*, Shakespeare has Hamlet speak a _____ on the question of "To be, or not to be."

9. Looking at the _____ field, the football coach realized he would have to adapt his game plan to wet conditions.

10. Before Charles Darwin proved the close biological relation between human beings and apes, many people saw human _____ characteristics as comical and inconsequential.

Sense or Nonsense

Indicate whether each sentence makes good sense or not.
Put S (SENSE) if it does, and put N (NONSENSE) if it does not.

1. The philosopher Bertrand Russell was skeptical of Idealist philosophies, believing they are based on false assumptions about knowledge. _____

2. The philosophy student compared following the treatise's long, subtle argument to following the path of a sinuous river for thousands of miles. _____

3. The poem's central simile is that the nation's leader is like a captain of a ship. _____

4. Italian mothers are famous for being so solicitous of their sons that they spend most of the day cooking for them. _____

5. The farmers are hoping for rain after the long period of hot and sodden weather. _____

UNIT 70

solvent / ˈsɑːlvənt / *adj.* able to meet financial obligations 有偿付能力的
During the financial crisis several large banks had difficulty remaining *solvent*. 金融危机中，数家大银行都难以维持偿付能力。

somatic / soʊˈmætɪk / *adj.* relating to or affecting the body; corporeal 躯体的；肉体的；身体的
A psychosomatic disorder is a malady caused by a mental disturbance that adversely affects *somatic* functioning. 身心失调是由对人体机能产生不利影响的心理障碍而引起的疾病。

soporific / ˌsɑːpəˈrɪfɪk / *adj.* sleep producing 催眠的 *n.* hypnotic 催眠药
For some people the best *soporific* is reading a boring book. 对某些人来说，阅读一本无聊的书就是最好的催眠方法。

sordid / ˈsɔːrdɪd / *adj.* filthy; contemptible and corrupt 肮脏的；卑鄙的；腐败的

The Monica Lewinsky scandal, which led to President Bill Clinton's impeachment in 1998, must certainly rank as one of the most *sordid* affairs in American history. 导致前总统比尔·克林顿在1998年遭到弹劾的莫妮卡·莱温斯基丑闻，堪称美国历史上最龌龊的风流韵事之一。

specious / ˈspiːʃəs / *adj.* seeming to be logical and sound, but not really so 似是而非的

The article systematically rebuts the *specious* argument advanced by the so-called expert in the field. 这篇文章系统地反驳了所谓业界专家貌似有理的论点。

spectrum / ˈspektrəm / *n.* ① band of colors produced when sunlight passes through a prism 【物】光谱 ② a broad range of related ideas or objects 范围；系列

The political science course deals with the whole *spectrum* of political ideologies. 政治科学研究涉及所有种类的政治意识形态。

spendthrift / ˈspendθrɪft / *n.* a person who spends money recklessly 挥霍无度的人 *adj.* wasteful and extravagant 挥霍无度的，奢侈的

A Chinese proverb describes a paradox: Rich *spendthrifts* never save enough, but the poor always manage to save something. 中国有句谚语道出了一个悖论：克勤克俭粮满仓，大手大脚仓底光。（字面意思也可翻译成：挥霍无度，富人没钱花；勤俭节约，穷人有钱攒。）// Tom's *spendthrift* habits resulted in his accumulating a huge amount of credit card debt. 汤姆大手大脚的花钱习惯使得他信用卡负债累累。

sporadic / spəˈrædɪk / *adj.* irregular 零星的；不定时的

Despite the ceasefire, there have been *sporadic* outbreaks of violence between the warring factions. 尽管已经停战了，但对战双方之间还是零星地发生了几起暴力事件。

squalor / ˈskwɑːlər / *n.* filthy, wretched condition 肮脏；卑劣

The family lives in *squalor* in the slums of Mexico City. 这家人住在墨西哥城肮脏的贫民窟里。

staccato / stəˈkɑːtoʊ / *adj.* marked by abrupt, clear-cut sounds 断奏的，断音的；不连贯的

We listened to the *staccato* steps of the woman in high heels running down the street. 我们听到那个女人跑过街道时她的高跟鞋发出的断断续续的声音。

REVIEW 70

Matching

Match each word with its definition:

1. solvent		a.	filthy; corrupt
2. somatic		b.	a broad range of
3. soporific		c.	irregular
4. sordid		d.	able to meet financial obligations
5. specious		e.	a person who spends recklessly
6. spectrum		f.	seeming to be logical and sound, but not really so
7. spendthrift		g.	filthy, wretched condition
8. sporadic		h.	affecting the body
9. squalor		i.	marked by abrupt, clear-cut sounds
10. staccato		j.	sleep producing

Fill-ins

Choose the best word to fill in the blank in each sentence.

solvent	somatic	soporific	sordid	specious
spectrum	spendthrift	sporadic	squalor	staccato

1. Newspapers sometimes publish stories with _____ claims to increase sales.
2. A _____ most of his life, Alex has only recently begun to save for his retirement.
3. Many towns have an area where people live in _____.
4. The salesperson has a sort of machine-gun way of speaking, fast and _____.
5. The various portions of the electromagnetic _____ are allocated to broadcasters, commercial operators, amateur hobbyists, and other users.
6. _____ outbreaks of violence marred the ceasefire.
7. Economists are concerned that some of the poorest countries will have difficulty remaining _____ as interest rates rise and the amount of their debt repayments increase.
8. The long car ride was a _____ for the family's small children; soon they were fast asleep in the back of the car.
9. In recent years, medicine has placed greater emphasis on how psychological factors contribute to _____ disorders such as heart disease and cancer.
10. The governor issued a complete and public apology to put the _____ affair behind him.

Sense or Nonsense

Indicate whether each sentence makes good sense or not.
Put S (SENSE) if it does, and put N (NONSENSE) if it does not.

1. The novels of Mickey Spillane portray the sordid world of criminals. _____
2. In the logic class, students were asked to identify specious lines of reasoning in several arguments. _____
3. If you absolutely have to stay awake you should take a soporific. _____
4. The bank's president warned its directors that it could not remain solvent if it kept making bad loans. _____
5. What the tourist brochure described as "local color" was called "squalor" by a plain-speaking member of the tour group. _____

UNIT 71

stanch / stæntʃ / *v.* to stop or check the flow of 使不漏；使不流失；制止

The country's government has put controls on currency movement to *stanch* the flow of money out of the country. 该国政府对现金去向进行调控，防止本国资金外流。

stentorian / sten'tɔːriən / *adj.* extremely loud 洪亮的

The *stentorian* speaker prefers not to use a microphone so that the audience can appreciate what he calls "the full effect of my powerful oratory." 声音洪亮的演讲者不想用话筒，他说这样听众能更好地欣赏"我激昂演讲的完美声效"。

stigma / 'stɪgmə / *n.* mark of disgrace or inferiority 污点；耻辱的印记

A problem with giving formal psychological treatment to a child who is believed to be poorly adjusted to society is that he may acquire a *stigma* as a result of officially being labeled as deviant, and he may act to corroborate society's expectation. 对那些不太适应社会的孩子进行正式的心理治疗可能会使他们因为被正式烙上"不正常的人"的印记，而做出一些事情去证实社会对他们的消极评价。

【派】**stigmatize** *v.* 污蔑，玷污；给…打上烙印

The civil rights movement helped to *stigmatize* racism, augmenting legal efforts to desegregate American society. 民权运动给种族主义打上了耻辱的烙印，增强了为废除种族隔离而进行的立法努力。

stint / stɪnt / *v.* to be sparing 节俭，节省 *n.* a period of time spent doing something 定额工作

Stinting on funding for education strikes many people as shortsighted. 对很多人来说，限制教育投资是缺乏远见的。 // Isaac Asimov did a short involuntary *stint* in the army as a conscript during the 1950s. 20世纪50年代，艾萨克·阿西莫夫作为义务兵被征召入伍，极不情愿地服役了一段时间。

stipulate / 'stɪpjuleɪt / *v.* to specify as an essential condition 规定；保证

The President's lawyer *stipulated* that he would appear before the investigative committee, but would answer only questions directly relevant to the issue at hand. 总统的律师保证他会在调查委员会前现身，但是只回答与当前案件有直接关系的问题。

【派】**stipulation** *n.* 规定；条款

Stipulations in a contract should be clear in order to obviate the need for parties to resort to litigation. 合同上的条款须清楚明确，以免双方发生冲突时诉诸法律。

stolid / 'stɑːlɪd / *adj.* having or showing little emotion 冷淡的，冷漠的

Behind the professor's *stolid* appearance is a fun-loving, gregarious character. 教授虽然外表冷漠，但其实是个喜开玩笑、爱交朋友的人。

stratified / 'strætɪfaɪd / *adj.* arranged in layers 分层次的

One of the implications of an increasingly *stratified* economy for America might be increased social unrest. 美国日渐分化的经济预示着社会将日益动荡不安。

【派1】**stratum** *n.* a layer 一层（*pl.* strata）

In the English-speaking world many members of the upper classes historically have had a deprecatory attitude toward slang, a form of language they regard as indecorous and thus suitable only for the lowest *stratum* of society. 长期以来，英语国家的许多上层人士一直反对说俚语，在他们看来俚语难登大雅之堂，

只适合社会最底层的人使用。// As it matured as a science, geology began to complement biology, a process that helped it to gain a more comprehensive view of the history of life on Earth by allowing fossils to be dated and identified (paleontology), often using knowledge gained from stratigraphy—the study of the deposition, distribution, and age of rock *strata*. 作为一门逐渐成熟的科学，地质学使生物学日趋完善。在这一过程中，地质学家通常运用地层学(一门研究沉积物、地层分布以及岩层年代的科学)知识来确定化石的年代和身份(古生物学研究的范畴)，从而使生物学家对地球上生命的起源有了更全面的认识。

【派2】**stratification** *n.* 分层

striated / ˈstraɪeɪtɪd / *adj.* marked with thin, narrow grooves or channels 凸凹不平的；有条纹的

The *striated* surface suggested to the geologist that he was walking over an area in which there once had been a torrent of water. 从千沟万壑的地表来看，这位地质学家脚下的这个地区曾有湍急的水流。

【派】**striation** *n.* 纹理；条纹

The geologist examined *striations* in the rock to learn about the glacier that had made them 10,000 years ago. 为了研究一万年前造就这些岩石的冰川，地质学家仔细观察了岩石表面的纹理。

stricture / ˈstrɪktʃər / *n.* ① something that restrains 限制，约束 ② negative criticism 指摘；非难

As professionals, lawyers are expected to abide by a set of ethical *strictures* in their practice of the law. 作为专业人员，律师在法律实践中应该受到道德准则的约束。

strident / ˈstraɪdnt / *adj.* loud; harsh; unpleasantly noisy 大声的；刺耳的

Calls for the prime minister's resignation became more *strident* after it was discovered that he had strong connections to organized crime. 首相与有组织的犯罪活动密切相关的丑闻被揭露后，群众要求其辞职的呼声更高了。

REVIEW 71

Matching

Match each word with its definition:

1. stanch	a. to be sparing
2. stentorian	b. arranged in layers
3. stigma	c. something that restrains
4. stint	d. to specify as an essential condition
5. stipulate	e. unpleasantly noisy
6. stolid	f. showing little emotion
7. stratified	g. marked with thin, narrow grooves
8. striated	h. extremely loud
9. stricture	i. to stop or check the flow of
10. strident	j. mark of disgrace

Fill-ins

Choose the best word to fill in the blank in each sentence.

stanch	stentorian	stigma	stint	stipulate
stolid	stratified	striated	strictures	strident

1. The baseball stadium's ground rules _____ that a batter who hits a ball that bounces off the ground into the left field bleachers gets a double.
2. Luke was one of those _____ individuals who rarely show their feelings.
3. The geologists examined _____ rocks left by the retreating glaciers.
4. Modern societies tend to be _____ into classes determined by such factors as wealth and occupation.
5. They sat silently in the room, listening to the telephone's _____ ringing.
6. The medic used a tourniquet to _____ the woman's bleeding wound.
7. The speaker's _____ voice rang through the hall.
8. A two-year _____ in the navy allowed Janet to visit 22 countries.
9. Perhaps the central paradox of poetry is that the _____ imposed by form on a poet of talent can help produce works of great power.
10. In most societies there is a _____ attached to mental illness.

Sense or Nonsense

Indicate whether each sentence makes good sense or not.

Put S (SENSE) if it does, and put N (NONSENSE) if it does not.

1. The young doctor learned a lot about both medicine and human nature during her stint in the emergency room. _____
2. The contract stipulates that the agreement will remain in force unless both sides agree to cancel it. _____
3. The banker deliberately cultivated his image as a careful, stolid, conservative person. _____
4. The Greeks and Persians fought a stentorian battle at Thermopylae in 480 B.C. _____
5. Anthropologists believe that the society is stratified by occupation, with warriors at the top and workers at the bottom. _____

UNIT 72

strut / strʌt / *v.* to swagger; display to impress others 昂首阔步；炫耀
> The star quarterback *strutted* around campus the entire week after he led his team to a 42∶0 win over the county's top-ranked team. 在率领队伍以42∶0大胜县里排名第一的球队后，那位橄榄球四分卫明星在学校整整一周都神气十足。

stultify / ˈstʌltɪfaɪ / *v.* to impair or reduce to uselessness 损害；使无价值
> The professor of education believes that overreliance on rote learning *stultifies* students' creativity. 这位教育学教授认为，过分依赖死记硬背的学习方法会损害学生的创新能力。

stupefy / ˈstuːpɪfaɪ / *v.* to dull the senses of; stun; astonish 使感觉迟钝；使昏迷；使震惊
> After drinking three glasses of wine, Linda was *stupefied*. 三杯葡萄酒下肚后，琳达感到昏昏沉沉的。

stygian / ˈstɪdʒiən / *adj.* dark and gloomy; hellish 黑暗的；阴暗的；阴森的

Wilfred Owens's famous poem "Dulce Et Decorum Est" describes an unfortunate soldier who was unable to get his gas mask on in time, seen through the *stygian* gloom of poison gas:

GAS! Gas! Quick, boys! —An ecstasy of fumbling,

Fitting the clumsy helmets just in time;

But someone still was yelling out and stumbling

And floundering like a man in fire or lime. —

Dim, through the misty panes and thick green light

As under a green sea, I saw him drowning.

在威尔弗雷德·欧文的名诗《为国捐躯》中，作者描写了一个没能及时戴上防毒面具而被阴森恐怖的毒气所淹没的士兵的悲惨命运：

毒气！毒气！快，孩子们！

一阵疯狂的摸索之后，

笨重的"头盔"及时戴好。

但仍有人在呼救，摇摇摆摆，拼命挣扎，

就好像有一个人被抛进了熊熊燃烧的大火，

或沸腾的石灰浆。

屋外灰蒙蒙一片，

透过模糊的镜片，和浓艳的绿光

我看到他淹没在绿色的海洋里。

subpoena / səˈpiːnə / *n.* notice ordering someone to appear in court 传票 *v.* to summon with a writ（作传票）传唤

The judge issued a *subpoena* for the man but the prosecutor had little hope that he would appear because he was living abroad. 法官给那人发了传票要求他出庭，但公诉人觉得他出庭的希望很渺茫，因为他住在国外。

subside / səbˈsaɪd / *v.* to settle down; grow quiet 平息；减弱；沉没

Army personnel told the civilians to wait for the violence to *subside* before reentering the town. 军方人员劝诫人们等暴力事件平息后再重返家园。

substantiate / səbˈstænʃieɪt / *v.* to support with proof or evidence 证实；证明

The validity of fossil identification is *substantiated* by data from geology and carbon-14 dating. 科学家根据地质学及碳14断代法得出的数据证实了化石鉴定的准确性。

substantive / ˈsʌbstəntɪv / *adj.* essential; pertaining to the substance 本质的；实质性的

The judge cautioned the attorney to present only information that was *substantive* to the case at hand. 法官提醒律师只能陈述与在审案件密切相关的信息。

subsume / səbˈsuːm / *v.* to include; incorporate 包含，包括

The philosopher described his work as an attempt to arrive at a final generalization that will *subsume* all previous generalizations about the nature of logic. 那位哲学家表示他的作品将尝试进行最终的总结，将前人对逻辑本质的所有概括都包含在内。

subversive / səbˈvɜːrsɪv / *adj.* intended to undermine or overthrow, especially an established government 颠覆性的；破坏性的 *n.* a person intending to undermine something 颠覆分子

【派】subvert *v.* 摧毁，推翻

Anything that *subverts* the market mechanism is believed to cause anomalies in prices, making the economy less efficient. 任何颠覆市场机制的行为都会导致物价出现异常，并降低经济体系的效率。

REVIEW 72

Matching

Match each word with its definition:

1.	strut	a.	dark and gloomy
2.	stultify	b.	to support with proof
3.	stupefy	c.	to dull the senses of
4.	stygian	d.	intended to undermine or overthrow
5.	subpoena	e.	to display to impress others
6.	subside	f.	to settle down
7.	substantiate	g.	notice ordering someone to appear in court
8.	substantive	h.	to include; incorporate
9.	subsume	i.	to impair or reduce to uselessness
10.	subversive	j.	essential

Fill-ins

Choose the best word to fill in the blank in each sentence.

strutted	stultifying	stupefied	stygian	subpoenaed
subside	substantiate	substantive	subsumes	subversive

1. Several people at the party were _____ from overdrinking.
2. The experiment provided such _____ evidence for the new theory that most scientists now accept it.
3. The drill team _____ into the stadium to perform the half-time show.
4. The scientist was able to formulate a general principle that _____ five more specific principles.
5. Businesses complained that government regulations are _____ free competition and innovation.
6. The critic called Emily Bronte's novel *Wuthering Heights* _____ because it attacks capitalist beliefs.
7. The news that the country was being invaded plunged it into a _____ gloom.
8. The prosecution _____ three witnesses it considered vital to its case.
9. The engineers waited for the floodwaters to _____ before assessing the damage.
10. Advocates of the theory that Atlantis existed more than 6,000 years ago sometimes use evidence of dubious authenticity to _____ their claims.

Sense or Nonsense

Indicate whether each sentence makes good sense or not.
Put S (SENSE) if it does, and put N (NONSENSE) if it does not.

1. Prosecutors obtained a subpoena to require the witness to testify. _____

2. The old miser is so stygian he refuses to buy his grandchildren birthday presents. _____

3. After the excitement of the election subsided, the new administration settled down to the serious business of governance. _____

4. The theory was substantiated by new evidence, so scientists were forced to abandon it. _____

5. The Army-McCarthy hearings of the 1950s investigated many citizens alleged to be engaged in subversive activities. _____

UNIT 73

succor / ˈsʌkər / *n.* relief; help in time of distress or want 救援；援助者

The woman was accused of providing *succor* to the enemy in the form of food and medical help. 那位妇女因向敌人提供食品和医疗援助而遭到起诉。

suffrage / ˈsʌfrɪdʒ / *n.* the right to vote 选举权；投票权

The pivotal feminist goal of *suffrage* was not obtained in the United States until 1920, and in Britain not until 1928. 直到1920年，美国妇女才取得女权主义追求的重要权利——选举权，而英国妇女直到1928年才获得这一权利。

sundry / ˈsʌndri / *adj.* various 各种各样的

The main character in the novel returns home safely after his *sundry* adventures. 小说主人公在经历了各种各样的冒险后，平安地回到了家乡。

supersede / ˌsuːpərˈsiːd / *v.* to replace, especially to displace as inferior or antiquated 取代；接替

Malay was the lingua franca of the Malay peninsula for centuries, but in many parts of that region it is being *superseded* in that role by a European interloper, English. 几个世纪以来，马来语一直是马来半岛上的通用语，然而在该地区许多地方，它正被英语这种来自欧洲的外来语所替代。

supine / ˈsuːpaɪn / *adj.* lying on the back; marked by lethargy 仰卧的；懒得动的

The captured robbery suspects were held *supine* on the floor. 被抓获的抢劫嫌疑犯被制服，仰面躺在地上。

supplant / səˈplænt / *v.* to replace; substitute 取代；代替

The "Frankenstein monster" fear of some people is that AI machines will eventually *supplant* biological life forms, making such life redundant or even subservient. 一些人对"科学怪人"怀有恐惧心理，他们害怕人工智能机器最终会取代生命形式，使其变得多余，甚至服从于这些智能机器。

suppliant / ˈsʌpliənt / *adj.* beseeching 恳求的，哀求的，乞求的 *n.* one who asks humbly and earnestly 恳求者；哀求者；乞求者 (=supplicant)

The worshippers raised their *suppliant* voices to God, praying for forgiveness. 做礼拜的人提高了恳求的声音，祈求上帝原谅他们。// The mother of the man sentenced to be executed appeared as a *supplicant* before the governor, asking him to grant her son clemency. 死刑犯的母亲以哀求者的身份来到长官面前，求他从轻发落她的儿子。

supposition / ˌsʌpəˈzɪʃn / *n.* the act of assuming to be true or real 假定，假设

Science proceeds on the *supposition* that knowledge is possible. 基于认识皆有可能的假设，科学不断取得进展。

syllogism / ˈsɪlədʒɪzəm / *n.* a form of deductive reasoning that has a major premise, a minor premise, and a conclusion 三段论法（一种演绎推理形式，包括大前提、小前提和结论）

The following *syllogism* is often taught in logic courses: "All Xs are Ys, all Ys are Zs; therefore, all Xs are Zs." 在逻辑课上，下述的三段论经常被提到："所有的X都是Y，所有的Y又都是Z，所以，所有的X都是Z。"

REVIEW 73

Matching

Match each word with its definition:

1. succor	a. beseeching
2. suffrage	b. various
3. sundry	c. lying on the back
4. supersede	d. one who asks humbly and earnestly
5. supine	e. to replace, especially as inferior or antiquated
6. supplant	f. a form of deductive reasoning
7. suppliant (*adj.*)	g. relief
8. suppliant (*n.*)	h. the act of assuming to be true
9. supposition	i. to replace; substitute
10. syllogism	j. the right to vote

Fill-ins

Choose the best word to fill in the blank in each sentence.

succor	suffrage	sundry	superseded	supine
supplanted	suppliant	suppliants	supposition	syllogism

1. Some experts predict that books made from paper will one day be _____ by electronic books.

2. The book tells the story of the protagonist's _____ adventures in Africa over the last 20 years.

3. The _____ approached the king, begging him to forgive their offences.

4. The depressed man found _____ by going inside the church to pray.

5. After eating our picnic lunch, we all lay _____ on the ground, looking at the clouds.

6. The logic instructor asked her class to consider whether the following _____ was true: Some A are B, some B are C. Therefore, some A are C.

7. The astronomers searching for extraterrestrial life are proceeding on the _____ that life requires water.

8. The Twenty-sixth Amendment to the United States Constitution extended _____ to both men and women from the age of 18 years, largely because of the fact that many men younger than 21 were being conscripted to fight in the Vietnam War but had no vote.

9. The first generation of digital computers based on vacuum tube technology were _____ by a second generation of transistorized computers in the late 1950s and 1960s that could perform millions of operations a second.

10. The painter portrays a _____ sinner begging for forgiveness.

Sense or Nonsense

Indicate whether each sentence makes good sense or not.
Put S (SENSE) if it does, and put N (NONSENSE) if it does not.

1. The political scientist predicts that by the year 2050 China will supplant Japan as Asia's most powerful nation. _____

2. The President ordered a halt to the bombing to end the suffrage of the people. _____

3. The astronomer's theory makes several suppositions about the nature of the early universe that are not well supported by the evidence. _____

4. The poem makes use of sophisticated figurative language, notably syllogism. _____

5. The science fiction novel speculates that human beings will one day be superseded by a race of specially bred superintelligent cyborgs. _____

UNIT 74

sylvan / ˈsɪlvən / *adj.* related to the woods or forest 森林的；多树木的

The house's *sylvan* setting provides the family with beauty and tranquility. 房子周围长满郁郁葱葱的树木，给这家人带来宜人的美景和安宁的心境。

tacit / ˈtæsɪt / *adj.* silently understood; implied 不言而喻的；隐含的，默示的

During the Cold War, there was a *tacit* assumption on the part of both the Soviet Union and the United States that neither side would launch an unprovoked nuclear attack against the other side. 冷战期间的一个潜规则是：前苏联和美国都不得无端对对方发动核武器袭击。

────── ● 常见学科术语 ● ──────

Cold War: the ideological, geopolitical, and economic conflict between capitalist nations (led by the United States) and communist nations (led by the Soviet Union) from around 1947 to 1991.

冷战： 1947至1991年间，以美国为首的资本主义国家和以前苏联为首的社会主义国家之间在意识形态、地缘政治和经济上的对立。

talisman / ˈtælɪzmən / *n.* charm to bring good luck and avert misfortune 护身符；驱邪物

The soldier's mother gave him a *talisman* to protect him from harm during battle. 士兵的母亲给了他一个护身符以保护他在战场上免受伤害。

tangential / tæn'dʒenʃl / *adj.* peripheral; digressing 次要的；离题的

The judge ruled that the evidence had only a *tangential* bearing on the case and directed the lawyer to present only a brief summary of it. 法官认为这些证据和案件没有太多关联，他要求律师简要概括一下即可。

tautology / tɔ'tɑːlədʒi / *n.* unnecessary repetition 同义反复；无谓的重复

Unless the phrase "repeat again" is being used to refer to something that has occurred more than twice, it is a *tautology*. 短语"再重复一遍"只有用来指一件事情发生了不止两次时才有意义，否则，它就是"赘语"。

taxonomy / tæk'sɑːnəmi / *n.* ① science of classification 分类学 ② in biology, the process of classifying organisms in categories（生物）分类

In the late seventeenth century and the eighteenth century accurate observation of organisms developed, leading to the development of the sciences of *taxonomy* and morphology（the study of the form and structure of organisms.）17世纪末和18世纪，人们得以更准确地观察有机物，从而促进了分类学和形态学（研究有机物的形态和结构的学科）的发展。

tenet / 'tenɪt / *n.* belief; doctrine 信条；教义

In his novel *Walden II*, the psychologist B. F. Skinner depicts a brave new world based on the *tenets* of a behavioral psychology that frees human beings from the inhibitions and preconceptions of traditional society. 心理学家B. F. 斯金纳在其小说《桃源二村》中描述了一个建立在行为主义心理学信条基础上的美丽新世界。这个世界使人们从传统社会的压抑和偏见中解脱出来。

─────── • 常见学科术语 • ───────

behavioral psychology: the school of psychology that seeks to explain behavior entirely in terms of observable responses to environmental stimuli.

行为主义心理学：心理学的一个流派，它试图完全通过人们对环境刺激所作出的可观察到的反应来解释人类行为。

tenuous / 'tenjuəs / *adj.* weak; insubstantial 脆弱的；缥缈的

Study of the historical evidence has shown that there is only a *tenuous* connection between the country Plato describes in *The Republic* and the legendary land of Atlantis. 史料研究表明，柏拉图在《理想国》中描述的国家与传说中的亚特兰蒂斯岛的关联微乎其微。

terrestrial / tə'restriəl / *adj.* ① earthly 地球的；陆地的 ② commonplace 普遍的

Much of our information about Mars comes from the Mariner 9 spacecraft, which orbited the planet in 1971; Mariner 9, photographing 100% of the planet, uncovered many spectacular geological formations, including a vast Martian canyon that dwarfs the *terrestrial* Grand Canyon. 我们关于火星的知识很多都来源于1971年环绕火星运行的"水手9号"飞船，它对火星进行全景拍摄，发现了许多壮观的地质构造，其中包括一座令美国大峡谷都相形见绌的火星峡谷。

theocracy / θi'ɑːkrəsi / *n.* government by priests representing a god 神权政治；僧侣政体

Some fundamentalists are opposed to secularism, and some of them support *theocracy*. 一些原教旨主义者反对现世主义，有些人甚至支持神权政治。

─────── • 常见学科术语 • ───────

secularism: a political movement that advocates making society less religious. Secularization is a process by which society gradually changes from close identification with the institutions of religion to a greater separation of religion from the rest of social life.

REVIEW 74

Matching

Match each word with its definition:

1.	sylvan	a.	science of classification
2.	tacit	b.	implied
3.	talisman	c.	government by priests
4.	tangential	d.	weak; insubstantial
5.	tautology	e.	digressing; diverting
6.	taxonomy	f.	related to the woods or forest
7.	tenet	g.	unnecessary repetition
8.	tenuous	h.	earthly; commonplace
9.	terrestrial	i.	charm to bring good luck
10.	theocracy	j.	belief; doctrine

Fill-ins

Choose the best word to fill in the blank in each sentence.

sylvan	tacit	talismans	tangential	tautologies
taxonomy	tenet	tenuous	terrestrial	theocracy

1. By _____ agreement no one in the group talked about the controversial subject of the war.

2. The judge asked everyone involved in the hearing to avoid introducing information _____ to the main issue.

3. The poet lives in _____ seclusion, writing about the beauty of nature.

4. A good pair of binoculars is very useful, not only for viewing _____ objects, but also for looking at relatively close astronomical objects.

5. The aim of the revolutionaries was to establish a _____ in the country run by senior clergy.

6. Archeologists have discovered objects they believe were used as _____ by warriors to ward off death.

7. A central _____ of democracy is that the law should treat everyone equally, regardless of his or her race, gender, or social status.

8. Linnaean _____, used in biology, classifies living things into a hierarchy, assigning each a unique place in the system.

9. The study has established a relationship, albeit a _____ one, between brain size in mammals and intelligence.

10. The English teacher asked the class to consider whether the phrases "past history" and "old adage" are _____.

Sense or Nonsense

Indicate whether each sentence makes good sense or not.
Put S (SENSE) if it does, and put N (NONSENSE) if it does not.

1. The landlord went to court to evict his tenets. _____
2. Research has demonstrated only a tenuous connection between the two phenomena. _____
3. Terrestrial observers north of the Equator were able to see the comet last night. _____
4. Members of the tribe believe that the talisman protects them from the evil spirits of the dead.

   _____
5. Religious leaders are arguing that the only way to save the country is to establish a theocracy.

   _____

UNIT 75

thespian / ˈθespiən / *n.* an actor or actress 演员

Every year the Edinburgh Festival in Scotland gives *thespians* from around the world the opportunity to perform before a diverse audience. 每年在苏格兰的"爱丁堡电影节"上，来自世界各地的演员均有机会在不同的观众面前一展风采。

timbre / ˈtɪmbər / *n.* the characteristic quality of sound produced by a particular instrument or voice; tone color 音质；音色

The audience was delighted by the rich *timbre* of the singer's soprano. 听众被那位女歌手富有特色的高音震撼了。

tirade / ˈtaɪreɪd / *n.* a long, violent speech; verbal assault 激烈的长篇指责或演说

The students had no choice but to sit and wait for the principal's *tirade* about poor discipline to end. 学生们别无选择，只得坐在那等待校长结束他那批评学生目无校纪的长篇大论。

toady / ˈtoʊdi / *n.* flatterer; hanger-on; yes-man 谄媚者，马屁精；唯唯诺诺的人

The boss had no respect for the employee because he considered him a *toady* who would do anything he said. 老板对那个职员缺乏最起码的尊重，因为在他眼里，他只不过是个惟命是从的人。

tome / toʊm / *n.* a book, usually large and academic 大部头书，(尤指学术性的)巨著

Despite being an abridged edition of the 20-volume *Oxford English Dictionary*, the *Shorter Oxford English Dictionary* consists of two *tomes* that define over half a million words. 虽然已经是20卷的《牛津英语词典》的缩减版，但《简明牛津英语词典》仍然包含了两本大部头的书，阐释的词条超过50万。

torpor / ˈtɔːrpər / *n.* lethargy; dormancy; sluggishness 迟钝；死气沉沉；懒散

After returning home from his coast-to-coast trip, the truck driver sank into a peaceful *torpor*, watching TV and dozing. 结束了海岸间的奔波，卡车司机回到家便懒洋洋地瘫作一团，边看电视边打盹。

torque / tɔːrk / *n.* ① a turning or twisting force 扭转力，弯曲力 ② the moment of a force; the measure of a force's tendency to produce twisting or turning and rotation around an axis 转矩，力矩

Internal combustion engines produce useful *torque* over a rather circumscribed range of rotational speeds. 内燃机能提供必要的旋转力，在一定范围内加快物体的转速。

tortuous / ˈtɔːrtʃuəs / *adj.* having many twists and turns; highly complex 弯曲的；拐弯抹角的；极其复杂的

Only the world's leading mathematicians are able to follow the *tortuous* line of reasoning used by the English mathematician Andrew Wiles to prove Fermat's Last Theorem via the Taniyama-Shimura conjecture. 只有世界上最优秀的数学家才有可能理解英国数学家安德鲁·怀尔斯利用谷山-志村猜想来证明费马大定理的曲折推理过程。

tout / taʊt / *v.* to promote or praise energetically 标榜；吹捧，吹嘘

The critic *touted Moby Dick* as the greatest book in American literature. 这位评论家标榜《大白鲸》是美国文学史上最伟大的著作。

tractable / ˈtræktəbl / *adj.* obedient; yielding 驯服的；温顺的

The country's leader found that the people became more *tractable* when he made them believe there was a great threat facing them that only he could overcome. 这个国家的领袖发现，使国民相信他们正面临严重威胁，而只有他才能消除这种威胁时，民众就会更加服从他的领导。

REVIEW 75

Matching

Match each word with its definition:

1. thespian		a.	a long, violent speech
2. timbre		b.	a turning or twisting force
3. tirade		c.	to promote
4. toady		d.	an actor or actress
5. tome		e.	obedient; yielding
6. torpor		f.	flatterer
7. torque		g.	tone color
8. tortuous		h.	a large, academic book
9. tout		i.	having many twists and turns
10. tractable		j.	lethargy; sluggishness

Fill-ins

Choose the best word to fill in the blank in each sentence.

thespians	timbre	tirade	toady	tome
torpor	torque	tortuous	touts	tractable

1. The musician has a special affinity for the guitar because of its beautiful _____.
2. The college _____ plan to perform three of Shakespeare's comedies this year.
3. The café _____ its cappuccino as the best in town.
4. The violent prisoner became _____ after he was given a sedative.

5. Every day the talk show host launches into a _____ against the failings of modern society.

6. In his *Malayan Trilogy*, the British novelist Anthony Burgess describes the _____ induced by hot Malaysian afternoons.

7. The book describes the author's _____ journey from cynicism and despair to faith and hope.

8. The diesel model of the Nissan Patrol is popular in Australia because it develops sufficient _____ to drive through steep, muddy terrain.

9. This 800-page _____ called *Biology* contains most of the information students need to learn for the introductory biology course.

10. Yes, the _____ won his promotion, but at what cost to his self-respect?

Sense or Nonsense

Indicate whether each sentence makes good sense or not.
Put S (SENSE) if it does, and put N (NONSENSE) if it does not.

1. Many high church officials are interred in tomes in the cathedral. _____

2. The farmer leased 100 acres of tractable land to grow corn. _____

3. The enemy launched a tirade of artillery and missiles against our position. _____

4. Timbre in the forests of most of the developed countries is self-sustaining. _____

5. The group of experts working on the space probe includes mechanical engineers, electrical engineers, physicists, and thespians. _____

UNIT 76

transgression / trænzˈgreʃn / *n.* the act of trespassing or violating a law or rule 违反；越轨

The teacher made it clear on the first day of the term that she would not countenance any *transgression* of classroom rules. 开学第一天，老师就明确表示她绝不会容忍任何触犯班级规定的行为。

【派】**transgress** *v.* 越界；违反；侵犯

Western medicine *transgressed* Hippocrates' prescriptions for medicine when doctors debilitated patients through the administration of purges and bloodletting. 当医生们开始采用通便、放血等疗法以减轻患者的痛苦时，西方医学就已经超出了希波克拉底药物疗法的限定范围。

────── • 常见学科术语 • ──────

Hippocrates: an ancient Greek physician who is often called "the father of medicine." He believed that medicine should stress prevention rather than cure of illness and that a regimen of a good diet and a sensible lifestyle is healthy, building a person's ability to withstand disease.

希波克拉底：古希腊医生，被公认为"医学之父"。他认为药物应该更为侧重预防疾病，而非治疗疾病。他认为合理膳食、理性生活才是健康的生活方式，并能有助于人体提高抗病能力。

transient / ˈtrænziənt / *adj.* temporary; short-lived; fleeting 短暂的，转瞬即逝的；临时的，不稳定的

A hypothesis to explain the fact that American states in which the population is composed of a large number of recently settled people (California, for example) tend to have high rates of crime, suicide, divorce, and other social problems is that anomie is higher in *transient* populations than in more stable populations, resulting in more antisocial behavior. 在美国，那些新近有大量移民定居的州(如加利福尼亚州)通常会出现更高的犯罪率、自杀率、离婚率以及更多其他社会问题。有种假说认为，这是因为较之常住人口，流动人口更容易出现行为失范，从而导致更多的反社会行为。

● 常见学科术语 ●
---

anomie: a social condition marked by a breakdown of social norms
社会道德沦丧：由于社会规范败坏而引起的社会状态。

translucent / trænsˈluːsnt / *adj.* partially transparent 半透明的

The architect decided to install a *translucent* door in the room to allow outside light to shine in. 为了能使阳光照射进来，建筑师决定在房间内安装一扇半透明的门。

travail / trəˈveɪl / *n.* work, especially arduous work; tribulation; anguish 艰苦劳作；磨难；痛苦
v. to work strenuously 艰苦劳作

America's early pioneers endured great *travail*, but persevered and eventually settled much of the vast continent. 美国早期的开拓者们历经了千辛万苦，但他们坚持了下来，并最终在这片广阔的土地上安家落户。

travesty / ˈtrævəsti / *n.* parody; exaggerated imitation; caricature 夸张的模仿；滑稽的模仿

The playwright complained that the musical comedy version of his play was a *travesty* of his work. 这位剧作家抱怨说，这出根据他的剧作改编的音乐喜剧是对他作品的拙劣模仿。

treatise / ˈtriːtɪs / *n.* article treating a subject systematically and thoroughly (专题)论文

The thesis of the philosopher's *treatise* is that reality is, ultimately, opaque to human understanding. 这位哲学家的论文主题是：就人类的理解力而言，现实根本就是难以洞悉的。

tremulous / ˈtremjələs / *adj.* ① trembling; quivering 战栗的，颤抖的 ② frugal 节俭的 ③ timid 胆怯的，怯生生的

One of the most famous poems in English literature is Matthew Arnold's "Dover Beach," in which the speaker listens to the "*tremulous* cadence slow" of waves on the shore. 英国文学史上最著名的一首诗歌是马修·阿诺德的《多佛海岸》，其中写道诗人在海滩上聆听着波涛"徐缓的旋律抖擞擞(编者注：来自卞之琳的译文)"。

trepidation / ˌtrepɪˈdeɪʃn / *n.* fear and anxiety 紧张；恐惧，惊慌；不安

John tried to hide his *trepidation* when he proposed to Susi, the girl he loved. 约翰向他心爱的苏西求婚时极力隐藏自己的紧张不安。

truculence / ˈtrʌkjələns / *n.* aggressiveness; ferocity 攻击性；凶猛；残暴

The principal warned the student that his *truculence* might one day land him in jail. 校长警告那个学生说，他早晚会因为寻衅闹事进监狱。

tryst / trɪst / *n.* an agreement between lovers to meet; rendezvous 约会，幽会

In his novel *The Mayor of Casterbridge*, Thomas Hardy describes an ancient Roman amphitheater where lovers often arranged secret *trysts*. 在其小说《卡斯特桥市长》中，托马斯·哈代描绘了一座古罗马式圆形露天剧场，恋人经常在此幽会。

REVIEW 76

Matching

Match each word with its definition:

1. transgression		a.	article treating a subject systematically
2. transient		b.	partially transparent
3. translucent		c.	fear and anxiety
4. travail		d.	temporary; fleeting
5. travesty		e.	exaggerated imitation; parody
6. treatise		f.	aggressiveness
7. tremulous		g.	arduous work
8. trepidation		h.	the act of violating a law
9. truculence		i.	rendezvous
10. tryst		j.	quivering; timid

Fill-ins

Choose the best word to fill in the blank in each sentence.

transgressed	transient	translucent	travails	travesty
treatise	tremulous	trepidation	truculence	tryst

1. The pastor urged the members of his congregation to face life's _____ cheerfully.
2. The gang has such a reputation for _____ that even the police approach its members with great caution.
3. This afternoon's solar eclipse will be a _____ phenomenon, so make sure you are ready to observe it as soon as it begins.
4. The philosophic _____ deals with Spinoza's metaphysics.
5. The soldier, his voice _____, begged his captor not to kill him.
6. A prism is a _____ piece of glass or crystal that creates a spectrum of light separated according to colors.
7. The judge in the most recent of the many times Dr. Jack Kevorkian was tried for murder for assisting a terminally ill person to kill himself held that the law is sacrosanct and cannot be _____ by an individual, even for reasons of conscience.
8. Bill and Sue arranged a _____ for Saturday afternoon.
9. The defense attorney called the trial of the soldier accused of war crimes a _____ of justice since the judges were all citizens of the nation that had defeated the country for which her defendant had been fighting.
10. The young scholar approached the problem with considerable _____, knowing that it had been thoroughly discussed by many of the great thinkers through the ages.

Sense or Nonsense

Indicate whether each sentence makes good sense or not.
Put S（SENSE）if it does, and put N（NONSENSE）if it does not.

1. Beth's father said he would prefer that she wore the opaque top, but her mother said she could wear the translucent one. _____

2. The transient nature of the phenomenon makes it difficult for scientists to study. _____

3. The professor's treatise on the influence of structuralism on modern thought was published last year. _____

4. The principal congratulated the student for successfully transgressing every school regulation. _____

5. The doctor in the soap opera spends so much of her time arranging trysts with her lover that she has no time left to practice medicine. _____

UNIT 77

tumid / ˈtjuːmɪd / *adj.* swollen; distended 肿起的，肿胀的；夸张的
> The prose of writers discussing lofty subjects sometimes becomes *tumid*. 有时讨论高尚主题的散文会变得很浮夸。

turbid / ˈtɜːrbɪd / *adj.* muddy; opaque; in a state of great confusion 浑浊不清的；极度混乱的
> The poem captures the restless and *turbid* state of the soldier's mind the night before the decisive battle was set to begin. 这首诗准确刻画了决战前夜士兵们惶恐不安的心理状态。

turgid / ˈtɜːrdʒɪd / *adj.* swollen; bloated; pompous 膨胀的，肿胀的；言辞浮夸的
> The professor's editor advised him to change his writing style so that it was less pedantic and *turgid* if he wanted to appeal to a mass audience. 编辑建议教授，要想吸引大众，要改变他的写作风格，少些学究气和浮华辞藻。

tutelary / ˈtuːtɪləri / *adj.* serving as a guardian or protector 守护的；保护的
> Most of the people of ancient Rome believed in the existence of *tutelary* spirits. 大多数古罗马人都相信守护神的存在。

───── • 常见学科术语 • ─────

tutelary spirit: the guardians of a particular area or person
守护神：保护某个地区或某个人的神灵

uncanny / ʌnˈkæni / *adj.* mysterious; strange 异常的；难以解释的；不可思议的
> Some people believe that the psychic has an *uncanny* ability to accurately predict the future. 一些人相信巫师拥有准确预言未来的特异功能。

undulating / ˈʌndʒəleɪtɪŋ / *adj.* moving in waves 起伏的；波浪的
> The *undulating* terrain of the area has made it difficult for engineers to build roads there. 这个地区连绵起伏的地形给工程师在该地修路造成困难。

unfeigned / ʌnˈfeɪnd / *adj.* not false; not made up; genuine 不虚伪的；不做作的；真诚的

The child smiled in *unfeigned* delight when she opened the Christmas present. 小女孩带着发自内心的微笑打开了圣诞礼物。

untenable / ʌnˈtenəbl / *adj.* indefensible 站不住脚的；难以捍卫的

Skeptics are inclined to regard arguments for God's existence from design as meaningless, since they rely on a logically *untenable* position that assumes the conclusion of their argument—God's existence. 怀疑论者倾向于认为坚信上帝存在的设计论证本身是毫无意义的，因为其所基于的观点在逻辑上就站不住脚，该观点预先假定了设计论证的结论，即上帝是存在的。

● 常见学科术语 ●

The argument from **design** is a philosophical argument for God's existence stating that God must exist because the universe is too complex to have been created any other way.
设计论证是哲学上关于上帝是否存在问题的一种论点。它认为，上帝一定存在，因为如此纷繁复杂的世界是不可能通过其他方式被创造出来的。

---

untoward / ʌnˈtɔːrd / *adj.* not favorable; adverse; troublesome; unruly 不利的；棘手的，麻烦的；难以控制的

Police were called in to investigate whether anything *untoward* had happened to the missing man. 警察被找来调查那位失踪的男士是否已经遭遇不测。

usury / ˈjuːʒəri / *n.* practice of lending money at exorbitant rates 高利贷

In the 1980s, Delaware Governor Pierre S. Du Pont succeeded in having the state's *usury* laws liberalized, with the result that many large New York banks set up subsidiaries in Delaware. 20世纪80年代，特拉华州州长皮埃尔·S·杜邦成功放宽了对高利贷的法律限制，这一举措使得许多纽约大银行纷纷在特拉华州设立分行。

【派】**usurious** *adj.* 放高利贷的

The consumer advocate's group complained about the bank's *usurious* interest rates. 消费者保护小组抱怨银行的利率跟高利贷的差不多高。

REVIEW 77

Matching

Match each word with its definition:

1. tumid		a.	serving as a guardian
2. turbid		b.	moving in waves
3. turgid		c.	swollen; distended
4. tutelary		d.	not made up; genuine
5. uncanny		e.	mysterious
6. undulating		f.	practice of lending money at exorbitant rates
7. unfeigned		g.	muddy; opaque; in a state of great confusion
8. untenable		h.	not favorable; adverse; troublesome
9. untoward		i.	swollen; bloated; pompous
10. usury		j.	indefensible

Fill-ins

Choose the best word to fill in the blank in each sentence.

tumid	turbid	turgid	tutelary	uncanny
undulating	unfeigned	untenable	untoward	usury

1. The student looked up with _____ astonishment—"You mean I got a perfect score on the GRE?"

2. The prime minister's position became _____ after he lost the support of his own party, so he resigned from office.

3. The consumer organization accused the credit card company of _____ after it raised its interest rate to 22% per year.

4. The head of the commission said that she did not want the report written in the _____ prose too often found in official documents.

5. The British writer George Orwell often satirized _____ political prose.

6. The commander told his troops that _____ circumstances had prevented victory, but that if they fought on valiantly, victory would be achieved eventually.

7. The orbiting spacecraft sent a manned vehicle down to the Martian surface, where it explored the area's _____ surface.

8. Steve's _____ ability to predict the outcome of college basketball games has helped him to win a lot of money on bets.

9. Many people believe that they have a guardian angel, a/an _____ being that guides and protects them.

10. After the storm the river was _____ because of all the soil that had flowed into it from the nearby stream.

Sense or Nonsense

Indicate whether each sentence makes good sense or not.
Put S (SENSE) if it does, and put N (NONSENSE) if it does not.

1. When chess grand masters find themselves in an untenable position they generally resign.
   _____

2. The tumid weather has made it difficult for the soccer team to train. _____

3. Despite its entertaining plot, the novel's turgid prose makes it rather difficult to enjoy.
   _____

4. The professor holds an extra tutelary class every Saturday morning. _____

5. The loan shark's usurious interest rates have attracted the attention of the district attorney.
   _____

UNIT 78

vacillate / ˈvæsəleɪt / *v.* to waver; oscillate 摇摆；动摇

The senator's position keeps *vacillating* between remaining neutral and lending his support to the proposal. 这位议员在保持中立和支持提议之间举棋不定。

vacuous / ˈvækjuəs / *adj.* empty; void; lacking intelligence; purposeless 空的；空洞的；愚蠢的；心灵空虚的，无目的的

In Jane Austen's novel *Pride and Prejudice*, the youngest of the five Bennett daughters, Lydia, is portrayed as a *vacuous* young woman with few interests other than having fun. 在简·奥斯汀的小说《傲慢与偏见》中，贝内特家的五个女儿中最小的莉迪亚，被描绘成一个脑袋空空如也、成天除了玩乐之外别无他好的年轻姑娘。

valedictory / ˌvælɪˈdɪktəri / *adj.* pertaining to a farewell 告别的，告辞的

The 80-year-old actor will give a *valedictory* performance on Broadway. 这位80岁高龄的男演员将在百老汇举办一场告别演出。

vapid / ˈvæpɪd / *adj.* tasteless; dull 乏味的，枯燥的

To relax in the evening the judge likes to watch *vapid* situation comedies on TV. 作为晚间消遣，这位法官爱看些无聊的电视情景喜剧。

variegated / ˈveriɡeɪtɪd / *adj.* varied; marked with different colors 各式各样的；色彩斑斓的

Botanists are still working to catalog the *variegated* species of the tropical rain forest. 植物学家仍致力于为品种繁多的热带雨林植物归类。

vaunt / vɔːnt / *v.* to boast; brag 吹嘘；夸耀

The head coach warned her players not to *vaunt* their undefeated record. 主教练警告队员们不要一味吹嘘自己不败的纪录。

【派】**vaunted** *adj.* boasted about 吹嘘的，吹牛的

Since every human activity depends on the integrity and proper functioning of the biological system, its destruction through pollution would cause our *vaunted* technological and economic systems to founder. 由于人类每一项活动都离不开生物界井然有序的运作，所以污染对生物界造成的破坏会动摇我们引以为豪的技术和经济体系。

venal / ˈviːnl / *adj.* bribable; mercenary; corruptible 贪赃枉法的；见利忘义的

The depressing though inescapable conclusion the journalist reached is that the mayor went into politics for motives that were almost entirely *venal*. 记者得出了一项令人沮丧的必然结论：市长从政的动机不过是为了从中渔利。

vendetta / venˈdetə / *n.* prolonged feud marked by bitter hostility 家族世仇；宿怨

The judge warned both families that the *vendetta* between them had to end at once. 法官告诫两个家族必须立刻放下长久以来对彼此的怨恨。

venerate / ˈvenəreɪt / *v.* to adore; honor; respect 敬重，崇敬，敬仰

Mother Theresa is *venerated* for her compassion for the poor people of India. 特雷莎修女因其对印度贫苦人民的同情而为人所敬重。

【派】venerable *adj.* respected because of age, character, or position 令人敬重的；德高望重的

In the plain-language edition of the *venerable Merck Manual of Diagnosis and Therapy* the original definition of a hangnail—"Acute or chronic inflammation of the periungual tissues"—is transmogrified into "An infection around the edge of a fingernail or toenail." 极具权威性的《默克诊疗手册》在其通俗版中，将指甲旁倒拉刺的最初定义——"甲周组织的急性或慢性炎症"——修改为"在指甲或趾甲周围出现的感染现象"。

veracious / vəˈreɪʃəs / *adj.* truthful; accurate 真实的；准确的

The witness' testimony appeared to be *veracious* at first, but under cross-examination, several inconsistencies appeared. 目击者的证词起初听起来很真实，但经过反复盘问，出现了几处前后不一致的地方。

REVIEW 78

Matching

Match each word with its definition:

1. vacillate		a.	bribable; corruptible
2. vacuous		b.	varied
3. valedictory		c.	to waver; oscillate
4. vapid		d.	to boast; brag
5. variegated		e.	truthful; accurate
6. vaunt		f.	tasteless; dull
7. venal		g.	to adore; honor
8. vendetta		h.	pertaining to a farewell
9. venerate		i.	prolonged feud
10. veracious		j.	empty; lacking intelligence

Fill-ins

Choose the best word to fill in the blank in each sentence.

vacillating	vacuous	valedictory	vapid	variegated
vaunted	venal	vendetta	venerated	veracious

1. The saint is _____ for her compassion toward all living things.
2. It is a mystery to critics how the writer went from producing _____ and sentimental stories to turning out some of the best stories ever written in America.
3. The jury's decision was based largely on the testimony of a single witness they believed to be _____.
4. The historian's book describes America's allies in Vietnam during the 1960s and 1970s as _____ and corrupt.
5. The booster club held a _____ breakfast for the football team.
6. The plot of *Romeo and Juliet* is centered around a _____ between two noble families, the Capulets and the Montagues.

7. Despite its _____ high-tech weapons, the invading army could not defeat the peasants, who were armed only with rifles.

8. The actress, a highly intelligent and well-educated young woman, plays the stereotyped part of the _____ "bimbo" in the film.

9. From odd bits of material the artist has achieved _____ effects.

10. Philip is _____ between going to medical school and law school.

Sense or Nonsense

Indicate whether each sentence makes good sense or not.
Put S (SENSE) if it does, and put N (NONSENSE) if it does not.

1. A veracious reader, Heather is planning to read five of Joseph Conrad's novels this month. _____

2. The president of the university has prepared some valedictory remarks for the Commencement ceremony. _____

3. The district attorney was elected mayor largely on his promise to prosecute venal government officials whenever possible. _____

4. The plot of the movie centers around a family's vendetta against another family that they believed had disgraced them. _____

5. The editor knew that the reporter's claim could not be true because it was clearly veracious. _____

UNIT 79

verbose / vɜːrˈboʊs / *adj.* wordy 冗长的，赘余的

The skillful editor cut 20% of the words from the *verbose* manuscript without appreciably altering its meaning. 资深编辑能从一份手稿中删去20%的冗余文字，而丝毫不改变其原意。

vertigo / ˈvɜːrtɪɡoʊ / *n.* dizziness 眩晕

The physician diagnosed the patient's *vertigo* as being caused by an acute anxiety attack. 医生诊断说患者的眩晕是急性焦虑发作造成的。

vexation / vekˈseɪʃn / *n.* irritation; annoyance; confusion; puzzlement 烦恼，恼怒；苦闷

Some people have the ability to prosper and live happily despite life's inevitable *vexations*. 人生难免有不如意，但有人总能走向成功，过得和和美美。

viable / ˈvaɪəbl / *adj.* practicable; capable of developing 切实可行的；能发展的

Since the early 1950s, government planners have faced a dilemma: Spend a great deal of money to keep cities *viable* by rebuilding decrepit infrastructure, or allow them to decay. 政府规划者自20世纪50年代初以来一直面临着这样一个进退维谷的局面：要么投入大笔资金重建损毁的基础设施以维持城市生机，要么任由这些城市自生自灭。

【派】viability *n.* 可行性；生存能力

According to the historian Arnold Toynbee, there is a strong relationship between a society's view of itself relative to other societies and its continued *viability*. 历史学家阿诺德·汤因比认为，一个社会相对于其他社会的自我定位与其自身的可持续发展之间有着密切的联系。

vindictive / vɪnˈdɪktɪv / *adj.* spiteful; vengeful; unforgiving 怀恨的；报复性的

The Treaty of Versailles, which concluded World War I, was deliberately *vindictive*, imposing tremendous penalties on the defeated nation. 标志着"一战"结束的《凡尔赛条约》蓄意报复战败国，对其施以重罚。

virtuoso / ˌvɜːrtʃuˈoʊsoʊ / *n.* someone with masterly skills; an expert musician 艺术大师；音乐名家 *adj.* 行家的；艺术爱好者的

The British guitar *virtuoso* John Williams has entertained thousands of people during his long career. 英国吉他演奏大师约翰·威廉姆斯在其漫长的演奏生涯中给成千上万的观众带来欢乐。// Raymond is a *virtuoso* pianist. 雷蒙德是一位技艺精湛的钢琴演奏家。

visage / ˈvɪzɪdʒ / *n.* countenance; appearance; aspect 脸，面庞；外貌；方面

The infant studied its mother's *visage* intently. 那个婴儿专注地注视着母亲的面庞。

viscous / ˈvɪskəs / *adj.* thick, syrupy, and sticky 黏稠的；黏滞的

The maple syrup is so *viscous* we had trouble pouring it. 枫糖浆太黏了，我们费了好大劲才把它倒出来。

vitiate / ˈvɪʃieɪt / *v.* to impair the quality of; corrupt morally; make inoperative 使变质；使失效；使堕落

Unfortunately, one error in the study's methodology *vitiates* the entire body of work. 遗憾的是，研究方法中的一个错误令整项工作都失去了意义。

vituperative / vɪˈtjuːpərətɪv / *adj.* using or containing harsh, abusive censure 责骂的；辱骂的

The young music critic's *vituperative* comments aroused the wrath of nearly every serious composer. 那位年轻音乐评论家尖酸刻薄的评论几乎令所有严肃音乐作曲家都愤怒不已。

【派】vituperate *v.* 谩骂，责骂

REVIEW 79

Matching

Match each word with its definition:

1. verbose
2. vertigo
3. vexation
4. viable
5. vindictive
6. virtuoso
7. visage
8. viscous
9. vitiate
10. vituperative

a. thick, syrupy, and sticky
b. to impair the quality of
c. spiteful; vengeful
d. countenance; appearance
e. practicable; capable of developing
f. wordy
g. someone with masterly skills
h. using or containing abusive censure
i. dizziness
j. irritation; annoyance

Fill-ins

Choose the best word to fill in the blank in each sentence.

verbose	vertigo	vexations	viable	vindictive
virtuoso	visage	viscous	vitiated	vituperative

1. The judge cautioned the attorney not to use his summing up as an opportunity to make _____ remarks about imperfections in the criminal justice system.
2. Heathcliff, the protagonist of *Wuthering Heights*, is _____ in seeking revenge against those he believes have harmed him.
3. Many people experience _____ when they stand near the edge of a cliff.
4. Sergei Rachmaninoff, a distinguished Russian-born composer, was also a _____ pianist who is famous for his interpretations of late romantic composers.
5. On the night before the battle, the soldier had a dream in which he saw the smiling _____ of his beloved mother.
6. The candidate's advisor warned her not to make her acceptance speech _____.
7. The engineer designed the motor to be lubricated with very _____ oil.
8. The congressional committee is trying to work out a _____ plan to give every American access to affordable, high-quality medical care.
9. The effectiveness of the new government will probably be _____ by factors beyond its control.
10. Returning home after the war, the soldier reflected that the _____ of daily civilian life would seem like nothing compared to the suffering he had endured as a conscript on the front line.

Sense or Nonsense

Indicate whether each sentence makes good sense or not.
Put S (SENSE) if it does, and put N (NONSENSE) if it does not.

1. The verbose speaker kept digressing to tell anecdotes about her life. _____
2. The government is studying the plan to provide universal health care to see whether it is economically viable. _____ .
3. According to the English professor, virtuosos of the novel form include Nathaniel Hawthorne, Henry James, Willa Cather, and Joseph Conrad. _____
4. The children enjoyed their visage to their uncle's house during the summer vacation. _____
5. Attacks of vertigo can be a symptom of a serious underlying malady. _____

UNIT 80

vivisection / ˌvɪvɪˈsekʃn / *n.* dissection, surgery, or painful experiments performed on a living animal for the purpose of scientific research 活体解剖

The book *Animal Rights* by the philosopher Tom Regan contains a long discussion of *vivisection*. 哲学家汤姆·里根所著的《动物权利》一书用了很大篇幅来讨论动物的活体解剖问题。

vogue / voʊg / *n.* prevailing fashion or practice 流行，风尚；风行

Although protectionist policies are not in *vogue* today, great capitalist democracies, such as Great Britain and the United States, flourished for long periods of their histories under protectionist trade policies that were nearly mercantilist—policies that imposed high tariffs on many foreign goods to promote domestic production. 尽管现在贸易保护政策已不再流行，但英美这样的资本主义民主大国却凭借其历史上长期施行的贸易保护主义政策而兴旺发达。它们的做法堪比重商主义，即通过对外国商品征收高额关税来保护本国商品。

volatile / ˈvɑːlətl / *adj.* tending to vary frequently; fickle 易变的，无常的

【派】**volatility** *n.* 易变

Some contemporary economists believe that advances in the understanding of the business cycle virtually preclude a recurrence of the crash of 1929, because governments can take steps to forestall depression. However, others worry that new factors are developing that are, to a significant extent, beyond the control of governments: notably, the ability of investors to quickly switch capital into and out of markets, a situation that could lead to *volatility* in prices and destabilize markets. 当代一些经济学家认为，随着人们对经济周期认识的深入，政府能够预先采取措施阻止危机的发生，进而避免再次爆发1929年那样的经济大萧条。但是也有一些经济学家担心，现在出现了一些新的因素，它们在很大程度上已经超出了政府的可控范围，尤其是投资者能够迅速地将资本注入或抽离市场的能力，其可能导致物价的波动和市场的不稳定。

vortex / ˈvɔːrteks / *n.* whirlpool; whirlwind; center of turbulence（水、风等的）漩涡；感情（或事件的）漩涡

Inexorably, the country was drawn into the *vortex* of war. 这个国家也未能幸免，被卷入战争的漩涡。

warrant / ˈwɔːrənt / *v.* to attest to the accuracy or quality; justify; grant authorization 保证；担保；批准

The book argues that a new investigation into Marilyn Monroe's death is *warranted* by new evidence released by the FBI under the Freedom of Information Act. 这本书指出，美国联邦调查局基于《信息自由法》公布了新的证据，所以有必要对玛丽莲·梦露的死因展开新的调查。// Throughout most of America, procedures in criminal law cases are essentially the same: The government, through a prosecutor, presents its case against a suspect to a grand jury, which decides if there is sufficient evidence to *warrant* a full trial. 在美国大多数地区，刑法案件的审理程序大致相同：政府的公诉人向大陪审团陈述对嫌疑人的诉讼，由其决定是否有足够的证据来确保进行全面审讯。

【派】**warranted** *adj.* justified 许可的；有担保的；合情合理的

wary / ˈweri / *adj.* careful; cautious 小心的，谨慎的

According to psychologists, human beings are naturally *wary* of strangers. 心理学家认为，天性使然，人们在与陌生人接触时总是很谨慎。

welter / ˈweltər / *v.* to wallow or roll; toss about; be in turmoil 打滚；翻动；混乱，骚动 *n.* 混乱

The pigs *weltered* about happily in the mud. 猪在泥浆里快活地滚来滚去。

whimsical / ˈwɪmzɪkl / *adj.* ① fanciful 异想天开的；幻想奇特的 ② unpredictable 反复无常的

Many children appreciate Dr. Seuss' *whimsical* stories. 很多孩子都喜欢瑟斯博士那些充满奇思妙想的故事。

【派】**whimsy** *n.* a playful or fanciful idea 怪念头；异想天开

Despite its rigorous and systematic methodology, there is still considerable room in science for imagination and even *whimsy*. 虽然科学讲究严谨性和条理性，但想象力甚至怪念头仍有不少发挥的余地。

wistful / ˈwɪstfl / *adj.* vaguely longing; sadly thoughtful 渴望的；留恋的；沉思的

The poem casts a *wistful* look back at a way of life that has vanished forever. 这首诗表达了诗人对一种永远逝去的生活方式的留恋之情。

zealot / ˈzelət / *n.* one who is fanatically devoted to a cause 狂热者，狂热分子

The Crusades of the eleventh to thirteenth centuries were conceived of by Christian *zealots* as a way to drive the Islamic interlopers from the Holy Land. 发生于11–13世纪的十字军东征运动是由基督教狂热分子谋划的，目的是将伊斯兰人驱逐出"圣地"。

【派1】**zealotry** *n.* fanaticism 狂热的态度或行为

The fact that the judicial branch is relatively undemocratic compared to the other two branches of government is justified by some theorists of democracy on the grounds that it serves as a check not only on the legislative branch and executive branch, but also on democratic *zealotry*. 司法机构不仅可以制衡立法和行政机构，还可以制约民主狂热行为。基于此，一些民主理论家认为较之政府的其他两个部门，司法机构不那么民主这一实情也是合理的。

【派2】**zealous** *adj.* enthusiastically devoted to a cause 狂热的；热心的，热情的

It is heretical to suggest to a *zealous* capitalist that free enterprise is not the only conceivable realistic economic system. 在狂热的资本主义者眼中，"可能的现实经济体制并非只有自由企业这一种"的观点简直就是异端邪说。

REVIEW 80

Matching

Match each word with its definition:

1. vivisection
2. vogue
3. volatile
4. vortex
5. warranted
6. wary
7. welter

a. tending to vary frequently
b. dissection performed on a living animal for scientific research
c. fanciful
d. one who is fanatically devoted to a cause
e. whirlpool; center of turbulence
f. to wallow or roll; be in turmoil
g. prevailing fashion

8. whimsical
9. wistful
10. zealot

h. careful; cautious
i. sadly thoughtful
j. justified

Fill-ins

Choose the best word to fill in the blank in each sentence.

vivisections	vogue	volatile	vortex	warranted
wary	welter	whimsical	wistful	zealot

1. Brad is such a party _____ that he has never even considered voting for a candidate who does not belong to his party.
2. Joan's friend said that she should be _____ of the man loitering around campus.
3. Lost in the _____ of conflicting information was the fact that there was no decisive proof of the theory's validity.
4. In James Boswell's *Life of Johnson* (1775), Samuel Johnson comments that the American colonists are "a race of convicts;" Boswell, however, expresses a contrary view: "I had now formed a clear and settled opinion, that the people of America were well _____ to resist a claim that their fellow subjects in the mother country should have the entire command of their fortunes, by taxing them without their consent."
5. Militant feminism reached its zenith in the 1960s, and since then a less confrontational approach to asserting women's rights has been in _____.
6. Steve advised his friend not to invest in the stock market until it became less _____.
7. The animal rights group organized a protest against the _____ being performed in the university biology laboratory.
8. The Swiss painter Paul Klee is famous for his humorous, personal, and often _____ paintings.
9. All of the people visiting the war memorial had _____ looks on their faces.
10. The young people of the country were drawn steadily into the _____ of revolutionary activity.

Sense or Nonsense

Indicate whether each sentence makes good sense or not.
Put S (SENSE) if it does, and put N (NONSENSE) if it does not.

1. Mini-skirts were in vogue in the 1960s. _____
2. The panel is considering the legal and moral implications of vivisection. _____
3. The coach decided that his team's excellent performance in the game warranted a day off practice. _____
4. The psychologist excels in helping patients learn to understand their volatile emotions.

   _____
5. The English novelist Evelyn Waugh was a practicing Roman Catholic, though hardly a zealot.

   _____

Final Review

Matching

Match each word with its definition:

Part A:

1. desuetude		a.	growth in size
2. extraneous		b.	unrehearsed
3. bifurcate		c.	self-control
4. fulminate		d.	to divide into two parts
5. continence		e.	to complain
6. extemporaneous		f.	moving away from the center
7. accretion		g.	to denounce
8. centrifugal		h.	a state of disuse
9. grouse		i.	moving toward the center
10. centripetal		j.	not essential

Part B:

11. impervious		a.	a fleeting feeling of hurt pride
12. labile		b.	not candid
13. affinity		c.	impossible to appease
14. plethora		d.	to waver; oscillate
15. implacable		e.	fondness; similarity
16. vitiate		f.	overabundance
17. disingenuous		g.	likely to change
18. pique		h.	incapable of being affected
19. subsume		i.	to include; incorporate
20. vacillate		j.	to impair the quality of

Sense or Nonsense

Indicate whether each sentence makes good sense or not.
Put S (SENSE) if it does, and put N (NONSENSE) if it does not.

21. Artwork of the classical period can seem austere to the uninitiated, but to the discerning audience it is satisfying to have feelings expressed in this form because they are transmuted in the crucible of art into a more stygian form. _____

22. Although he is remembered chiefly as a novelist, D.H. Lawrence also had an enervation for writing verse. _____

23. In his poetry and novels, writer Thomas Hardy often portrayed a contumacious God who interfered almost maliciously in human affairs. _____

24. The nineteenth-century British satirist Thomas Love Peacock lampooned the metaphysical speculation of thinkers like Samuel Taylor Coleridge as pretentious and limpid. _____

25. Skeptics believe that the Green Revolution can only mitigate the effects of a rapidly increasing demand for food, and that in the long run starvation will reappear when pestilence and other disasters decrease food supplies. _____

26. The scientist is in an ethical quandary about whether he should repudiate his past involvement in developing a weapon of mass destruction. _____

27. In 1787, when the U.S. Constitution was being framed, it was proposed that slavery be abolished, but opponents of the measure forced a compromise whereby slavery would not be prescribed until early in the next century. _____

28. Evolution is a process that results in the overall improvement of life; paradoxically, however, that process of improvement is driven by aberrations in the process of DNA's self-replication.

_____

29. In the so-called "clockwork universe" of the deists, God is relegated to the role of a "clockmaker" who creates the cosmos and then withdraws to allow man autonomous action.

_____

30. In his argument against conscription, Joseph conceded that there might be rarefied situations in which it is justified, but warned that allowing it in these cases might be a step down the slippery slope to totalitarianism. _____

Fill-ins

Choose the best word or set of words to fill in the blanks in each sentence.

31. The Hubble Space Telescope—in orbit around the Earth to offer observations not _____ by the earth's atmosphere—has been a boon to astronomers; it is one of the finest astronomical instruments ever developed, greatly expanding man's gaze into space.

　(A) attenuated
　(B) mitigated
　(C) imploded
　(D) subsumed
　(E) intimated

32. The literary critic Susan Sontag uttered a famous _____ dictum: "Taste has no system and no proofs"—by which she meant that artistic taste is subjective, since there are no unbiased criteria for assessing art.

　(A) desultory
　(B) aesthetic
　(C) existential
　(D) linguistic
　(E) capricious

33. _____ of primitivism is that there is no progress in art, and thus the art of so-called "primitive" cultures is as _____ as that of so-called "high" civilization.

(A) An exigency .. plastic

(B) A precept .. felicitous

(C) A credo .. gauche

(D) A supposition .. whimsical

(E) A tenet .. evocative

34. In 1787, when the United States Constitution was written, it was proposed that slavery be abolished, but opponents of the measure forced a compromise whereby slavery would not be _____ until early in the next century.

(A) admonished

(B) emulated

(C) proscribed

(D) interpolated

(E) obviated

35. The following _____, called Olber's paradox, long puzzled astronomers: If the universe is infinite in extent and age, and filled with stars, why is the sky dark at night?

(A) apothegm

(B) stricture

(C) valedictory

(D) conundrum

(E) vendetta

36. _____ was an academic discipline at many universities in the early twentieth century, and was supported by such _____ figures such as Winston Churchill and George Bernard Shaw until it became closely associated with abuses of the Nazis of the 1940s in Germany, who carried out atrocities such as the extermination of undersized population groups.

(A) Epistemology .. impassive

(B) Eugenics .. redoubtable

(C) Necromancy .. discerning

(D) Hieroglyphics .. beneficent

(E) Cartography .. avuncular

37. _____ generally believe that determinism is incompatible with human dignity, and _____ attempts to limit man's freedom.

(A) Libertines .. aver

(B) Existentialists .. disparage

(C) Neophytes .. repudiate

(D) Conscripts .. aggrandize

(E) Anarchists .. admonish

38. Scholars are sometimes tempted into _____ off the main topic to discuss esoteric areas of interest to them, but which are regarded by many readers as _____ display of _____.

    (A) diatribes .. a formidable .. miscellany
    (B) soliloquies .. a megalomaniacal .. propriety
    (C) digressions .. a pedantic .. erudition
    (D) homilies .. an egotistical .. sagacity
    (E) expositions .. a bombastic .. chivalry

39. When the word "gay" began to be widely adopted to refer to homosexuals, some commentators, presumably unaware of the word's complex history and long association with homosexuality, _____ it as a/an _____ with connotations of merriment that was being foisted by homosexuals on the heterosexual majority.

    (A) defamed .. tautology
    (B) denigrated .. syllogism
    (C) derided .. euphemism
    (D) disparaged .. neologism
    (E) maligned .. mnemonic

40. _____ student of literature remembers that literary terms are notoriously _____ in that their meanings are ever shifting depending on the premises of the writer using them and the nature of the work under discussion.

    (A) A jejune .. inevitably
    (B) A craven .. poignantly
    (C) A judicious .. impetuously
    (D) An astute .. querulously
    (E) A sagacious .. plastic

41. The fact that social welfare programs existed only in embryonic form during the Great Depression _____ the effects of that depression because there was virtually no mechanism for coping with sudden and _____ unemployment.

    (A) negated .. perennial
    (B) forestalled .. precipitate
    (C) alleviated .. ineluctable
    (D) exacerbated .. pervasive
    (E) impeded .. substantive

42. _____ believe that because people are _____ agents, they should not allow themselves to be circumscribed by the restrictions of the state.

    (A) Misanthropes .. covert
    (B) Mavericks .. complaisant
    (C) Iconoclasts .. viable
    (D) Zealots .. guileless
    (E) Anarchists .. autonomous

43. Because it is very quickly destroyed by ordinary matter, antimatter has _____ existence in our locality of the universe.

(A) a derivative

(B) an intangible

(C) a viable

(D) an ephemeral

(E) a poignant

44. To make your writing _____, it is a good idea to read what you have written from a reader's perspective, looking for any language that is _____.

(A) execrable .. bombastic

(B) banal .. convoluted

(C) pellucid .. equivocal

(D) discordant .. tangential

(E) amenable .. disjointed

45. Modern _____ uses _____ techniques involving methodologies such as photogrammetry, which utilizes photographs taken from airplanes and satellites to measure topography with extreme accuracy.

(A) meteorology .. salutary

(B) paleontology .. hermetic

(C) entomology .. audacious

(D) ornithology .. recondite

(E) cartography .. esoteric

46. The _____, "Women are more intelligent than men" needs to be _____, because not all women are smarter than all men.

(A) axiom .. jibed

(B) stricture .. refuted

(C) extrapolation .. queried

(D) contention .. qualified

(E) credo .. vitiated

47. The concept of the biosphere has helped to _____ the idea of life on earth as a fragile and interdependent system that humanity disrupts at its peril.

(A) supplant

(B) bifurcate

(C) burnish

(D) disseminate

(E) amalgamate

48. It seems likely that herd mentality plays a part in depressions; as an economy slumps, some people panic, others _____ this panic, and something akin to mass hysteria ensues.

(A) arrest

(B) foreswear

(C) impede

(D) subsume

(E) emulate

49. In burning fossil fuels so _____, humanity is squandering a legacy from _____ times.

(A) ostentatiously .. indeterminate

(B) presumptuously .. antediluvian

(C) precipitously .. sidereal

(D) prodigally .. primordial

(E) abstemiously .. anachronistic

50. Because of its political problems and _____ inflation for long periods after World War II, some economists have cited Argentina as a developed country that was nearly _____ to the rank of an underdeveloped country.

(A) insuperable .. divested

(B) intractable .. relegated

(C) ineluctable .. accrued

(D) implacable .. goaded

(E) nugatory .. interpolated

End of Final Review

ANSWERS

1. h	2. j	3. d	4. g	5. c	6. b	7. a	8. f	9. e	10. i
11. h	12. g	13. e	14. f	15. c	16. j	17. b	18. a	19.i	20. d
21. N	22. N	23. N	24. N	25. S	26. S	27. N	28. S	29. S	30. N
31. A	32. B	33. E	34. C	35. D	36. B	37. B	38. C	39. C	40. E
41. D	42. E	43. D	44. C	45. E	46. D	47. D	48. E	49. D	50. B

300 High-Frequency
Word Roots and Prefixes

掌握常见词根、前缀，有效扩充词汇量

我们已经学习了GRE考试800个核心单词，但这远远不足以应对实际考试，还需要积累更多的词汇。那么如何才能高效地掌握更多词汇呢？

答案就是：通过词根、词缀的学习，积累更多核心词汇。

本部分从构词角度对GRE常考词汇进行分析，精选出300个常见词根、前缀（后缀见P326），以及1500个由这些词根和前缀衍生而来的单词。本部分共分为60个列表，每个列表后均附有10道词汇释义连线题，帮助考生加深对单词的理解与记忆。每5个列表后附有1个回顾练习（Review），检测考生对前5个列表的词根、前缀和词汇的学习效果，包括10道词根及前缀释义连线题、10道单词释义题、5道单词用法判断题。

通过词根、词缀的学习，深入掌握英语词汇的基本构成，加深对GRE核心词汇的记忆与理解。更重要的是，它能展示如何分解、破译GRE阅读材料中出现的学术词汇，为考生以后的学术生涯打下基础。

如何通过词根、词缀来学习词汇

大多数英语词汇都由源于盎格鲁-撒克逊时期的古英语、希腊语、拉丁语、法语、意大利语和德语的词根或词干加上一些特定词缀构成，这些词缀（也称词素，包括前缀和后缀）有助于界定词义或改变其语法结构。在超过100万的英语词汇中源自拉丁或希腊词根的约占60%，这就意味着只要掌握了这些高频词根，就能更好地理解大部分单词的起源和意思。例如，我们知道exacerbate一词指"使恶化，使加剧"，但你知道它的构词吗？它由ex-(前缀，表加强)＋拉丁词根acer(严酷的；痛苦的)＋-ate(动词后缀，使、做)组成。再如aberrant(脱离常规的)一词，它由ab-(远离)＋err(徘徊)＋-ate组成。因此，如果你掌握了词根err(徘徊)以及常见后缀，如-or(表性质或状态)、-ous(充满…的)、-ant(表状态)，那么你能否推断出下列单词的含义？

err	**error**	**errant**	**erratic**	**erroneous**

下面是正确答案，看看你猜得对不对：

err	*v.* to make a mistake 犯错，做错
error	*n.* a mistake 错误
errant	*adj.* mistaken; straying from the proper course 错误的；偏离正路的
erratic	*adj.* deviating from the customary course 偏离的
erroneous	*adj.* mistaken 不正确的；错误的

下面再进行一个拓展练习，用词根、词缀"分解"GRE高难词汇。

acuminate	**ergatocracy**	**orthotropism**	**neonate**	**noctilucent**
osseous	**paleography**	**sacrosanct**	**sequacious**	**somniloquy**

写下你对每个单词词义的理解。如果你不知道准确的意思，就试着猜测一下。然后参照下面的正确词义进行自评。完全准确的得10分，部分正确的得5分。

acuminate	*v.* to make sharp; taper to a point 使尖锐；（使）变尖
ergatocracy	*n.* government by workers 劳工执政
orthotropism	*n.* vertical growth 直生性
neonate	*n.* a newborn child 婴儿
noctilucent	*adj.* shining at night 夜光的
osseous	*adj.* bony 骨的；多骨的
paleography	*n.* study of ancient writings 古文书学
sacrosanct	*adj.* extremely sacred 极神圣的；神圣不可侵犯的
sequacious	*adj.* disposed to follow another 盲从的
somniloquy	*n.* the act of talking in one's sleep 说梦话

现在来计算一下得分。如果低于50分，说明你对GRE词汇词根的掌握有待提高，需要强化学习本部分的词根、词缀。如果得分在50和80之间，则需要再复习一遍希腊和拉丁词根，以在GRE考试中取得更加优异的成绩。

我们来分析一下上述单词的具体构成：

acuminate	acu(尖的) + -ate(动词后缀，使)
ergatocracy	erg(工作) + ato + cracy(政府)
orthotropism	ortho-(直的；正确的) + trop(变化) + -ism
neonate	neo-(新的) + natur(出生)
noctilucent	nocti(夜晚) + luc(光，闪光)
osseous	oss(骨) + -ous(形容词后缀，充满…的、具有…特征的)
paleography	paleo(古的) + graph(写) + y
sacrosanct	sacr(神圣的) + (o)sanct(奉献)
sequacious	sequ(跟随) + aci + ous(形容词后缀；充满…的、具有…特征的)
somniloquy	somn(i)(睡觉) + loqu(说话) + y

有些考生可能会认为没必要掌握orthotropism、sequacious之类的单词。但如果想获得硕士或博士学位，并有志于从事医学、法律或其他极具学术性、专业性的领域的研究工作，掌握大量类似词汇就非常必要。学完本书这300多个常见词根、词缀后，在以后的学习中遇见高难度的专业学术词汇，也能轻松自如地进行破译，并稳步扩充词汇量。

当然，词根学习不能仅止于此。考生在平时的学习中就应该有意识地积累新的词根，遇到不认识或不会解释的单词时，可以查询带有词源注释的词典，如*The American Heritage College Dictionary*（《美国传统词典–大学版》）、*Merriam-Webster's Collegiate Dictionary*（《韦氏大学词典》）等。

现在，开始学习这些常见词根、词缀吧！

ROUNDUP 1

- **A-/AN-*** (WITHOUT, ABSENSE OF, NOT 没有，无；缺乏）[G]**

  atheist   *n.* a person who does not believe in the existence of a god 无神论者

  agnostic   *n.* a person who is doubtful about something 不可知论者

  anarchy   *n.* absence of political authority 无政府状态

  anemia   *n.* deficiency in the part of the blood that carries oxygen 贫血

  anachronism   *n.* something out of the proper time 不合潮流的事物

- **AB-/ABS-** (FROM, AWAY, OFF 来自；远离，离开）[L]

  abduct   *v.* to carry away by force; kidnap 绑架；诱拐

  aberrant   *adj.* deviating away from the expected or normal course 脱离常规的

  abrade   *v.* to wear away by friction; erode 磨损，擦伤；磨蚀

  abdicate   *v.* to formally relinquish power or responsibility 退位；放弃

  abstinence   *n.* refraining from something 节制

- **ACER/ACID/ACRI** (HARSH, BITTER, SOUR 严酷的；痛苦的；酸的）[L]

  acrid   *adj.* sharp or bitter to the taste or smell; sharp in language or tone 辛辣的；苦的；刻薄的

  acrimonious   *adj.* bitter and sharp in language and tone 辛辣的；刻薄的

  acerbate   *v.* to annoy 使烦恼

  acerbity   *n.* sourness or bitterness of taste, character, or tone 酸，涩；刻薄

  ex**acer**bate   *v.* to increase bitterness; make worse 使加剧；使恶化

- **ACT/AG** (DRIVE, DO, LEAD, ACT, MOVE 驱动；做；引导；行动；移动）[L]

  active   *adj.* being in physical motion 活跃的；积极的

  actuate   *v.* to put into motion; activate 开动；驱使

  agenda   *n.* list or program of things to be done 议程；日常工作事项

  agency   *n.* condition of being in action 代理；作用，效力

  agitation   *n.* act of causing to move with violent force 搅动；煽动

- **ACU** (SHARP 尖的）[L]

  acumen   *n.* keenness of judgment 聪明；敏锐

  acuminate   *adj.* tapering to a point 锐利的

                   v. to make sharp; taper 使尖锐；（使）变尖

  acupuncture   *n.* therapeutic technique that uses needles to relieve pain 针刺疗法

  aculeate   *adj.* having a stinger; having sharp prickles 有刺的，多刺的

  acuity   *n.* sharpness of perception or vision 敏锐；尖锐

---

*本部分所有的前缀和后缀都加有英文连字符。

**［G］表示该词根或前缀源于希腊语，［L］表示源于拉丁语，［OE］表示源于古英语。

Work 1

Match each word with its definition:

1. agency		a.	to formally relinquish power
2. exacerbate		b.	sharpness of vision
3. actuate		c.	deficiency in the blood
4. abstinence		d.	to increase bitterness
5. anarchy		e.	condition of being in action
6. acuity		f.	to make sharp; taper
7. abdicate		g.	sharp or bitter to the taste or smell
8. anemia		h.	absence of political authority
9. acrid		i.	to put into motion
10. acuminate		j.	refraining from something

ROUNDUP 2

- **AD-/AC-/AF-/AG-/AL-/AN-/AP-/AR-/AS-/AT-** (TO, TOWARD 去; 朝向) [L]

accord	*v.* to cause to agree; bring into harmony 使一致; 符合
acquiesce	*v.* to consent quietly to something 默许; 勉强同意
advent	*n.* arrival; coming 到来; 出现
aggregate	*adj.* amounting to a whole 集合的; 合计的
	v. total 合计; 总计
appease	*v.* to bring peace or calm to; soothe 使平息; 使和缓

- **AEV/EV** (AGE, ERA 时代; 年代) [L]

prim**ev**al	*adj.* belonging to the earliest age 原始的; 初期的
medi**ev**al	*adj.* belonging to the Middle Ages 中世纪的
medi**ev**alism	*n.* devotion to the ideas of the Middle Ages 中世纪精神; 中世纪性质
co**ev**al	*adj.* existing during the same era 同时代的
long**ev**ity	*n.* long life; long duration 长寿; 长期

- **AGOG** (LEADER 领导) [G]

ped**agog**ue	*n.* teacher; a dogmatic teacher 教师; 学究
syn**agog**ue	*n.* a place of meeting for worship in the Jewish faith 犹太教堂
emmen**agog**ue	*n.* agent that induces menstrual flow 通经剂, 调经剂
an**agog**y	*n.* mystical interpretation that detects allusions to the afterlife 神秘解释; 寓意诠释
hypn**agog**ic	*adj.* inducing sleep 催眠的

- **AGR** (FIELD 土地) [L]

agribusiness	*n.* farming done as a large-scale business 农业综合企业
agriculture	*n.* farming 农业
agrarian	*adj.* relating to farming or rural matters 土地的; 耕地的; 农业的
agritourism	*n.* form of tourism that lets people experience life on a farm 农业旅游
agronomy	*n.* application of science to farming 农学; 农艺学

- **ALI** (ANOTHER 另外的) [L]

alien	*adj.* characteristic of another place or society; strange 外国的；相异的
alienation	*n.* emotional isolation or disassociation 疏远；精神错乱
in**ali**enable	*adj.* not capable of being surrendered 不可分割的；不可剥夺的；不能让与的
alibi	*n.* fact of absence from the scene of a crime 不在犯罪现场的证明
alienage	*n.* official status as an alien 外国人的身份

Work 2

Match each word with its definition:

1.	agrarian	a.	application of science to farming
2.	primeval	b.	from another place or society
3.	inalienable	c.	existing during the same era
4.	pedagogue	d.	relating to farming
5.	agronomy	e.	inducing sleep
6.	appease	f.	belonging to the earliest age
7.	coeval	g.	arrival; coming
8.	advent	h.	to bring peace or calm to
9.	hypnagogic	i.	teacher; a dogmatic teacher
10.	alien	j.	not capable of being surrendered

ROUNDUP 3

- **ALIM** (SUPPORT, NOURISH, CHERISH 支持；滋养；珍惜) [L]

aliment	*n.* something that nourishes 滋养品；养料
alimony	*n.* allowance for support to a divorced person by the former chief provider 赡养费；生活费
alible	*adj.* nourishing 有营养的
alimentary	*adj.* concerned with nutrition or food 滋养的；食物的
alimentation	*n.* giving or receiving of nourishment 滋养；营养

- **ALTER** (OTHER 其他的) [L]

alter	*v.* to change; modify; become different 改变，变换；更改，修改；变得不同
alternate	*v.* to proceed by turns 交替；轮流
alternative	*n.* one of two mutually exclusive possibilities 二中择一；可替代的选择
alter ego	second self or another side of oneself 第二个我；个性的另一面
altercate	*v.* to argue vehemently 争吵，发生口角；争论

- **ALT** (HIGH, DEEP 高的；深的) [L]

altar	*n.* elevated structure before which religious ceremonies are performed 祭坛；圣坛
ex**alt**ation	*n.* condition of being raised up in rank 提拔；欣喜
altimeter	*n.* instrument that measures elevation 测高仪，高度计
altiplano	*n.* high plateau 高原
altitude	*n.* height of something above a certain reference level 高度；海拔

- **AM** (LOVE, LIKING 爱，喜欢) [L]

amiable	*adj.* friendly; likeable 友好的；和蔼可亲的，亲切的
en**am**ored	*adj.* captivated 迷恋的；倾心的
amicable	*adj.* friendly 友好的；友善的
amity	*n.* friendship 友谊；友好关系
amatory	*adj.* inclined toward love 恋爱的；情人的

- **AMB/AMBUL** (GO, WALK 走) [L]

ambulate	*v.* to walk from place to place 走动；移动
amble	*v.* to walk slowly 缓行；从容漫步
ambulance	*n.* vehicle to transport injured people 救护车；野战医院
per**ambul**ate	*v.* to walk about 巡行；巡游；漫步
ambulatory	*adj.* capable of walking 能走动的；步行的

Work 3

Match each word with its definition

1. perambulate
2. alter ego
3. amatory
4. alter
5. amicable
6. altiplano
7. alimentary
8. exaltation
9. amble
10. alible

a. to walk slowly
b. friendly
c. to become different
d. nourishing
e. high plateau
f. to walk about
g. another side of oneself
h. concerned with nutrition
i. being raised up in rank
j. inclined toward love

ROUNDUP 4

- **AMBI-** (AROUND, ON BOTH SIDES 周围；两边) [L]

ambient	*n. /adj.* surrounding 周围环境(的)
ambidextrous	*adj.* able to use both hands well 灵巧的
ambivalent	*adj.* having conflicting feelings 矛盾的；好恶相克的
ambiguous	*adj.* doubtful or unclear 引起歧义的；模糊不清的
ambiversion	*n.* personality trait that combines both introversion and extroversion 中向性格，中间性格

- **AMPH-/AMPHI-** (AROUND, DOUBLE, ON BOTH SIDES 周围；双的；两边) [G]

amphibian	*n.* animal that can live both on land and in water 两栖动物
amphora	*n.* a two-handled Greek or Roman jar 双耳瓶；土罐
amphitheater	*n.* round structure with levels of seats rising upward from central area 圆形露天剧场；古罗马剧场
amphidiploid	*adj.* having a diploid set of chromosomes from each parent 二倍体的
amphibolous	*adj.* having a grammatical structure that allows two interpretations 词义暧昧的

- **ANIM** (LIFE, BREATH, SPIRIT 生命；呼吸；精神) [L]

  animal   *n.* multicellular organism of the kingdom Animalia 动物

  animation   *n.* enthusiasm; excitement 活泼；生气

  animism   *n.* belief that individual spirits inhabit natural phenomena 万物有灵论，泛灵论

  animosity   *n.* hostility; hatred 憎恶；仇恨；敌意

  in**anim**ate   *adj.* not exhibiting life 无生命的；无生气的

- **ANNU/ANNI/ENNI** (YEARLY 每年的) [L]

  annuity   *n.* yearly income payment 年金

  anniversary   *n.* yearly recurring date of an event that occurred in the past 周年纪念日

  bi**enni**al   *adj.* happening every two years 两年一次的

  per**enni**al   *adj.* lasting throughout the year or for several years 常年的；多年生的；常在的

  mill**enni**um   *n.* thousand-year period 千禧年；一千年

- **ANT-/ANTE-** (BEFORE 在…之前) [L]

  antecedent   *n.* something that comes before 先行词；祖先；前情

  antediluvian   *adj.* extremely old; happening before the Flood 远古的；大洪水前的

  antedate   *v.* to come before in time 先于；前于

  anterior   *adj.* placed before; earlier 前面的；先前的

  antler   *n.* bony growth on the head of a deer 鹿角

Work 4

Match each word with its definition:

1. inanimate
2. ambiguous
3. antediluvian
4. animation
5. millennium
6. amphibian
7. ambivalent
8. amphora
9. annuity
10. antecedent

a. enthusiasm

b. having conflicting feelings

c. yearly income payment

d. animal able to live on land or in water

e. not exhibiting life

f. doubtful; unclear

g. something coming before

h. a two-handled Greek or Roman jar

i. thousand-year period

j. extremely old

ROUNDUP 5

- **ANT-/ANTI-** (AGAINST, OPPOSITE 对立的，反对的) [G]

  antibiotic   *n.* substance that can kill microorganisms 抗生素，抗菌素

  antiseptic   *n.* substance that can kill disease-causing organisms 防腐剂；抗菌剂

  antipathy   *n.* dislike 反感；厌恶；憎恶

  antithesis   *n.* opposite of 对照，对立；对立面

  antagonistic   *adj.* hostile 敌对的；反对的；对抗的

- **ANTHROP**（MANKIND, HUMAN BEING 人类，人）[G]

anthropic	*adj.* related to the human race 有关人类的；人类的
anthropoid	*adj.* resembling human beings 似人的，类人的
anthropology	*n.* study of man 人类学
mis**anthrop**y	*n.* hatred of humanity 厌恶人类；厌世
anthropocentric	*adj.* regarding human beings as the center of the universe 以人类为中心的

- **ANTIQU**（OLD, ANCIENT 旧的；古老的）[L]

antiquate	*v.* to make old-fashioned or obsolete 使过时；废弃
antiquated	*adj.* too old to be useful or fashionable 陈旧的；过时的
antique	*adj.* belonging to an earlier period 古老的，年代久远的；古董的，过时的；古式的
antiquity	*n.* ancient times; an object from ancient times 古代；古物，古代遗物
antiquarian	*adj.* relating to the study of antiquities 古文物研究的

- **APPELL**（NAME, CALL UPON 名字；号召）[L]

appellation	*n.* name or title 名称；名目；称呼
appellative	*adj.* relating to the assignment of names 命名的；通称的
appeal	*n.* earnest or urgent request 呼吁；恳求，请求
appellant	*adj.* relating to an appeal 上诉的
appellate	*adj.* having the power to hear court appeals 受理上诉的

- **APT/EPT**（SKILL, ABILITY 技巧；能力）[L]

in**ept**	*adj.* not suitable; having a lack of judgment or reason 不适当的；笨拙的
apt	*adj.* exactly suitable 恰当的，适当的
un**apt**	*adj.* not suitable 不合适的；不适合的
ad**apt**	*v.* to make suitable to a specific situation 使适应
aptitude	*n.* inherent ability; talent 天资；能力；才能

Work 5

Match each word with its definition:

1.	antiquated	a.	exactly suitable
2.	misanthropy	b.	name or title
3.	inept	c.	hatred of humanity
4.	antithesis	d.	relating to the assignment of names
5.	appellative	e.	dislike
6.	anthropic	f.	not suitable; lacking judgment
7.	appellation	g.	belonging to an earlier period
8.	antipathy	h.	related to the human race
9.	apt	i.	too old to be useful
10.	antique	j.	the opposite of

REVIEW 1–5

Matching

Match each of the following roots or prefixes to its meaning:

1. ANTHROP
2. ACER/ACID/ACRI
3. ACT/AG
4. AMBI-
5. ANTE-
6. AD-/AF-
7. ALTER
8. AP/EPT
9. AM
10. AGOG

a. harsh, bitter, sour
b. skill, ability
c. leader
d. to, toward
e. other
f. human being
g. around, on both sides
h. love, liking
i. drive, do, lead, act, move
j. before

Fill-ins

Fill in the blanks with the word that fits the definition:

| aliment | anarchy | annuity | acumen | pedagogue |
| unapt | antiquate | agrarian | inanimate | perambulate |

1. teacher; a dogmatic teacher _____
2. to walk about _____
3. to make old-fashioned or obsolete _____
4. something that nourishes _____
5. not exhibiting life _____
6. absence of political authority _____
7. not suitable _____
8. yearly income payment _____
9. relating to farming or rural matters _____
10. keenness of judgment _____

True or False

If the statement is correct, put (T) True; if it is incorrect, put (F) False.

1. An anachronism is something that is in tune with the times. _____
2. Things that are coeval are equally evil. _____
3. An altimeter is an instrument that measures elevation. _____
4. An amphora is a Greek or Roman jar with two handles. _____
5. Antagonistic people do not usually display hostility. _____

ROUNDUP 6

- **AQU/AQUA** (WATER 水) [L]

  aquarium   *n.* a tank for holding fish and sea plants 水族馆；养鱼池；金鱼缸

  aqueduct   *n.* a large pipe or canal that carries water to large communities 沟渠，导水管

  aquatic   *adj.* relating to things that occur in or on water 水生的，水栖的

           n. aquatic plants or sports 水生植物；水上运动

  sub**aqu**eous   *adj.* created or existing under water 水中的；水下的

  aquifer   *n.* underground rock formation that bears water 蓄水层；含水土层

- **ARCH** (FIRST, CHIEF, RULE, SUPERIOR 第一的；主要的；统治；高级的) [G]

  archangel   *n.* chief angel 大天使；天使长

  archaic   *adj.* out of date 古代的；陈旧的；过时的

  patri**arch**y   *n.* family or community governed by men 父系社会；父权制；家长制

  archeology   *n.* study of material evidence of past human life 考古学

  archetype   *n.* original model after which others are patterned 原型

- **ARM/ARMA** (WEAPONS 武器) [L]

  armistice   *n.* truce; temporary stop to fighting 休战；停战

  armada   *n.* fleet of warships 舰队

  dis**arma**ment   *n.* reduction of a nation's weapons and military forces 裁军

  armor   *n.* covering that protects one's body against weapons 盔甲；装甲

  armadillo   *n.* burrowing mammal that has armorlike long plates 犰狳

- **ART** (ART 技术；艺术) [L]

  artisan   *n.* craftsperson 工匠；技工

  artifact   *n.* object made by human craft 人工制品；手工艺品

  art nouveau   a late nineteenth-century style of art 新艺术(十九世纪末的艺术风格)

  artificial   *adj.* made by human action 人造的；人工的

  artifice   *n.* artful expedient 诡计；权宜之计；巧妙的方法

- **ASTR/ASTER** (STAR 星) [G]

  asterisk   *n.* the sign 星号(*)

  astral   *adj.* relating to stars 星的；星际的

  astronaut   *n.* a person who travels in space 宇航员

  astrology   *n.* study of the influence of the stars and planets on human beings 占星术；占星学

  astronomy   *n.* scientific study of the stars and other bodies in the universe 天文学

Work 6

Match each word with its definition:

1. aqueduct
2. patriarchy
3. archetype
4. artisan

    a. craftsperson

    b. fleet of warships

    c. existing underwater

    d. community or family governed by men

5. armada
6. astronomy
7. subaqueous
8. astral
9. disarmament
10. artifact

e. scientific study of the stars and other bodies in the universe
f. reduction of a nation's weapons and military forces
g. object made by human craft
h. relating to the stars
i. original model after which others are patterned
j. a canal that carries water to communities

ROUNDUP 7

- **AUD/AUDI/AUS** (BOLD, DARING, LISTEN, HEAR 大胆的；英勇的；听，听见)［L］

  auditorium   *n.* part of a theater where the audience sits 观众席

  audible   *adj.* capable of being heard 听得见的

  audacious   *adj.* bold, daring 无畏的；大胆的

  audacity   *n.* fearless, daring, and adventurousness 无畏；大胆；敢作敢为

  auscultation   *n.* listening to the heart or other organs 听诊

- **AUG/AUX** (INCREASE 增加)［L］

  augment   *v.* to make greater 增加；增大

  in**aug**urate   *v.* to begin or start officially 开创，开辟；开幕

  august   *adj.* dignified; awe-inspiring 威严的；令人敬畏的

  augur   *v.* to foretell 预言；占卜

  auxiliary   *n. /adj.* supplementary 辅助物（的）；补助物（的）

- **AUTO-** (SELF 自己)［G］

  automatic   *adj.* self-acting or self-regulating 自动的

  autograph   *n.* person's signature 亲笔签名

  autonomic   *adj.* occurring involuntarily 自发的；自动的

  autonomous   *adj.* self-governing 自治的；自主的

  autobiography *n.* self-written account of one's own life 自传

- **BE-** (MAKE 使)［OE］

  befuddled   *adj.* confused; perplexed 迷惑的；糊里糊涂的

  beguile   *v.* to delude; deceive by guile 迷惑；使着迷；欺骗

  besmirched   *adj.* stained; soiled 被玷污的；被污染的

  bedecked   *adj.* adorned in a showy manner 过分装饰的；过分点缀的

  bedizen   *v.* to dress in a showy manner 俗丽地穿着；过分地打扮

- **BEL/BELL** (WAR 战争)［L］

  re**bel**   *v.* to carry out armed resistance to the government 造反；反叛，反抗

  bellicose   *adj.* aggressive; warlike 好斗的；好战的

  belligerent   *adj.* hostile; tending to fight 好战的；交战的

  ante**bell**um   *adj.* existing before a war (美国南北)战争前的

  post**bell**um   *adj.* existing after a war (美国南北)战争后的

Work 7

Match each word with its definition:

1. autonomic
2. august
3. audacious
4. antebellum
5. auscultation
6. bedizen
7. befuddled
8. autonomous
9. belligerent
10. augment

a. to make greater
b. existing before a war
c. self-governing
d. confused; perplexed
e. hostile; tending to fight
f. bold; daring
g. occurring involuntarily
h. to dress in a showy manner
i. dignified; awe-inspiring
j. listening to the heart or other organs

ROUNDUP 8

- **BEN-/BON-** (WELL, GOOD, FAVORABLE 好的；有利的；良好的) [L]

  beneficent   *adj.* kindly; doing good 慈善的；善行的

  benediction   *n.* blessing 祝福

  benevolent   *adj.* generous; charitable 慈善的；仁慈的

  benign   *adj.* harmless; kind 良性的；和蔼的，亲切的

  bonanza   *n.* large amount 大量

- **BI-** (TWO, TWICE, DOUBLE 二；两次；两倍) [L]

  bicycle   *n.* light-framed vehicle mounted on two wheels 自行车

  biannual   *adj.* happening twice each year 一年两次的

  bifurcate   *v.* to divide into two parts (使) 分叉，分开

  bicuspid   *adj.* having two points 有两尖头的

  bivalve   *adj.* having a shell composed of two valves 双壳的

- **BIO** (LIFE 生物) [G]

  biologist   *n.* a scientist who studies life 生物学家

  biosphere   *n.* part of the Earth's surface and atmosphere in which life exists 生物圈

  bionics   *n.* science concerned with applying biological systems to engineering problems 仿生学

  biotic   *adj.* produced by living organisms 生物的；有关生命的

  sym**bio**tic   *adj.* relating to a relationship of mutual benefit or dependence 共生的

- **BREV** (SHORT 短的) [L]

  ab**brev**iate   *v.* to make shorter 缩短，缩写；使缩略

  ab**brev**iation   *n.* act or product of shortening 省略，简略；缩写

  brevity   *n.* a state of briefness in duration 短促，短暂，简洁，简短

  breve   *n.* symbol over a vowel to indicate a short sound 短音符号

  breviary   *n.* a book containing hymns and prayers for canonical hours 祈祷书

- **CAP/CAPT/CEPT/CIP** (HOLD, SEIZE, TAKE 抓；拿；握) [L]

capable	*adj.* having ability or capacity 有能力的
inter**cep**t	*v.* to interrupt the course of 拦截；截住
captious	*adj.* faultfinding; intending to entrap, as in an argument 挑剔的；吹毛求疵的
pre**cept**	*n.* principle that prescribes a course of action 规矩，规则
capture	*v.* to take captive; seize 捕获；占领

Work 8

Match each word with its definition:

1. biotic	a.	to interrupt the course of
2. capture	b.	happening twice a year
3. bicuspid	c.	shortness in duration
4. breve	d.	harmless; kind
5. biannual	e.	produced by living organisms
6. intercept	f.	having two points
7. benign	g.	symbol over a vowel that indicates a short sound
8. biosphere	h.	generous; charitable
9. benevolent	i.	part of the Earth's surface and atmosphere in which life exists
10. brevity	j.	to seize

ROUNDUP 9

- **CAP/CAPIT** (HEAD 头) [L]

per **capit**a	per unit of population 按人口计算；人均
capitol	*n.* building in which a state legislature meets 国会大厦
de**capit**ate	*v.* to behead 斩首
capitulate	*v.* to surrender 投降，屈服
captain	*n.* someone who commands others 队长；首领，领袖

- **CARD/CORD** (HEART 心) [L]

cardiac	*adj.* relating to the heart 心脏的
cardiology	*n.* branch of medicine concerned with the heart 心脏病学
cordial	*adj.* warm and sincere 热忱的，诚挚的
con**cord**	*n.* harmony; agreement 和谐；和睦；一致
dis**cord**ant	*adj.* disagreeable in sound; conflicting 不和谐的，刺耳的；有冲突的

- **CARN** (FLESH, BODY 肉；身体) [L]

carnal	*adj.* of the flesh or body 肉体的
carnation	*n.* perennial plant with showy flowers 康乃馨
carnivore	*n.* animal or plant that feeds on flesh 肉食动植物
in**carn**ate	*v.* to give bodily form to 使具体化；使实体化；体现
carnage	*n.* massive slaughter, as in war 大屠杀，残杀

- **CATA-** (DOWN, DOWNWARD 向下；朝下方) [G]

  catalyst   *n.* something causing change 催化剂；促进因素

  cataract   *n.* a high waterfall; a great downpour 大瀑布；暴雨

  catapult   *n.* an ancient military machine for hurling missiles 弩炮，石弩

  cataclysm   *n.* violent upheaval 剧变，激变；动乱

  catastrophic   *adj.* relating to a great calamity 灾难的；浩劫的

- **CED/CEED/CESS** (YIELD, SURRENDER, MOVE, GO 喊叫；让步；移动) [L]

  cede   *v.* to surrender; yield 放弃；屈服；让步

  ac**ced**e   *v.* to agree to 同意，准许

  pre**ced**e   *v.* to go before 领先于；先于

  ante**ced**ent   *n.* something that comes before 先例；祖先

  in**cess**ant   *adj.* never ceasing 不停的；持续不断的

Work 9

Match each word with its definition:

1. concord
2. incarnate
3. captain
4. antecedent
5. cordial
6. cataract
7. decapitate
8. catastrophic
9. cede
10. carnivore

a. warm and sincere
b. animal or plant that feeds on flesh
c. a high waterfall; a great downpour
d. relating to a great calamity
e. to surrender; yield
f. something that comes before
g. harmony; agreement
h. to behead
i. someone who commands others
j. to give bodily form to

ROUNDUP 10

- **CELER** (SWIFT 快速的) [L]

  ac**celer**ate   *v.* to increase speed 加速

  ac**celer**ant   *n.* substance used as a catalyst 促进剂，催化剂

  celerity   *n.* swiftness; speed 敏捷；快速

  de**celer**ation   *n.* decrease the velocity of 降速，减速

  ac**celer**ando   *n.* musical direction for a dual quickening in time 渐速音

- **CENTR** (CENTER 中心) [L]

  con**centr**ic   *adj.* having a common center 同中心的；同轴的

  centrifugal   *adj.* moving or directed away from a center 离心的

  centripetal   *adj.* moving or directed toward a center 向心的

  con**centr**ate   *v.* to direct toward a center 集中；聚集；浓缩

  centric   *adj.* situated near or at the center of something 中央的；中心的

- **CENT-** (HUNDRED 百) [L]

  centimeter   *n.* unit of length equal to one hundredth of a meter 厘米

  centenary   *adj.* relating to a 100-year period 百年的

  centenarian   *n.* one who is 100 years old or more 百岁老人

  century   *n.* period of 100 years 世纪

  centennial   *adj.* relating to a period of 100 years; occurring every 100 years 百年的，世纪的；百年一次的

- **CERN** (PERCEIVE 感觉；觉察) [L]

  con**cern**   *v.* to regard for or be interest in 关系到，涉及，关心，关注

  dis**cern**   *v.* to perceive; detect 辨别；识别

  dis**cern**ing   *adj.* showing good judgment; perceptive 有识别力的；有眼力的

  indis**cern**ible   *adj.* difficult to perceive 难识别的；难以分辨的

  uncon**cern**edly   *adv.* in a way that is unworried 不在乎地；漠不关心地

- **CERT** (CERTAIN 确信，确定) [L]

  certify   *v.* to confirm formally as genuine 证明；保证

  certificate   *n.* document confirming the truth of something 证书；证明

  certainty   *n.* the state or fact of being certain 确定性；必然性

  certitude   *n.* a state of being certain; sureness of occurrence 确信；确实

  as**cert**ain   *v.* to discover with certainty 查明，弄清；确定

Work 10

Match each word with its definition:

1.	centrifugal	a.	moving toward a center
2.	certitude	b.	swiftness; speed
3.	centennial	c.	substance used as a catalyst
4.	centenarian	d.	to discover with certainty
5.	indiscernible	e.	relating to a period of 100 years
6.	celerity	f.	showing good judgment; perceptive
7.	discerning	g.	moving away from a center
8.	accelerant	h.	difficult to perceive
9.	centripetal	i.	a state of being certain; sureness of occurrence
10.	ascertain	j.	someone 100 years old or more

REVIEW 6–10

Matching

Match each of the following roots or prefixes to its meaning:

1.	ASTR/ASTER	a.	short
2.	ARM/ARMA	b.	flesh, body
3.	AUG/AUS	c.	weapons
4.	BE-	d.	swift
5.	BIO	e.	down

6.	BREV	f.	perceive
7.	CARN	g.	make
8.	CATA-	h.	star
9.	CELER	i	increase
10.	CERN	j.	life

Fill-ins

Fill in the blanks with the word that fits the definition:

benediction	augur	symbiotic	archaic	captious
catapult	incessant	centripetal	centrifugal	subaqueous

1. relating to a relationship of mutual benefit or dependence _____
2. to foretell _____
3. created or existing underwater _____
4. out of date _____
5. never ceasing _____
6. moving away from a center _____
7. blessing _____
8. an ancient military machine for hurling missiles _____
9. moving toward a center _____
10. faultfinding; intending to entrap, as in argument _____

True or False

If the statement is correct, put (T) True; if it is incorrect, put (F) False.

1. Antebellum refers to a period after a war. _____
2. Archeology is the study of the influence of stars and planets on human life. _____
3. Auscultation means speaking clearly and fluently. _____
4. A patriarchy is a family or community governed by men. _____
5. Centennial relates to a period of 1,000 years. _____

ROUNDUP 11

- **CHRON** (TIME, A LONG TIME 时间；长期）[G]
chronic	*adj.* constant; prolonged 慢性的；长期的
chronicle	*n.* a record of historical events 编年史；年代记
chronometer	*n.* instrument that measures time 计时器
ana**chron**ism	*n.* something out of the proper time 不合时代的事物
chronology	*n.* arrangement in order of occurrence 年表

- **CID/CIS** (CUT, KILL 切；杀) [L]

homi**cid**e	*n.* killing of one person by another 杀人
s**cis**sors	*n.* cutting instrument with two blades 剪刀
exor**cis**e	*v.* to expel evil spirits 驱邪；除怪
ex**cis**ion	*n.* remove by cutting 切除
abs**cis**sion	*n.* natural separation of flowers, leaves, etc. from plants 脱落，脱离

- **CIRCU-/CIRCUM-** (AROUND 周围，环绕) [L]

circumvent	*v.* to avoid; get around 规避；绕行
circumflex	*adj.* curving around 弯曲的
circuitous	*adj.* taking a roundabout course 迂回的；绕行的
circumlocution	*n.* indirect way of saying something 委婉的说法；遁词
circumscribe	*v.* to limit 限制

- **CIT/CITAT** (CALL, START 召唤；开始) [L]

cite	*v.* to mention as illustration or proof; quote as an example 引证；引用
citable	*adj.* able to be brought forward as support or proof 可引用的
citation	*n.* the act of citing; quotation 引证；引文；引句
re**cit**e	*v.* to say aloud before an audience something rehearsed 背诵
re**citat**ive	*adj.* having the character of a recital 背诵的；叙述的

- **CIVI** (CITIZEN 市民) [L]

civil	*adj.* relating to a citizen or citizens; of ordinary citizens or ordinary community life 公民的；民间的；民事的
civic	*adj.* relating to a city, a citizen, or citizenship 城市的；市民的，公民的
civilize	*v.* to raise from barbarism to civilization; educate in matters of culture 使文明；使开化
civilian	*n.* a citizen who is not an acting member of the military or police 平民，百姓
civility	*n.* courteous behavior 礼貌；礼仪

Work 11

Match each word with its definition:

1.	excision	a.	constant; prolonged
2.	circumflex	b.	relating to a city or a citizen
3.	cite	c.	to say aloud before an audience something rehearsed
4.	anachronism	d.	natural separation of flowers and leaves from plants
5.	recite	e.	to mention as an illustration
6.	civic	f.	to avoid; get around
7.	abscission	g.	a citizen who is not a member of the military
8.	civilian	h.	curving around
9.	chronic	i.	something out of the proper time
10.	circumvent	j.	remove by cutting

ROUNDUP 12

- **CLAM/CLAIM** (CALL OUT, SHOUT 喊叫) [L]

ex**claim**	v. to cry out suddenly; utter vehemently 突然呼喊; 惊叫
ex**clam**ation	n. an abrupt forceful utterance; an outcry 感叹; 惊叫
clamor	n. loud outcry 吵闹, 喧嚷
re**claim**	v. to demand the return of something 要求归还
ac**clam**ation	n. shout of enthusiastic approval 欢呼, 喝彩

- **CLEMEN** (MILD, KIND, MERCIFUL 温和; 善良; 仁慈) [L]

clemency	n. disposition to show mercy; merciful act; mildness 仁慈; 宽容; 温厚
clement	adj. inclined to be merciful; mild 仁慈的; 温和的
in**clemen**t	adj. stormy; showing no mercy 狂风暴雨的; 冷酷无情的
in**clemen**cy	n. a state of showing no mercy 严酷; 冷酷无情
in**clemen**tly	adv. in a way that shows no mercy 严酷地

- **CLAUD/CLAUS/CLOS/CLUD/CLUS** (SHUT, CLOSE 关闭) [L]

clause	n. a stipulation or provision in a document 条款
ex**clud**e	v. to keep out; reject; put out 排除; 排斥; 逐出
se**clus**ion	n. isolation; solitude 隔离; 隐退; 孤立
re**clus**e	n. a person who lives in seclusion 隐居者, 隐士
oc**clud**e	v. to cause to become closed; obstruct 使闭塞; 封闭

- **CLI/CLIN/CLIV** (LEAN, INCLINE, SLOPE 倾斜; 趋向, 趋势) [L]

climax	n. point of greatest intensity in an ascending progression 高潮; 顶点
in**clin**ation	n. a tendency toward a certain condition 倾向; 爱好
dis**inclin**ation	n. lack of inclination; reluctance 不感兴趣; 不情愿
syn**clin**al	adj. sloping downward from opposite directions and meeting in a common point 向斜的
pro**cliv**ity	n. tendency; inclination 趋向; 倾向

- **CO-/COL-/COM-/CON-/COR-** (TOGETHER, WITH 一起, 共同) [L]

coherent	adj. understandable; sticking together 连贯的; 清晰的; 黏在一起的
collaborate	v. to work together 合作; 合谋; 勾结, 通敌
communicate	v. to exchange thoughts and information 交流; 通信
conformity	n. harmony; agreement 符合; 一致
corroborate	v. to confirm 证实; 使坚固

Work 12

Match each word with its definition:

1. collaborate
2. clamor
3. occlude
4. conformity
5. acclamation

a. a person who lives in seclusion
b. shout of enthusiastic approval
c. inclined to be merciful
d. harmony; agreement
e. to work together

6. disinclination
7. clement
8. inclement
9. proclivity
10. recluse

f. to cause to become closed
g. tendency; inclination
h. lack of inclination
i. loud outcry
j. stormy; showing no mercy

ROUNDUP 13

- **COD**（BOOK 书）[L]

code	*n.* systematic, comprehensive collection of laws 法规，法典
	system of symbols used for sending messages that require secrecy 密码；编码；代码
de**cod**e	*v.* to convert from code into text 解码，译码
codify	*v.* to reduce to a code 把…编成法典，使法律成文化
codex	*n.* manuscript volume of a classic work 抄本
codicil	*n.* an appendix to a will 遗嘱的附录

- **COGNI/GNO**（LEARN, KNOW 学习；知道）[L/G]

cognition	*n.* mental process by which knowledge is acquired 认知
in**cogni**to	*adj.* in disguise; concealing one's identity 隐瞒身份的；隐姓埋名的
dia**gno**sis	*n.* process of determining the nature and cause of a disease 诊断
pro**gno**sticate	*v.* to predict on the basis of present conditions 预测，预言
a**gno**sia	*n.* loss of the ability to interpret sensory stimuli 失认(症)

- **CONTRA-/CONTRO-**（AGAINST, OPPOSITE 相反）[L]

contradict	*v.* to speak against 反驳；与…矛盾
contrary	*adj.* opposed 相反的
contravene	*v.* to act contrary to; to violate 抵触；反驳；违反
contraindicate	*v.* to indicate the inadvisability of the use of a medicine 显示(治疗或用药)不当
controversy	*n.* dispute between sides holding opposing views 争议；争论

- **CORP**（BODY 身体）[L]

corpse	*n.* a dead body 尸体
corpulent	*adj.* excessively fat 肥胖的
corporeal	*adj.* concerned with the body 肉体的；身体的
corpus	*n.* a large collection of writings 全集；文集
in**corp**orate	*v.* to unite one thing with something else already in existence 把…并入；包含

- **COSM**（UNIVERSE 宇宙）[G]

cosmic	*adj.* relating to the universe; infinite; vast 宇宙的；无限的
micro**cosm**	*n.* a small system having analogies to a larger system 缩影
cosmology	*n.* study of the physical universe 宇宙学
cosmos	*n.* the universe as a harmonious whole 宇宙
cosmopolitan	*adj.* common to or having elements from all over the world 世界性的；四海一家的

Work 13

Match each word with its definition:

1.	cognition	a.	manuscript volume of a classic work
2.	contradict	b.	concerned with the body
3.	codex	c.	study of the physical universe
4.	cosmos	d.	mental process by which knowledge is acquired
5.	corporeal	e.	to speak against
6.	code	f.	to predict on the basis of present conditions
7.	contravene	g.	the universe as a harmonious whole
8.	cosmology	h.	to act contrary to
9.	corpus	i.	systematic, comprehensive collection of laws
10.	prognosticate	j.	a large collection of writings

ROUNDUP 14

- **CRACY/CRAT** (GOVERNMENT, RULE, STRENGTH 政府；统治；势力) [G]

  aristo**cracy**　　*n.* hereditary ruling class 贵族

  bureau**cracy**　　*n.* administration of a government or a large complex 官僚主义；官僚机构

  pluto**cracy**　　*n.* society ruled by the wealthy 财阀政治

  theo**cracy**　　*n.* government by priests 神权统治

  techno**crat**　　*n.* a strong believer in technology 技术统治论者

- **CREA** (BRING FORTH, CREATE 创造) [L]

  create　　*v.* to bring into being 创造

  creature　　*n.* something created 创造物；a living being 生物

  re**crea**te　　*v.* to give fresh life to 再创造；to refresh mentally or physically 消遣，娱乐

  pro**crea**tion　　*n.* the conceiving of offspring; producing or creating 生育，生殖；生产

  mis**crea**te　　*v.* to make or shape badly 误创；拙劣地创造

- **CRED** (BELIEVE, TRUST 信任) [L]

  credo　　*n.* statement of belief or principle; creed 信条；教义

  credentials　　*n.* evidence concerning one's right to confidence or authority 资格证书；信任状

  credible　　*adj.* believable; plausible 可信的；可靠的

  credence　　*n.* acceptance of something as true 相信；信赖

  in**cred**ulous　　*adj.* skeptical; doubtful 怀疑的

- **CRE/CRESC/CRET/CRU** (RISE, GROW 上升；生长，成长) [L]

  ac**cru**e　　*v.* to increase; come about as a result of growth 增长；获得；积累

  crescent　　*adj.* increasing; waxing, as the moon 逐渐增加的；月亮渐满的

  crescendo　　*n.* in music, a gradual increase in the volume or intensity of sound 声音渐强

  in**cre**ment　　*n.* something added; process of increasing 增量；增加；增额；盈余

  in**cresc**ent　　*adj.* waxing; showing a surface that is ever larger and lighted 渐盈的

- **CRIT** (SEPARATE, JUDGE 分开；判断) [G]

critical	*adj.* inclined to judge severely; characterized by careful judgment 严厉批评的；吹毛求疵的	
criterion	*n.* a standard on which a judgment can be made (评判的) 标准	
hypo**crit**ical	*adj.* professing beliefs that one does not possess; false 伪善的；虚伪的	
criticism	*n.* a critical comment or judgment 批评；指责	
critique	*n.* a critical review or commentary 批评；评论性的文章	

Work 14

Match each word with its definition:

1. technocrat
2. incredulous
3. accrue
4. miscreate
5. critical
6. procreation
7. criterion
8. increscent
9. theocracy
10. credible

a. believable; plausible
b. producing or creating
c. government by priests
d. waxing
e. a standard on which a judgment can be made
f. a strong believer in technology
g. to increase; come about as a result of growth
h. to inclined to judge severely
i. to make or shape badly
j. skeptical; doubtful

ROUNDUP 15

- **COUR/CUR** (RUN, COURSE 跑；路程) [L]

con**cur**rence	*n.* agreement in opinion; simultaneous occurrence 赞同；同时发生
courier	*n.* messenger 信使；情报员，通讯员
curriculum	*n.* the courses offered by an educational institution 课程
pre**cur**sor	*n.* a forerunner or predecessor 先锋，先驱；先兆
current	*n.* a steady, smooth, onward movement 趋势；倾向

- **CUR/CURA** (CARE 关心；照看，照顾) [L]

curator	*n.* someone who overseas a museum collection 博物馆馆长
curé	*n.* a parish priest 教区牧师
curette	*n.* surgical instrument that removes growths from a body cavity 耳匙
curative	*adj.* tending to cure 有疗效的
curate	*n.* a cleric who is in charge of a parish 教堂牧师

- **CYCL/CYCLO** (CIRCLE, WHEEL, CYCLE 圆圈；轮子；周期) [G]

cyclical	*adj.* characterized by cycles; moving in cycles 循环的，周期的
cyclosis	*n.* rotary motion of protoplasm within a cell 胞质环流
cycloid	*adj.* resembling a circle 圆形的
cyclops	*n.* in Greek mythology, any of a race of one-eyed giants 独眼巨人
cyclothymia	*n.* affective disorder characterized by alternating periods of depression and elation 躁郁症

- **DE-** (INTENSIVE; FROM, DOWN, AWAY, AGAINST, THOROUGHLY 表加强; 从; 向下; 离开; 相反; 彻底) [L]

demolish	*v.* to tear down completely 摧毁; 拆除; 破坏
deplore	*v.* to disapprove of; regret 谴责; 哀叹, 悲叹
deride	*v.* to mock 嘲笑; 嘲弄
denounce	*v.* to condemn 谴责, 指责; 抨击
deprecate	*v.* to belittle; express disapproval 轻视; 反对

- **DEC-/DECA-** (TEN 十) [G]

decalogue	*n.* the Ten Commandments 摩西十诫
decimate	*v.* to destroy a large part of; inflict great destruction on 大破坏; 大毁灭
decade	*n.* a period of ten years 十年(期)
decahedron	*n.* a polyhedron with ten faces 十面体
decapod	*n.* a crustacean having ten legs 十足目动物

Work 15

Match each word with its definition:

1. deride		a.	to tear down completely
2. decahedron		b.	a crustacean having ten legs
3. curative		c.	one who oversees a museum collection
4. cyclical		d.	forerunner
5. precursor		e.	resembling a circle
6. concurrence		f.	simultaneous occurrence
7. decapod		g.	to mock
8. cycloid		h.	characterized by cycles
9. curator		i.	a polyhedron with ten faces
10. demolish		j.	tending to cure

REVIEW 11–15

Matching

Match each of the following roots or prefixes to its meaning:

1. CID/CIS		a.	body
2. CIRCU-/CIRCUM-		b.	call out, shout
3. CLAM/CLAIM		c.	believe, trust
4. CLEMEN		d.	book, writing
5. COD		e.	run, course
6. CORP		f.	mild, kind, merciful
7. CRED		g.	cut, kill
8. CRIT		h.	from, down, away, against, thoroughly
9. COUR/CUR		i.	around
10. DE-		j.	separate, judge

Fill-ins

Fill in the blanks with the word that fits the definition:

criterion	synclinal	cosmopolitan	civil	coherent
corpulent	cyclothymia	miscreate	deprecate	cite

1. relating to a citizen or citizens; of ordinary citizens or ordinary community life _____
2. common to or having elements from all over the world _____
3. sticking together; understandable _____
4. to mention as illustration or proof; quote as an example _____
5. a standard on which a judgment can be made _____
6. excessively fat _____
7. to make or shape badly _____
8. to belittle; express disapproval _____
9. sloping downward from opposite directions and meeting in a common point _____
10. an affective disorder characterized by alternating periods of depression and elation _____

True or False

If the statement is correct, put（T）True; if it is incorrect, put（F）False.

1. A chronometer is an instrument that measures wind speed. _____
2. A proclivity is a tendency or inclination. _____
3. To prognosticate is to predict based on present conditions. _____
4. Something increscent is growing or showing a surface that is ever larger and lighted. _____
5. Decahedrons are polyhedrons with nine faces. _____

ROUNDUP 16

- **DEI/DIV**（GOD 神；上帝）[L]

divine	*adj.* having the nature of a god 神的；神圣的
divinity	*n.* the state of being divine 神性；神力
deify	*v.* to raise to the condition of a god 把…神化，把…奉若神明
deism	*n.* belief that a God has created the universe, but exerts no control or influence on it 自然神论
deific	*adj.* making divine; characterized by a godlike nature 神圣的；予以神化的

- **DEMI-**（PART 局部的，一部分的）[L]

demigod	*n.* the male offspring of a god and a mortal; a minor god 半神半人；小神
demimonde	*n.* a group whose respectability is questionable 名声不好的人
demirelief	*n.* structural relief having modeled forms projecting halfway from a background 半浮雕
demirep	*n.* a person whose reputation is doubtful 名声不好的人
demitasse	*n.* a small cup of espresso 小杯咖啡

- **DEM** (COMMON PEOPLE 普通民众) [G]

  demographic   *adj.* related to population balance 人口统计的

  epidemic   *n.* a widespread disease that affects many people at the same time 传染病；流行病

  pandemic   *adj.* spread over a whole area or country 广泛的；普遍的；流行的

  demagogue   *n.* a leader who appeals to emotion or prejudice 煽动者

  democratic   *adj.* of or for the people; popular 大众的；民主的

- **DERM** (SKIN 皮肤) [G]

  dermatology   *n.* branch of medicine concerned with pathology of the skin 皮肤科；皮肤病学

  dermatitis   *n.* inflammation of the skin 皮炎

  epidermis   *n.* the outer layer of the skin 表皮，上皮

  taxidermist   *n.* one who works in the art of stuffing and mounting skins of dead animals (动物标本) 录制师

  pachyderm   *n.* a thick-skinned hoofed animal like the elephant or hippopotamus 厚皮动物

- **DI-** (TWO, DOUBLE 两，双数) [G]

  diphase   *adj.* having two phases 双相的，复相的

  dichotomy   *n.* division into two usually contradictory parts 二分法

  dilemma   *n.* situation necessitating a choice between two unsatisfactory options 进退两难的窘境

  dibromide   *n.* chemical compound having two bromine atoms 二溴化物

  dihedral   *adj.* two-sided 二面的

Work 16

Match each word with its definition:

1. demigod	a.	a leader who appeals to emotion or prejudice
2. pachyderm	b.	one who works in the art of stuffing and mounting skins of dead animal
3. deific	c.	chemical compound having two bromine atoms
4. diphase	d.	a minor god
5. taxidermist	e.	a person whose reputation is doubtful
6. demirep	f.	to raise to the condition of a god
7. deify	g.	making divine; having a godlike nature
8. demagogue	h.	spread over a whole area or country
9. pandemic	i.	a thick-skinned hoofed animal
10. dibromide	j.	having two phases

ROUNDUP 17

- **DIA-** (ACROSS, THROUGH, BETWEEN 交叉；穿过；两者之中) [G]

  diagram   *n.* drawing that explains the relationship between parts of a whole 图解；图表

  diachronic   *adj.* concerned with phenomena as they change through time 历时的

  diatribe   *n.* an abusive denunciation 诽谤；谩骂；苛评

  dialogue   *n.* a conversation between two or more people 对话

  diaphanous   *adj.* so fine as to be almost transparent or translucent 透明的；清澈的

- **DIC/DICT**（SAY, SPEAK, PRONOUNCE 说，讲；宣布）[L]

  e**dict**　　　　　*n.* a formal command 法令；布告；诏书；谕旨

  bene**dict**ion　　*n.* blessing 祝福；赐福；恩赐

  in**dict**　　　　　*v.* to charge with a crime 控告，起诉

  male**dict**ion　　*n.* curse 咒骂，诅咒；坏话

  dictum　　　　*n.* authoritarian statement 声明

- **DIF-/DIS-**（APART, AWAY, NOT 分离；离开；不，没有）[L]

  diffuse　　　　*v.* to spread out 四散，扩散；传播

  disparity　　　*n.* difference 不同；不等；差异

  dissuade　　　*v.* to persuade someone to alter intentions 劝阻，劝止

  dispassionate　*adj.* impartial; unaffected by emotion 不带感情的，无偏见的，公平的；平心静气的

  disseminate　　*v.* to spread; scatter 散布；广为传播；宣传

- **DOC/DOCT**（TEACH, PROVE 教；证明）[L]

  doctrinaire　　*adj.* relating to a person who cannot compromise about points of a theory or doctrine 空谈理论的；教条主义的

  docent　　　　*n.* lecturer 讲师；解说员

  doctrine　　　*n.* principle or system presented for acceptance or belief 教义；信条；主义；学说

  in**doct**rinate　　*v.* to instruct in a body of principles 灌输；教导

  docile　　　　*adj.* willing to be taught; yielding to supervision 容易教的；驯服的，温顺的

- **DON**（GIVE 给予）[L]

  donate　　　　*v.* to give 捐赠；捐献

  donation　　　*n.* the act of giving to a cause or charity 捐赠；捐献；捐款

  donor　　　　*n.* one who contributes a donation to a cause or charity 捐赠者

  donee　　　　*n.* one who receives a gift 受赠者

  donatio mortis causa　gift by reason of death 死因赠与

Work 17

Match each word with its definition:

1. dispassionate
2. dictum
3. donatio mortis causa
4. malediction
5. donate
6. diaphanous
7. diffuse
8. docent
9. dialogue
10. docile

a. a conversation between two or more people

b. lecturer

c. to spread out

d. authoritarian statement

e. willing to be taught

f. gift by reason of death

g. unaffected by emotion

h. so fine as to be almost transparent or translucent

i. curse

j. to give

ROUNDUP 18

- **DOG/DOX** (OPINION, BELIEF, PRAISE 观点；信念；赞颂) [G]

  dogmatic   *adj.* characterized by an authoritarian assertion of unproved principles 教条的；武断的

  ortho**dox**   *adj.* adhering to what is commonly accepted or traditional 正统的；传统的；惯常的

  para**dox**   *n.* self-contradictory assertion based on valid deduction from acceptable premises 悖论

  hetero**dox**   *adj.* not in agreement with accepted beliefs 非正统的；异端的

  doxology   *n.* an expression of praise to God 荣耀颂；颂歌；上帝赞美诗

- **DOM/DOMIN** (MASTER, LORD 主人) [L]

  dominate   *v.* to control by authority or power 支配，控制；占优势

  dominion   *n.* control; sovereignty 支配；主权，统治权

  pre**domin**ant   *adj.* having greatest authority, influence, or force 主要的；有影响的；有力的；卓越的

  domination   *n.* control or power over another 控制；支配

  in**dom**itable   *adj.* unconquerable; not able to be subdued 不气馁的，不屈不挠的；不服输的

- **DORM** (SLEEP 睡眠) [L]

  dormant   *adj.* inactive; asleep 不活动的，静止的；休眠的；睡着的

  dormitory   *n.* a room used for sleeping quarters for many people 宿舍

  dormient   *adj.* sleeping; dormant; latent 冬眠的；蛰伏的

  dormitive   *adj.* causing sleep 催眠的；安眠的

  dormouse   *n.* a squirrel-like rodent 榛睡鼠

- **DROM/DROME** (RUN, STEP, ARENA 跑；步；场地) [G]

  dromedary   *n.* one-humped camel 单峰骆驼

  aero**drome**   *n.* an airport; military air base 飞机场；军用飞机基地

  hippo**drome**   *n.* arena for equestrian shows 赛马场，跑马场；竞技场

  dromond   *n.* a medieval sailing ship (中世纪的) 大型快速帆船

  cata**drom**ous   *adj.* inhabiting fresh water but migrating to the ocean to breed 为产卵而入海的

- **DU-** (DOUBLE, TWO 双，两) [L]

  duplicity   *n.* double-dealing; being twofold; deceptiveness 口是心非；表里不一；不诚实

  duplex   *adj.* twofold; double 二倍的；双重的

  duplicate   *adj.* identically copied from an original 复制的，副本的

  duplicator   *n.* machine that copies printed material 复印机

  duple   *adj.* consisting of two; double 二倍的；双重的

Work 18

Match each word with its definition:

1. indomitable   a. control; sovereignty
2. dormitive   b. not in agreement with accepted beliefs
3. dromond   c. arena for equestrian shows
4. doxology   d. asleep; inactive
5. duplicity   e. consisting of two

6. dominion   f.   unconquerable

7. hippodrome   g.   a medieval sailing ship

8. duple   h.   an expression of praise to God

9. heterodox   i.   causing sleep

10. dormant   j.   being twofold; deceptiveness

ROUNDUP 19

- **DUC/DUCT**（LEAD, PULL 导致；拉）[L]

in**duc**e	*v.* to bring about 导致；引诱，诱导
se**duc**e	*v.* to lead away from duty or proper conduct 唆使；引诱；怂恿
ab**duc**t	*v.* to carry off by force 绑架；诱拐
via**duc**t	*n.* series of arches used to carry a road over a valley or other roads 高架桥；高架铁路
ductile	*adj.* easily drawn into wire; easily molded 易延展的；有韧性的；柔软的

- **DUR**（HARD, LASTING 坚固；持久）[L]

durable	*adj.* able to withstand wear and tear 持久的，耐用的
duration	*n.* persistence in time; a period of existence 持续，持久；持续时间
en**dur**e	*v.* to carry on through hardships; bear tolerantly 忍受，忍耐
duress	*n.* constraint by threat; forcible confinement 强迫；监禁
ob**dur**ate	*adj.* hardened; hardhearted; inflexible 顽固的，执拗的；冷酷无情的；不易变通的

- **DYN/DYNAM**（POWER, ENERGY 力量，能量）[G]

dynamite	*n.* a class of powerful explosives 炸药
dynamo	*n.* a generator that produces current 发电机；an energetic person 精力充沛的人
dynasty	*n.* succession of rulers from the same line 王朝，朝代
dynamic	*adj.* marked by intensity and vigor 有活力的；精力充沛的
hetero**dyn**e	*adj.* having alternating currents with two different frequencies【电】外差的

- **DYS-**（BAD, IMPAIRED, ABNORMAL 不好的；受损的；不正常的）[G]

dysfunctional	*adj.* functioning abnormally 反常的
dyslexia	*n.* learning disorder causing impairment of the ability to read 诵读困难，阅读障碍
dystopia	*n.* an imaginary place in which life is bad 反面乌托邦
dysentery	*n.* disorder of the lower intestinal tract 痢疾
dyspepsia	*n.* indigestion 消化不良

- **E-/EX-**（APART, ABOVE, AWAY, BEYOND, FROM, OUT 分离，离开；超越；来自；出去）[L]

emit	*v.* to send out 放射；喷出；发射
enervate	*v.* to weaken 使衰弱；使失去活力
extricate	*v.* to free from 使解脱；使解除
exhale	*v.* to breathe out 呼出，发出
exotic	*adj.* unusual 异国的；异域风情的；不寻常的

Work 19

Match each word with its definition:

1. dynasty
2. obdurate
3. emit
4. endure
5. dystopia
6. ductile
7. dysentery
8. exhale
9. dynamo
10. seduce

a. an imaginary place where life is bad
b. easily molded
c. an energetic person
d. hardhearted
e. to breathe out
f. succession of rulers from the same line
g. to lead away from duty or proper conduct
h. disorder of lower intestinal tract
i. to send out
j. to carry on through hardships

ROUNDUP 20

- **ECTO-** (OUTSIDE, EXTERNAL 外在的；外的) [G]

  ectogenous   *adj.* able to develop outside a host 外生的；体外生活的

  ectoplasm   *n.* outer part of the cytoplasm of a cell 外质

  ectoderm   *n.* outermost germ layer of an embryo 外胚层

  ectopia   *n.* abnormal location of an organ or body part 异位（器官等的位置异常，一般是先天性的）

  ectopic pregnancy   development of an ovum outside the uterus 宫外孕

- **EGO** (I, SELF 自我) [L]

  egocentric   *adj.* self-centered 以自我为中心的；利己主义的

  egomania   *n.* extreme egocentrism 自大狂

  egotistical   *adj.* excessively self-centered 自我本位的；自负的

  egoist   *n.* one devoted to his or her own interests 利己主义者，自我主义者

  super **ego**   the part of the mind that opposes the desires of the id 超我

- **ENDO-** (WITHIN, INSIDE 内部，里面) [G]

  endomorph   *n.* a mineral enclosed inside another mineral 内容矿物

  endogenous   *adj.* growing from within; produced inside an organism 内生的；内源性的

  endoscope   *n.* instrument for viewing the inside of an organ of the body 内窥镜

  endobiotic   *adj.* living as a parasite within a host 体内寄生的

  endocardial   *adj.* relating to a membrane that lines the heart's interior 心脏内的；心内膜的

- **EPI-** (UPON, OVER, NEAR 在…之上；附近) [G]

  epidermis   *n.* outer layer of skin covering the dermis 表皮，上皮

  epidemic   *adj.* widely prevalent 流行的；传染性的

  epigeal   *adj.* living in or near the surface of the ground 贴地生长的；生长在地面上的

  epitaph   *n.* inscription on a tombstone 墓志铭，碑文

  epicenter   *n.* point in the Earth directly above the center of an earthquake 震中

    equator   *n.* the imaginary circle around the Earth, which is equidistant from the poles 赤道

    equation   *n.* statement asserting the equality of two mathematical expressions 方程式；等式

    equivocal   *adj.* ambiguous; misleading 模棱两可的；可疑的

    equanimity   *n.* composure 镇静，沉着

    in**equ**ity   *n.* unfairness 不平等，不公正

Work 20

Match each word with its definition:

1. egoist	a. able to develop outside a host
2. ectoderm	b. instrument to look inside an organ of the body
3. epigeal	c. excessively self-centered
4. endobiotic	d. composure
5. epitaph	e. inscription on a tombstone
6. ectogenous	f. unfairness
7. equanimity	g. outermost germ layer of an embryo
8. inequity	h. living near the surface of the ground
9. egotistical	i. living as a parasite within a host
10. endoscope	j. one devoted to his or her own interests

REVIEW 16–20

Matching

Match each of the following roots or prefixes to its meaning:

1. DEI/DIV	a. teach, prove
2. DEMI-	b. power, energy
3. DON	c. sleep
4. DOC/DOCT	d. within
5. DOM/DOMIN	e. apart, above, beyond, from
6. DORM	f. I, self
7. DYN/DYNAM	g. God
8. ENDO-	h. give
9. EGO	i. master, lord
10. E-/EX-	j. partly

Fill-ins

Fill in the blanks with the word that fits the definition:

dichotomy	obdurate	malediction	duple	ductile	inequity
pandemic	dermatitis	epigeal	donatio mortis causa		

1. spread over an entire area _____
2. consisting of two _____
3. hardened; inflexible; hardhearted _____
4. gift by reason of death _____
5. unfairness _____
6. division into two usually contradictory parts _____
7. living near or in the surface of the ground _____
8. easily molded _____
9. inflammation of the skin _____
10. curse _____

True or False

If the statement is correct, put（T）True; if it is incorrect, put（F）False.

1. A taxidermist is a thick-skinned hoofed animal. _____
2. Diachronic means concerned with phenomena of a particular time. _____
3. An ectoderm is the outermost germ layer of an embryo. _____
4. Doxology is adherence to unorthodox beliefs. _____
5. A dystopia is an imaginary place in which life is bad. _____

ROUNDUP 21

- **ERG**（WORK 工作；劳动）[G]

ergatocracy	n. government by workers 劳工执政
ergonomics	n. science of the design of equipment for maximizing productivity 人体工程学；工效学
erg	n. a unit of work 尔格(功和能的单位)
ergograph	n. instrument for measuring work capacity of a muscle while contracting 测功器；测力器（测量肌肉收缩时的力量的工具）
syn**erg**ic	adj. working together 合作的，协作的

- **ERR**（WANDER, MISTAKE 徘徊；错误）[L]

errant	adj. mistaken; straying from the proper course 错误的；偏离正路的
erratic	adj. lacking regularity; deviating from the customary course 不稳定的；偏离的；古怪的
erroneous	adj. mistaken 错误的；不正确的
err	v. to make a mistake 犯错；做错
erratum	n. mistake in writing or printing (印刷或书写中的)错误

- **ETH/ETHOS**（CHARACTER 特性）[G]

ethos	n. character peculiar to a person, people, or culture 气质；民族精神；社会思潮
bio**eth**ics	n. study of ethical implications of scientific discoveries, as in genetic engineering 生物伦理
ethic	n. set of principles of correct conduct; system of moral values 伦理；道德规范；价值体系
ethics	n. rules that govern conduct of people or members of a profession 伦理观；道德规范
ethology	n. the study of human ethos 性格学

- **EU-** (GOOD, WELL 好的；美的) [G]

  eulogy   *n.* high praise 颂词；赞词；颂扬；悼词

  euphemism   *n.* use of inoffensive language in place of offensive language 委婉语；委婉说法

  eugenics   *n.* a philosophy that advocates the improvement of human traits through various means 优
                    生学

  euphoria   *n.* a feeling of extreme happiness 精神欢快；幸福愉快感

  euphony   *n.* pleasant and harmonious sound 悦耳之音；和谐之音

- **EXTRA-/EXTRO-** (BESIDES, BEYOND, OUTSIDE OF, MORE 额外；超出；更多) [L]

  extraordinary   *adj.* beyond the ordinary 特别的，不寻常的；非凡的

  extracurricular *adj.* outside of the regular curriculum 课外的

  extraterrestrial *adj.* outside Earth 地球外的；宇宙的

  extraneous   *adj.* not essential 非主要的；不相干的

  extroversion   *n.* behavior directed outside one's self 外向性；外倾

Work 21

Match each word with its definition:

1. euphony
2. erratic
3. ethos
4. erg
5. ethic
6. erroneous
7. extraterrestrial
8. eulogy
9. synergic
10. extraneous

a. character peculiar to a person or people

b. high praise

c. working together

d. set of principles of correct conduct

e. deviating from the customary course

f. outside Earth

g. a unit of work

h. harmonious sound

i. mistaken

j. not essential

ROUNDUP 22

- **FAC/FIC/FEC** (DO, MAKE 做；使) [L]

  bene**fic**ent   *adj.* performing acts of kindness 慈善的；仁慈的

  manu**fac**ture   *v.* to make or process 生产；制造；加工

  con**fec**tion   *n.* act of making a sweet preparation 调制；a sweet preparation 糖果，蜜饯

  sopori**fic**   *n.* something that produces sleep 安眠药；催眠剂

  facile   *adj.* done with little effort; easy 易做到的；容易的

- **FALL/FALS** (DECEPTIVE, FALSE, ERRONEOUS 欺骗的；假的；错误的) [L]

  false   *adj.* untrue; mistaken; wrong; misleading 不真实的；虚假的；错误的；误导的

  fallacious   *adj.* based on a false idea or fact; misleading 谬误的，荒谬的；使人误解的

  falsify   *v.* to state untruthfully; misrepresent 撒谎；伪造；篡改；掺假

  fallible   *adj.* capable of making an error 易犯错误的；不可靠的

  in**fall**ible   *adj.* incapable of making a mistake 不会犯错的，绝无错误的；万无一失的

- **FED**（LEAGUE, PACT 联盟；合约）[L]

  federal   *adj.* related to a system of government in which power is divided between a central government and constituent states 联邦的；同盟的

  federation   *n.* the act of joining into a league or federal union 联合；联盟；联邦

  federacy   *n.* alliance; contederacy 联盟；联邦

  federative   *adj.* forming, belonging to, or having the nature of a federation 联合的；联邦性的

  con**fed**erate   *n.* a member of a league; an ally 同盟者；同盟国

- **FER**（BEAR, CARRY 拥有，持有；携带）[L]

  coni**fer**ous   *adj.* pertaining to needle-leaved cone-bearing trees such as pines or firs 结球果的；松柏科的

  aqui**fer**   *n.* stratum of permeable rock that bears water 含水层

  pesti**fer**ous   *adj.* bearing moral contagion; pestilent; deadly 传播疾病的；有害的；致命的

  voci**fer**ous   *adj.* loud, vocal, and noisy 大声的；喧嚣的

  spori**fer**ous   *adj.* producing spores 产孢子的；生芽孢的

- **FID**（FAITH, TRUST 信仰；忠实；信任）[L]

  con**fid**e   *v.* to tell in confidence 吐露

  fidelity   *n.* loyalty; exact correspondence 忠诚；精确；保真度，逼真

  con**fid**ence   *n.* trust or faith in someone or something 信心；信任

  per**fid**ious   *adj.* faithless; disloyal; untrustworthy 不忠的；背信弃义的

  con**fid**ante   *n.* a person to whom one's private affairs or thoughts are disclosed 知己

Work 22

Match each word with its definition:

1. fidelity
2. facile
3. vociferous
4. beneficent
5. federation
6. fallacious
7. federacy
8. coniferous
9. infallible
10. perfidious

a. loud, vocal, and noisy
b. based on a false idea
c. loyalty
d. done with little effort
e. pertaining to cone-bearing trees
f. the act of joining into a federal union
g. performing acts of kindness
h. disloyal
i. alliance
j. incapable of making a mistake

ROUNDUP 23

- **FIN**（END 结束；末端）[L]

  finite   *adj.* limited; impermanent 有限的；暂时的

  finale   *n.* concluding part of a musical composition 终曲；最后乐章；尾声

  de**fin**itive   *adj.* conclusive; authoritative; precisely defined 最后的；权威的；明确的

  fin de siècle   end of a century 世纪末

  ad in**fin**itum   forever; again and again 永久地；无限地；无穷地

- **FLECT/FLEX** (BEND 弯曲) [L]

  flexible   *adj.* capable of being bent 柔韧的，易弯曲的；弹性的；灵活的

  re**flex**   *adj.* bent or thrown back; reflected 反射的；反省的；反作用的

  re**flect**ion   *n.* the act of bending back or throwing back from a surface 反射

  de**flect**   *v.* to turn aside; bend; deviate 使转向；使弯曲；使偏斜

  circum**flex**   *adj.* curving around 弯曲的

- **FLU/FLUCT/FLUX** (FLOW 流) [L]

  fluctuate   *v.* to vary irregularly; rise and fall in waves 变动；波动；起伏

  in**flu**ent   *adj.* flowing into 流入的

  con**flu**ence   *n.* a flowing together; a juncture of two or more streams (人或物的)聚集；(河流的)汇合处

  flux   *n.* flowing; a continuous moving 流量；流出，流动；不断的变动

  re**flu**x   *n.* a flowing back; ebbing 逆流；退潮

- **FORT** (BRAVE, STRONG, CHANCE 勇敢的；强壮的；机会) [L]

  fortify   *v.* to strengthen; reinforce 加固；加强；增强

  forte   *n.* a person's strong point 强项；长处；特长

  fortitude   *n.* quality that enables a person to face pain and suffering with courage 坚毅；勇气；坚韧

  fortuitous   *adj.* occurring by chance 偶然的；意外的

  fortress   *n.* a large military stronghold 堡垒；要塞

- **FRAC/FRAG/FRING** (BREAK 打破) [L]

  fractional   *adj.* very small; being in fractions or pieces 极小的；微不足道的；部分的

  re**frac**t   *v.* to deflect sound or light (使)折射

  in**fring**e   *v.* to transgress; violate 侵犯；违反

  fractious   *adj.* unruly; rebellious 易怒的；难以控制的

  fragmentary   *adj.* consisting of small disconnected parts 残缺不全的；碎片的

Work 23

Match each word with its definition:

1. fortuitous		a.	curving around
2. definitive		b.	a person's strong point
3. fractious		c.	a flowing together
4. confluence		d.	conclusive
5. forte		e.	to deflect sound or light
6. circumflex		f.	end of a century
7. deflect		g.	occurring by chance
8. refract		h.	to rise and fall in waves
9. fluctuate		i.	unruly; rebellious
10. fin de siècle		j.	to turn aside; bend

ROUNDUP 24

- **FRAT** (BROTHER 兄弟) [L]

fraternity	*n.* a social organization of men students 兄弟会
con**frat**ernity	*n.* an association of persons united in a common purpose 协会；团体
fraternal	*adj.* brotherly 兄弟般的
fraternize	*v.* to mingle on friendly terms 使亲如兄弟；友善
fratricide	*n.* the killing of one's brother or sister 弑兄弟(或姐妹)的行为；自相残杀

- **FUNC** (PERFORM, DISCHARGE 作用；做事；释放) [L]

function	*n.* assigned duty or activity 功能；职责
de**func**t	*adj.* no longer existing 已故的；非现存的
per**func**tory	*adj.* performed really as a duty; superficial 例行公事的；敷衍的
functionary	*n.* someone who performs a particular function 工作人员；公职人员
mal**func**tion	*n.* failure to work 故障；失灵

- **GAM** (MARRIAGE 婚姻) [G]

poly**gam**ous	*adj.* having more than one wife or husband at a time 一夫多妻的；一妻多夫的
endo**gam**y	*n.* marriage within a particular group 同族结婚
exo**gam**y	*n.* marriage outside a social unit 异族结婚
gamic	*adj.* requiring fertilization to reproduce (需)受胎的；(需)受精的
mono**gam**ous	*adj.* relating to marriage to one person at a time 一夫一妻制的

- **GEN** (BIRTH, CLASS, DESCENT, RACE, GENERATE 出生；阶级；后裔；种族；发生) [L]

en**gen**der	*v.* to cause; produce 引起；产生；酿成
genesis	*n.* beginning; origin 发生；起源；创始
genetics	*n.* branch of biology that deals with heredity 基因学；遗传学
gentry	*n.* a people of standing; class of people just below nobility 贵族；绅士
genre	*n.* type, class; distinct literary or artistic category 类型；流派；文体

- **GEO** (EARTH 地球) [G]

geology	*n.* science that studies the structure and composition of the Earth 地质学
geography	*n.* science that studies the Earth and the distribution of life on it 地理学
geocentric	*adj.* having the Earth as center 以地球为中心的；地心说的
geothermal	*adj.* produced by the heat in the Earth's interior 地热的
geophysics	*n.* the physics of the Earth 地球物理学

Work 24

Match each word with its definition:

1. polygamous
2. fratricide
3. defunct
4. geothermal
5. fraternal

a. to cause; produce
b. relating to marriage to one person at a time
c. type; class
d. no longer existing
e. the physics of the Earth

6. monogamous
7. engender
8. genre
9. geophysics
10. perfunctory

f. the killing of one's brother or sister
g. produced by heat in the Earth's interior
h. performed really as a duty
i. having more than one wife or husband at a time
j. brotherly

ROUNDUP 25

- **GLOSS/GLOT** (LANGUAGE, TONGUE 语言；舌) [L]

glossa	*n.* the tongue 舌
poly**glot**	*n.* a speaker of many languages 通晓数门语言的人
glossolalia	*n.* fabricated and meaningless speech associated with trance states 语意不清；言语不清
glossary	*n.* list of words and their meanings, usually at the back of a book 词汇表
glottis	*n.* opening between the vocal chords and the larynx 声门

- **GRAD/GRESS** (STEP 步) [L]

re**gress**	*v.* to move backward; revert to an earlier state 后退；倒退
pro**gress**ive	*adj.* going step-by-step; favoring progress 前进的；进步的
e**gress**	*n.* exit 出口
in**gress**	*n.* entrance 入口
graduate	*v.* to advance to a new level of skill or achievement 升级

- **GRAPH/GRAM** (WRITE, DRAW, RECORD 写；画；记录) [G]

graphology	*n.* study of handwriting, particularly for the purpose of character analysis 笔迹学
bio**graph**ical	*adj.* relating to facts and events of a person's life 传记的；传记体的
gramophone	*n.* a record player 留声机
epi**gram**	*n.* short and witty saying 隽语；警句
grammar	*n.* the system of rules of a language 语法

- **GRAT** (PLEASING 快乐的) [L]

gratify	*v.* to please 使高兴；使满意；使满足
gratitude	*n.* thankfulness 致谢；感激，感恩
gratuitous	*adj.* free; voluntary 免费的；自愿的
ex**grat**ia	*adj.* done voluntarily, out of kindness or grace 作为优惠的；通融的；出于恩惠而做的
persona non **grat**a	a person who is not acceptable or welcome 不受欢迎的人

- **GRAV/GRIEV** (SERIOUS, HEAVY, HARMFUL 严肃的；重的；有害的) [L]

gravity	*n.* seriousness 严肃性
grave	*adj.* requiring serious thought 严肃的
gravitas	*n.* seriousness in demeanor or treatment 庄严
grievous	*adj.* causing grief or pain 痛苦的；悲切的
ag**griev**ed	*adj.* afflicted; distressed 受委屈的；受折磨的；悲痛的

Work 25

Match each word with its definition:

1.	epigram	a.	to please
2.	progressive	b.	entrance
3.	polyglot	c.	free; voluntary
4.	gratify	d.	the tongue
5.	gravity	e.	afflicted; distressed
6.	ingress	f.	short and witty saying
7.	aggrieved	g.	study of handwriting
8.	graphology	h.	a speaker of many languages
9.	glossa	i.	going step-by-step
10.	gratuitous	j.	seriousness

REVIEW 21–25

Matching

Match each of the following roots or prefixes to its meaning:

1.	ERR	a.	league, pact
2.	EU-	b.	earth
3.	FER	c.	language, tongue
4.	FED	d.	flow
5.	FLECT/FLEX	e.	pleasing
6.	FLU/FLUCT/FLUX	f.	good, well
7.	FRAT	g.	bear, carry
8.	GEO	h.	brother
9.	GRAT	i.	wander, mistake
10.	GLOSS/GLOT	j.	bend

Fill-ins

Fill in the blanks with the word that fits the definition:

genre	**gravitas**	**soporific**	**egress**	**perfidious**
extraneous	**fractious**	**perfunctory**	**euphony**	**fin de siècle**

1. seriousness in demeanor _____
2. faithless; disloyal; untrustworthy _____
3. unruly; rebellious _____
4. type; class _____
5. performed really as a duty _____
6. pleasant and harmonious sound _____
7. exit _____

8. end of a century _____

9. not essential _____

10. something that produces sleep _____

True or False

If the statement is correct, put（T）True; if it is incorrect, put（F）False.

1. Endogamy refers to marriage outside a particular group. _____

2. Something fallacious is based on a false idea or fact. _____

3. An erg is a mistake in writing or printing. _____

4. Fortitude enables one to face pain and suffering with courage. _____

5. Ethos is a feeling of extreme happiness. _____

ROUNDUP 26

- **GREG**（FLOCK, HERD 群）[L]

  ag**greg**ate   *n.* collective mass or sum; total 合计；总计

  con**greg**ation   *n.* gathering 集会；集合

  gregarious   *adj.* sociable 社交的；爱交际的，合群的

  gregarine   *n.* various parasitic protozoans in the digestive tracts of invertebrates 簇虫

  se**greg**ate   *v.* to separate from a main body or group 使分离；使隔离

- **GYN**（WOMAN 女性）[G]

  miso**gyn**ist   *n.* one who hates women 厌恶女人者

  gynecology   *n.* branch of medicine dealing with women's health care 妇科

  gynarchy   *n.* government by women 女人当政；妇女政治

  gynophobia   *n.* fear of women 女性恐惧症

  gynecoid   *adj.* characteristic of a woman 有女性特征的；女性的

- **HELIO**（SUN 太阳）[G]

  heliocentric   *adj.* having the Sun as a center 以太阳为中心的

  heliolatry   *n.* Sun worship 太阳崇拜

  heliotaxis   *n.* an organism's movement in response to the Sun's light 趋日性，向日性

  heliotrope   *n.* kind of plant that turns toward the Sun 向阳植物

  heliotherapy   *n.* therapy based on exposure to sunlight 日光浴疗法

- **HEMO**（BLOOD 血液）[G]

  hemorrhage   *n.* heavy bleeding（大）出血

  hemoglobin   *n.* respiratory pigment in red blood cells 血红素；血红蛋白

  hemophilia   *n.* blood coagulation disorder 血友病

  hemoptysis   *n.* the expectoration of blood 咳血；咯血

  hemophobia   *n.* fear of blood 恐血症

- **HERB** (VEGETATION 草) [L]

herbal	*adj.* relating to or containing herbs 草药的；草本的
herbicide	*n.* chemical that destroys plants or weeds 除草剂
herbaceous	*adj.* characteristic of a herb 草本的
herbivorous	*adj.* feeding mainly on plants 食草的
herbalism	*n.* herbal medicine 草药医术学

Work 26

Match each word with its definition:

1. herbaceous
2. hemophobia
3. aggregate
4. heliotrope
5. gregarious

6. gynarchy
7. hemophilia
8. herbivorous
9. heliotaxis
10. gynecoid

a. blood coagulation disorder
b. kind of plant that turns toward the Sun
c. characteristic of a herb
d. collective mass or sum
e. an organism's movement in response to the Sun's light
f. feeding mainly on plants
g. sociable
h. fear of blood
i. characteristic of a woman
j. government by women

ROUNDUP 27

- **HETERO-** (DIFFERENT, MIXED, UNLIKE 不同的；混合的；不同) [G]

heterosexual	*adj.* sexually oriented to persons of the opposite sex 异性恋的
heterodox	*adj.* unorthodox, not widely accepted 非正统的；异端的
heterogeneous	*adj.* composed of unlike parts, different, diverse 异种的，混杂的
heterodyne	*adj.* having alternating currents of two different frequencies producing two new ones 电外差的
heterochromatic	*adj.* characterized by different colors 异色的

- **HOMO-** (SAME, ALIKE 相同的；相似的) [G]

homologous	*adj.* similar in value or function 相应的；同源的；类似的
homonym	*n.* word identical in pronunciation and sometimes spelling to one or more other words but different in meaning 同形同音异义词
homogeneous	*adj.* composed of identical parts; uniform in composition 同种的；均匀的
homocentric	*adj.* having the same center 同心的
homogenize	*v.* to make uniform in consistency 使类同

- **HOM/HOMO/HUMAN** (MAN, HUMANITY 人，人类) [L]

humane	*adj.* characterized by kindness or compassion 仁慈的；人道的
humanity	*n.* humans as a group 人类

humanism   *n.* system of thought focusing on humans, their values, and capacities 人文主义，人本主义

humanitarian   *adj.* relating to the promotion of human welfare 人道主义的

hominoid   *adj.* belonging to the family Hominidae, which includes apes and man 类人猿的；类人的

- **HYDR/HYDRA/HYDRO** （WATER 水）［G］

  hydroelectric   *adj.* producing electricity through action of falling water 水力发电的

  hydroponics   *n.* science of growing plants in water reinforced with nutrients 营养液种植法，水耕法

  hydrant   *n.* a large pipe for drawing water 水龙头；给水栓

  de**hydr**ate   *v.* to remove water from（使）脱水；使干燥

  hydrophyte   *n.* a water plant 水生植物

- **HYPER-** （ABOVE, EXCESSIVE, OVER 在…之上；过多的；超过）［G］

  hyperbole   *n.* purposeful exaggeration for effect 夸张

  hyperactive   *adj.* excessively active 极度活跃的；亢奋的

  hypertension   *n.* high blood pressure 高血压

  hypercritical   *adj.* excessively critical 吹毛求疵的；苛评的

  hyperventilate   *v.* to breathe abnormally fast【医】换气过度；呼吸急促

Work 27

Match each word with its definition:

1.	homologous	a.	characterized by kindness or compassion
2.	dehydrate	b.	composed of identical parts
3.	heterodox	c.	to breathe abnormally fast
4.	heterochromatic	d.	characterized by different colors
5.	hyperbole	e.	to remove water from
6.	humane	f.	similar in value or function
7.	hydroponics	g.	purposeful exaggeration for effect
8.	humanity	h.	not widely accepted
9.	hyperventilate	i.	science of growing plants in water reinforced with nutrients
10.	homogeneous	j.	humans as a group

ROUNDUP 28

- **HYPO-** （BENEATH, LOWER, UNDER 在…之下；低于）［G］

  hypothetical   *adj.* based on assumptions or hypotheses 假设的；假想的

  hypothermia   *n.* abnormally low body temperature 低体温症

  hypoglycemia   *n.* abnormally low glucose level in the blood 低血糖症

  hypochondria   *n.* unfounded belief that one is likely to become ill 臆想病

  hypoplasia   *n.* arrested development of an organ（器官等）发育不全

- **IG-/IL-/IM-/IN-/IR-** (NOT, WITHOUT 不，没有) [L]

  ignominious   *adj.* disgraceful and dishonorable 可耻的；屈辱的

  impecunious   *adj.* poor; having no money 没钱的；一文不名的

  impoverish   *v.* to make poor or bankrupt 使贫困

  intractable   *adj.* not easily managed 难对付的；棘手的

  irrelevant   *adj.* not applicable; unrelated 无关的；不相干的

- **IN-** (IN, ON, UPON, NOT 在…里；在…上；不；没有) [L]

  incite   *v.* to arouse to action 煽动；激励；刺激

  incarnate   *adj.* having bodily form 化身的，人体化的

  indigenous   *adj.* native, occurring naturally in an area 本土的；土著的

  inclusive   *adj.* tending to include all 包括在内的

  incongruity   *n.* a state of not fitting 不协调；不一致

- **INTER-** (AMONG, BETWEEN, WITHIN, MUTUAL 之间，内部；共同的) [L]

  intervene   *v.* to come between 介入；干涉；干预

  interpose   *v.* to insert; intervene 插入；干预

  interregnum   *n.* interval between reigns 空位期；过渡期；间隔

  intersperse   *v.* to distribute among; mix with 散置；散布

  internecine   *adj.* deadly to both sides 自相残杀的；两败俱伤的

- **INTRA-/INTRO-** (INTO, INWARD, WITHIN 向内；在…里面) [L]

  intraocular   *adj.* occurring within the eyeball 眼内的

  intravenous   *adj.* within a vein 静脉内的

  intramural   *adj.* within an institution such as a school 校内的；内部的

  introvert   *n.* someone given to self-analysis 性格内向的人

  introspective   *adj.* contemplating one's own thoughts and feelings 内省的

Work 28

Match each word with its definition:

1. incongruity
2. interregnum
3. irrelevant
4. introspective
5. indigenous
6. hypothermia
7. intramural
8. hypochondria
9. interpose
10. intractable

a. within an institution

b. occurring naturally in an area

c. not easily managed

d. a state of not fitting

e. not applicable; unrelated

f. unfounded belief that one is likely to become ill

g. contemplating one's own thoughts and feelings

h. to insert; intervene

i. abnormally low body temperature

j. interval between reigns

ROUNDUP 29

- **JAC/JACT/JECT** (THROW, FLING 扔，掷；射出) [L]
  - re**ject**　　　　*v.* to refuse to accept or consider; deny 排斥；抵制；拒绝
  - e**ject**　　　　 *v.* to throw out 喷射；逐出
  - tra**ject**ory　　 *n.* path taken by a projectile 弹道；轨道
  - inter**ject**　　　*v.* to interpose; insert 插入
  - e**jac**ulate　　　*v.* to eject abruptly 突然说出；射出 (液体)

- **JUR/JUS/JUD** (SWEAR, LAW, JUDGE, JUST 宣誓；法律；法官；公正的) [L]
  - **jud**icious　　　*adj.* wise; sound in judgment 明智的；明断的
  - per**jur**e　　　　*v.* to tell a lie under oath 发假誓；作伪证
  - **jur**isdiction　　*n.* power to interpret and apply law; control 司法权；审判权；管辖权
  - **jur**isprudence *n.* philosophy of law 法理学；法学
  - **jus**tice　　　　*n.* quality of being honorable and fair 公正

- **LECT/LEG/LIG** (READ, CHOOSE 读；选) [L]
  - **leg**ible　　　　*adj.* readable 可读的；易读的
  - se**lect**　　　　 *v.* to make a choice 选择；挑选；选拔
  - **lect**or　　　　 *n.* someone who reads scriptural passages in a church service (专门在教堂读经的)读经师
  - e**lect**ion　　　　*n.* ability to make a choice 选择；推选
  - predi**lect**ion　　*n.* preference; liking 偏爱；嗜好

- **LEG** (LAW 法律) [L]
  - **leg**acy　　　　 *n.* a gift made by a will 遗产；遗赠
  - il**leg**al　　　　 *adj.* prohibited by law 非法的
  - **leg**alese　　　 *n.* abstruse vocabulary of the legal profession 法律措辞；法律术语
  - **leg**itimate　　 *adj.* in accordance with established standards; reasonable 合法的；正当的；合理的
  - **leg**islation　　 *n.* laws; decree; mandate 法律；法规

- **LEV** (LIGHT 轻的) [L]
  - **lev**ity　　　　 *n.* light manner or attitude 轻浮；轻率
  - **lev**itate　　　　*v.* to rise in the air or cause to rise (使)浮在空中
  - **lev**er　　　　　*n.* a means of accomplishing something 杠杆
  - al**lev**iate　　　 *v.* to relieve; improve partially 减轻；缓解；缓和
  - **lev**erage　　　 *n.* power to act effectively 影响力

Work 29

Match each word with its definition:

1. legitimate
2. jurisprudence
3. legislation
4. levity
5. perjure
6. legible
7. eject
8. trajectory
9. alleviate
10. predilection

a. law; decree; mandate
b. to relieve, improve partially
c. to tell a lie under oath
d. readable
e. preference, liking
f. to throw out
g. in accordance with established standards
h. path taken by a projectile
i. light manner or attitude
j. philosophy of law

ROUNDUP 30

- **LEX** (WORD 词) [G]

  lexicon   *n.* dictionary; list of words 词典，辞典；词汇

  lexicography   *n.* process of compiling a dictionary 词典编纂

  lexis   *n.* vocabulary; set of words in a language 词汇；词语

  lexical   *adj.* relating to the words of a language 词汇的

  lexeme   *n.* basic unit of the lexicon of a language 词素；词位

- **LIBER** (FREE 自由的) [L]

  liberal   *adj.* tolerant, broad-minded; generous, lavish 宽容的；慷慨的，大方的

  liberation   *n.* freedom, emancipation 自由；解放

  libertine   *n.* one without moral restraint 浪荡子；放荡不羁者

  il**liber**al   *adj.* bigoted; narrow-minded 狭隘的；偏执的

  libertarian   *n.* one who believes in unrestricted freedom (思想或行动等的)自由论者

- **LIBRAR/LIBR** (BOOK 书) [L]

  library   *n.* place where books are kept; collection of books 图书馆，藏书室；藏书

  librarianship   *n.* specialization in library work 图书馆管理；图书馆事业

  libel   *n.* defamatory statement; act of writing something that smears a person's character 诽谤；诋毁

  libretto   *n.* text of a dramatic musical work (歌剧等的)剧本

  librettist   *n.* author of a libretto 歌词作家；剧本作者

- **LITER** (LETTER 文字) [L]

  literati   *n.* scholarly or learned persons 文人；学者

  literature   *n.* a body of written works 文学；文献

  il**liter**ate   *adj.* unable to read and write 文盲的，不识字的

  literation   *n.* letter for letter 缩略字

  literal   *adj.* limited to the most obvious meaning of a word; word for word 字面的；逐字的

- **LOC/LOG/LOQU** (WORD, SPEAK, TALK 词；说；谈) [L]

  loquacious   *adj.* talkative 健谈的；多话的

  col**loqu**ial   *adj.* typical of informal speech 口语的，白话的；通俗的

  soli**loqu**y   *n.* literary or dramatic speech by one character, not addressed to others 独白

  circum**locu**tion   *n.* indirect way of saying something 委婉的话；遁词

  epi**log**ue   *n.* short speech at the end of a play 收场白；结语；尾声

Work 30

Match each word with its definition:

1. lexis   a. talkative
2. illiterate   b. indirect way of saying something
3. libertarian   c. word for word
4. loquacious   d. tolerant; broad-minded

5. lexicon	e. believer in unrestricted freedom
6. libretto	f. unable to read and write
7. circumlocution	g. list of words
8. libel	h. writing something to smear a character
9. literal	i. vocabulary
10. liberal	j. text of a musical work

REVIEW 26–30

Matching

Match each of the following roots or prefixes to its meaning:

1. HERB	a. free
2. HEMO	b. law
3. HETERO-	c. same, alike
4. HOMO-	d. into, inward, within
5. IN-	e. light
6. INTRA-/INTRO-	f. blood
7. LEG	g. in, on, upon, not
8. LEV	h. letter
9. LIBER	i. vegetation
10. LITER	j. different, mixed, unlike

Fill-ins

Fill in the blanks with the word that fits the definition:

internecine	literati	hominoid	impecunious	hyperbole
lector	lexical	misogynist	jurisprudence	hemoptysis

1. relating to the words of a language _____
2. expectoration of blood _____
3. one who reads scriptural passages in a church service _____
4. purposeful exaggeration for effect _____
5. scholarly or learned persons _____
6. deadly to both sides _____
7. philosophy of law _____
8. hater of women _____
9. having no money _____
10. belonging to the family that includes apes and man _____

True or False

If the statement is correct, put (T) True; if it is incorrect, put (F) False.

1. A homonym is a word identical in pronunciation and sometimes spelling to one or more other words but different in meaning. _____

2. Hypothermia is an abnormally high body temperature. _____
3. Heliotaxis refers to an organism's movement in response to the Sun's light. _____
4. Circumlocution is an extremely direct way of saying something. _____
5. To interject is to throw out or delete. _____

ROUNDUP 31

- **LUC/LUM/LUS** (LIGHT 光) [L]

lucid	*adj.* bright; clear; intelligible 透明的；清晰的；头脑清楚的	
trans**luc**ent	*adj.* partially transparent 半透明的	
e**luc**idation	*n.* clarification 清楚；澄清；阐明	
pel**luc**id	*adj.* transparent; translucent; easily understood 透明的；明了的；易懂的	
luminous	*adj.* bright; brilliant; glowing 光亮的；明亮的；闪光的	

- **LUD** (PLAY, GAME 游戏；戏剧) [L]

al**lud**e	*v.* to make an indirect reference to 暗指；影射
ludicrous	*adj.* laughable; ridiculous 好笑的；滑稽的；荒唐的
pre**lud**e	*n.* an introductory performance preceding the principal matter 序幕；序曲
inter**lud**e	*n.* an entertainment between acts of a play 幕间节目；插曲
e**lud**e	*v.* to evade 逃避，躲避

- **MACRO-** (LARGE, LONG 大的；长的) [G]

macrocosm	*n.* the universe 宇宙
macroeconomics	*n.* study of the overall workings of the economy 宏观经济学
macroscopic	*adj.* large enough to be seen with the naked eye 肉眼可见的；宏观的
macronutrient	*n.* an element needed in large proportion for a plant's growth【生】大量养料
macrocyte	*n.* an abnormally large red blood cell 大红细胞

- **MAGN-** (GREAT 巨大的) [L]

magnify	*v.* to enlarge 放大；夸大
magnate	*n.* a powerful person 富豪；巨头；大人物；要人
magnitude	*n.* extent; greatness of size 大小；震级；重要
magnanimity	*n.* generosity; nobility 宽宏大量
magna cum laude	with high honors (以) 优异的成绩

- **MAL-** (BAD 坏的) [L]

malign	*v.* to speak evil of 诽谤，污蔑；中伤，说坏话
malaise	*n.* feeling of discomfort; general sense of depression 不舒服；心神不定
malicious	*adj.* full of animosity and hatred 邪恶的；憎恨的
malefactor	*n.* doer of evil 坏人
malfeasance	*n.* misconduct 渎职；恶行；不正当

Work 31

Match each word with its definition:

1.	pellucid	a.	large enough to be seen with the naked eye
2.	elucidation	b.	a powerful person
3.	macroscopic	c.	the universe
4.	malfeasance	d.	to evade
5.	magnate	e.	clarification
6.	malefactor	f.	to make an indirect reference to
7.	allude	g.	misconduct
8.	macrocosm	h.	transparent; translucent
9.	magnanimity	i.	generosity; nobility
10.	elude	j.	doer of evil

ROUNDUP 32

- **MAN** (HAND 手) [L]

e**man**cipate	*v.* to liberate 解放
manipulate	*v.* to operate or control by the hands 操纵；操作
manubrium	*n.* a body part that is shaped like a handle 柄状体
maniable	*adj.* easy to handle; flexible 易于操作的；灵活顺手的
quadru**man**us	*adj.* having four feet with the first digits being opposable 四足如手的

- **MAND** (ORDER 命令) [L]

mandate	*n.* authoritative order or instruction 授权；命令；指令
mandatory	*adj.* commanded by authority 强制的；命令的
com**mand**ment	*n.* command 命令
mandamus	*n.* an order issued by a superior court to a lower court 书面训令
repri**mand**	*n.* a strong formal rebuke 训诫；谴责；申诉

- **MANIA** (OBSESSION 迷住；着魔) [G]

mania	*n.* mental disorder characterized by excessive gaiety; wild enthusiasm 狂热；热衷
maniac	*n.* someone who has excessive enthusiasm for something; an insane person 狂热分子；疯子
megalo**mania**	*n.* delusions of power or importance 妄自尊大
maniacal	*adj.* characterized by excessive enthusiasm; marked by insanity 狂热的；疯狂的
manic-depressive	*n.* affective disorder marked by alternating periods of mania and depression 躁狂抑郁症

- **MAR/MARI** (SEA 海) [L]

maritime	*adj.* relating to the sea 海洋的
marine	*adj.* native to the sea; relating to the sea 海的；海生的
marina	*n.* a boat basin for small boats 码头
aqua**mari**ne	*n.* pale blue to light greenish blue 青绿色，碧绿色
sub**mari**ne	*adj.* undersea 海底的，水下的

- **MATER/MATR** (MOTHER 母亲) [L]

maternal	*adj.* relating to or characteristic of a mother 母亲的；母性的；母系的
matron	*n.* a mother of mature age and social position 已婚妇女；夫人
matrix	*n.* the womb 子宫
matrilineal	*adj.* tracing ancestry through the mother's line 母系的
matriarchy	*n.* family or community governed by women 母权社会；母系氏族

Work 32

Match each word with its definition:

1. reprimand
2. matriarchy
3. submarine
4. mandate
5. mania
6. maritime
7. matrilineal
8. maniable
9. manubrium
10. maniacal

a. characterized by excessive enthusiasm
b. a body part shaped like a handle
c. easy to handle
d. community governed by women
e. undersea
f. wild enthusiasm
g. authoritative order or instruction
h. tracing ancestry through the mother's line
i. relating to the sea
j. a strong formal rebuke

ROUNDUP 33

- **MEGA-** (GREAT, LARGE 大的；伟大的) [G]

megaphone	*n.* device used to amplify the voice 扩音器
megalomania	*n.* delusions of power or importance 妄想自大狂
megalith	*n.* huge stone used in prehistoric structures (史前建筑所用的)巨石
megalopolis	*n.* vast city 大都市
megalophonous	*adj.* having a loud voice 大声的

- **META** (CHANGE, AT A LATER TIME, BEYOND 变化；后来；超越) [G]

metaphor	*n.* figure of speech that compares two different things 暗喻，隐喻
metamorphosis	*n.* change; transformation 变形；变质；蜕变
metaplasia	*n.* change of one kind of tissue into another kind 转化，化生；组织变形
metanoia	*n.* spiritual conversion 悔改
metaphysical	*adj.* pertaining to speculative philosophy 形而上学的

- **METER/METR** (MEASURE 测量) [G]

baro**meter**	*n.* instrument used in weather forecasting for measuring atmospheric pressure 气压表
peri**meter**	*n.* the outer limits of an area 周长
micro**meter**	*n.* device that measures small distances or objects 千分尺，测微计
am**meter**	*n.* instrument that measures electric current in amperes 安培计；电流表
metrology	*n.* study of weights and measures 度量衡学

- **MICRO-** (SMALL 小的) [G]

  microbiota   *n.* the microscopic life of an area 微生物区

  micrology   *n.* excessive devotion to small details 显微学；拘泥于细节的研究

  microclimate   *n.* the climate of a small area 小气候

  microcosm   *n.* a small system having analogies to a larger system; small world 微观世界；缩影

  microdont   *adj.* having small teeth 有微齿的

- **MIN-** (SMALL 小的) [L]

  di**min**ution   *n.* lessening; reduction 减少；降低

  di**min**utive   *adj.* small 微小的；小的；小型的

  minute   *adj.* very small 微小的

  minutia   *n.* petty details 细节；琐事

  minuscule   *adj.* very small 非常小的；极微细的

Work 33

Match each word with its definition:

1.	microcosm	a.	huge stone used in prehistoric structures
2.	megalomania	b.	very small
3.	metamorphosis	c.	study of weights and measures
4.	micrometer	d.	spiritual conversion
5.	metanoia	e.	device that measures small distances or objects
6.	minuscule	f.	having small teeth
7.	microdont	g.	small world
8.	metrology	h.	delusions of importance or power
9.	megalith	i.	petty details
10.	minutia	j.	transformation

ROUNDUP 34

- **MIS-** (HATRED, BAD, IMPROPER, WRONG 怀恨；坏的；不合适的；错误的) [G]

  misconstrue   *v.* to misunderstand 误解，曲解；误会

  misapprehension   *n.* a misunderstanding 误会；误解

  misnomer   *n.* incorrect name 误称；错误的名称

  misanthropy   *n.* hatred of humanity 厌恶人类

  misogynist   *n.* hater of women 厌恶女人者

- **MISS/MIT** (MOVE, SEND 移动；散播) [L]

  trans**mit**   *v.* to send from one place to another; cause to spread 传输；传播；发射；传达

  re**mit**tance   *n.* something sent as payment 汇款，汇付

  missive   *n.* letter 信件，信函；公文，公函

  dis**miss**   *v.* to put away from consideration; reject 解散，开除；驳回

  mittimus   *n.* writ that commits one to prison 收押令

- **MOB/MOT/MOV** (MOVE 移动) [L]

im**mob**ile	*adj.* fixed; motionless 固定的；不可移动的；不变的
mobility	*n.* a state of being capable of moving 流动性；移动性
auto**mob**ile	*n.* passenger vehicle having four wheels and an engine 汽车
e**mot**ive	*adj.* appealing to or expressing emotion 感情的；情绪的
movie	*n.* sequence of images on a screen so rapid that they create the illusion of movement 电影

- **MONO-** (ONE, SINGLE 一个；单独的) [G]

monogamy	*n.* marriage to one person at a time 一夫一妻制
monologue	*n.* speech performed by one actor 独白
monocline	*n.* in geology, a single upward fold 单斜层
monochromatic	*adj.* having one color 单色的
monolithic	*adj.* constituting a single, unified whole 构成整体的

- **MON/MONIT** (WARN 警告) [L]

monitor	*v.* to maintain continuous observation of 监控，监测，监视；监督，监管
ad**mon**ish	*v.* to caution or reprimand 警告，劝诫
ad**monit**ion	*n.* mild reproof 警告；劝诫
pre**monit**ion	*n.* forewarning; presentiment 事先警告；预兆；预感
re**mon**strate	*v.* to object or protest 反对；抗议

Work 34

Match each word with its definition:

1.	premonition	a.	speech performed by one actor
2.	misogynist	b.	something sent as payment
3.	movie	c.	expressing emotion
4.	misnomer	d.	letter
5.	monologue	e.	incorrect name
6.	monochromatic	f.	images on a screen that give the illusion of movement
7.	missive	g.	forewarning
8.	emotive	h.	to caution
9.	remittance	i.	hater of women
10.	admonish	j.	having one color

ROUNDUP 35

- **MORI/MORT** (DEATH 死) [L]

moribund	*adj.* dying 垂死的；濒死的
mortorio	*n.* sculpture of the dead Christ 受难耶稣雕像
im**mort**al	*adj.* not subject to death; everlasting 不朽的；永生的
mortification	*n.* shame or humiliation 屈辱；羞愧
mortician	*n.* funeral director 殡仪业者；丧事承办人

- **MORPH** (FORM, SHAPE 形态) [G]

  morphous   *adj.* having definite form 有固定形状的

  a**morph**ous   *adj.* lacking definite form 无固定形态的

  morphometry   *n.* measurement of form 形态测量学

  morphology   *n.* the form and structure of an organism 形态学

  anthropo**morph**ic   *adj.* attributing human qualities to nonhumans 拟人的；赋予人性的

- **MULTI-** (MANY 多的) [L]

  multipara   *n.* mother of two or more children 经产妇

  multifaceted   *adj.* made up of many parts 多层面的

  multifarious   *adj.* diverse 各式各样的；多样的；多种的

  multiplicity   *n.* a state of being numerous 多样性；多重性

  multeity   *n.* a state of being many 多样性；多重性；多方面性

- **MUT** (CHANGE 改变) [L]

  mutative   *adj.* in grammar, expressing change of state or place 变化的

  mutation   *n.* significant genetic change 突变；变异

  trans**mut**ation   *n.* change in appearance, shape, or nature 变形；变化；演变

  im**mut**able   *adj.* unchangeable 不可改变的；永恒不变的

  mutable   *adj.* changeable 可改变的；易变的；不定的

- **NAS/NAT** (BIRTH, BE FROM, SPRING FORTH 出生；来自) [L]

  nationality   *n.* a state of belonging to a particular nation by birth or by naturalization 国籍

  nativity   *n.* place or circumstances of birth 出生；出生地或环境

  natal   *adj.* relating to birth 出生的；分娩的

  native   *n.* an original inhabitant of a particular place 本地人；当地居民

  nascent   *adj.* starting to develop; coming into existence 初期的；开始形成的

Work 35

Match each word with its definition:

1. multifarious
2. natal
3. nascent
4. moribund
5. immutable
6. morphous
7. morphology
8. mortician
9. mutation
10. multipara

a. having definite form

b. significant genetic change

c. mother of two or more children

d. funeral director

e. the form and structure of an organism

f. dying

g. diverse

h. unchangeable

i. starting to develop; come into existence

j. relating to birth

REVIEW 31–35

Matching

Match each of the following roots or prefixes to its meaning:

1. LUD	a. sea
2. MAGN-	b. small
3. MANIA	c. one, single
4. MAR/MARI	d. great
5. METER/METRE	e. change
6. MICRO-	f. death
7. MON/MONIT	g. play
8. MONO-	h. obsession
9. MORI/MORT	i. warn
10. MUT	j. measure

Fill-ins

Fill in the blanks with the word that fits the definition:

mandamus	**morphology**	**matrilineal**	**missive**	**diminution**
nascent	**misogynist**	**macrocosm**	**metanoia**	**malfeasance**

1. letter _____
2. starting to develop _____
3. lessening; reduction _____
4. misconduct _____
5. hater of women _____
6. tracing ancestry through the mother's line _____
7. the form and structure of an organism _____
8. an order issued by a superior court to a lower court _____
9. spiritual conversion _____
10. the universe _____

True or False

If the statement is correct, put (T) True; if it is incorrect, put (F) False.

1. Pellucid means cloudy, vague, or unintelligible. _____
2. Manubrium refers to a body part that is shaped like an egg. _____
3. A person's nativity refers to his or her place of birth. _____
4. Metrology means urban planning. _____
5. In geology, a monocline is a single upward fold. _____

ROUNDUP 36

- **NAV** (SHIP 船) [L]

naval	adj. relating to ships or shipping 船的；船运的
navigation	n. theory and practice of charting a ship's course 航海术；航行术
navarch	n. commander of a fleet (古希腊)舰队指挥官
naviform	adj. boat-shaped 船形的
circumnavigate	v. to go completely around 环航

- **NEC/NIC/NOC/NOX** (KILL, DEATH, HARM 杀死；死亡；伤害) [L]

internecine	adj. deadly to both sides 自相残杀的；两败俱伤的
pernicious	adj. very harmful 有害的；恶性的
nocent	adj. causing injury 有害的，伤害的
innocuous	adj. not harmful 无害的；无伤大雅的
noxious	adj. injurious to health 有害健康的，有毒的

- **NECRO-** (DEAD, CORPSE 死的；尸体) [G]

necromancy	n. divination through communicating with spirits 巫术；妖术；通灵术
necrophobia	n. fear of dead bodies 死亡恐怖；尸体恐怖
necrotype	n. extinct species 灭绝的物种
necrophilia	n. intercourse with dead bodies 恋尸狂，恋尸癖
necromorphous	adj. feigning death 装死的，假死的

- **NEG** (NO 否，不) [L]

negate	v. to nullify; cancel out 否定；否认；取消
negative	adj. indicating opposition 否定的；消极的
renege	v. to go back on one's word 违约；食言
negligent	adj. careless; inattentive 疏忽的；粗心大意的
negligible	adj. not worth considering 微不足道的；无足轻重的；可以忽略的

- **NEO-** (NEW, RECENT 新的) [G]

neologism	n. a new word or expression; an existing word or expression used in a new way 新词，新义；新词的使用
neophyte	n. novice, beginner 新手；初学者
neonate	n. a newborn child 新生儿，婴儿
neoplasia	n. formation of new tissue 瘤形成
neolithic	adj. of New Stone Age 新石器时代的

Work 36

Match each word with its definition:

1. necrotype   a. boat-shaped
2. negligible   b. deadly to both sides
3. navarch   c. to nullify
4. pernicious   d. fear of dead bodies

5. neonate
6. necrophobia
7. neophyte
8. internecine
9. naviform
10. negate

e. novice
f. commander of a fleet
g. a newborn child
h. very harmful
i. not worth considering
j. extinct species

ROUNDUP 37

- **NEUR** (NERVE 神经) [G]

  neurology   *n.* study of the nerves and the brain 神经学，神经病学

  neurosis   *n.* disorder of the nervous system 神经官能症

  neuroid   *adj.* nervelike 类神经的

  neurergic   *adj.* pertaining to nerve action 神经作用的

  neuralgia   *n.* pain along nerve 神经痛

- **NEUT/NEUTR** (NOT EITHER 也不是) [L]

  neutral   *adj.* belonging to neither side in a war or controversy 中立的

  neutralize   *v.* to make neutral; counterbalance the effect of 中和；抵消；使中立

  neutrality   *n.* a state of being neutral 中立；中立立场

  neutron   *n.* an electrically neutral subatomic particle 中子

  neuter   *adj.* neither masculine nor feminine 中性的

- **NOCT/NOX** (NIGHT 夜晚) [L]

  nocturnal   *adj.* pertaining to night; active at night 夜间的；夜间活动的

  equi**nox**   *n.* either of two times in a year when the Sun crosses the celestial equator 昼夜平分点（春分或秋分）

  noctambulant   *adj.* walking in one's sleep 夜间步行的；梦游的

  noctivagant   *adj.* wandering around at night 夜游的

  noctilucous   *adj.* shining at night 夜光的

- **NOM/NOMEN/NYM** (NAME 名字) [L/G]

  nominal   *adj.* existing in name only 名义上的；有名无实的；象征性的

  nom de guerre   war name; pseudonym 化名，艺名；假名

  ig**nom**inious   *adj.* disgraceful and dishonorable 耻辱的，屈辱的；下流的

  nomenclature   *n.* terms used in a particular science or discipline 术语

  mis**nom**er   *n.* incorrect name 误称；错误的名称

- **NON-** (NOT 不) [L]

  nonplussed   *adj.* bewildered 困惑的；不知所措的，陷于窘境的

  nonchalant   *adj.* casual, unconcerned 漠不关心的；无动于衷的

  non sequitur   conclusion not following from apparent evidence 不根据前提的推理；不合逻辑的推论

  nondescript   *adj.* lacking interesting or distinctive qualities; dull 单调乏味的；莫可名状的；难以形容的

  non licet   not lawful 【法】不准许；不合法

Work 37

Match each word with its definition:

1. noctambulant
2. misnomer
3. nonplussed
4. neuroid
5. nom de guerre
6. neuralgia
7. non licet
8. noctilucous
9. neuter
10. neutralize

a. to counterbalance the effect of
b. shining at night
c. pain along nerve
d. not lawful
e. neither masculine nor feminine
f. nervelike
g. incorrect name
h. walking in one's sleep
i. bewildered
j. war name

ROUNDUP 38

- **NOV** (NEW 新的)[L]

  re**nov**ate   v. to restore to an earlier condition 翻修，整修；翻新

  novice   n. apprentice; beginner 新手；初学者

  novel   adj. new or original 新颖的；新奇的；独创的

  novitiate   n. a state of being a beginner or novice 见习(期)

  in**nov**ation   n. something newly introduced 改革；创新，革新

- **NUM** (NUMBER 数)[L]

  numismatics   n. coin collecting 收集钱币

  numeral   n. a symbol that represents a number 数字

  numerate   v. to count 数

  e**num**erate   v. to count off; list 计算；列举，枚举

  numerology   n. study of mystical meanings in numbers 数字命理学

- **OB-/OC-/OF-/OP-** (AGAINST 反)[L]

  obdurate   adj. stubborn 顽固的，执拗的

  occlude   v. to shut; block 堵塞；阻隔，挡住；封闭

  obliterate   v. to destroy completely 消灭；废除；彻底破坏

  opprobrious   adj. disgraceful; contemptuous 无礼的，轻蔑的；可耻的

  obfuscate   v. to obscure; confuse 使糊涂；使迷乱

- **OLIG-** (FEW, LITTLE 少的；小的)[G]

  oligopoly   n. situation with only a few sellers so that action by any one of them will affect price 卖方寡头垄断

  oligarchy   n. government by only a few 寡头政治

  oligodontous   adj. having few teeth 牙少的

  oligophagous   adj. eating only a few kinds of food 寡食性的，狭食性的

  oligosyllable   n. a word with only a few syllables 音节少的单词

- **OMNI-** (ALL, EVERY 全的；所有的) [L]
omnipotent	*adj.* having unlimited power 全能的；无所不能的	
omnivorous	*adj.* eating everything; absorbing everything 杂食的；无所不吃的	
omnipresent	*adj.* present everywhere 无所不在的	
omniscient	*adj.* having infinite knowledge 全知的；无所不知的	
omneity	*n.* a state of including all things 包罗万象	

Work 38

Match each word with its definition:

1.	obdurate	a.	to shut; block
2.	novice	b.	coin collecting
3.	oligarchy	c.	eating everything
4.	innovation	d.	stubborn
5.	oligodontous	e.	study of mystical meanings in numbers
6.	occlude	f.	a state of including all things
7.	omnivorous	g.	something newly introduced
8.	numerology	h.	government by only a few
9.	omneity	i.	having few teeth
10.	numismatics	j.	beginner

ROUNDUP 39

- **OPER** (WORK 工作) [L]
opera	*n.* musical work 歌剧
opere citato	already mentioned in the work 在前面所引用的书中
operon	*n.* a group of genes that operate as a unit 操纵子
operative	*adj.* functioning; working 有效的；运转着的
operose	*adj.* working hard 费力的；勤勉的, 辛勤的

- **OPTI/OPTO** (EYE, VISION 眼睛；视觉) [L]
optimistic	*adj.* looking on the positive side 乐观的
optician	*n.* someone who makes eyeglasses 眼镜(制造)商
optometry	*n.* measuring and testing of vision 验光；视力测定
optogram	*n.* an image fixed on the retina 视网膜像
optical	*adj.* of or relating to sight 眼睛的, 视觉的；光学的

- **ORTHO-** (STRAIGHT, CORRECT 直的；正确的) [L]
orthodox	*adj.* traditional; conservative 正统的；传统的
orthopraxy	*n.* correct action 正确的做法
orthodontics	*n.* correction of irregularity of teeth 畸齿矫正(术), 正牙学
orthognathism	*n.* condition of having straight jaws 正颌, 直颌
orthopedic	*adj.* correcting physical deformities 整形外科的

- **OS/OSS/OST/OSTEO**（BONE 骨）［L/G］

  osseous   *adj.* bony 骨的；多骨的

  ossify   *v.* to turn into bone 骨化；硬化；僵化

  osteitis   *n.* bone inflammation 骨炎

  ostosis   *n.* formation of bone 骨质生成；骨形成

  osteoma   *n.* bone tumor 骨瘤

- **PAC**（PEACE 和平）［L］

  pact   *n.* treaty 条约；公约；协定；契约

  pacifist   *n.* a person opposed to war or violence between nations 和平主义者；反战主义者

  pacify   *v.* to restore calm; bring peace 使镇静；使平静

  pacific   *adj.* calm; peaceful 镇静的；和平的

  pacification   *n.* appeasement 和解；平定；绥靖

Root Work 39

Match each word with its definition:

1. optician
2. pacify
3. orthopraxy
4. operon
5. pacifist
6. optometry
7. ostosis
8. orthodontics
9. operative
10. osseous

a. bony
b. correction of teeth irregularity
c. functioning
d. bone formation
e. to restore calm
f. testing of vision
g. correct action
h. a group of genes operating as a unit
i. a person opposed to war
j. maker of eyeglasses

ROUNDUP 40

- **PAL/PALEO**（ANCIENT 古的；旧的）［G］

  paleontology   *n.* study of past geological eras through fossil remains 古生物学

  paleoethnic   *adj.* relating to the earliest races of man 古人种的

  paleography   *n.* study of ancient writings 古文书学

  paleology   *n.* study of antiquities 考古学

  paleogenetic   *adj.* of past origin 遗传性的

- **PAN-**（ALL, EVERY 全部的；每个）［G］

  panorama   *n.* broad view; comprehensive picture 全景；全貌

  panacea   *n.* cure-all 灵丹妙药；万能药

  pantheon   *n.* all the gods of a people; group of highly regarded persons 众神；名流，伟人

  panoply   *n.* impressive array 雄伟的阵式

  pandemic   *adj.* spread over a whole area（疾病）大流行的；普遍的

- **PAR** (EQUAL 相等；平等) [L]

  parable   *n.* simple story that teaches a lesson 寓言

  parity   *n.* equality 平等；同等；相等

  par   *n.* equality of status or value 等值

  dis**par**ity   *n.* difference 不同；差异，不一致

  a**par**theid   *n.* a system of discrimination based on race 种族隔离

- **PARA-** (BEYOND, RELATED, ALONGSIDE 超越；相关的；在…旁) [G]

  paradigm   *n.* model; example; pattern 式样；典范，楷模

  paradisiacal   *adj.* heavenly; wonderful 天堂的；奇妙无比的

  paramount   *adj.* supreme; primary 至高无上的；最重要的；最主要的

  paragon   *n.* model of excellence 典范，模范

  parasite   *n.* a person or an animal that lives at another's expense 寄生虫；寄生物；食客

- **PAS/PATH** (FEELING, DISEASE, SUFFERING 感觉，感情；疾病；痛苦) [G]

  a**path**y   *n.* indifference 冷淡无情；漠不关心

  anti**path**y   *n.* dislike 反感，厌恶；憎恶

  pathos   *n.* pity; compassion 同情；怜悯

  pathogen   *n.* agent that causes disease 病菌；病原体

  dis**pass**ionate   *adj.* impartial; unaffected by emotion 公正的，不带偏见的；不动感情的

Work 40

Match each word with its definition:

1. paradigm   a. all the gods of a people
2. pantheon   b. study of ancient writings
3. paramount   c. dislike
4. disparity   d. comprehensive picture
5. paleogenetic   e. difference
6. pathos   f. equality
7. panorama   g. of past origin
8. antipathy   h. supreme
9. parity   i. model
10. paleography   j. pity; compassion

REVIEW 36–40

Matching

Match each of the following roots or prefixes to its meaning:

1. NECRO-   a. kill, death, harm
2. NEC/NIC/NOC/NOX   b. against
3. NEUR   c. peace
4. NOCT/NOX   d. ancient
5. NOV   e. nerve

6. OB-/OC-/OF-/OP-   f. dead, corpse
7. OPER   g. new
8. PAL/PALEO   h. feeling, disease, suffering
9. PAC   i. work
10. PAS/PATH   j. night

Fill-ins

Fill in the blanks with the word that fits the definition:

| paramount | noctivagant | oligophagous | omniscient | navarch |
| paragon | apartheid | ignominious | orthopraxy | osteoma |

1. correct action _____
2. disgraceful and dishonorable _____
3. supreme; primary _____
4. bone tumor _____
5. having infinite knowledge _____
6. commander of a fleet _____
7. wandering around at night _____
8. eating only a few kinds of food _____
9. a system of discrimination based on race that formerly existed in South Africa _____
10. model of excellence _____

True or False

If the statement is correct, put (T) True; if it is incorrect, put (F) False.

1. To renege is to repeat an offer of negotiation. _____
2. A neologism can be an existing word or expression used in a new way. _____
3. A neutron is an electrically neutral subatomic particle. _____
4. Numerology is the study of mystical meanings in natural phenomena. _____
5. A non sequitur is a conclusion that follows from apparent evidence. _____

ROUNDUP 41

- **PATER/PATR** (FATHER 父亲) [L]
  paternity   *n.* fatherhood; descent from father's ancestors 父权；父系；父系血统
  patronize   *v.* to condescend to; disparage; buy from 光顾，惠顾；资助
  patronage   *n.* support of a sponsor or benefactor, as for a cause or an institution 赞助；资助；光顾
  patricide   *n.* murder of one's father 弑父
  patrimony   *n.* inheritance or heritage derived from one's father 祖传的财物；继承物；遗产

- **PED** (CHILD 儿童) [G]

pedant	*n.* uninspired, boring academic who makes a display of his or her learning 卖弄学问的人；书呆子；学究
pedantic	*adj.* showing off learning 迂腐的；卖弄学问的；学究式的
pedagogue	*n.* teacher 教师
pedodontics	*n.* dentistry dealing with the treatment of children's teeth 儿童牙科学
encyclo**ped**ia	*n.* reference work that contains articles on a broad range of subjects 百科全书

- **PED/POD** (FOOT 脚) [G]

pediform	*adj.* shaped like a foot 脚形的，足状的
pedestrian	*adj.* commonplace 平淡的；一般的 *n.* a person traveling on foot 行人；步行者
pedate	*adj.* having feet 有脚的
pedometer	*n.* a device that measures distance by the number of steps of a walker 计步器
podiatry	*n.* the diagnosis and treatment of diseases of the foot 足部医疗；脚病学

- **PEL/PULS** (DRIVE, URGE 驱动，推动) [L]

pulse	*n.* a regular or rhythmical beating 律动
pulsate	*v.* to beat; vibrate 搏动；脉动；跳动；颤抖
re**pel**lant	*n.* something that repels or drives back 排斥力；抗耐剂
re**puls**e	*v.* to drive back; repel 击退；驱逐
pro**pel**lant	*n.* something that provides thrust 推进燃料；推进剂

- **PER-** (THROUGH, COMPLETELY 彻底，完全) [L]

peregrinate	*v.* to wander through 徒步旅行；漫游
percutaneous	*adj.* effecting something through the skin 经皮的；通过皮肤的
permeable	*adj.* penetrable 可渗透的
pervasive	*adj.* spread throughout every part 无处不在的；普遍的
permeate	*v.* to diffuse through 渗入；透入；弥漫

Work 41

Match each word with its definition:

1.	pedate	a.	fatherhood
2.	pedodontics	b.	murder of one's father
3.	repellant	c.	something that provides thrust
4.	patricide	d.	dentistry dealing with children's teeth
5.	propellant	e.	shaped like a foot
6.	pedantic	f.	having feet
7.	peregrinate	g.	something that drives back
8.	paternity	h.	to diffuse through
9.	permeate	i.	showing off learning
10.	pediform	j.	to wander through

ROUNDUP 42

- **PERI-** (AROUND, NEAR 周围；附近) [G]

periosteal	*adj.* around a bone 骨膜的
peripatetic	*adj.* moving about or from place to place 漫游的；徒步游历的
perihelion	*n.* the point in orbit nearest the Sun 近日点
perigee	*n.* the point in orbit nearest the Earth 近地点
periphrasis	*n.* circumlocution 迂回说法

- **PET** (SEEK, REQUEST, ASSAIL 追求；要求；打击) [L]

petition	*n.* request to a superior authority 情愿；祈求，恳求
com**pet**ition	*n.* the act of striving against others to attain a goal 竞争；竞赛
petulant	*adj.* contemptuous; peevish 暴躁的；任性的；易怒的
re**pet**itive	*adj.* given to the act of repeating 重复的
petitio principii	begging the question 预期理由

- **PHIL** (LOVE, FONDNESS, PREFERENCE 爱，喜欢；嗜好) [G]

philanthropist	*n.* lover of mankind; doer of good 慈善家；乐善好施的人
techno**phil**e	*n.* lover of technology 技术爱好者
philogynist	*n.* lover of women 喜欢女子的人
philhellene	*n.* lover of Greek culture 希腊文化爱好者
philtre	*n.* love potion 催情药，春药

- **PHOB** (FEAR 恐惧) [G]

phobia	*n.* abnormal, irrational fear of a situation or thing 恐惧症
arachno**phob**ia	*n.* abnormal fear of spiders 蜘蛛恐惧症
agora**phob**ia	*n.* fear of places that are public or open 广场恐惧症；旷野恐惧症
claustro**phob**ic	*n.* fear of being in enclosed spaces 幽闭恐惧症
hydro**phob**ia	*n.* fear of water 恐水症

- **PHON** (SOUND, VOICE 声，声音) [G]

micro**phon**e	*n.* an instrument that changes sound waves into electric current 麦克风，扩音器
phonogram	*n.* a symbol that represents sound 表音符号，音符
phonic	*adj.* relating to sound 有声的；声音的；声学的
phonetics	*n.* study of speech sounds 发音学；语音学
caco**phon**y	*n.* jarring, unpleasant noise 刺耳的声音，不和谐音

Work 42

Match each word with its definition:

1. petition
2. philtre
3. perihelion
4. hydrophobia
5. cacophony

a. lover of mankind
b. begging the question
c. moving about
d. relating to sound
e. request to a superior authority

6. peripatetic   f. love potion
7. phonic   g. the point in orbit nearest the Sun
8. petitio principii   h. fear of water
9. philanthropist   i. fear of places that are public or open
10. agoraphobia   j. unpleasant, jarring sound

ROUNDUP 43

- **PHOS/PHOTO**（LIGHT 光）［G］

  photosensitive   *adj.* sensitive to light or radiant energy 光敏的；感光的

  photograph   *n.* an image recorded by a camera and reproduced on a photosensitive surface 照片，相片

  phototaxis   *n.* growth directed by light 趋光性

  photophile   *n.* loving light 适光性；喜光性

  photometry   *n.* measurement of the properties of light 光度测定；光测量

- **PHYS/PHYSIO**（NATURE 自然）［G］

  physiology   *n.* functions of a living organism 生理；生理机能

  physical   *adj.* relating to the body 身体的

  physiolatry   *n.* worship of nature 自然崇拜

  physiocracy   *n.* government that is in accord with the operation of natural laws 重农主义

  physiognomy   *n.* divination of character from a person's face 相面术，占相术

- **PICT**（PAINT 描绘）［L］

  picture   *n.* an image rendered on a flat surface 图片

  de**pict**   *v.* to represent in a picture 绘画；描画

  pictograph   *n.* a picture that represents a word or idea 象形文字

  picturesque   *adj.* of a picture; quaintly attractive 如画的；生动的

  pictorial   *adj.* relating to or composed of pictures 绘画的

- **PLAC**（PLEASE 使高兴）［L］

  placid   *adj.* calm 温和的；平静的；沉着的

  placate   *v.* to lessen another's anger; pacify 安抚，抚慰；使和解

  im**plac**able   *adj.* inflexible, incapable of being appeased 无法平息的；难以和解的

  com**plac**ent   *adj.* self-satisfied 自满的；得意的；满足的

  placebo   *n.* something given to please or quiet 安慰剂；安慰的话(或行为)

- **POLI**（CITY, STATE, CITIZEN 城市；政府；市民）［G］

  politics   *n.* the art of governing a state and the control of its affairs 政治

  metro**poli**tan   *adj.* relating to a major city 大都市的

  cosmo**poli**tan   *adj.* common to the whole world 世界性的；四海一家的

  political   *adj.* relating to the affairs of the state 政治的

  polity   *n.* political organization of a state 政体；国体

Work 43

Match each word with its definition:

1. implacable
2. physiology
3. metropolitan
4. polity
5. phototaxis
6. depict
7. placebo
8. physiolatry
9. picturesque
10. photophile

a. something given to please
b. growth directed by light
c. worship of nature
d. incapable of being appeased
e. functions of a living organism
f. of a picture
g. loving light
h. relating to a major city
i. to represent in a picture
j. political organization of a state

ROUNDUP 44

- **POLY-**（MANY 多的）[G]

  polyphony　　*n.* use of one symbol for many sounds 多音；复调
  polymorphic　*adj.* having many forms 多形的；多形态的
  polyglot　　　*n.* speaker of many languages 通晓多种语言的人
  polygamy　　*n.* having more than one wife or husband at a time 一夫多妻，一妻多夫
  polytheist　　*n.* one who believes in more than one god 多神论者

- **PON/POS**（PUT, PLACE 放，置）[L]

  com**pos**e　　*v.* to constitute or form 组成；构成
  com**pon**ent　*n.* element; ingredient 成分；组件；元件
  com**pos**ite　*adj.* made up of components 复合的；合成的
  op**pos**e　　　*v.* to place so as to be opposite something else 反对；对抗；抗争
  re**pos**e　　　*v.* to place; lay down 休息；安眠；静卧

- **POPUL**（THE PEOPLE 人民）[L]

  populate　　*v.* to supply with inhabitants; people 构成人口；居住于
  popular　　*adj.* reflecting the taste of the people at large 受欢迎的；大众的，普及的；流行的，通俗的
  populace　　*n.* the masses 大众；平民
  population　*n.* all of the people who inhabit an area 人口；种群，群体
  populous　　*adj.* containing many inhabitants 人口稠密的

- **PORT**（CARRY, GATE 搬运；门）[L]

  portage　　*n.* the act of transporting or carrying 搬运；运输
  portal　　　*n.* entrance; gate 大门；入口
  portable　　*adj.* able to be carried easily 便于携带的；轻便的
  de**port**　　　*v.* to expel from a country 将…驱逐出境
  portfolio　　*n.* case to carry papers 公文包

- **POST-** (AFTER, BEHIND 在…之后) [L]

posterity	*n.* future generations; all of a person's descendants 子孙，后裔，后代，后世
posterior	*n.* bottom; rear 后部；后面
postdiluvian	*adj.* after the flood 大洪水后的
posthumous	*adj.* after a person's death 死后的；身后的
post factum	after the event 事后，事后行为

Work 44

Match each word with its definition:

1.	repose	a.	future generations
2.	posterity	b.	having many forms
3.	populace	c.	to people
4.	polytheist	d.	after the event
5.	portal	e.	entrance; gate
6.	populate	f.	to place; lay down
7.	oppose	g.	to place so as to be opposite something else
8.	portfolio	h.	one who believes in more than one god
9.	polymorphic	i.	case to carry papers
10.	post factum	j.	the masses

ROUNDUP 45

- **PRE-** (BEFORE, EARLIER 在…之前；早于…的) [L]

prenatal	*adj.* before birth 出生前的；产前的
preclude	*v.* to make impossible in advance 排除；妨碍；阻止
premise	*n.* proposition upon which an argument is based 前提
precept	*n.* principle; law 规则；训诫；格言；箴言
precedent	*n.* a model for something that follows 先例，前例

- **PREHEND/PREHENS** (SEIZE, GRASP 抓住) [L]

re**prehend**	*v.* to censure; reprove 斥责，指摘，责备
com**prehend**	*v.* to take in the meaning; grasp 理解；领会
ap**prehens**ion	*n.* act of seizing; understanding 逮捕；理解，领悟
prehensile	*adj.* able to grasp 可盘卷的
prehension	*n.* act of grasping 抓住；理解

- **PRIM** (BEFORE, FIRST 在…之前；第一的) [L]

prima facie	at first sight; on the face of it 乍看上去，据初步印象
primapara	*n.* a woman having her first child 首产妇
primeval	*adj.* ancient, primitive 原始的；太古的；初期的
primordial	*adj.* original; existing from the beginning 初生的；原始的
primogeniture	*n.* a state of being the eldest child 长子身份

- **PRO-**（FORTH; IN FAVOR OF 向前；赞同，支持）［L］

pro re nata	for an emergency (for the thing born) 临机应变；必要时
proponent	*n.* supporter 支持者
prodigy	*n.* a highly gifted child; marvel 天才；奇迹；奇观
propensity	*n.* inclination; tendency 倾向；癖好
proclivity	*n.* tendency; inclination 倾向；癖好

- **PROTO-**（FIRST, EARLIEST 起初的；最早的）［G］

protogenic	*adj.* formed at the beginning 原生的
prototype	*n.* an original model 原型；雏形；蓝本
protomorphic	*adj.* primitive 原始的
protoplast	*n.* an original ancestor 原人
protolithic	*adj.* relating to the first Stone Age 原始石器时代的，旧石器时代的

Work 45

Match each word with its definition:

1. prehension	a.	supporter
2. primordial	b.	at first sight
3. precedent	c.	a highly gifted child
4. protoplast	d.	an original ancestor
5. prima facie	e.	able to grasp
6. prodigy	f.	a model for something that follows
7. proponent	g.	act of grasping
8. protogenic	h.	original
9. prenatal	i.	formed at the beginning
10. prehensile	j.	before birth

REVIEW 41–45

Matching

Match each of the following roots or prefixes to its meaning:

1. PATER	a.	seek, request, assail
2. PEL/PULS	b.	put, place
3. PET	c.	father
4. PHIL	d.	in favor of
5. PHOS/PHOTO	e.	city, state, citizen
6. POLI	f.	before, first
7. PON/POS	g.	drive, urge
8. POPUL	h.	light
9. PRIM	i.	love, fondness, preference
10. PRO-	j.	the people

Fill-ins

Fill in the blanks with the word that fits the definition:

pedagogue	prehensile	placate	depict	percutaneous
protogenic	cacophony	portage	postdiluvian	agoraphobia

1. able to grasp _____
2. to represent in a picture _____
3. fear of places that are open or public _____
4. teacher _____
5. formed at the beginning _____
6. affecting something through the skin _____
7. after the flood _____
8. to lessen another's anger; pacify _____
9. jarring, unpleasant noise _____
10. the act of transporting or carrying _____

True or False

If the statement is correct, put（T）True; if it is incorrect, put（F）False.

1. The perigee is the point in orbit farthest from the Earth. _____
2. A physiocracy is a government that is in accord with the operation of natural laws. _____
3. Pro re nata means for an emergency. _____
4. Polyphony refers to the use of one symbol for many sounds. _____
5. A pedometer is a device that measures distance by the number of steps of a walker. _____

ROUNDUP 46

- **PSEUDO-**（FALSE 假的）［G］
  pseudonym   *n.* pen name; fictitious or borrowed name 笔名；假名
  pseudopsia   *n.* optical illusion 假视觉；视幻觉
  pseudodox   *n.* false doctrine 错误观点；谬论
  pseudomorph *n.* false or irregular form 伪形；假象
  pseudocyesis *n.* false pregnancy 假孕；假妊娠

- **PSYCH**（MIND 心灵）［G］
  psyche   *n.* the mind 灵魂；心智
  psychic   *adj.* perceptive of nonmaterial, spiritual forces; originating in the mind 精神的；心灵的
  psychiatrist   *n.* a doctor who treats disorders of the mind 精神病医生，精神病专家
  psychedelic   *adj.* mind-expanding 出现幻觉的
  psychology   *n.* study of the mind 心理学

- **PUB** (THE PUBLIC 公众) [L]

  public   *adj.* concerning the community or the people 公共的；公立的

  re**pub**lic   *n.* a political order in which a body of citizens has supreme power 共和国；共和政体

  publication   *n.* communication of information to the public 公布；发表

  publicity   *n.* act of communicating information to attract public interest 宣传，宣扬；公开

  publish   *v.* to announce; bring to the attention of the public 出版；发表；公布

- **PUNCT** (POINT, PRICK 点；刺) [L]

  punctilious   *adj.* strictly attentive to small details of form in conduct 一丝不苟的；谨慎的

  punctilio   *n.* a fine point of etiquette 细节

  punctual   *adj.* prompt 准时的；守时的，按时的

  puncture   *n.* a hole made by a sharp object 小孔；刺痕

  punctate   *adj.* like a point; ending in a point 点状的；有小点的

- **PUT/PUTAT** (THINK, CALCULATE 思考；计算) [l]

  putative   *adj.* supposed 推定的；假定的

  re**put**e   *v.* to consider; suppose 考虑；称为；认为

  re**put**ed   *adj.* supposed to be such 被普遍认为的；号称的

  re**putat**ion   *n.* a state of being held in high esteem 声望，名望；名誉

  com**put**e   *v.* to determine an amount or number 计算；估算

Work 46

Match each word with its definition:

1. psychic   a. concerning the people
2. punctate   b. the mind
3. compute   c. to bring to the attention of the public
4. public   d. a fine point of etiquette
5. putative   e. optical illusion
6. pseudodox   f. to determine an amount
7. punctilio   g. false doctrine
8. psyche   h. supposed
9. publish   i. originating in the mind
10. pseudopsia   j. like a point

ROUNDUP 47

- **QUER/QUES/QUIR/QUIS** (ASK, SEEK 问，追问) [L]

  query   *n./v.* (to) question 疑问；质问

  in**ques**t   *n.* investigation; court or legal proceeding 调查；审讯；审理；讯问

  in**quis**ition   *n.* investigation; act of inquiring 调查；审讯

  in**quir**er   *n.* one who asks a question 询问者；调查者

  re**quis**ite   *adj.* required 需要的；必要的

- **RE-** (BACK, AGAIN, REPEAT 后；再；重复) [L]

  recant   *v.* to retract a statement or opinion 宣布撤回；宣布放弃

  rebut   *v.* to refute by evidence or argument 反驳

  retract   *v.* to withdraw; take back 收回

  recurrence *n.* repetition 重现

  redundant   *adj.* exceeding what is necessary; unnecessarily repetitive 多余的，过剩的；累赘的

- **RECT** (STRAIGHT 直的) [L]

  e**rect**   *v.* to fix in an upright position 直立

  e**rect**ile   *adj.* able to be raised to an upright position 能够直立的

  rectitude   *n.* moral uprightness 诚实；公正；正直

  rectilinear *adj.* bounded by straight lines 直线的

  recto   *n.* right-hand page of a book (书的) 右页

- **RECT/REG/REGN** (RULE, GOVERN 统治；控制) [L]

  rector   *n.* an Anglican cleric in charge of a parish 教区长

  cor**rect**   *v.* to remove the errors from; punish for the purpose of improving 改正；纠正；责罚

  regime   *n.* government in power 政权；政体

  regulation *n.* law to govern conduct 法规；规章，制度

  regular   *adj.* conforming with fixed procedure or discipline 定期的；有规律的

- **RETRO-** (BACKWARD 向后) [L]

  retrospect *n.* review or contemplation of the past 回顾；追忆

  retrograde *adj.* having a backward motion or direction 后退的；倒退的；退化的

  retroactive *adj.* applying to an earlier time 追溯的；有追溯力的

  retroject   *v.* to throw back 向后抛；掷回

  retrovirus *n.* a virus that synthesizes DNA from RNA instead of the reverse 逆转录酶病毒

Work 47

Match each word with its definition:

1. retrograde   a. applying to an earlier time
2. redundant   b. （to）question
3. rectitude   c. right-hand page of a book
4. query   d. having a backward motion
5. recto   e. law to govern conduct
6. retroactive   f. government in power
7. regulation   g. required
8. regime   h. unnecessarily repetitive
9. requisite   i. moral uprightness
10. retract   j. to take back

ROUNDUP 48

- **RID/RIS**（LAUGH 笑）[L]

  de**rid**e   *v.* to mock 嘲笑；嘲弄；讥笑

  ridicule   *n.* words that evoke contemptuous laughter at a person 嘲笑；愚弄

  de**ris**ion   *n.* ridicule 嘲笑

  ridiculous   *adj.* deserving ridicule; absurd 可笑的，荒谬的

  ridibund   *adj.* easily moved to laughter 爱笑的

- **ROG**（ASK 问）[L]

  inter**rog**atory   *adj.* asking a question 质问的；疑问的

  pre**rog**ative   *n.* a special right or privilege 特权

  rogatory   *adj.* requesting information 咨询的；调查的

  rogation   *n.* solemn prayer 祈祷

  de**rog**atory   *adj.* disparaging; belittling 贬损的；贬抑的；轻视的

- **SACR/SANCT**（SACRED, HOLY 神圣的；圣洁的）[L]

  sanctuary   *n.* haven; retreat 避难所；庇护所

  sanctify   *v.* to set apart as holy; consecrate 使圣洁；使神圣；奉献于

  sanction   *n.* approval; ratification; permission 认可；批准；许可

  sacrosanct   *adj.* extremely sacred; beyond criticism 神圣不可侵犯的；极神圣的

  sanctimonious   *adj.* pretending to be pious or righteous 伪装虔诚的；伪装圣洁的；伪装正直的

- **SCI**（KNOW 知道）[L]

  scibile   *n.* something that is possible to know 可认知的事物

  sciolism   *n.* conceited and shallow knowledgeability 一知半解；学识浅薄

  con**sci**entious   *adj.* careful and thorough; governed by conscience 认真的，尽责的；本着良心的

  pre**sci**ent   *adj.* having foresight 有先见之明的；预知的

  ne**sci**ence   *n.* absence of knowledge; ignorance 无知

- **SCOP**（EXAMINE, OBSERVE, WATCH 检查；观察，注视）[G]

  scopic   *adj.* visual 视觉的

  tele**scop**e   *n.* device used to observe distant objects 望远镜

  peri**scop**e   *n.* optical instrument used to see things from a position not in a direct line of sight 潜望镜

  micro**scop**ic   *adj.* too small to be seen with the naked eye 微观的；用显微镜可见的

  colono**scop**e   *n.* long, flexible instrument used to visually examine the colon 结肠镜

Work 48

Match each word with its definition:

1. prescient
2. ridibund
3. sacrosanct
4. rogatory
5. telescope

a. absence of knowledge
b. to set apart as holy
c. to mock
d. visual
e. having foresight

6. interrogatory   f. extremely sacred
7. nescience   g. easily moved to laughter
8. deride   h. device used to observe distant objects
9. sanctify   i. asking a question
10. scopic   j. requesting information

ROUNDUP 49

- **SCRIB/SCRIP** (WRITE 写) [L]

  a**scrib**e   *v.* to attribute to a cause or source 归于；归因于；归咎于

  circum**scrib**e *v.* to limit; confine 限制

  pre**scrib**e   *v.* to set down a rule; recommend a treatment 规定；开药方

  manu**scrip**t   *n.* a document written by hand 手抄本；手稿

  nonde**scrip**t *adj.* lacking interesting or distinctive qualities; dull 莫可名状的；难以区别的

- **SE-** (AWAY, APART 离开；分开) [L]

  secede   *v.* to withdraw from membership in an alliance 从(组织)中脱离或退出

  select   *v.* to pick out; choose 挑选；选拔

  seclusion   *n.* act of keeping apart from social contact 隔离；隔绝；隐退

  seduce   *v.* to lead away from accepted principles; attract 唆使；引诱；怂恿；吸引

  secretive   *adj.* not open or frank 秘密的；偷偷摸摸的

- **SEC/SECT/SEGM** (CUT 切割) [L]

  sectile   *adj.* relating to a mineral that can be cut smoothly by a knife 可切的

  dis**sect**   *v.* to cut apart 切开

  inter**sect**ion *n.* the process or result of cutting across or through 交集，交叉；横断

  secant   *n.* a straight line that intersects a curve at two or more points 割线

  segmented *adj.* divided into parts 分段的；切割的

- **SECU/SEQU** (FOLLOW 跟随) [L]

  pro**secu**tor   *n.* one who initiates a civil or criminal court action 检察官；公诉人；起诉人

  sequel   *n.* something that follows 结局，后果；续集，续篇

  incon**sequ**ential *adj.* insignificant; unimportant 无关紧要的；不重要的

  ob**sequ**ious   *adj.* overly submissive 谄媚的；奉承的；顺从的

  sequacious *adj.* disposed to follow another 顺从的；盲从的

- **SEMI-** (HALF, PARTLY 半的；部分的) [L]

  semiterrestrial *adj.* partially living on land 半陆生的；半陆栖的

  semiannual *adj.* occurring twice a year 一年两次的；每半年的

  semiaquatic *adj.* not entirely adapted for living in water 半水生的；半水栖的

  semicircle   *n.* half of a circle 半圆

  semitaur   *n.* in mythology, a creature that is half-man and half-bull 神话中半人半牛的生物

Work 49

Match each word with its definition:

1. secede
2. obsequious
3. sectile
4. sequel
5. manuscript
6. semitaur
7. seclusion
8. semiaquatic
9. dissect
10. prescribe

a. act of keeping apart from social contact
b. a document written by hand
c. something that follows
d. to cut apart
e. to withdraw from membership in an alliance
f. half-man and half-bull
g. to set down a rule
h. not entirely adapted for living in water
i. overly submissive
j. relating to a mineral that can be cut smoothly by a knife

ROUNDUP 50

- **SENS/SENT**（FEEL, BE AWARE 感觉；认知）［L］

  sensate   *adj.* perceived by the senses 感觉到的；知觉的

  in**sens**ible   *adj.* unconscious; unresponsive 无知觉的；昏迷的；无反应的

  sentiment   *n.* a view based on emotion rather than reason 感情，情绪；感想

  sentient   *adj.* aware; conscious; able to perceive 有知觉的，有意识的

  sentisection   *n.* vivisection performed without the use of anesthesia 活体解剖

- **SOL**（SUN 太阳）［L］

  solarium   *n.* a room exposed to sunlight 阳光充足的房间；日光浴室

  solarize   *v.* to expose to sunlight 曝光

  solstice   *n.* point or time when the Sun is furthest from the Equator 至；至日

  soliterraneous   *adj.* relating to the meteorological effect of the Sun and the Earth 日对地的关系的

  solarimeter   *n.* device that measures the flux of the Sun's radiation 太阳辐射强度计，日射表

- **SOLV/SOLU**（FREE, LOOSEN, DISSOLVE 释放；放松；融化）［L］

  dis**solv**e   *v.* to make something pass into solution; melt; dispel 溶解；解散；消失

  soluble   *adj.* able to be dissolved; possible to solve 可溶解的；可解决的

  solute   *n.* substance dissolved in another one 溶剂；溶解物

  dis**solu**tion   *n.* disintegration; debauchery 溶解；解散；解除；放荡，纵情酒色

  irre**solu**te   *adj.* undecided 优柔寡断的；踌躇不定的

- **SOMN**（SLEEP 睡觉）［L］

  somnambulance   *n.* walking in one's sleep 梦游(症)

  somniloquence   *n.* talking in one's sleep 说梦话；梦呓(症)

  in**somn**ia   *n.* inability to fall asleep or remain asleep 失眠(症)

  somnolent   *adj.* sleepy 昏昏欲睡的；嗜睡的

  somniferous   *adj.* inducing sleep 催眠的

- **SOPH** (WISE, SKILLFUL, SHREWD 智慧的；有技巧的；精明的) [G]

  sophist　　　*n.* one who is skilled in deceptive argumentation 诡辩家

  sophistry　　*n.* plausible but misleading argumentation 诡辩

  sophisticate　*v.* to make more worldly; refine 使世故；使精巧

  sophomoric　　*adj.* showing lack of judgment and immaturity 一知半解的；幼稚的

  philo**soph**y　　*n.* love of wisdom 哲学

Work 50

Match each word with its definition:

1.	solarium	a.	able to perceive
2.	somniferous	b.	able to be dissolved or solved
3.	philosophy	c.	inducing sleep
4.	dissolution	d.	point when the Sun is furthest from the Equator
5.	sentiment	e.	sleepy
6.	soluble	f.	disintegration; debauchery
7.	somnolent	g.	to refine; make more worldly
8.	sophisticate	h.	a view based on emotion
9.	solstice	i.	a room exposed to sunlight
10.	sentient	j.	love of wisdom

REVIEW 46–50

Matching

Match each of the following roots or prefixes to its meaning:

1.	PSYCH	a.	sacred, holy
2.	PUB	b.	backward
3.	RECT	c.	know
4.	RETRO-	d.	free, loosen, dissolve
5.	SCI	e.	the public
6.	SACR/SANCT	f.	follow
7.	SE-	g.	straight
8.	SECU/SEQU	h.	feel, be aware
9.	SENS/SENT	i.	mind
10.	SOLV/SOLUT	j.	away, apart

Fill-ins

Fill in the blanks with the word that fits the definition:

retrospect	secant	punctilio	ridibund	pseudodox
somniloquence	sophistry	sequacious	recant	rogation

1. easily moved to laughter _____
2. plausible but misleading argumentation _____
3. contemplation of the past _____
4. a straight line that intersects a curve at two or more points _____
5. talking in one's sleep _____
6. false doctrine _____
7. to retract a statement or opinion _____
8. solemn prayer _____
9. a fine point of etiquette _____
10. disposed to follow another _____

True or False

If the statement is correct, put（T）True; if it is incorrect, put（F）False.

1. A punctilious person is inattentive to small details of form in conduct. _____
2. Rectilinear means bounded by straight lines. _____
3. Sectile relates to a mineral that can be cut smoothly by a knife. _____
4. A semitaur is a mythological creature that is half-man and half-lion. _____
5. Soliterraneous refers to the meteorological effect of the Moon and the Earth. _____

ROUNDUP 51

- **SPEC/SPECT/SPIC**（SEE, LOOK AT 看见，看）[L]

  specimen   *n.* a representative of a class or whole; a sample 样品；样本；范例

  specter   *n.* apparition 幽灵

  speculate   *v.* to take something as true based on insufficient evidence 推测，推断

  retro**spect**ive   *n.* review of the past 回顾

  per**spic**acious *adj.* shrewd; astute; keen-witted 精明的，敏锐的；伶俐的

- **SPIR**（BREATH, ENERGY, ANIMATION 呼吸；能量；生气）[L]

  re**spir**ation   *n.* breathing 呼吸

  a**spir**ation   *n.* expulsion of breath in speaking 送气

  spirit   *n.* animating force within living things 灵魂；灵气

  spirited   *adj.* animated; courageous 生机勃勃的；英勇的

  spirograph   *n.* device that records the movements of breathing 呼吸运动记录器

- **STAS/STAT**（STAND, BEING IN A PLACE, POSITION 站立；立场，位置）[G]

  stationary   *adj.* not moving 静止的；固定的

  static   *adj.* having no motion; fixed; stationary 不动的；静止的；固定的

  state   *n.* condition of being 状态

  status   *n.* position or standing in relation to that of others 地位

  status quo   existing state of affairs 现状

- **STRICT/STRING** (TIGHT, DRAWN TOGETHER 紧的；拉到一起的) [L]

  re**strict**   *v.* to keep within limits 限制，限定；约束

  stricture   *n.* limit; restriction 限制，约束，束缚

  stringent   *adj.* imposing rigorous standards; constricted; tight 严格的，严厉的；紧迫的

  strict   *adj.* precise; within narrow limits; rigorous in discipline 精确的，严格的；严谨的

  con**strict**   *v.* to squeeze or compress; restrict the scope of 压缩；束紧；限制

- **STRUCT** (BUILD 建造) [L]

  de**struct**ion   *n.* act of destroying 毁灭；破坏；摧毁

  structure   *n.* something built 结构；构造

  con**struct**   *v.* to build 建造，构建

  in**struct**ion   *n.* act of methodically providing with knowledge 指导；教导；传授

  inde**struct**ible *adj.* impossible to destroy 坚不可摧的

Work 51

Match each word with its definition:

1. spirited   a. impossible to destroy
2. stricture   b. existing state of affairs
3. retrospective   c. limit; restriction
4. stringent   d. device that records the movements of breathing
5. constrict   e. to restrict the scope of
6. status quo   f. review of the past
7. spirograph   g. fixed; stationary
8. indestructible   h. imposing rigorous standards; constricted
9. static   i. apparition
10. specter   j. animated

ROUNDUP 52

- **SUB-/SUC-/SUF-/SUG-/SUP-/SUS-** (BELOW, UNDER, LESS 在⋯之下；少于⋯的) [L]

  subtle   *adj.* hard to detect or describe 微妙的

  subterfuge   *n.* trick or tactic used to avoid something 遁词；借口；诡计

  subsume   *v.* to include; incorporate 包含，包括；把⋯归入

  suppress   *v.* to put down by force; restrain 镇压；抑制

  suspend   *v.* to defer; interrupt 推迟；中断，暂停；dangle, hang 悬(浮)；挂

- **SUPER-/SUR-** (OVER, ABOVE 超过；在⋯之上) [L]

  superior   *adj.* higher than another in rank or authority 上级的；优秀的

  supersede   *v.* to take the place of 代替，取代

  in**super**able   *adj.* insurmountable; unconquerable 不能克服的；不能征服的；不可逾越的

  supernal   *adj.* celestial; heavenly 天上的；神圣的

  surtax   *n.* additional tax 附加税

- **SYL-/SYM-/SYN-/SYS-** (TOGETHER, WITH 一起；和) [G]

  syllogism   *n.* argument with a conclusion deduced from two premises 三段论

  synchronous   *adj.* occurring at the same time; moving at the same rate 同时的；同步的

  syndicate   *n.* association of people who undertake a duty or transact business 辛迪加；企业联盟

  synthesis   *n.* blend；combination 合成，综合

  system   *n.* group of interrelated elements that form a whole 系统；体系

- **TACT/TANG** (TOUCH 触摸) [L]

  con**tact**   *n.* coming together or touching 接触；联系

  tactile   *adj.* relating to the sense of touch 触觉的

  tactus   *n.* sense of touch 触觉

  tangible   *adj.* able to be touched 可见的；有形的；可触摸的

  tangent   *n.* digression; diversion 离题；改变

- **TELE-** (DISTANCE, FAR 距离；远的) [G]

  telemeter   *n.* instrument that measures distance 遥测计；测距仪

  telemetry   *n.* science of transmitting data from someplace remote to a distant receiving station 遥感勘测

  telecommunication   *n.* science of communicating over distances by electronic transmission 电信学

  teleseism   *n.* tremor from a distant earthquake 远震

  telephony   *n.* sound transmission between distant stations 电话通讯；电话学

Work 52

Match each word with its definition:

1.	suspend	a.	blend
2.	supernal	b.	sense of touch
3.	suppress	c.	heavenly
4.	tactus	d.	to interrupt; dangle
5.	synchronous	e.	able to be touched
6.	teleseism	f.	insurmountable
7.	synthesis	g.	instrument that measures distance
8.	telemeter	h.	to put down by force
9.	tangible	i.	tremor from a distant earthquake
10.	insuperable	j.	occurring at the same time

ROUNDUP 53

- **TEMPOR** (TIME 时间) [L]

  con**tempor**ary   *adj.* belonging to the same time period 同时代的；当代的，现代的

  temporal   *adj.* related to time 当时的；暂时的；现世的

  temporize   *v.* to act evasively to gain time, avoid an argument, or postpone a decision 敷衍；拖延

  ex**tempor**aneous   *adj.* unrehearsed 无准备的；即席的；临时的

  temporality   *n.* being bounded in time 暂时性

- **TEN/TAIN**（HOLD 抓住）[L]

detain	v. to delay; keep from proceeding 耽搁
pertain	v. to relate to 属于；关于
tenacious	adj. stubborn; holding firm 顽强的；坚韧的；固执的；紧握的
content	n. something that is contained 内容；含量
tenure	n. a period during which something is held 任期；占有期

- **TEND/TENS/TENT**（STRETCH, STRIVE 伸展；争斗）[L]

tension	n. act of stretching tight 紧张；绷紧，拉紧
contend	v. to strive in opposition; struggle 主张；奋斗，斗争；竞争
contention	n. act of striving in controversy 争论，争辩；竞争
tense	adj. tightly stretched 紧张的；拉紧的
tensor	n. a muscle that stretches a body part 张肌

- **TERM**（END, LIMIT 结尾；界限）[L]

terminal	adj. concluding; final; fatal 终点的；末端的；晚期的
midterm	n. middle of an academic term 期中的
terminate	v. to end 结束；终止；满期
interminable	adj. endless 冗长的；无限的；无止境的
termless	adj. having no limits; unending 无限期的；无条件的

- **TERR**（LAND, THE EARTH 土地；地球）[L]

terraqueous	adj. consisting of land and water 水陆的；水陆两栖的
terraceous	adj. earthen 土的，土质的
terrestrial	adj. related to the land of the Earth 地球的；陆地的；地上的
terra firma	dry land 陆地
terra incognita	unknown land 未知地区；未知领域

Work 53

Match each word with its definition:

1. interminable		a.	earthen
2. terminal		b.	to act evasively to gain time
3. tensor		c.	stubborn; holding firm
4. contend		d.	consisting of land and water
5. temporal		e.	endless
6. tenacious		f.	a muscle that stretches a body part
7. detain		g.	final
8. terraqueous		h.	to strive in opposition
9. temporize		i.	related to time
10. terraceous		j.	to delay

ROUNDUP 54

- **TERTI** (THIRD 第三的) [L]

  tertial   *adj.* relating to the third row of flight feathers on the basal section of a bird's wing （指鸟翼基部关节上的拨风羽）第三列的

  tertian   *adj.* recurring after three days 每三日复发一次的；间日的

  tertiary   *adj.* third in degree or rank 第三的；第三位的

  tertium quid   a third thing of indeterminate character 中间物；第三者

  tertiary color   a color that results from mixing two secondary colors 两种颜色混合后的第三色，三次色

- **THE/THEI/THEO** (GOD 神) [G]

  atheist   *n.* a person who does not believe in the existence of God 无神论者

  theocracy   *n.* government by priests representing a god 神权政治

  theology   *n.* study of God and religion 神学；宗教学

  apo**theo**sis   *n.* glorification; glorified ideal 神化；崇拜；颂扬

  theogamy   *n.* marriage of gods 神神联姻

- **THERAP** (ATTEND, TREAT 关注；处理；治疗) [G]

  therapy   *n.* treatment of illness 治疗；疗法

  therapeutic   *adj.* having healing powers 治疗的；有益于健康的

  therapist   *n.* specialist in a particular therapy 治疗学家；特定疗法专家

  bio**therap**y   *n.* treatment of disease with preparations synthesized from living organisms 生物疗法

  physio**therap**y   *n.* treatment of physical injury with therapeutic exercise 物理疗法

- **THERM/THERMO** (WARM, HOT 温暖的；热的) [G]

  thermochemistry   *n.* the chemistry of heat 热化学

  thermal   *adj.* relating to, or caused by heat 热的；热量的

  thermoduric   *adj.* able to survive high temperatures 耐热的

  thermodynamic   *adj.* resulting from heat conversion 热力学的；使用热动力的

  thermolabile   *adj.* subject to change or destruction by heating 不耐热的；受热即分解的

- **TOM/TOME/TOMY** (CUT, SECTION 切，割；截面；部分) [G]

  tome   *n.* one book in a work of many volumes 册，卷

  derma**tome**   *n.* instrument used to cut slices of the skin in skin grafts 皮刀

  micro**tome**   *n.* instrument that cuts specimens into slices for examination with microscopes （显微镜用）切片机

  gastro**tomy**   *n.* surgical incision into the stomach 胃切开术

  vasec**tomy**   *n.* surgical removal of a duct that carries semen 输精管切除术

Work 54

Match each word with its definition:

1. tertian   a. marriage of gods

2. therapy   b. surgical incision into the stomach

3. thermoduric   c. having healing powers

4. apotheosis
5. thermal
6. tertium quid
7. gastrotomy
8. therapeutic
9. tome
10. theogamy

d. recurring after three days
e. one book in a work of many volumes
f. caused by heat
g. glorified ideal
h. able to survive high temperatures
i. a third thing of an indeterminate character
j. treatment of illness

ROUNDUP 55

- **TOP/TOPO** (PLACE, REGION 地点；地区) [G]

topography	n. the configuration of a land surface 地势；地貌；地形
topology	n. regional anatomy 局部解剖学
toponym	n. name of a place 地名
topophobia	n. fear of certain places 特殊场所恐惧
topos	n. a traditional theme (文学创作上的)传统主题

- **TORS/TORT/TORQU** (TWIST, TURN 扭转；转动) [L]

re**tort**	n. quick caustic reply that turns the first speaker's words to one's own advantage 反驳；顶嘴
torsion	n. act of twisting or turning 扭曲；扭转
con**tort**	v. to twist out of shape 扭曲；曲解
torque	n. a turning or twisting force 转矩；力矩
tortuous	adj. winding; twisting; circuitous 扭曲的，弯曲的；啰唆的

- **TRACT** (DRAG, PULL 拉；拖；拔) [L]

at**tract**	v. to cause to draw near 吸引
tractor	n. vehicle for pulling machinery 拖拉机；牵引机
tractable	adj. easy to manage or control; easy to manipulate 易于管教的；易驾驭的；驯良的，听话的
in**tract**able	adj. not easily managed 不易于管教的；棘手的
pro**tract**	v. to draw out; prolong 绘制；延长，伸展

- **TRAN-/TRANS-** (ACROSS, THROUGH 通过，穿过) [L]

transcend	v. to rise above; go beyond 超越；胜过
transmute	v. to change in appearance, shape or nature 变形；变质；变相
transgression	n. the exceeding of a limit or boundary 越界；侵犯
translucent	adj. clear; lucid 清楚的；透明的；明晰的
transmogrify	v. to change into a different shape or form (使)变形

- **TREM/TREMU** (TREMBLE, SHAKE 晃动，抖动) [L]

tremendous	adj. enormous; able to make one tremble 巨大的；惊人的
tremulous	adj. marked by shaking or trembling 战栗的；震颤的
tremble	v. to shake involuntarily; quake; feel fear 颤抖；战栗
tremor	n. a shaking movement; a trembling or quivering 抖动；颤抖；震颤
tremolo	n. a quivering effect produced by quickly repeating a single tone 颤声，颤音

Work 55

Match each word with its definition:

1.	tortuous	a.	a turning or twisting force
2.	attract	b.	name of a place
3.	topophobia	c.	to go beyond
4.	protract	d.	to change in appearance or nature
5.	transmute	e.	to cause to draw near
6.	torque	f.	winding; twisting
7.	tremulous	g.	fear of certain places
8.	toponym	h.	a shaking movement
9.	tremor	i.	marked by trembling
10.	transcend	j.	to draw out; prolong

REVIEW 51–55

Matching

Match each of the following roots or prefixes to its meaning:

1.	SPIR	a.	far
2.	STRUCT	b.	end, limit
3.	TACT/TANG	c.	place, region
4.	TELE-	d.	attend, treat
5.	TEMPOR	e.	warm, hot
6.	TERM	f.	build
7.	THERAP	g.	touch
8.	THERM/THERMO	h.	time
9.	TOP/TOPO	i.	drag, pull
10.	TRACT	j.	breath, energy, animation

Fill-ins

Fill in the blanks with the word that fits the definition:

supernal	tenacious	theogamy	synchronous	stricture
thermoduric	toponym	torque	status quo	contention

1. marriage of gods _____
2. act of striving in controversy _____
3. able to survive high temperatures _____
4. existing state of affairs _____
5. stubborn; holding firm _____
6. occurring at the same time; moving at the same rate _____
7. a twisting or turning force _____

318

8. celestial; heavenly _____

9. limit; restriction _____

10. name of a place _____

True or False

If the statement is correct, put（T）True; if it is incorrect, put（F）False.

1. To transmogrify is to change into a different shape or form. _____

2. To subsume is to regard something as assumed. _____

3. A spirograph is an instrument used to measure wind direction. _____

4. Tertial refers to the second row of flight feathers on the basal section of a bird's wing.

   _____

5. A tremolo is a quivering effect produced by quickly repeating a single tone. _____

ROUNDUP 56

- **TURB**（SPINNING, CONFUSION, DISTURBANCE 旋转；混乱；扰乱）［G］

turbid	*adj.* in a state of turmoil 浑浊的；混乱的
turbine	*n.* machine that converts the energy of moving fluid to rotary mechanical power 涡轮机
turbojet	*n.* jet engine with a turbine-driven compressor 涡轮喷气发动机
turbulent	*adj.* violently agitated 混乱的，骚乱的；狂暴的
dis**turb**ance	*n.* commotion 扰乱；不安；骚乱

- **TYP/TYPE**（TYPE 种类）［G］

typal	*adj.* relating to or serving as a type 典型的
typical	*adj.* conforming to a type 典型的；特有的；代表性的
typify	*v.* to represent as a typical example of; symbolize 代表；作为典型
typology	*n.* the study or classification of types 类型学
stereo**type**	*n.* a formulaic conception or image 陈规，陈腔滥调；老套

- **ULTRA-**（BEYOND, EXCESSIVE, ON THE OTHER SIDE OF 超越；过多的；在另一边）［L］

ultrasonic	*adj.* relating to acoustic frequencies above the ear's audible range 超声的
ultramodern	*adj.* extremely modern in style or ideas 超现代的
ultraconservative	*adj.* conservative to an extreme 超级保守的，极端保守的
ultranationalism	*n.* extreme nationalism 极端民族主义；狭隘民族主义
ultramundane	*adj.* extending beyond the world or the universe 世界之外的；超然的，超俗的

- **UN-**（NOT, REVERSE, UNDO, REMOVE 不；相反；解开；去除）［L］

unfeigned	*adj.* not feigned; not made up; genuine; real 真实的；非虚伪的
untenable	*adj.* not viable; indefensible 不能防守的；不能维持的，支持不住的
unyielding	*adj.* firm; resolute 不屈服的，不屈不挠的
unequivocal	*adj.* absolute; certain 绝对的；明白的，明确的；不含糊的
unfetter	*v.* to free from restraints; liberate 解放，释放

- **UNI-** (ONE 一个) [L]

unique	*adj.* one of a kind 独特的，独一无二的
universal	*adj.* characterizing or affecting all; present everywhere 全世界的；普遍的；通用的
unipolar	*adj.* having a single magnetic or electric pole 单极的
unicorn	*n.* a mythological creature, usually represented as a horse, with a single horn projecting from its forehead 独角兽，麒麟
unanimity	*n.* a state of total agreement or unity 同意；全体一致

Work 56

Match each word with its definition:

1. unfeigned
2. unipolar
3. unanimity
4. typify
5. turbid
6. ultramodern
7. typal
8. untenable
9. disturbance
10. ultramundane

a. commotion
b. extending beyond the world or universe
c. in a state of turmoil
d. not made up; genuine
e. serving as a type
f. not viable
g. a state of total agreement
h. to represent as an example
i. extremely modern in ideas or style
j. having a single magnetic or electric pole

ROUNDUP 57

- **URB** (CITY 城市) [L]

urban	*adj.* related to a city 城市的；市区的
sub**urb**	*n.* residential area outlying a city 郊区；市郊
urbane	*adj.* refined; sophisticated; suave 温文尔雅的；彬彬有礼的
urbanite	*n.* city dweller 城市居民；都市人
urbanologist	*n.* specialist in city life 都市问题专家；都市学专家

- **US/UT** (USE; USEFUL 用；用途；有用的) [L]

usage	*n.* act of using 使用；用途；用法
usurp	*v.* to seize by force 篡夺，夺取；侵占
usury	*n.* lending money at exorbitant rates 高利贷
utilitarian	*adj.* concerned with usefulness rather than beauty 实用的；实际的；实用主义的；功利主义的
utile	*adj.* useful 有用的；有益的

- **VAC/VACA/VACU** (EMPTY 使空；空的) [L]

vacate	*v.* to empty of occupants 空出；腾出；搬出
vacuum	*n.* space empty of matter 真空
vacuous	*adj.* empty; void; lacking intelligence; purposeless 空的；空虚的；空洞的；无意义的
vacuity	*n.* emptiness of mind; lack of ideas 空虚；空白；思想贫乏
vacuole	*n.* small cavity in cell cytoplasm 液泡

- **VEH/VECT**（CARRY 携带；搬运）［L］

  vehicular   *adj.* relating to vehicles 车辆的；用车辆运载的

  vehemently   *adv.* vigorously; energetically 热烈地；激烈地

  vector   *n.* a course or direction 向量，矢量

  vectoring   *n.* guiding by radio communication according to vectors 引导；确定航向

  convection   *n.* transmission 对流；传送，传导

- **VEN/VENT**（COME 来）［L］

  invent   *v.* to produce or contrive by ingenuity 发明；创造

  prevention   *n.* act of impeding; hindrance 阻止；妨碍；预防

  conventional *adj.* customary 传统的，符合习俗的

  circumvent   *v.* to avoid 绕行；避免

  contravene   *v.* to act contrary to; violate 抵触；违反

Work 57

Match each word with its definition:

1. vacuity
2. urbanite
3. conventional
4. usage
5. vehemently
6. utilitarian
7. convection
8. urbanologist
9. circumvent
10. vacuole

a. act of using
b. vigorously
c. concerned with usefulness rather than beauty
d. city dweller
e. small cavity in cell cytoplasm
f. to avoid
g. specialist in city life
h. customary
i. emptiness of mind; lack of ideas
j. transmission

ROUNDUP 58

- **VER/VERAC/VERI**（TRUE 真的）［L］

  veritable   *adj.* real; genuine 真正的；名副其实的

  verity   *n.* truthfulness 真实性；确实

  aver   *v.* to affirm; declare to be true 断言；主张；极力声明

  veracity   *n.* accuracy; truthfulness 准确性，精确性；真实性；确实

  verisimilitude *n.* quality of appearing true or real 逼真

- **VERB**（WORD 词）［L］

  verbatim   *adj.* corresponding word for word 逐字的

  verbal   *adj.* associated with words 言语的；口头的

  proverbial   *adj.* widely referred to 公认的；众所周知的

  verbiage   *n.* an excess of words; wordiness 冗长；累赘

  verbose   *adj.* wordy; long-winded 冗长的；啰嗦的

- **VERS/VERT** (TURN, CHANGE 转；变化) [L]

versatile	*adj.* adaptable, all-purpose 多才多艺的；多方面的；通用的，万能的
re**vers**ion	*n.* return to an earlier stage 返回；逆转
a**vert**	*v.* to turn away; prevent 转开，转移；避免，防止
extro**vert**	*n.* a person whose psychological energy is directed toward other people 性格外向者
vertigo	*n.* dizziness 眩晕，头晕

- **VIA** (WAY, ROAD 途径；道路) [L]

via	*prep.* by way of 经由；取道；通过
via media	middle way or course 中间道路；中庸之道
viaduct	*n.* series of spans that carry a road over another road or a valley 高架桥
viatical	*adj.* relating to a road or traveling 道路的
viaticum	*n.* traveling provisions 旅行必需品；旅费

- **VICT/VINC/VANQ** (CONQUER 征服) [L]

victor	*n.* one who defeats an adversary 胜利者
victory	*n.* defeat of an enemy; triumph 胜利；成功；凯旋
e**vict**	*v.* to force out; expel 逐出，赶出，驱逐
in**vinc**ible	*adj.* impossible to overcome or defeat 不可征服的，难以制服的
vanquish	*v.* to conquer in battle; subjugate 征服；击败；克服

Work 58

Match each word with its definition:

1.	verbose	a.	an excess of words
2.	aver	b.	to turn away; prevent
3.	via media	c.	relating to a road or traveling
4.	verisimilitude	d.	to declare to be true
5.	vanquish	e.	adaptable
6.	avert	f.	wordy; long-winded
7.	viatical	g.	to conquer in battle; subjugate
8.	verbiage	h.	middle way or course
9.	invincible	i.	quality of appearing true or real
10.	versatile	j.	impossible to defeat

ROUNDUP 59

- **VID/VIS** (SEE, LOOK 看见，看) [L]

video	*adj.* relating to televised images 视频的，电视的；录像的
visible	*adj.* perceptible to the eye 可见的
super**vis**or	*n.* one who is in charge 管理人；监督人
vista	*n.* a distant view or prospect 远景
visage	*n.* appearance; aspect; countenance 外貌；面容；方面

- **VIR** (MAN 男人) [L]

virile	*adj.* having the characteristics of an adult male 男性的，有男子气概的，刚健的
virtue	*n.* moral excellence and righteousness 正直；善良
virago	*n.* woman who is noisy and scolding, or domineering 泼妇，悍妇
virility	*n.* manly characteristic; potency 男子气；生殖力
virilism	*n.* male sexual characteristics in a female（女性）男性化

- **VIT** (LIFE 生命) [L]

vital	*adj.* characteristic of or relating to life 至关重要的；生死攸关的；有活力的，充满生机的
vitalize	*v.* to endow with life; invigorate 赋予生命；激发；使有活力，使有生气
curriculum **vit**ae	a summary of a person's education and professional life 履历，简历
vitamin	*n.* organic substance needed for normal growth and body activity 维生素
vitality	*n.* capacity to live and grow 活力，生气；生命力

- **VIV/VIVA** (ALIVE, LIVELY, ANIMATED 活着的；活跃的，给以生命的) [L]

sur**viv**e	*v.* to remain alive 存活；幸存
vivacious	*adj.* lively 欢快的，活泼的；有生气的
con**viv**iality	*n.* the state of being merry 欢乐；高兴
vivarium	*n.* enclosure where living things are raised for observation and research 植物园；动物园
vivisection	*n.* the practice of cutting into or otherwise injuring living animals, especially for the purpose of scientific research 活体解剖

- **VOC/VOKE** (CALL 大声喊叫) [L]

ad**voc**ate	*v.* to recommend; plead for 提倡；主张；拥护；请求
equi**voc**al	*adj.* ambiguous; misleading 模棱两可的；可疑的
irre**voc**able	*adj.* conclusive; irreversible 不可改变的；不可逆转的；不可撤销的
vociferous	*adj.* loud, vocal, and noisy 大声喊叫的；吵吵嚷嚷的
e**voke**	*v.* to produce a reaction 引起，唤起

Work 59

Match each word with its definition:

1. virtue
2. conviviality
3. vista
4. advocate
5. vitalize
6. virile
7. vociferous
8. vitality
9. visage
10. vivacious

a. capacity to live and grow
b. appearance; countenance
c. to endow with life
d. having the characteristics of an adult male
e. a distant view
f. loud, vocal, and noisy
g. lively
h. moral excellence
i. to plead for
j. the state of being merry

ROUNDUP 60

- **VOL/VOLI** (WISH, CHOICE 愿望；选择) [L]

  voluntary   *adj.* done of one's own free will 自愿的，自发的

  volition   *n.* act of making a conscious choice 选择；决定

  bene**vol**ent   *adj.* characterized by doing good 善意的；仁慈的；慈善的

  male**vol**ent   *adj.* showing ill will; wishing harm to others 恶毒的；有恶意的

  volitive   *adj.* relating to the will; expressing a wish 意志的；表示意愿的

- **VOLV/VOLU** (ROLL, TURN 滚动；转动) [L]

  e**volu**tion   *n.* changing of a thing into a more complex or better form 进化，进展；演变，演化

  de**volv**e   *v.* to pass on or transfer to another 移交；转移

  re**volu**tion   *n.* a turning around an axis 旋转

  volution   *n.* a turn or twist around a center 旋转，螺旋

  volvulus   *n.* abnormal twisting of the intestine 肠扭结，肠扭转

- **VOR/VORAC** (DEVOUR; GREEDY 吞噬；贪婪的) [L]

  voracious   *adj.* having an insatiable appetite; ravenous 贪吃的；狼吞虎咽的；贪婪的

  voracity   *n.* condition of being eager to consume great amounts of food 贪婪；贪食

  carni**vor**e   *n.* flesh-eating animal 食肉动物

  herbi**vor**e   *n.* animal that feeds mainly on plants 食草动物

  omni**vor**ous   *adj.* eating both animals and plants 杂食性的

- **XEN/XENO** (STRANGER, FOREIGNER 陌生人；外国人) [G]

  xenophobe   *n.* person who is afraid of strangers or foreigners 惧外者

  xenophile   *n.* one who is attracted to foreigners 崇洋媚外者

  xenobiotic   *adj.* foreign to living organisms 异型生物质的

  xenocryst   *n.* foreign crystal in an igneous rock 捕获晶

  xenogenesis   *n.* production of children that are very different from either parent 异种生殖

- **ZO/ZOO** (ANIMAL 动物) [G]

  zoology   *n.* study of the structure and classification of animals 动物学

  zoolatry   *n.* animal worship 动物崇拜

  zoogenic   *adj.* produced by animals 由动物产生的

  zoonosis   *n.* animal disease that can be transmitted to human beings 动物传染病，人畜共患病

  zoophilia   *n.* affection for animals 嗜兽癖；动物爱好

Work 60

Match each word with its definition:

1. volvulus
2. malevolent
3. herbivore
4. xenobiotic
5. revolution
6. zoogenic
7. xenophile

a. foreign to living organisms

b. relating to the will

c. animal worship

d. a turning around an axis

e. abnormal twisting of the intestine

f. wishing harm to others

g. ravenous

8. volitive
9. zoolatry
10. voracious

h. animal that feeds on plants
i. produced by animals
j. one who is attracted to foreigners

REVIEW 56–60

Matching

Match each of the following roots or prefixes to its meaning:

1. TURB
2. UNI-
3. VEH/VECT
4. VEN/VENT
5. VERB
6. VICT/VINC/VANQ
7. VIT/VITA
8. VOC/VOKE
9. VOR/VORAC
10. XEN/XENO

a. life
b. word
c. one
d. conquer
e. devour, greedy
f. carry
g. spinning, confusion, disturbance
h. stranger, foreigner
i. come
j. call

Fill-ins

Fill in the blanks with the word that fits the definition:

invincible	**vacuous**	**virago**	**convection**	**ultramundane**
usurp	**urbane**	**unfeigned**	**viatical**	**curriculum vitae**

1. extending beyond the world or the universe _____
2. empty; void _____
3. impossible to defeat or overcome _____
4. sophisticated; refined; suave _____
5. woman who is domineering _____
6. not made up; genuine; real _____
7. relating to a road or traveling _____
8. to seize by force _____
9. a summary of a person's education and professional life _____
10. transmission _____

True or False

If the statement is correct, put (T) True; if it is incorrect, put (F) False.

1. Unanimity is a state of total chaos. _____
2. A utilitarian is concerned with aesthetics rather than usefulness. _____
3. The quality of appearing real or true is verisimilitude. _____
4. Xenogenesis is the production of children that are very similar to one parent. _____
5. Zoophilia is an abnormal fear of animals. _____

Common Suffixes

-able, -ible: capable of, subject to, prone to; worthy of, deserving of 能…的；易于…的；倾向于；值得…的

impeccable	*adj.* 无瑕疵的；没有缺点的
incorrigible	*adj.* 无可救药的；积习难改的
irrefutable	*adj.* 不能驳倒的
mutable	*adj.* 易变的；不定的
feasible	*adj.* 可行的；可能的
affable	*adj.* 和蔼可亲的；友善的
gullible	*adj.* 易受骗的；轻信的
laudable	*adj.* 值得赞赏的
reprehensible	*adj.* 应受斥责的，应受指摘的
culpable	*adj.* 该责备的；有罪的

-ac: relating to 与…相关的；person affected with 受…感染的人

ammoniac	*adj.* 氨的；含有氨的
celiac	*adj.* 腹腔的
maniac	*adj.* 发狂的，发疯的 *n.* 疯子；狂热分子
cardiac	*adj.* 心脏的；心脏病的 *n.* 心脏病患者
hypochondriac	*adj.* 忧郁症的 *n.* 忧郁症患者

-age: relationship; condition; action or result; place 表关系、状态、行为或结果、处所

parentage	*n.* 出身；门第；血统
bondage	*n.* 奴役；束缚
carnage	*n.* 大屠杀；残杀
anchorage	*n.* 锚地，停泊地点；抛锚，停泊

-al, -ial: of, pertaining to 属于…的；与…相关的；the act of 表行为

logical	*adj.* 合逻辑的；合理的
ephemeral	*adj.* 短暂的；朝生暮死的
equivocal	*adj.* 模棱两可的；可疑的
glacial	*adj.* 冰川的；冰冷的
peripheral	*adj.* 外围的；次要的
polemical	*adj.* 好辩的；好争论的 *n.* 辩论
prodigal	*adj.* 挥霍的；浪费的；奢侈的
provincial	*adj.* 省的；地方性的；褊狭的
rhetorical	*adj.* 修辞的
satirical	*adj.* 讽刺的；讥讽的；挖苦人的
superficial	*adj.* 表面的；浅薄的

terrestrial	adj. 地球的；陆地的 n. 陆地生物
whimsical	adj. 异想天开的；反复无常的；古怪的
denial	n. 否认；否定；拒绝
rehearsal	n. 排演；预演；排练

-an, -ian: belonging to, related to, characteristic of, resembling 属于…的；与…相关的；具有…特征的；像…的；one that is 表人

Canadian	adj. 加拿大(人)的 n. 加拿大人
Freudian	adj. 弗洛伊德式的 n. 弗洛伊德学者
reptilian	adj. 爬虫类的 n. 爬虫类动物
civilian	adj. 民用的，百姓的 n. 平民，百姓
antediluvian	adj. 大洪水前的；远古的；陈旧的 n. 大洪水以前的人；不合时宜的人
subterranean	adj. 地下的；秘密的 n. 地下工作者
authoritarian	adj. 独裁主义的；专制的 n. 独裁主义者
partisan	adj. 党派的；偏袒的 n. 党羽
artisan	n. 工匠，技工

-ance, -ence: action or process; state of being 表行为、过程、状态

emergence	n. 出现，浮现；发生
dependence	n. 依赖；依靠
arrogance	n. 自大；傲慢
compliance	n. 顺从；服从
vigilance	n. 警戒；警觉
exuberance	n. 丰富；茂盛
impudence	n. 冒失；厚颜无耻
nonchalance	n. 冷淡；漠不关心
opulence	n. 富裕；丰富
quiescence	n. 静止；沉默
reticence	n. 沉默寡言；勉强

-ant, -ent: causing or performing something 引起某种行为或表现的；state of being; one who does or undergoes 表状态、从事某事的人

document	n. 文件；公文；文档
flagrant	adj. 公然的；臭名昭著的
ardent	adj. 热情的；热切的；热烈的
benevolent	adj. 仁慈的；慈善的
indifferent	adj. 漠不关心的
inherent	adj. 固有的；内在的
munificent	adj. 慷慨的；宽宏的
strident	adj. 刺耳的；尖锐的
virulent	adj. 剧毒的；致命的
contestant	n. 竞争者；争辩者
pedant	n. 学究，书呆子；卖弄学问的人

-ar, -ary: relating to; connected to 与…相关的；与…有联系的

solar	*adj.* 太阳的；日光的
polar	*adj.* 极地的；两极的
jocular	*adj.* 诙谐的；滑稽的
arbitrary	*adj.* 任意的；武断的，专制的
exemplary	*adj.* 典范的；可仿效的
mercenary	*adj.* 雇用的；唯利是图的
centenary	*adj.* 一百年的

-ate: act upon; having; characterized by 对…起作用；拥有…的；以…为特征的

obliterate	*v.* 消灭；涂去；涂掉
mitigate	*v.* 使缓和；使减轻
deprecate	*v.* 反对；抨击；轻视
emulate	*v.* 仿真；模仿；尽力赶上
debilitate	*v.* 使衰弱；使虚弱
extricate	*v.* 使解脱；使摆脱
facilitate	*v.* 促进；帮助
instigate	*v.* 唆使；教唆；煽动
perpetuate	*v.* 使不朽；长存 *adj.* 长存的
truncate	*v.* 截短；缩短 *adj.* 截短的；被删节的
placate	*v.* 安慰；抚慰；平息
intimidate	*v.* 恐吓，威胁；胁迫
repudiate	*v.* 拒绝；否定；批判
ornate	*adj.* 华丽的；装饰的；绚丽的
innate	*adj.* 先天的；固有的；与生俱来的
articulate	*adj.* 发音清晰的；口才好的

-cy: state of being; quality 表状态、性质

ascendancy	*n.* 优势；支配地位
bankruptcy	*n.* 破产
lunacy	*n.* 精神失常
dependency	*n.* 从属；依赖
complacency	*n.* 自满；自鸣得意

-dom: domain; rank; state of being 表领域、等级、状态

fiefdom	*n.* 封地；权力机构
boredom	*n.* 无聊；厌倦
martyrdom	*n.* 殉难，牺牲；受苦，受难
officialdom	*n.* 官场；官僚作风

-eer, -er, -or: person who does something 从事…的人

auctioneer	*n.* 拍卖商
engineer	*n.* 工程师
contender	*n.* 竞争者
director	*n.* 监督者；主管；导演
executor	*n.* 执行者
orator	*n.* 演说者；雄辩家

-ery: a place for; the act of; state of; qualities of 表场所、行为、状态、性质

bakery	*n.* 面包店	
bribery	*n.* 行贿；受贿；贿赂	
chicanery	*n.* 狡辩；欺骗	
slavery	*n* 奴隶制	
snobbery	*n.* 势利；摆架子	

-(esc)ent: becoming; beginning to be; characterized by（开始）成为…的；以…为特征的

crescent	*adj.* 逐渐增加的；新月的
nascent	*adj.* 初期的；初生的
evanescent	*adj.* 容易消散的；逐渐消失的
phosphorescent	*adj.* 发出磷光的

-ferous: producing; carrying 产生的；带来的

coniferous	*adj.* 结球果的；松柏科的
vociferous	*adj.* 喊叫的；喧嚷的
aquiferous	*adj.* 含水的；蓄水的
calciferous	*adj.* 含钙的
carboniferous	*adj.* 含碳或煤的；产碳或煤的

-fic: making; causing 制成的；引起的

terrific	*adj.* 可怕的；恐怖的
horrific	*adj.* 可怕的；恐怖的
beatific	*adj.* 幸福的；快乐的
prolific	*adj.* 多产的；丰富的
soporific	*adj.* 催眠的；昏昏欲睡的
benefic	*adj.* 有益的
malefic	*adj.* 有害的

-fy: make; cause to become 制作，做；使成为

falsify	*v.* 伪造；篡改；掺假
magnify	*v.* 放大，夸大
exemplify	*v.* 例证，例示
ratify	*v.* 批准，认可
rectify	*v.* 改正；纠正；整顿
personify	*v.* 使人格化
purify	*v.* 净化，使纯净
mortify	*v.* 抑制；约束

-ia: abnormal condition 表非正常状态

anorexia	*n.* 厌食
toxemia	*n.* 毒血症
septicemia	*n.* 败血症
memorabilia	*n.* 大事记；值得纪念的事件或经历
personalia	*n.* 轶事

-ic: having to do with 与…相关的; one characterized by 以…为特征的人或物

cosmic	*adj.* 宇宙的
hedonistic	*adj.* 快乐主义的; 快乐论的
caustic	*adj.* 腐蚀性的; 刻薄的 *n.* 腐蚀剂
aesthetic	*adj.* 审美的; 美学的
altruistic	*adj.* 利他的, 无私心的
archaic	*adj.* 古代的; 陈旧的; 古体的
ascetic	*adj.* 苦行的; 禁欲主义的 *n.* 苦行者; 禁欲者
bombastic	*adj.* 夸大的; 言过其实的
cryptic	*adj.* 神秘的; 含义模糊的
dogmatic	*adj.* 教条的; 武断的
eclectic	*adj.* 折中的 *n.* 折中主义者
ironic	*adj.* 讽刺的; 挖苦的
sporadic	*adj.* 零星的; 分散的
lunatic	*adj.* 精神错乱的; 疯狂的 *n.* 疯子
heretic	*adj.* 异端的; 异教的 *n.* 异教徒; 异端者

-ide: group of related chemical compounds; binary compound; chemical element with properties that are similar to another 一组相关的化合物; 二元化合物; 化学性质相似的元素

diglyceride	*n.* 甘油二酯
monosaccharide	*n.* 单糖
chloride	*n.* 氯化物
potassium	*n.* 钾
bromide	*n.* 溴化物
boride	*n.* 硼化物

-il, -ile: pertaining to; capable of being 与…相关的; 能…的

puerile	*adj.* 幼稚的, 孩子气的
ductile	*adj.* 柔软的; 易延展的; 易教导的
infantile	*adj.* 婴儿的; 幼稚的; 初期的
senile	*adj.* 高龄的
servile	*adj.* 奴性的; 卑屈的
tensile	*adj.* 可拉长的; 可伸长的
versatile	*adj.* 多才多艺的; 多方面的; 通用的, 万能的

-ine: having the nature of; relating to; resembling; made of 具有…性质的; 和…相关的; 像…的; 由…构成(或制成)的; chemical substance 化学物质

divine	*adj.* 有神性的; 神圣的
feline	*adj.* 猫的, 猫科的; 似猫的
marine	*adj.* 海洋的; 海运的; 船舶的
leonine	*adj.* 狮子的; 狮子般的
saturnine	*adj.* 忧郁的; 阴沉的
opaline	*adj.* 乳白色的 *n.* 乳白玻璃
crystalline	*adj.* 水晶般的; 晶体的; 透明的

tourmaline	n. 电气石
incarnadine	n. 肉色 adj. 肉色的
gasoline	n. 汽油

-ion, -tion, -ation: state or condition; the result of 表状态、条件、结果

criterion	n. 标准，准则
oblivion	n. 遗忘，忘却；忽视
limitation	n. 限制；限度；极限
adulation	n. 奉承；谄媚
affirmation	n. 主张；肯定；断言
apprehension	n. 理解；逮捕；恐惧；忧虑
aversion	n. 厌恶；嫌恶
conviction	n. 信念；深信；定罪
degradation	n. 退化，恶化；降级；堕落
disinclination	n. 不感兴趣；厌恶
innovation	n. 改革；创新，革新
sanction	n. 认可，批准；许可；制裁
seclusion	n. 隔绝；隐退；隐居

-ise, -ize: make; become like 使；制作；成为

surmise	v. 猜测；推测
maximize	v. 使最大化
scrutinize	v. 详细检查；仔细观察
vaporize	v. (使)蒸发
hypothesize	v. 假设；假定
cauterize	v. 灼烧；使麻木不仁

-ism: belief; doctrine; devotion to; act of 主义，信仰；教义；行为

ethnocentrism	n. 民族(或种族)优越感
egotism	n. 自我中心论
fanaticism	n. 狂热，着迷；盲信
criticism	n. 批评；苛求
witticism	n. 妙语；俏皮话

-ist: one who does something; one who believes or adheres to something; an expert 做某事的人；持某种信仰的人；专家

opportunist	n. 机会主义者；投机取巧者
cartoonist	n. 漫画家
ventriloquist	n. 腹语术者；口技表演者
altruist	n. 利他主义者
pacifist	n. 和平主义者
nihilist	n. 虚无主义者
prohibitionist	n. 禁酒主义者

linguist	n. 语言学家
geologist	n. 地质学家；地质学者
psychiatrist	n. 精神病学家
scientist	n. 科学家

-ite: make, do 使，做; inhabitant or native of; descendant of; adherent of 居民；后裔；信徒

ignite	v. 点燃，使着火
Israelite	n. 以色列人；犹太人
Luddite	n. 路德分子(反对新技术或新工作方法的人)

-itis: inflammatory disease 炎症

dermatitis	n. 皮炎
phlebitis	n. 静脉炎
appendicitis	n. 阑尾炎
tendonitis	n. 肌腱炎
osteoarthritis	n. 骨关节炎

-ity, -ty: state of; quality 表状态、性质

animosity	n. 憎恶，仇恨，敌意
paucity	n. 缺乏；少数，少量
reality	n. 现实；实体；真实性
uniformity	n. 一致；同样；均匀
similarity	n. 相似，类似；相似性
enmity	n. 敌意；憎恨
duplicity	n. 口是心非；表里不一
depravity	n. 堕落；邪恶；败坏；腐化
insularity	n. 褊狭；僵化；岛国性质
notoriety	n. 恶名；臭名；声名狼藉
novelty	n. 新颖；新奇
integrity	n. 完整；正直；诚实；廉正
virility	n. 男子气概；生殖力
tenacity	n. 坚韧不拔；不屈不挠
veracity	n. 诚实；老实；真实性

-ive: tending toward an action; belonging, quality of 倾向于某种行为的；表属性、性质

argumentative	adj. 好辩的；争辩的
introspective	adj. 内省的；反省的
collective	adj. 集体的；共同的 n. 集体
comprehensive	adj. 综合的；广泛的 n. 综合学校
derivative	adj. 派生的 n. 派生物；衍生物
elusive	adj. 逃避的；难以捉摸的
exhaustive	adj. 详尽的；彻底的
furtive	adj. 鬼鬼祟祟的；秘密的
inclusive	adj. 包括的；包含的；包罗万象的

-let: small one; small object worn on the body 小东西；佩戴的小物件

eaglet	n. 小鹰
islet	n. 小岛
piglet	n. 小猪
ringlet	n. 小圈；小环
amulet	n. 护身符；辟邪物
rivulet	n. 小溪；小河
pamphlet	n. 小册子

-(o)logy: expression; theory; science; study of 表达；理论；学科；研究

eulogy	n. 悼词；颂词；赞扬
phraseology	n. 措辞；用词
ideology	n. 意识形态；思想意识
geology	n. 地质学；地质情况

-ly: like; to the extent of, recurring at specified intervals; in a specified way 像…的；到…程度的；以一定间隔重复发生的；特定的（或地）

miserly	adj. 吝啬的；贪婪的
daily	adj. 日常的；每日的
slowly	adv. 缓慢地；慢慢地

-ment: act; state; means 表行为、状态、方法

entertainment	n. 娱乐；消遣
admonishment	n. 训诫；警告
abatement	n. 减少；减轻
detachment	n. 分离，拆开；超然
instrument	n. 仪器，器械；工具

-oid: form, shape 形态，外形；resembling; relating to 像…的；与…相关的

android	n. 机器人 adj. 具有人类特征的
humanoid	n. 类人动物 adj. 像人的
planetoid	n. 小行星
asteroid	n. 小行星 adj. 星状的
spheroid	n. 球状体
paranoid	n. 偏执狂患者 adj. 多疑的

-or: a person or thing that does something; a quality or condition 做某事的人或物；表性质、状态

inspector	n. 检查员；巡视员
progenitor	n. 祖先；起源
incisor	n. 门牙；切牙

-ory: relating to; characterized by 与…相关的；以…为特征的；a place used for 表场所

obligatory	*adj.*	义务的；必需的
conciliatory	*adj.*	安抚的，抚慰的；缓和的
cursory	*adj.*	粗略的；草率的；匆忙的
observatory	*n.*	天文台；气象台；瞭望台

-ose: full of; characterized by 充满…的；以…为特征的；a form of sugar 一种糖

verbose	*adj.*	冗长的；啰嗦的
lachrymose	*adj.*	爱哭的；易流泪的
jocose	*adj.*	诙谐的
sucrose	*n.*	蔗糖
dextrose	*n.*	葡萄糖

-osis: condition; disease 状态；疾病

apotheosis	*n.*	神化；崇拜
metamorphosis	*n.*	变形；变质
morphosis	*n.*	形态形成
apoptosis	*n.*	细胞凋亡
neurosis	*n.*	神经官能症
psychosis	*n.*	精神病；神经错乱

-ous: full of; characterized by 充满…的；以…为特征的

assiduous	*adj.*	刻苦的；勤勉的
autonomous	*adj.*	自治的；自主的
capricious	*adj.*	任性的；善变的
contentious	*adj.*	有争议的；爱争论的
erroneous	*adj.*	错误的
fastidious	*adj.*	挑剔的；苛求的
gregarious	*adj.*	社交的；群居的
ingenious	*adj.*	有独创性的；心灵手巧的
innocuous	*adj.*	无害的；无伤大雅的
nefarious	*adj.*	邪恶的
pretentious	*adj.*	自命不凡的；矫揉造作的
querulous	*adj.*	喜欢抱怨的，爱发牢骚的；易怒的；暴躁的
raucous	*adj.*	沙哑的；粗声的
scrupulous	*adj.*	小心谨慎的；一丝不苟的

-tude: state of being 表状态

magnitude	*n.*	震级；量级
solitude	*n.*	孤独
solicitude	*n.*	关心，挂念；渴望
verisimilitude	*n.*	逼真
lassitude	*n.*	疲乏；懒散
pulchritude	*n.*	美丽；标致
turpitude	*n.*	卑鄙；奸恶

Posttest

It's time to put your new knowledge of words and roots to the test. If you studied carefully and did the exercises diligently, you should see a significant improvement in your score compared to your score on the Pretest. Good luck!

Choose the best word or set of words to fill in the blanks in each of the sentences below.

1. It is not _____ to term the post-World War II developments in computer technology a revolution.
   (A) doggerel
   (B) debauchery
   (C) hyperbole
   (D) demographic
   (E) agnostic

2. To the modern sensibility, Baroque art seems to rely too much on _____, or even bizarre, ornamentation.
   (A) ephemeral
   (B) incongruous
   (C) invidious
   (D) loquacious
   (E) puissant

3. The phrase "true fact" may prompt one to _____ whether a fact can be untrue.
   (A) gainsay
   (B) foreswear
   (C) jibe
   (D) query
   (E) juxtapose

4. The statement "Men can run faster than women" is not true because it is an overgeneralization; some women can run faster than some men. The statement could be made valid by _____ it: "Many men can run faster than many women."

(A) substantiating

(B) rescinding

(C) sanctioning

(D) distilling

(E) qualifying

5. Until his death in 2004, John Mack, who was a professor of psychiatry at Harvard Medical School, had a reputation as _____ investigator who believed that many scientists are reluctant to investigate reports of humans being abducted by aliens because such events are incompatible with the prevailing Western materialist and _____ worldview.

(A) a subversive .. salacious

(B) a laconic .. doctrinaire

(C) a suppliant .. dogmatic

(D) an iconoclastic .. anthropocentric

(E) an ambiguous .. egotistical

6. Language purists pounce on errors as though they were ghastly offences against the natural order; however, it is wise to remember that language is a wonderfully _____ tool that is sometimes at its best when it is most _____ .

(A) florid .. fettered

(B) glib .. compliant

(C) malleable .. unfettered

(D) demotic .. whimsical

(E) plastic .. tortuous

7. Some observers contend that the alliance of big business with big science and technology has created a _____ that is _____ government, creating an elite that is insensitive to society's true needs.

(A) tautology .. obviating

(B) technocracy .. supplanting

(C) theocracy .. admonishing

(D) juggernaut .. forswearing

(E) matriarchy .. superseding

8. The sociologist Stanley Milgram theorized that the rise of mass society has made it easier for individuals to ignore responsibility than in more cohesive societies, because the individual is frequently "an intermediate link in a chain of evil," making it possible for a person to rationalize

his actions by saying, "I was only carrying out my social responsibilities as given in the orders of my superiors; it is not for me to decide the ultimate morality of socially _____ actions, even if they appear _____."

(A) warranted .. perfidious

(B) venerated .. malign

(C) subversive .. meretricious

(D) substantiated .. Machiavellian

(E) sanctioned .. execrable

9. In _____ Singapore, the _____ that _____ communication between speakers of Chinese, Malay, and Tamil is English.

(A) hermetic .. rubric .. impedes

(B) polyglot .. lingua franca .. facilitates

(C) multifarious .. mnemonic .. proscribes

10. Steeped in mysticism and allegory, _____ has been a favorite subject of people speculating about the existence of _____ tradition concealed behind _____ facade.

(A) alchemy .. an occult .. a mundane

(B) metaphysics .. a singular .. a sedulous

(C) necromancy .. a hermetic .. an avuncular

Read the following passage carefully. Then answer the questions that follow.

"You cannot plumb the depths of the human heart, nor find what a man is thinking; how do you expect to search out God, who made all these things, and find out his mind or comprehend his thoughts?"

—*Apocrypha,* Judith 8:14

(5)   Experience has repeatedly confirmed that well-known maxim of Bacon's that "a little philosophy inclineth man's mind to atheism, but depth in philosophy bringeth men's minds about to religion." In every age the most comprehensive thinkers have found in the religion of their time and country something they could accept, interpreting and illustrating that religion so as to give it depth and universal application. Even the heretics and atheists, if they have had

(10) profundity, turn out after a while to be forerunners of some new orthodoxy. What they rebel against is a religion alien to their nature; they are atheists only by accident, and relatively to a convention which inwardly offends them, but they yearn mightily in their own souls after the

religious acceptance of a world interpreted in their own fashion. So it appears in the end that their atheism and loud protestation were in fact the hastier part of their thought, since what

(15) emboldened them to deny the poor world's faith was that they were young wits and worm-eaten old satirists, who plume themselves on detecting the scientific ineptitude of religion—something which the blindest half see—is not nearly enlightened enough; it points to notorious fact incompatible with religious tenets literally taken, but it leaves unexplored the habits of thought from which those tenets sprang; their original meaning, and their true function. Such

(20) studies would bring the skeptic face to face with the mystery and pathos of mortal existence. They would make him understand why religion is so profoundly moving and in a sense so profoundly just. There must needs be something humane and necessary in an influence that has become the most general sanction of virtue, the chief occasion for art and philosophy, and the source, perhaps, of the best human happiness.

—*Reason in Religion,* George Santayana

11. The word "profundity" as it is used in line 10 most nearly means
   (A) vertigo
   (B) fidelity
   (C) depth
   (D) knowledge
   (E) faith

12. The word "convention" as it is used in line 12 most nearly means
   (A) misogynist
   (B) widely accepted belief
   (C) gathering of people
   (D) cosmology
   (E) decorum

13. The word "plume" as it is used in line 16 most nearly means
   (A) enrich
   (B) plumb
   (C) reward
   (D) convince oneself
   (E) congratulate oneself in a self-satisfied way

14. The word "skeptic" as it is used in line 20 most nearly means
   (A) person who doubts

(B) misanthrope

(C) person who adopts a liberal view

(D) atheist

(E) zealot

15. The word "pathos" as it is used in line 20 most nearly means

(A) intransigence

(B) quality that causes pity or sorrow

(C) meaninglessness

(D) capriciousness

(E) existential purpose

Read the following passage carefully. Then answer the questions that follow.

The author refers to articles by several scholars in two collections of papers on Mediterranean anthropology.

"Mediterranean honor," according to David Gilmore's introduction, "is a 'libidinized' social reputation; and it is this eroticized aspect of honor—albeit unconscious or implicit—that

(5) seems to make the Mediterranean variant distinctive." Again: "Mediterranean...unity is at least partly derived from the primordial values of honor and shame, and these values are deeply tied up with sexuality and power, with masculine and gender relations." Again: "If a gender based honor-and-shame moral system defines a Mediterranean World, then this category emerges not simply as an example of butterfly collecting, but as a mutually intelligible framework of moral

(10) choices by which people communicate and gain an identity both with and within the group." That same specification is underlined in the collection's concluding essay by Stanley Brandes. "It is this pervasive sexuality that is particularly characteristic of Mediterranean value systems, of Mediterranean codes of honor and shame. In this, the codes may be distinguished from parallel moral systems elsewhere, in Japan, for example."

(15) In his 1977 survey of Mediterranean anthropology, John Davis claims, "There are three main forms of stratification which have been observed in the Mediterranean: bureaucracy, class, and honor. Each of them is related to the distribution of wealth, more or less directly. They are, for the purpose of analysis, ideal types, distinct elementary forms which, in substantive politics, are intertwined, mixed in varying degrees, variously important. Each is associated with an

(20) appropriate mode of political representation — again, ideal types, elementary forms, which in the hugger-mugger* of actual political activity have variable importance. These are: insistence on citizen's rights; class struggle; patronage."

---

* hugger-mugger: disorderly confusion

Those three stratification systems are exemplified very clearly in John G. Peristiany's essay. His fieldwork concentrated on the Greek Cypriot mountain village of Alona in the middle-

(25) 1950s. Stratification by bureaucracy and power is clear when the villager has to approach a government civil servant and when "in the impersonal interaction between citizen and civil servant the only claim upon the latter's philotimo** is that of this own sectional interests, and these call for the assertion of his administrative dignity, for arrogance and the marking of social distance." Stratification by wealth and class is clear "when the returned expatriate

(30) who had achieved success in a city environment wished to trade on this success as a means of achieving immediate recognition in the village... [and] considered...further that his financial success raised him above the confines of the village hierarchy." But neither of those other stratifications is confused by the villagers with their own hierarchy of honor and shame. Peristiany concludes by comparing honor and honesty:

(35)   "The punctiliousness of honor must be referred to the code of an exclusive and agonistic*** microsociety: that of honesty to an inclusive, egalitarian macrosociety. Duty, in the first instance, is to those with whom one shares honor. In the second, the un-Greek macrosociety, one's duty is to all fellow citizens or, even further, to all humans...Honor is active. Here insecurity and the daily reevaluation of one's standing breed constant self-assertion and

(40) even heroism. The ideals of honesty and equality breed passive conformity and are more congenial to a conception of duty wide in its application, but more accommodating in its expectation."

—*The Historical Jesus, The Life of a Mediterranean Jewish Peasant*, John Dominic Crossan

16. According to David Gilmore, honor and shame are
    (A) analogous values
    (B) anachronistic codes of honor found only in Mediterranean culture
    (C) original values of Mediterranean culture
    (D) immutable values in all cultures studied by anthropologists
    (E) perennial truths

17. The word "stratification" as it used in line 16 can most accurately be described as referring to
    (A) discrimination based on gender and social class
    (B) individual income as a determinant of social class
    (C) archaeological layers revealing life in a succession of Mediterranean towns through the millennia

---

** philotimo: a Greek word meaning "love of honor"
*** agonistic: combative

(D) vendettas

(E) the hierarchical arrangement of individuals in a society into classes or castes

18. The word "patronage" as it is used in line 22 most nearly means

(A) the power to appoint people to high positions in society

(B) trade given to a business by its customers

(C) fatherhood

(D) patriarchy

(E) old age

19. The word "punctiliousness" as it is used in line 35 most nearly means

(A) carelessness in being punctual

(B) petulance about perceived threats to masculine pride

(C) pusillanimity in obeying authority

(D) carefulness in observing rules of behavior

(E) irascibility

20. The word "congenial" as it is used in line 41 most nearly means

(A) friendly

(B) suited to

(C) chivalrous

(D) conciliatory

(E) convivial

End of Posttest

ANSWERS

1. C	2. B	3. D	4. F	5. D
6. C	7. B	8. E	9. B	10. A
11. C	12. B	13. E	14. A	15. B
16. C	17. E	18. A	19. D	20. B

YOUR POSTTEST SCORE

1—3	CORRECT ANSWERS: VERY POOR
4—6	CORRECT ANSWERS: POOR
7—9	CORRECT ANSWERS: BELOW AVERAGE
10—12	CORRECT ANSWERS: AVERAGE
13—15	CORRECT ANSWERS: GOOD
16—18	CORRECT ANSWERS: VERY GOOD
19—20	CORRECT ANSWERS: EXCELLENT

Answer Key

UNIT 1

Matching

1. g   2. c   3. j   4. b   5. f   6. a   7. i   8. e   9. h   10. d

Fill-ins

1. abdicated   2. aberrations   3. abeyance   4. abstemious   5. abate

6. abstinence   7. abject   8. abjured   9. abscission   10. absconded

Sense or Nonsense

1. S   2. S   3. N   4. N   5. S

UNIT 2

Matching

1. b   2. f   3. a   4. i   5. d   6. j   7. e   8. c   9. g   10. h

Fill-ins

1. affected   2. affinity   3. accretion   4. aesthetic   5. admonished

6. accrued   7. abysmal   8. adamant   9. adulterated   10. adjunct

Sense or Nonsense

1. S   2. N   3. S   4. N   5. N

UNIT 3

Matching

1. d   2. g   3. a   4. j   5. f   6. h   7. b   8. c   9. e   10. i

Fill-ins

1. allure   2. alacrity   3. alleviate   4. aggrandize   5. alchemy

6. ambiguous   7. aggregate   8. alloys   9. allay   10. amalgamate

Sense or Nonsense

1. N   2. S   3. N   4. N   5. S

UNIT 4

Matching

1. c   2. i   3. g   4. a   5. j   6. e   7. f   8. b   9. h   10. d

Fill-ins

1. ambivalent   2. anarchy   3. amulet   4. ambrosia   5. analgesic

6. analogy   7. ameliorate   8. amenable   9. anachronism   10. amenities

Sense or Nonsense

1. N   2. S   3. N   4. S   5. S

UNIT 5

Matching

1. g   2. i   3. c   4. b   5. e   6. a   7. h   8. f   9. j   10. d

Fill-ins

1. antecedents   2. antipathy   3. apathy   4. anomalous   5. appease

6. antediluvian   7. apothegms   8. anodyne   9. apogee   10. apex

Sense or Nonsense

1. N   2. S   3. N   4. N   5. S

UNIT 6
Matching

1. e   2. g   3. j   4. h   5. b   6. a   7. d   8. i   9. c   10. f

Fill-ins

1. apropos   2. apprised   3. arduous   4. ardor   5. Archeology

6. appropriated   7. arabesque   8. appellation   9. apposite   10. approbation

Sense or Nonsense

1. S   2. N   3. S   4. S   5. N

UNIT 7
Matching

1. h   2. e   3. c   4. a   5. j   6. g   7. b   8. f   9. d   10. i

Fill-ins

1. artless   2. asperity   3. ascetic   4. astringent   5. artifact

6. arrest   7. assuage   8. assiduously   9. argot   10. aspersions

Sense or Nonsense

1. N   2. N   3. S   4. S   5. S

UNIT 8
Matching

1. h   2. b   3. j   4. e   5. a   6. g   7. c   8. i   9. d   10. f

Fill-ins

1. autonomous   2. austere   3. atavism   4. avuncular   5. avocation

6. asylum   7. audacious   8. avarice   9. avers   10. attenuate

Sense or Nonsense

1. N   2. S   3. S   4. S   5. N

UNIT 9
Matching

1. h   2. c   3. f   4. a   5. i   6. e   7. j   8. d   9. g   10. b

Fill-ins

1. bawdy   2. bard   3. axiomatic   4. belie   5. behemoths

6. banal   7. bedizen   8. beatification   9. bacchanalian   10. banter

Sense or Nonsense

1. N   2. S   3. S   4. N   5. S

UNIT 10
Matching

1. c   2. i   3. a   4. e   5. g   6. j   7. h   8. b   9. d   10. f

Fill-ins

1. blasé   2. bifurcation   3. beneficence   4. broached   5. bovine

6. blandishments   7. brazen   8. boorish   9. bombastic   10. bolstered

Sense or Nonsense

1. N   2. N   3. S   4. S   5. N

UNIT 11

Matching

1. f   2. h   3. a   4. b   5. i   6. c   7. g   8. j   9. d   10. e

Fill-ins

1. burgeoning   2. buttress   3. canard   4 bucolic   5. cadge

6. burnish   7. calumny   8. cacophonous   9. callous   10. canon

Sense or Nonsense

1. S   2. N   3. N   4. S   5. S

UNIT 12

Matching

1. d   2. i   3. b   4. j   5. a   6. e   7. g   8. c   9. f   10. h

Fill-ins

1. caste   2. cant   3. captious   4. capricious   5. cardinal

6. carnal   7. cartography   8. castigated   9. carping   10. cantankerous

Sense or Nonsense

1. N   2. S   3. N   4. S   5. N

UNIT 13

Matching

1. e   2. h   3. b   4. j   5. a   6. i   7. c   8. f   9. d   10. g

Fill-ins

1. championed   2. causal   3. categorical   4. catalysts   5. cataclysm

6. centripetal   7. centrifugal   8. celestial   9. caucus   10. caustic

Sense or Nonsense

1. S   2. S   3. N   4. S   5. N

UNIT 14

Matching

1. e   2. c   3. h   4. a   5. d   6. j   7. f   8. i   9. b   10. g

Fill-ins

1. chivalric   2. coagulates   3. clique   4. clamor   5. circuitous

6. churlish   7. chicanery   8. chastened   9. clairvoyant   10. cloistered

Sense or Nonsense

1. S   2. S   3. N   4. N   5. S

UNIT 15

Matching

1. b   2. h   3. a   4. j   5. c   6. e   7. i   8. f   9. d   10. g

Fill-ins

1. coda   2. complaisant   3. coalesced   4. commensurate   5. codification

6. compendium   7. complement   8. complacent   9. cognizant   10. collage

Sense or Nonsense

1. S   2. S   3. S   4. N   5. N

UNIT 16
Matching

1. b   2. i   3. a   4. g   5. d   6. j   7. e   8. c   9. h   10. f

Fill-ins

1. concomitant   2. compliant   3. conjugal   4. compunction   5. congenial

6. confounded   7. concocted   8. concave   9. condoned   10. conciliatory

Sense or Nonsense

1. N   2. S   3. S   4. S   5. S

UNIT 17
Matching

1. g   2. e   3. b   4. j   5. f   6. c   7. a   8. i   9. d   10. h

Fill-ins

1. contentious   2. contends   3. conscripted   4. conundrums   5. continence

6. connoisseur   7. contumacious   8. contiguous   9. consecrated   10. contrite

Sense or Nonsense

1. N   2. S   3. S   4. N   5. S

UNIT 18
Matching

1. f   2. d   3. b   4. j   5. a   6. g   7. h   8. e   9. c   10. i

Fill-ins

1. cosmology   2. conventions   3. convoluted   4. Convex   5. convivial

6. copious   7. converges   8. covert   9. coquette   10. cornucopia

Sense or Nonsense

1. N   2. S   3. N   4. S   5. N

UNIT 19
Matching

1. d   2. h   3. a   4. e   5. i

6. c   7. b   8. g   9. j   10. f

Fill-ins

1. dearth   2. craven   3. cozens   4. daunting   5. credence

6. decorum   7. covets   8. credo   9. debauchery   10. defaming

Sense or Nonsense

1. S   2. N   3. S   4. S   5. S

UNIT 20
Matching

1. f   2. b   3. j   4. g   5. d   6. i   7. a   8. e   9. c   10. h

Fill-ins

1. denouement   2. demographic   3. denizens   4. defunct   5. delineated

6. demurred   7. demotic   8. default   9. deference   10. denigrated

Sense or Nonsense

1. N   2. S   3. N   4. S   5. S

UNIT 21

Matching

1. j   2. f   3. c   4. h   5. d   6. a   7. e   8. i   9. b   10. g

Fill-ins

1. dichotomy   2. diaphanous   3. desiccated   4. deterrent   5. derided
6. derivative   7. desultory   8. desuetude   9. diatribe   10. detraction

Sense or Nonsense

1. N   2. S   3. S   4. S   5. S

UNIT 22

Matching

1. f   2. b   3. d   4. h   5. a   6. j   7. c   8. g   9. i   10. e

Fill-ins

1. disabuse   2. discrepancy   3. dirge   4. digressions   5. discredited
6. discerning   7. diffidence   8. diffuse   9. discomfited   10. discordant

Sense or Nonsense

1. S   2. S   3. N   4. S   5. S

UNIT 23

Matching

1. i   2. f   3. h   4. b   5. a   6. j   7. d   8. c   9. g   10. e

Fill-ins

1. disinterested   2. disseminated   3. disjointed   4. disparate   5. discrete
6. dismissed   7. discretion   8. disingenuous   9. disparaged   10. dissembled

Sense or Nonsense

1. N   2. S   3. N   4. N   5. N

UNIT 24

Matching

1. i   2. c   3. j   4. e   5. b   6. g   7. f   8. d   9. h   10. a

Fill-ins

1. distill   2. dissolution   3. distended   4. dissonance   5. divested
6. dissidents   7. diverged   8. distrait   9. divulge   10. doctrinaire

Sense or Nonsense

1. N   2. N   3. S   4. S   5. S

UNIT 25

Matching

1. c   2. b   3. f   4. h   5. j   6. a   7. g   8. e   9. d   10. i

Fill-ins

1. eclectic   2. documented   3. duped   4. doggerel   5. effete
6. dogmatic   7. effervescent   8. dormant   9. dross   10. ebullient

Sense or Nonsense

1. N   2. S   3. S   4. S   5. N

UNIT 26

Matching

1. i   2. e   3. d   4. f   5. b   6. h   7. c   8. a   9. g   10. j

Fill-ins

1. elixirs   2. egoism   3. elicit   4. emaciated   5. egotistical
6. embellish   7. efficacious   8. effrontery   9. Elysian   10. elegy

Sense or Nonsense

1. N   2. N   3. N   4. S   5. S

UNIT 27

Matching

1. c   2. e   3. i   4. j   5. b   6. h   7. f   8. a   9. d   10. g

Fill-ins

1. emulated   2. enhance   3. empirical   4. enervating   5. enunciate
6. endemic   7. engendered   8. Encomiums   9. emollient   10. entomologist

Sense or Nonsense

1. N   2. S   3. S   4. S   5. S

UNIT 28

Matching

1. h   2. b   3. d   4. j   5. e   6. f   7. i   8. c   9. g   10. a

Fill-ins

1. esoteric   2. ephemeral   3. equanimity   4. errant   5. erudition
6. epistemology   7. equivocate   8. essayed   9. equable   10. estimable

Sense or Nonsense

1. N   2. S   3. N   4. S   5. N

UNIT 29

Matching

1. c   2. a   3. g   4. i   5. b   6. f   7. d   8. h   9. j   10. e

Fill-ins

1. etymology   2. euphoria   3. evinces   4. etiology   5. eugenics
6. evocative   7. eulogy   8. ethnocentrism   9. euthanasia   10. euphemisms

Sense or Nonsense

1. S   2. N   3. S   4. N   5. S

UNIT 30

Matching

1. d   2. g   3. b   4. j   5. f   6. a   7. c   8. i   9. e   10. h

Fill-ins

1. exigency   2. exorcises   3. exacerbating   4. exacting   5. expatriate
6. exhorted   7. expatiate   8. execrable   9. Existential   10. exculpated

Sense or Nonsense

1. N   2. S   3. S   4. N   5. N

UNIT 31
Matching

1. i   2. f   3. h   4. d   5. a   6. c   7. j   8. b   9. g   10. e

Fill-ins

1. facetious   2. explication   3. extraneous   4. expository   5, extant
6. extemporaneous   7. extirpate   8 extrinsic   9. expiate   10. Extrapolating

Sense or Nonsense

1. N   2. N   3. S   4. S   5. S

UNIT 32
Matching

1. c   2. g   3. e   4. f   5. a   6. i   7. h   8. d   9. b   10. j

Fill-ins

1. fauna   2. fawning   3. Feral   4. factotum   5. felicitous
6. fallacious   7. fervor   8. fatuous   9. facilitate   10. fallow

Sense or Nonsense

1. N   2. N   3. S   4. N   5. S

UNIT 33
Matching

1. i   2. f   3. c   4. e   5. a   6. h   7. b   8. d   9. j   10. g

Fill-ins

1. filibuster   2. fetid   3. Fidelity   4. fiat   5. flag
6. fledgling   7. flora   8. fettered   9. finesse   10. fissures

Sense or Nonsense

1. N   2. S   3. S   4. S   5. S

UNIT 34
Matching

1. i   2. a   3. f   4. d   5. j   6. c   7. h   8. b   9. g   10. e

Fill-ins

1. flourishes   2. foundered   3. formidable   4. forswear   5. flux
6. forestall   7. foment   8. flouts   9. forbearance   10. florid

Sense or Nonsense

1. N   2. N   3. S   4. S   5. S

UNIT 35
Matching

1. i   2. e   3. a   4. f   5. c   6. j   7. g   8. b   9. h   10. d

Fill-ins

1. futile   2. fusion   3. fracas   4. frugality   5. froward
6. frieze   7. fulsome   8. Fractious   9. fulminated   10. fresco

Sense or Nonsense

1. N   2. N   3. S   4. S   5. S

UNIT 36
Matching
1. c   2. f   3. d   4. i   5. h   6. j   7. g   8. b   9. e   10. a
Fill-ins
1. garrulous   2. gambol   3. geniality   4. glib   5. gerrymandering
6. goaded   7. gossamer   8. gauche   9. gouged   10. gainsay
Sense or Nonsense
1. N   2. N   3. N   4. S   5. N

UNIT 37
Matching
1. f   2. j   3. h   4. a   5. g   6. d   7. b   8. e   9. i   10. c
Fill-ins
1. grouse   2. gregarious   3. hallowed   4. gullible   5. grandiloquent
6. gustatory   7. guises   8. guileless   9. halcyon   10. harangue
Sense or Nonsense
1. N   2. S   3. S   4. S   5. N

UNIT 38
Matching
1. b   2. i   3. e   4. a   5. j   6. f   7. c   8. h   9. g   10. d
Fill-ins
1. homily   2. hermetic   3. heterodox   4. herbivorous   5. harrowing
6. homogeneous   7. hirsute   8. homeostatic   9. hieroglyphics   10. histrionic
Sense or Nonsense
1. N   2. S   3. N   4. N   5. S

UNIT 39
Matching
1. c   2. g   3. d   4. i   5. a   6. f   7. b   8. j   9. h   10. e
Fill-ins
1. hyperbole   2. impecunious   3. idolatry   4. imbroglio   5. impeded
6. immutable   7. Igneous   8. iconoclastic   9. impassive   10. impaired
Sense or Nonsense
1. S   2. S   3. N   4. S   5. S

UNIT 40
Matching
1. f   2. j   3. h   4. b   5. i   6. a   7. e   8. d   9. c   10. g
Fill-ins
1. implausible   2. implacable   3. Implicit   4. implosions   5. impinging
6. impermeable   7. impervious   8. imperturbable   9. impute   10. imprecations
Sense or Nonsense
1. S   2. S   3. S   4. N   5. S

UNIT 41
Matching

1. f   2. h   3. a   4. j   5. c   6. b   7. d   8. i   9. g   10. e

Fill-ins

1. inconsequential   2. indolent   3. incursions   4. incorporates   5. indeterminate
6. incongruous   7. inchoate   8. inadvertently   9. incarnate   10. indigent

Sense or Nonsense

1. S   2. S   3. S   4. N   5. S

UNIT 42
Matching

1. f   2. c   3. i   4. g   5. j   6. d   7. a   8. e   9. b   10. h

Fill-ins

1. insensible   2. insularity   3. insipid   4. ingenuous   5. inert
6. insinuating   7. insouciance   8. inherent   9. ineluctable   10. innocuous

Sense or Nonsense

1. N   2. N   3. N   4. N   5. S

UNIT 43
Matching

1. b   2. d   3. i   4. e   5. j   6. g   7. f   8. c   9. a   10. h

Fill-ins

1. intransigence   2. intimate   3. insuperable   4. interdicting   5. intangible
6. interpolated   7. internecine   8. introspection   9. interregnum   10. intractable

Sense or Nonsense

1. N   2. N   3. S   4. S   5. S

UNIT 44
Matching

1. d   2. b   3. e   4. a   5. j   6. f   7. h   8. i   9. g   10. c

Fill-ins

1. invective   2. irascible   3. invidious   4. itinerant   5. inveigh
6. inundated   7. inveterate   8. inured   9. irresolute   10. inveigle

Sense or Nonsense

1. N   2. S   3. S   4. N   5. N

UNIT 45
Matching

1. h   2. e   3. a   4. c   5. j   6. g   7. b   8. f   9. d   10. i

Fill-ins

1. juggernaut   2. junta   3. jocose   4. itinerary   5. labile
6. juxtaposed   7. jaundiced   8. kudos   9. laconic   10. jibe

Sense or Nonsense

1. N   2. N   3. S   4. S   5. S

UNIT 46
Matching

1. b   2. d   3. j   4. g   5. c   6. e   7. a   8. h   9. f   10. i

Fill-ins

1. levee   2. lambasted   3. lassitude   4. lauded   5. liberal
6. latent   7. lethargic   8. lascivious   9. levity   10. libertine

Sense or Nonsense

1. N   2. S   3. S   4. S   5. S

UNIT 47
Matching

1. b   2. f   3. d   4. a   5. j   6. g   7. h   8. c   9. i   10. e

Fill-ins

1. libido   2. literati   3. logs   4. loquacious   5. limpid
6. litany   7. litigation   8. limning   9. linguistics   10. lilliputian

Sense or Nonsense

1. N   2. N   3. S   4. S   5. S

UNIT 48
Matching

1. g   2. b   3. a   4. j   5. i   6. d   7. f   8. c   9. h   10. e

Fill-ins

1. lucid   2. Machiavellian   3. luminous   4. maligned   5. lucre
6. magnanimity   7. lustrous   8. maelstrom   9. malingering   10. machinations

Sense or Nonsense

1. N   2. S   3. N   4. S   5. S

UNIT 49
Matching

1. h   2. a   3. e   4. b   5. j   6. d   7. i   8. g   9. c   10. f

Fill-ins

1. metaphysical   2. metamorphosed   3. mendicant   4. megalomania   5. malleable
6. mavericks   7. meretricious   8. mesmerized   9. mendacious   10. menagerie

Sense or Nonsense

1. N   2. N   3. S   4. N   5. S

UNIT 50
Matching

1. h   2. c   3. a   4. g   5. f   6. d   7. i   8. b   9. j   10. e

Fill-ins

1. mettle   2. Meteorological   3. misanthropic   4. militates   5. meticulous
6. minatory   7. microcosm   8. mettlesome   9. minuscule   10. minutiae

Sense or Nonsense

1. S   2. S   3. N   4. S   5. N

UNIT 51
Matching

1. e   2. b   3. f   4. i   5. g   6. c   7. j   8. a   9. d   10. h

Fill-ins

| 1. misogynist | 2. mollify | 3. monolithic | 4. mnemonic | 5. miscellany |
| 6. morose | 7. mitigate | 8. modicum | 9. miscreant | 10. motley |

Sense or Nonsense

1. N   2. S   3. S   4. S   5. S

UNIT 52
Matching

1. d   2. j   3. c   4. a   5. f   6. b   7. i   8. g   9. e   10. h

Fill-ins

| 1. negated | 2. mundane | 3. nonplussed | 4. nostrums | 5. nexus |
| 6. neologisms | 7. multifarious | 8. nostalgia | 9. neophyte | 10. necromancy |

Sense or Nonsense

1. S   2. S   3. N   4. S   5. N

UNIT 53
Matching

1. g   2. c   3. b   4. f   5. j   6. e   7. h   8. d   9. a   10. i

Fill-ins

| 1. obsequious | 2. obviated | 3. olfactory | 4. officious | 5. occult |
| 6. occludes | 7. obdurate | 8. odyssey | 9. nugatory | 10. obsequies |

Sense or Nonsense

1. N   2. S   3. S   4. N   5. S

UNIT 54
Matching

1. e   2. c   3. j   4. a   5. h   6. f   7. b   8. g   9. d   10. i

Fill-ins

| 1. paeans | 2. oligarchy | 3. oscillating | 4. Ornithologists | 5. onerous |
| 6. paleontologists | 7. ostentatious | 8. overweening | 9. opprobrium | 10. onomatopoeia |

Sense or Nonsense

1. N   2. N   3. S   4. S   5. S

UNIT 55
Matching

1. h   2. j   3. g   4. b   5. d   6. a   7. i   8. c   9. f   10. e

Fill-ins

| 1. pathology | 2. pellucid | 3. pedantic | 4. partisan | 5. patois |
| 6. pallid | 7. penchant | 8. paragons | 9. panegyric | 10. paucity |

Sense or Nonsense

1. N   2. N   3. S   4. S   5. S

UNIT 56
Matching

1. f   2. i   3. g   4. d   5. j   6. b   7. c   8. a   9. e   10. h

Fill-ins

1. perigee   2. permeable   3. pervasive   4. perennial   5. perfidious
6. penury   7. perfunctory   8. peregrinations   9. perturbed   10. peremptory

Sense or Nonsense

1. N   2. N   3. S   4. S   5. S

UNIT 57
Matching

1. c   2. b   3. f   4. d   5. j   6. h   7. g   8. i   9. a   10. e

Fill-ins

1. placid   2. piety   3. plaintive   4. piqued   5. physiognomy
6. petulant   7. phoenix   8. placated   9. piquant   10. phlegmatic

Sense or Nonsense

1. N   2. S   3. S   4. N   5. S

UNIT 58
Matching

1. g   2. a   3. f   4. d   5. i   6. e   7. h   8. b   9. j   10. c

Fill-ins

1. plethora   2. porous   3. platonic   4. plumbed   5. platitudes
6. poseur   7. plutocracy   8. pragmatic   9. plasticity   10. plummet

Sense or Nonsense

1. S   2. N   3. S   4. S   5. S

UNIT 59
Matching

1. b   2. e   3. c   4. i   5. g   6. h   7. j   8. f   9. a   10. d

Fill-ins

1. precursor   2. precepts   3. Prehensile   4. precarious   5. prattle
6. preamble   7. precipitated   8. preempted   9. precipitate   10. prated

Sense or Nonsense

1. S   2. S   3. N   4. S   5. S

UNIT 60
Matching

1. e   2. g   3. a   4. c   5. i   6. d   7. j   8. f   9. b   10. h

Fill-ins

1. preternatural   2. presage   3. premonition   4. primordial   5. prevaricating
6. pristine   7. problematic   8. prodigal   9. presumptuous   10. probity

Sense or Nonsense

1. N   2. N   3. N   4. S   5. S

UNIT 61
Matching

1. e   2. c   3. j   4. g   5. i   6. a   7. d   8. f   9. b   10. h

Fill-ins

1. proscribes	2. proliferating	3. punctilious	4. puissant	5. Propriety
6. profound	7. propensity	8. propitiated	9. prohibitive	10. provident

Sense or Nonsense

1. S   2. N   3. S   4. S   5. S

UNIT 62
Matching

1. e   2. c   3. g   4. a   5. i   6. f   7. j   8. h   9. b   10. d

Fill-ins

1. quagmire	2. purported	3. pungent	4. quailed	5. qualms
6. query	7. qualified	8. pusillanimous	9. quibble	10. quiescent

Sense or Nonsense

1. S   2. S   3. N   4. S   5. S

UNIT 63
Matching

1. j   2. e   3. h   4. d   5. b   6. c   7. a   8. i   9. f   10. g

Fill-ins

1. recalcitrant	2. ramifications	3. rationale	4. raiment	5. rails
6. quorum	7. raconteur	8. rarefied	9. rebus	10. recant

Sense or Nonsense

1. N   2. N   3. S   4. S   5. S

UNIT 64
Matching

1. f   2. c   3. i   4. g   5. a   6. e   7. b   8. j   9. d   10. h

Fill-ins

1. regaled	2. refractory	3. relegated	4. reneged	5. refulgent
6. recluse	7. recondite	8. redoubtable	9. remonstrated	10. refute

Sense or Nonsense

1. N   2. S   3. S   4. S   5. N

UNIT 65
Matching

1. g   2. b   3. i   4. a   5. f   6. e   7. j   8. c   9. d   10. h

Fill-ins

1. reproached	2. resolved	3. repudiated	4. rescinded	5. resolution
6. reparations	7. reticent	8. repine	9. reprobate	10. reprise

Sense or Nonsense

1. S   2. S   3. S   4. S   5. N

UNIT 66

Matching

1. f   2. h   3. d   4. j   5. g   6. a   7. c   8. b   9. i   10. e

Fill-ins

1. revere	2. riposte	3. rue	4. ruse	5. sage
6. salacious	7. salubrious	8. salutary	9. rubric	10. rococo

Sense or Nonsense

1. S   2. N   3. S   4. S   5. S

UNIT 67

Matching

1. d   2. g   3. a   4. f   5. j   6. h   7. b   8. i   9. c   10. e

Fill-ins

1. savored	2. satiate	3. saturnine	4. saturated	5. sanctions
6. sartorial	7. satyr	8. schematic	9. secrete	10. sardonic

Sense or Nonsense

1. N   2. S   3. S   4. S   5. S

UNIT 68

Matching

1. c   2. g   3. j   4. e   5. a   6. f   7. i   8. b   9. d   10. h

Fill-ins

1. servile	2. Sedition	3. sedulous	4. seismic	5. Shards
6. sextant	7. sidereal	8. sentient	9. sensual	10. sensuous

Sense or Nonsense

1. S   2. N   3. S   4. S   5. S

UNIT 69

Matching

1. i   2. c   3. a   4. e   5. j   6. f   7. b   8. d   9. h   10. g

Fill-ins

1. sobriety	2. singular	3. solicitous	4. skeptic	5. similes
6. sinecure	7. sinuous	8. soliloquy	9. sodden	10. simian

Sense or Nonsense

1. S   2. S   3. S   4. S   5. N

UNIT 70

Matching

1. d   2. h   3. j   4. a   5. f   6. b   7. e   8. c   9. g   10. i

Fill-ins

1. specious	2. spendthrift	3. squalor	4. staccato	5. spectrum
6. Sporadic	7. solvent	8. soporific	9. somatic	10. sordid

Sense or Nonsense

1. S   2. S   3. N   4. S   5. S

UNIT 71

Matching

1. i   2. h   3. j   4. a   5. d   6. f   7. b   8. g   9. c   10. e

Fill-ins

1. stipulate	2. stolid	3. striated	4. stratified	5. strident
6. stanch	7. stentorian	8. stint	9. strictures	10. stigma

Sense or Nonsense

1. S   2. S   3. S   4. N   5. S

UNIT 72

Matching

1. e   2. i   3. c   4. a   5. g   6. f   7. b   8. j   9. h   10. d

Fill-ins

1. stupefied	2. substantive	3. strutted	4. subsumes	5. stultifying
6. subversive	7. stygian	8. subpoenaed	9. subside	10. substantiate

Sense or Nonsense

1. S   2. N   3. S   4. N   5. S

UNIT 73

Matching

1. g	2. j	3. b	4. e	5. c
6. i	7. a	8. d	9. h	10. f

Fill-ins

1. superseded	2. sundry	3. suppliants	4. succor	5. supine
6. syllogism	7. supposition	8. suffrage	9. supplanted	10. suppliant

Sense or Nonsense

1. S   2. N   3. S   4. N   5. S

UNIT 74

Matching

1. f   2. b   3. i   4. e   5. g   6. a   7. j   8. d   9. h   10. c

Fill-ins

1. tacit	2. tangential	3. sylvan	4. terrestrial	5. theocracy
6. talismans	7. tenet	8. taxonomy	9. tenuous	10. tautologies

Sense or Nonsense

1. N   2. S   3. S   4. S   5. S

UNIT 75

Matching

1. d   2. g   3. a   4. f   5. h   6. j   7. b   8. i   9. c   10. e

Fill-ins

1. timbre	2. thespians	3. touts	4. tractable	5. tirade
6. torpor	7. tortuous	8. torque	9. tome	10. toady

Sense or Nonsense

1. N   2. N   3. N   4. N   5. N

UNIT 76
Matching
1. h   2. d   3. b   4. g   5. e   6. a   7. j   8. c   9. f   10. i
Fill-ins
1. travails   2. truculence   3. transient   4. treatise   5. tremulous
6. translucent   7. transgressed   8. tryst   9. travesty   10. trepidation
Sense or Nonsense
1. S   2. S   3. S   4. N   5. S

UNIT 77
Matching
1. c/i   2. g   3. i/c   4. a   5. e   6. b   7. d   8. j   9. h   10. f
Fill-ins
1. unfeigned   2. untenable   3. usury   4. turgid/tumid   5. tumid/turgid
6. untoward   7. undulating   8. uncanny   9. tutelary   10. turbid
Sense or Nonsense
1. S   2. N   3. S   4. N   5. S

UNIT 78
Matching
1. c   2. j   3. h   4. f   5. b   6. d   7. a   8. i   9. g   10. e
Fill-ins
1. venerated   2. vapid   3. veracious   4. venal   5. valedictory
6. vendetta   7. vaunted   8. vacuous   9. variegated   10. vacillating
Sense or Nonsense
1. N   2. S   3. S   4. S   5. N

UNIT 79
Matching
1. f   2. i   3. j   4. e   5. c   6. g   7. d   8. a   9. b   10. h
Fill-ins
1. vituperative   2. vindictive   3. vertigo   4. virtuoso   5. visage
6. verbose   7. viscous   8. viable   9. vitiated   10. vexations
Sense or Nonsense
1. S   2. S   3. S   4. N   5. S

UNIT 80
Matching
1. b   2. g   3. a   4. e   5. j   6. h   7. f   8. c   9. i   10. d
Fill-ins
1. zealot   2. wary   3. welter   4. warranted   5. vogue
6. volatile   7. vivisections   8. whimsical   9. wistful   10. vortex
Sense or Nonsense
1. S   2. S   3. S   4. S   5. S

WORK 1

1. e 2. d 3. i 4. j 5. h 6. b 7. a 8. c 9. g 10. f

WORK 2

1. d 2. f 3. j 4. i 5. a 6. h 7. c 8. g 9. e 10. b

WORK 3

1. f 2. g 3. j 4. c 5. b 6. e 7. h 8. i 9. a 10. d

WORK 4

1. e 2. f 3. j 4. a 5. i 6. d 7. b 8. h 9. c 10. g

WORK 5

1. i 2. c 3. f 4. j 5. d 6. h 7. b 8. e 9. a 10. g

REVIEW 1–5

Matching

1. f 2. a 3. i 4. g 5. j 6. d 7. e 8. b 9. h 10. c

Fill-ins

1. pedagogue 2. perambulate 3. antiquate 4. aliment 5. inanimate
6. anarchy 7. unapt 8. annuity 9. agrarian 10. acumen

True or False

1. F 2. F 3. T 4. T 5. F

WORK 6

1. j 2. d 3. i 4. a 5. b 6. e 7. c 8. h 9. f 10. g

WORK 7

1. g 2. i 3. f 4. b 5. j 6. h 7. d 8. c 9. e 10. a

WORK 8

1. e 2. j 3. f 4. g 5. b 6. a 7. d 8. i 9. h 10. c

WORK 9

1. g 2. j 3. i 4. f 5. a 6. c 7. h 8. d 9. e 10. b

WORK 10

1. g 2. i 3. e 4. j 5. h 6. b 7. f 8. c 9. a 10. d

REVIEW 6–10

Matching

1. h 2. c 3. i 4. g 5. j 6. a 7. b 8. e 9. d 10. f

Fill-ins

1. symbiotic 2. augur 3. subaqueous 4. archaic 5. incessant
6. centrifugal 7. benediction 8. catapult 9. centripetal 10. captious

True or False

1. F 2. F 3. F 4. T 5. F

WORK 11

1. j 2. h 3. e 4. i 5. c 6. b 7. d 8. g 9. a 10. f

WORK 12

1. e   2. i   3. f   4. d   5. b   6. h   7. c   8. j   9. g   10. a

WORK 13

1. d   2. e   3. a   4. g   5. b   6. i   7. h   8. c   9. j   10. f

WORK 14

1. f   2. j   3. g   4. i   5. h   6. b   7. e   8. d   9. c   10. a

WORK 15

1. g   2. i   3. j   4. h   5. d   6. f   7. b   8. e   9. c   10. a

REVIEW 11–15

Matching

1. g   2. i   3. b   4. f   5. d   6. a   7. c   8. j   9. e   10. h

Fill-ins

1. civil   2. cosmopolitan   3. coherent   4. cite   5. criterion
6. corpulent   7. miscreate   8. deprecate   9. synclinal   10. cyclothymia

True or False

1. F   2. T   3. T   4. T   5. F

WORK 16

1. d   2. i   3. g   4. j   5. b   6. e   7. f   8. a   9. h   10. c

WORK 17

1. g   2. d   3. f   4. i   5. j   6. h   7. c   8. b   9. a   10. e

WORK 18

1. f   2. i   3. g   4. h   5. j   6. a   7. c   8. e   9. b   10. d

WORK 19

1. f   2. d   3. i   4. j   5. a   6. b   7. h   8. e   9. c   10. g

WORK 20

1. j   2. g   3. h   4. i   5. e   6. a   7. d   8. f   9. c   10. b

REVIEW 16–20

Matching

1. g   2. j   3. h   4. a   5. i   6. c   7. b   8. d   9. f   10. e

Fill-ins

1. pandemic   2. duple   3. obdurate   4. donatio mortis causa   5. inequity
6. dichotomy   7. epigeal   8. ductile   9. dermatitis   10. malediction

True or False

1. F   2. F   3. T   4. F   5. T

WORK 21

1. h   2. e   3. a   4. g   5. d   6. i   7. f   8. b   9. c   10. j

WORK 22

1. c   2. d   3. a   4. g   5. f   6. b   7. i   8. e   9. j   10. h

WORK 23

1. g	2. d	3. i	4. c	5. b	6. a	7. j	8. e	9. h	10. f

WORK 24

1. i	2. f	3. d	4. g	5. j	6. b	7. a	8. c	9. e	10. h

WORK 25

1. f	2. i	3. h	4. a	5. j	6. b	7. e	8. g	9. d	10. c

REVIEW 21–25

Matching

1. i	2. f	3. g	4. a	5. j	6. d	7. h	8. b	9. e	10. c

Fill-ins

1. gravitas	2. perfidious	3. fractious	4. genre	5. perfunctory
6. euphony	7. egress	8. fin de siècle	9. extraneous	10. soporific

True or False

1. F	2. T	3. F	4. T	5. F

WORK 26

1. c	2. h	3. d	4. b	5. g	6. j	7. a	8. f	9. e	10. i

WORK 27

1. f	2. e	3. h	4. d	5. g	6. a	7. i	8. j	9. c	10. b

WORK 28

1. d	2. j	3. e	4. g	5. b	6. i	7. a	8. f	9. h	10. c

WORK 29

1. g	2. j	3. a	4. i	5. c	6. d	7. f	8. h	9. b	10. e

WORK 30

1. i	2. f	3. e	4. a	5. g	6. j	7. b	8. h	9. c	10. d

REVIEW 26–30

Matching

1. i	2. f	3. j	4. c	5. g	6. d	7. b	8. e	9. a	10. h

Fill-ins

1. lexical	2. hemoptysis	3. lector	4. hyperbole	5. literati
6. internecine	7. jurisprudence	8. misogynist	9. impecunious	10. hominoid

True or False

1. T	2. F	3. T	4. F	5. F

WORK 31

1. h	2. e	3. a	4. g	5. b	6. j	7. f	8. c	9. i	10. d

WORK 32

1. j	2. d	3. e	4. g	5. f	6. i	7. h	8. c	9. b	10. a

WORK 33

1. g	2. h	3. j	4. e	5. d	6. b	7. f	8. c	9. a	10. i

WORK 34

1. g   2. i   3. f   4. e   5. a   6. j   7. d   8. c   9. b   10. h

WORK 35

1. g   2. j   3. i   4. f   5. h   6. a   7. e   8. d   9. b   10. c

REVIEW 31–35

Matching

1. g   2. d   3. h   4. a   5. j   6. b   7. i   8. c   9. f   10. e

Fill-ins

1. missive   2. nascent   3. diminution   4. malfeasance   5. misogynist
6. matrilineal   7. morphology   8. mandamus   9. metanoia   10. macrocosm

True or False

1. F   2. F   3. T   4. F   5. T

WORK 36

1. j   2. i   3. f   4. h   5. g   6. d   7. e   8. b   9. a   10. c

WORK 37

1. h   2. g   3. i   4. f   5. j   6. c   7. d   8. b   9. e   10. a

WORK 38

1. d   2. j   3. h   4. g   5. i   6. a   7. c   8. e   9. f   10. b

WORK 39

1. j   2. e   3. g   4. h   5. i   6. f   7. d   8. b   9. c   10. a

WORK 40

1. i   2. a   3. h   4. e   5. g   6. j   7. d   8. c   9. f   10. b

REVIEW 36–40

Matching

1. f   2. a   3. e   4. j   5. g   6. b   7. i   8. d   9. c   10. h

Fill-ins

1. orthopraxy   2. ignominious   3. paramount   4. osteoma   5. omniscient
6. navarch   7. noctivagant   8. oligophagous   9. apartheid   10. paragon

True or False

1. F   2. T   3. T   4. F   5. F

WORK 41

1. f   2. d   3. g   4. b   5. c   6. i   7. j   8. a   9. h   10. e

WORK 42

1. e   2. f   3. g   4. h   5. j   6. c   7. d   8. b   9. a   10. i

WORK 43

1. d   2. e   3. h   4. j   5. b   6. i   7. a   8. c   9. f   10. g

WORK 44

1. f   2. a   3. j   4. h   5. e   6. c   7. g   8. i   9. b   10. d

WORK 45

1. g   2. h   3. f   4. d   5. b   6. c   7. a   8. i   9. j   10. e

REVIEW 41–45

Matching

1. c   2. g   3. a   4. i   5. h   6. e   7. b   8. j   9. f   10. d

Fill-ins

1. prehensile   2. depict   3. agoraphobia   4. pedagogue   5. protogenic
6. percutaneous   7. postdiluvian   8. placate   9. cacophony   10. portage

True or False

1. F   2. T   3. T   4. T   5. T

WORK 46

1. i   2. j   3. f   4. a   5. h   6. g   7. d   8. b   9. c   10. e

WORK 47

1. d   2. h   3. i   4. b   5. c   6. a   7. e   8. f   9. g   10. j

WORK 48

1. e   2. g   3. f   4. j   5. h   6. i   7. a   8. c   9. b   10. d

WORK 49

1. e   2. i   3. j   4. c   5. b   6. f   7. a   8. h   9. d   10. g

WORK 50

1. i   2. c   3. j   4. f   5. h   6. b   7. e   8. g   9. d   10. a

REVIEW 46–50

Matching

1. i   2. e   3. g   4. b   5. c   6. a   7. j   8. f   9. h   10. d

Fill-ins

1. ridibund   2. sophistry   3. retrospect   4. secant   5. somniloquence
6. pseudodox   7. recant   8. rogation   9. punctilio   10. sequacious

True or False

1. F   2. T   3. T   4. F   5. F

WORK 51

1. j   2. c   3. f   4. h   5. e   6. b   7. d   8. a   9. g   10. i

WORK 52

1. d   2. c   3. h   4. b   5. j   6. i   7. a   8. g   9. e   10. f

WORK 53

1. e   2. g   3. f   4. h   5. i   6. c   7. j   8. d   9. b   10. a

WORK 54

1. d   2. j   3. h   4. g   5. f   6. i   7. b   8. c   9. e   10. a

WORK 55

1. f   2. e   3. g   4. j   5. d   6. a   7. i   8. b   9. h   10. c

REVIEW 51–55

Matching

1. j   2. f   3. g   4. a   5. h   6. b   7. d   8. e   9. c   10. i

Fill-ins

1. theogamy   2. contention   3. thermoduric   4. status quo   5. tenacious

6. synchronous   7. torque   8. supernal   9. stricture   10. toponym

True or False

1. T   2. F   3. F   4. F   5. T

WORK 56

1. d   2. j   3. g   4. h   5. c   6. i   7. e   8. f   9. a   10. b

WORK 57

1. i   2. d   3. h   4. a   5. b   6. c   7. j   8. g   9. f   10. e

WORK 58

1. f   2. d   3. h   4. i   5. g   6. b   7. c   8. a   9. j   10. e

WORK 59

1. h   2. j   3. e   4. i   5. c   6. d   7. f   8. a   9. b   10. g

WORK 60

1. e   2. f   3. h   4. a   5. d   6. i   7. j   8. b   9. c   10. g

REVIEW 56–60

Matching

1. g   2. c   3. f   4. i   5. b   6. d   7. a   8. j   9. e   10. h

Fill-ins

1. ultramundane   2. vacuous   3. invincible   4. urbane   5. virago

6. unfeigned   7. viatical   8. usurp   9. curriculum vitae   10. convection

True or False

1. F   2. F   3. T   4. F   5. F

Terms Index

3500 Master Words

A

abase
abash
abate
abbreviate
abdicate
aberrant
aberration
abet
abeyance
abhor
abject
abjure
ablution
abnegation
abolish
abominable
abominate
aboriginal
abortive
abrasive
abridge
abrogate
abscission
abscond
absolute
absolve
abstain
abstemious
abstinence
abstract
abstruse
abusive
abut
abysmal

abyss
academic
accede
accelerate
accessible
accessory
acclaim
acclimate
acclivity
accolade
accommodate
accomplice
accord
accost
accoutre
accretion
accrue
acerbic
acerbity
acetic
acidulous
acknowledge
acme
acoustics
acquiesce
acquittal
acrid
acrimonious
acrophobia
actuarial
actuate
acuity
acumen
acute
adage
adamant

adapt
addendum
addiction
addle
address
adept
adhere
adherent
adjacent
adjunct
adjuration
adjutant
admonish
adorn
adroit
adulation
adulterate
advent
adventitious
adversary
adverse
adversity
advert
advocacy
advocate
aegis
aerie
aesthetic
affable
affected
affidavit
affiliation
affinity
affirmation
affix
affliction

affluence
affront
agape
agenda
agglomeration
aggrandize
aggregate
aggressor
aghast
agility
agitate
agnostic
agog
agrarian
alacrity
alchemy
alcove
alias
alienate
alimentary
alimony
allay
allege
allegiance
allegory
alleviate
alliteration
allocate
alloy
allude
allure
allusion
alluvial
aloft
aloof
altercation

altruistic
amalgamate
amass
amazon
ambidextrous
ambience
ambiguous
ambivalence
amble
ambrosia
ambulatory
ameliorate
amenable
amend
amenities
amiable
amicable
amiss
amity
amnesia
amnesty
amok
amoral
amorous
amorphous
amphibian
amphitheater
ample
amplify
amputate
amulet
anachronism
analgesic
analogous
analogy
anarchist

367

anarchy
anathema
ancestry
anchor
ancillary
anecdote
anemia
anesthetic
anguish
angular
animadversion
animated
animosity
animus
annals
anneal
annex
annihilate
annotate
annuity
annul
anodyne
anoint
anomalous
anomaly
anonymity
antagonism
antecede
antecedents
antediluvian
anthem
anthology
anthropoid
anthropologist
anthropomorphic
antic
anticlimax
antidote
antipathy
antiquated
antiseptic
antithesis

anvil
apathy
ape
aperture
apex
aphasia
aphorism
apiary
aplomb
apocalyptic
apocryphal
apogee
apolitical
apologist
apostate
apothecary
apothegm
apotheosis
appall
apparition
appease
appellation
append
application
apposite
appraise
appreciate
apprehend
apprehensive
apprise
approbation
appropriate
appurtenances
apropos
aptitude
aquiline
arabesque
arable
arbiter
arbitrary
arbitrate
arboretum

arcade
arcane
archaeology
archaic
archetype
archipelago
archives
ardor
arduous
argot
aria
arid
aristocracy
armada
aromatic
arraign
array
arrears
arrest
arrhythmic
arrogance
arroyo
arsenal
artful
articulate
artifact
artifice
artisan
artless
ascendancy
ascertain
ascetic
ascribe
aseptic
ashen
asinine
askance
askew
asperity
aspersion
aspirant
aspire

assail
assay
assent
assert
assessment
assiduous
assimilate
assuage
assumption
assurance
asteroid
astigmatism
astral
astringent
astronomical
astute
asunder
asylum
asymmetric
atavism
atheist
atone
atrocity
atrophy
attentive
attenuate
attest
attribute
attrition
atypical
audacious
audit
augment
augury
august
aureole
auroral
auspicious
austere
authenticate
authoritarian
authoritative

autocratic
automaton
autonomous
autopsy
auxiliary
avalanche
avarice
avenge
aver
averse
aversion
avert
aviary
avid
avocation
avow
avuncular
awe
awl
awry
axiom
azure

B

babble
bacchanalian
badger
badinage
baffle
bait
baleful
balk
ballast
balm
balmy
banal
bandy
bane
baneful
bantering
barb
bard

barefaced	berate	bode	bugaboo	canter
baroque	bereavement	bogus	bullion	canto
barrage	bereft	bohemian	bulwark	canvass
barrister	berserk	boisterous	bungle	capacious
barterer	beseech	bolster	buoyant	capacity
bask	beset	bolt	bureaucracy	capillary
bastion	besiege	bombardment	burgeon	capitulate
bate	besmirch	bombastic	burlesque	caprice
bauble	bestial	boon	burnish	capricious
bawdy	bestow	boorish	buttress	caption
beatific	betoken	bouillon	buxom	captious
beatify	betray	bountiful		carafe
beatitude	betroth	bourgeois	©	carapace
bedizen	bevy	bovine		carat
bedraggle	bicameral	bowdlerize	cabal	carcinogenic
beeline	bicker	boycott	cache	cardinal
befuddle	biennial	brackish	cacophonous	cardiologist
beget	bifurcated	braggadocio	cadaver	careen
begrudge	bigotry	braggart	cadaverous	caricature
beguile	bilious	brandish	cadence	carillon
behemoth	bilk	bravado	cadge	carnage
beholden	billowing	brawn	cajole	carnal
behoove	bivouac	brazen	calamity	carnivorous
belabor	bizarre	breach	calculated	carousal
belated	blanch	breadth	caldron	carping
beleaguer	bland	brevity	caliber	carrion
belie	blandish	brindled	calligraphy	cartographer
belittle	blandishment	bristling	callous	cascade
bellicose	blare	brittle	callow	caste
belligerent	blasé	broach	calorific	castigation
bemoan	blasphemy	brocade	calumny	casualty
bemused	blatant	brochure	camaraderie	cataclysm
benediction	bleak	brooch	cameo	catalyst
benefactor	blighted	brook	camouflage	catapult
beneficent	blithe	browbeat	canard	cataract
beneficial	bloated	browse	candor	catastrophe
beneficiary	blowhard	brunt	canine	catcall
benevolent	bludgeon	brusque	canker	catechism
benign	bluff	buccaneer	canny	categorical
benison	blunder	bucolic	canon	catharsis
bent	blurt	buffet	cant	cathartic
bequeath	bluster	buffoonery	cantankerous	catholic
			cantata	

caucus	chasten	cliché	combustible	concession
caulk	chastened	clientele	comely	conciliatory
causal	chastise	climactic	comestible	concise
caustic	chauvinist	clime	comeuppance	conclave
cauterize	check	clique	comity	conclusive
cavalcade	checkered	cloister	commandeer	concoct
cavalier	cherubic	clout	commemorative	concomitant
cavil	chicanery	cloying	commensurate	concord
cede	chide	coagulate	commiserate	concur
celerity	chimerical	coalesce	commodious	concurrent
celestial	chisel	coalition	communal	condescend
celibate	chivalrous	coda	compact	condign
censor	choleric	coddle	compatible	condiment
censorious	choreography	codicil	compelling	condole
censure	chortle	codify	compendium	condone
centaur	chronic	coercion	compensatory	conducive
centigrade	chronicle	coeval	compilation	conduit
centrifugal	churlish	cog	compile	confidant
centrifuge	ciliated	cogent	complacency	confine
centripetal	cipher	cogitate	complaisant	confiscate
centurion	circlet	cognate	complement	conflagration
cerebral	circuitous	cognitive	complementary	conflate
cerebration	circumlocution	cognizance	compliance	confluence
ceremonious	circumscribe	cohabit	compliant	conformity
certitude	circumspect	cohere	complicity	confound
cessation	circumvent	cohesion	component	congeal
cession	cistern	cohorts	comport	congenial
chafe	citadel	coiffure	composure	congenital
chaff	cite	coin	compound	conglomeration
chaffing	civil	coincidence	comprehensive	congruence
chagrin	clairvoyant	colander	compress	congruent
chalice	clamber	collaborate	comprise	conifer
chameleon	clamor	collage	compromise	conjecture
champion	clandestine	collate	compunction	conjugal
chaotic	clangor	collateral	compute	conjure
charisma	clapper	collation	concatenate	connivance
charlatan	clarion	colloquial	concave	connoisseur
chary	claustrophobia	colloquy	concede	connotation
chase	clavicle	collusion	conceit	connubial
chasm	cleave	colossal	concentric	consanguinity
chassis	cleft	colossus	conception	conscientious
chaste	clemency	comatose	concerted	conscript

exude
exult

F

fabricate
facade
facet
facetious
facile
facilitate
facsimile
faction
factious
factitious
factotum
faculty
fallacious
fallacy
fallible
fallow
falter
fanaticism
fancied
fancier
fancy
fanfare
farce
fastidious
fatalism
fathom
fatuous
fauna
fawning
faze
feasible
febrile
feckless
fecundity
feign
feint
felicitous

felicity
fell
felon
feral
ferment
ferret
fervent
fervid
fervor
fester
festive
fete
fetid
fetter
fiasco
fiat
fickle
fictitious
fidelity
figment
figurative
figurine
filch
filial
filibuster
filigree
filing
finale
finesse
finicky
finite
firebrand
fissure
fitful
flaccid
flag
flagrant
flail
flair
flamboyant
flaunt
flay

fleck
fledgling
fleece
flick
flinch
flippant
flit
floe
flora
florid
flotsam
flounder
flourish
flout
fluctuate
fluency
fluke
fluster
fluted
flux
fodder
foible
foil
foist
foliage
foment
foolhardy
fop
foray
forbearance
ford
forebears
foreboding
forensic
foreshadow
foresight
forestall
forgo
forlorn
formality
formidable
forsake

forswear
forte
forthright
fortitude
fortuitous
foster
founder
fracas
fractious
frail
franchise
frantic
fraudulent
fraught
fray
frenetic
frenzied
fresco
fret
friction
frieze
frigid
fritter
frivolous
frolicsome
frond
froward
fructify
frugality
fruition
frustrate
fugitive
fulcrum
fulminate
fulsome
functionary
fundamental
funereal
furor
furtive
fusillade
fusion

effet
effi
eff
e

gao
gaffe
gainsay
gait
galaxy
gale
gall
galleon
galvanize
gambit
gambol
gamely
gamut
gape
garbled
gargantuan
gargoyle
garish
garner
garnish
garrulous
gastronomy
gauche
gaudy
gaunt
gavel
gawk
gazette
genealogy
generality
generate
generic
genesis
geniality
genre
genteel
gentility
gentry

consecrate
consensus
consequential
conservatory
consign
consistency
console
consolidation
consonance
consort
conspiracy
constituent
constraint
construe
consummate
contagion
contaminate
contempt
contend
contention
contentious
contest
context
contiguous
continence
contingent
contortions
contraband
contravene
contrite
contrived
controvert
contumacious
contusion
conundrum
convene
convention
conventional
converge
conversant
converse
convert

convex
conveyance
conviction
convivial
convoke
convoluted
copious
coquette
cordial
cordon
cornice
cornucopia
corollary
corporeal
corpulent
correlation
corroborate
corrode
corrosive
corrugated
cosmic
coterie
countenance
countermand
counterpart
coup
couple
courier
covenant
covert
covetous
cow
cower
coy
cozen
crabbed
crass
craven
credence
credo
credulity
creed

crescendo
crestfallen
crevice
cringe
criteria
crone
crotchety
crux
crypt
cryptic
cubicle
cuisine
culinary
cull
culmination
culpable
culvert
cumbersome
cumulative
cupidity
curator
curmudgeon
cursive
cursory
curtail
cynical
cynosure

D

dabble
dais
dally
damp
dank
dapper
dappled
daub
daunt
dauntless
dawdle
deadlock
deadpan

dearth
debacle
debase
debauch
debilitate
debonair
debris
debunk
debutante
decadence
decant
decapitate
decelerate
deciduous
decimate
decipher
declivity
décolleté
decomposition
decorum
decoy
decrepitude
decry
deducible
deface
defame
default
defeatist
defection
defer
deference
defiance
defile
definitive
deflect
defoliate
defray
defrock
deft
defunct
degenerate
degradation

dehydrate
deify
deign
delete
deleterious
deliberate
delineate
delirium
delta
delude
deluge
delusion
delusive
delve
demagogue
demean
demeanor
demented
demise
demographic
demolition
demoniac
demotic
demur
demure
denigrate
denizen
denotation
denouement
denounce
depict
deplete
deplore
deploy
depose
deposition
depravity
deprecate
depreciate
depredation
derange
derelict

deride
derivative
dermatologist
derogatory
descry
desecrate
desiccate
desolate
desperado
despise
despoil
despondent
despot
destitute
desuetude
desultory
detached
determinate
determination
deterrent
detonation
detraction
detrimental
deviate
devious
devise
devoid
devolve
devotee
devout
dexterous
diabolical
diadem
dialectical
diaphanous
diatribe
dichotomy
dictum
didactic
die
diffidence
diffuse

digression
dilapidated
dilate
dilatory
dilemma
dilettante
diligence
dilute
diminution
din
dinghy
dingy
dint
diorama
dire
dirge
disabuse
disaffected
disapprobation
disarray
disavowal
disband
disburse
discernible
discerning
disclaim
disclose
discombobulated
discomfit
disconcert
disconsolate
discord
discordant
discount
discourse
discredit
discrepancy
discrete
discretion
discriminating
discursive
disdain

disembark
disenfranchise
disengage
disfigure
disgorge
disgruntle
dishearten
disheveled
disinclination
disingenuous
disinter
disinterested
disjointed
disjunction
dislodge
dismantle
dismember
dismiss
disparage
disparite
disparity
dispassionate
dispatch
dispel
disperse
dispirited
disport
disputatious
disquietude
disquisition
dissection
dissemble
disseminate
dissent
dissertation
dissident
dissimulate
dissipate
dissolution
dissonance
dissuade
distant

distend
distill
distinction
distort
distrait
distraught
diurnal
diva
diverge
divergent
diverse
diversion
diversity
divest
divine
divulge
docile
docket
doctrinaire
doctrine
document
doddering
doff
dogged
doggerel
dogmatic
doldrums
doleful
dolorous
dolt
domicile
domineer
don
dormant
dormer
dorsal
dossier
dotage
dote
dour
douse
dowdy

downcast
drab
draconian
dregs
drivel
droll
drone
dross
drudgery
dubious
ductile
dulcet
dumbfound
dupe
duplicity
duration
duress
dutiful
dwindle
dynamic
dyspeptic

E

earthy
ebb
ebullient
eccentric
eccentricity
ecclesiastic
eclectic
eclipse
ecologist
economy
ecstasy
eddy
edict
edify
eerie
efface
effectual
effeminate
effervescence

emolument
empathy
empirical
emulate
enamored
encipher
enclave
encomiastic
encomium
encompass
encroachment
encumber
endearment
endemic
endorse
endue
enduring
energize
enervate
enfranchise
engage
engaging
engender
engross
enhance
enigma
enigmatic
enjoin
enmity
ennui
enormity
emboss
embrace
embroider
embroil
embryonic
emend
emendation
emetic
eminent
emissary
emollient

acy
gy
ffluvium
effrontery
effusion
effusive
egoism
egotistical
egregious
egress
ejaculation
elaboration
elated
elegy
elicit
elixir
ellipsis
elliptical
eloquence
elucidate
elusive
elysian
emaciated
emanate
emancipate
embargo
embark
embed
embellish
embezzlement

entree
entrepreneur
enumerate
enunciate
environ
eon
epaulet
ephemeral
epic
epicure
epigram
epilogue
episodic
epistemologist
epitaph
epithet
epitome
epoch
equable
equanimity
equestrian
equilibrium
equine
equinox
equipoise
equitable
equity
equivocal
equivocate
erode
erotic
errant
erratic
erroneous
erudite
escapade
eschew
esoteric
espionage
espouse
essay
esteem
enrapture
ensconce
ensue
entail
enterprising
enthrall
entice
entity
entomology
entrance
entreat

estimable
estranged
ethereal
ethnic
ethnology
ethos
etymology
eugenic
eulogistic
eulogy
euphemism
euphony
euphoria
euthanasia
evanescent
evasive
evenhanded
evince
evenhanded
evocative
evoke
ewe
exacerbate
exact
exacting
exalt
exasperate
exceptionable
excerpt
excise
exclaim
excoriate
exculpate
execrable
execrate
execute
exegesis
exemplary
exemplify
exempt
exertion
exhilarating

exhort
exhume
exigency
exiguous
existential
exodus
exonerate
exorbitant
exorcise
exotic
expansive
expatiate
expatriate
expedient
expedite
expenditure
expertise
expiate
expletive
explicate
explicit
exploit
expository
expostulation
exposure
expropriate
expunge
expurgate
extant
extemporaneous
extenuate
extirpate
extol
extort
extradition
extraneous
extrapolation
extricate
extrinsic
extrovert
extrude
exuberance

genuflect
germane
germinal
germinate
gerontocracy
gerrymander
gestate
gesticulation
ghastly
gibberish
gibe
giddy
gingerly
girth
gist
glacial
glaring
glaze
glean
glib
glimmer
gloat
gloss over
glossary
glossy
glower
glut
glutinous
glutton
gnarled
gnome
goad
gorge
gory
gossamer
gouge
gourmand
gourmet
graduated
granary
grandeur
grandiloquent

grandiose
granulate
graphic
grapple
grate
gratify
gratis
gratuitous
gratuity
gravity
gregarious
grievance
grill
grimace
grisly
grotesque
grotto
grouse
grovel
grudging
gruel
grueling
gruesome
gruff
guffaw
guile
guileless
guise
gull
gullible
gustatory
gusto
gusty
guy
gyroscope

habituate
hackles
hackneyed
haggard
haggle

halcyon
hale
hallowed
hallucination
halting
hamper
hap
haphazard
hapless
harangue
harass
harbinger
harbor
hardy
harping
harrowing
harry
hatch
haughtiness
haven
hazardous
hazy
headlong
headstrong
heckler
hedonist
heedless
hegemony
heinous
herbivorous
heresy
hermetic
hermitage
herpetologist
heterodox
heterogeneous
hew
heyday
hiatus
hibernal
hibernate
hierarchy

hieroglyphic
hilarity
hindmost
hindrance
hinterlands
hireling
hirsute
histrionic
hoard
hoary
hoax
holocaust
holster
homage
homeostasis
homespun
homily
homogeneous
hone
hoodwink
horde
hortatory
horticultural
hostility
hovel
hover
hubbub
hubris
hue
hue and cry
humane
humdrum
humid
humility
hummock
humus
hurtle
husband
husbandry
hybrid
hydrophobia
hyperbole

hypercritical
hypochondriac
hypocritical
hypothetical

I

ichthyology
icon
iconoclastic
ideology
idiom
idiosyncrasy
idolatry
idyllic
igneous
ignite
ignoble
ignominy
illicit
illimitable
illuminate
illusion
illusive
illusory
imbalance
imbecility
imbibe
imbroglio
imbue
immaculate
imminent
immobility
immolate
immune
immure
immutable
impair
impale
impalpable
impartial
impassable
impasse

impassive
impeach
impeccable
impecunious
impede
impediment
impel
impending
impenetrable
impenitent
imperative
imperceptible
imperial
imperious
impermeable
impertinent
imperturbable
impervious
impetuous
impetus
impiety
impinge
impious
implacable
implausible
implement
implicate
implication
implicit
implode
implore
imply
impolitic
imponderable
import
importunate
importune
imposture
impotent
imprecation
impregnable
impromptu

impropriety
improvident
improvise
imprudent
impudence
impugn
impuissance
impunity
impute
inadvertently
inalienable
inane
inanimate
inarticulate
inaugurate
incandescent
incantation
incapacitate
incarcerate
incarnate
incarnation
incendiary
incense
incentive
inception
incessant
inchoate
incidence
incidental
incipient
incisive
incite
inclement
incline
inclined
inclusive
incognito
incoherent
incommodious
incompatible
incongruity
inconsequential

inconsistency
incontinent
incontrovertible
incorporate
incorporeal
incorrigible
incredulity
incredulous
increment
incriminate
incrustation
incubate
incubus
inculcate
incumbent
incur
incursion
indefatigable
indelible
indemnify
indentation
indenture
indeterminate
indicative
indices
indict
indifferent
indigence
indigenous
indigent
indignation
indignity
indiscriminate
indisputable
indissoluble
indite
indolent
indomitable
indubitable
induce
inductive
indulgent

industrious
inebriated
ineffable
ineffectual
ineluctable
inept
inequity
inerrancy
inert
inevitable
inexorable
infallible
infamous
infantile
infer
infernal
infidel
infiltrate
infinitesimal
infirmity
inflated
influx
infraction
infringe
ingenious
ingenuous
ingrained
ingrate
ingratiate
inherent
inhibit
inimical
inimitable
iniquitous
initiate
injurious
inkling
innate
innocuous
innovation
innuendo
inopportune

inordinate
inquisitor
insalubrious
insatiable
inscrutable
insensate
insensible
insidious
insightful
insinuate
insipid
insolence
insolvent
insomnia
insouciant
instigate
insubordination
insubstantial
insularity
insuperable
insurgent
insurmountable
insurrection
intangible
integral
integrate
integrity
intellect
intelligentsia
inter
interdict
interim
interloper
interminable
intermittent
internecine
interpolate
interregnum
interrogate
intervene
intimate
intimidate

intractable
intransigence
intrepid
intrinsic
introspective
introvert
intrude
intuition
inundate
inured
invalidate
invective
inveigh
inveigle
inverse
invert
inveterate
invidious
invincible
inviolable
invocation
invoke
invulnerable
iota
irascible
irate
iridescent
irksome
ironic
irony
irreconcilable
irrefutable
irrelevant
irremediable
irreparable
irrepressible
irreproachable
irresolute
irretrievable
irreverence
irrevocable
isotope

isthmus
itinerant
itinerary

J

jabber
jaded
jargon
jaundiced
jaunt
jaunty
jeopardize
jettison
jibe
jingoist
jocose
jocular
jocund
jollity
jostle
jovial
jubilation
judicious
juggernaut
juncture
junket
junta
jurisprudence
juxtapose

K

kaleidoscope
ken
kernel
killjoy
kindle
kindred
kinetic
kismet
kleptomaniac
knave
knead

knell
knit
knoll
knotty
kudos

L

labile
laborious
labyrinth
laceration
lachrymose
lackadaisical
lackluster
laconic
laggard
lagoon
laity
lambaste
lament
lampoon
lancet
languid
languish
languor
lank
lap
larceny
larder
largess
lascivious
lassitude
latent
lateral
latitude
laud
lavish
lax
leaven
lechery
lectern
leery

leeway
legacy
legend
legerdemain
leniency
leonine
lethal
lethargic
levee
levitate
levity
levy
lewd
lexicographer
lexicon
liability
liaison
libel
libertine
libidinous
libido
libretto
licentious
lien
ligneous
lilliputian
limber
limbo
limn
limpid
lineage
lineaments
linger
linguistic
lionize
liquidate
list
listless
litany
lithe
litigation
litotes

livid
loath
loathe
lode
lofty
log
loiter
loll
longevity
loom
lope
loquacious
lout
low
lucid
lucrative
lucre
ludicrous
lugubrious
lull
lumber
lumen
luminary
luminous
lunar
lunge
lurid
lurk
luscious
luster
lustrous
luxuriant

M

macabre
mace
macerate
Machiavellian
machinations
maculated
madrigal
maelstrom

magisterial
magnanimity
magnate
magniloquent
magnitude
maim
maladroit
malady
malaise
malapropism
malcontent
malediction
malefactor
malevolent
malfeasance
malicious
malign
malignant
malingerer
malleable
malodorous
mammal
mammoth
manacle
mandate
mandatory
mangy
maniacal
manifest
manifestation
manifesto
manifold
manipulate
mannered
manumit
marital
maritime
marked
marred
marshal
marsupial
martial

martinet
martyr
masochist
masticate
materialism
maternal
matriarch
matriculate
matrix
maudlin
maul
mausoleum
mauve
maverick
mawkish
maxim
mayhem
meager
mealymouthed
meander
meddlesome
mediate
mediocre
meditation
medium
medley
meek
megalomania
melancholy
melee
mellifluous
memento
memorialize
menagerie
mendacious
mendicant
menial
mentor
mercantile
mercenary
mercurial
meretricious

merger
mesmerize
metallurgical
metamorphosis
metaphor
metaphysical
mete
meteoric
methodical
meticulous
metropolis
mettle
miasma
microcosm
migrant
migratory
milieu
militant
militate
millennium
mimicry
minatory
mincing
minion
minuscule
minute
minutiae
mirage
mire
mirth
misadventure
misanthrope
misapprehension
miscellany
mischance
misconstrue
miscreant
misdemeanor
miserly
misgivings
mishap
misnomer

misogamy
misogynist
missile
missive
mite
mitigate
mnemonic
mobile
mock
mode
modicum
modish
modulate
mogul
molecule
mollify
mollycoddle
molt
molten
momentous
momentum
monarchy
monastic
monetary
monochromatic
monolithic
monotheism
monotony
monumental
moodiness
moratorium
morbid
mordant
mores
moribund
morose
mortician
mortify
mosaic
mote
motif
motility

motley
mottled
mountebank
muddle
muggy
mulct
multifarious
multiform
multilingual
multiplicity
mundane
munificent
mural
murky
muse
musky
muster
musty
mutability
muted
mutilate
mutinous
myopic
myriad

Ⓝ

nadir
naiveté
narcissist
narrative
nascent
natation
natty
nauseate
nautical
navigable
nebulous
necromancy
nefarious
negate
negligence
negligible

nemesis
neologism
neophyte
nepotism
nether
nettle
nexus
nib
nicety
niggardly
niggle
nihilist
nip
nirvana
nocturnal
noisome
nomadic
nomenclature
nominal
nonchalance
noncommittal
nondescript
nonentity
nonplus
nostalgia
nostrum
notable
notoriety
novelty
novice
noxious
nuance
nubile
nugatory
nullify
numismatist
nuptial
nurture
nutrient

O

oaf

obdurate
obeisance
obelisk
obese
obfuscate
obituary
objective
obligatory
oblique
obliterate
oblivion
oblivious
obloquy
obnoxious
obscure
obsequious
obsequy
obsessive
obsidian
obsolete
obstetrician
obstinate
obstreperous
obtrude
obtuse
obviate
Occident
occlude
occult
oculist
odious
odium
odoriferous
odorous
odyssey
offensive
offhand
officious
ogle
olfactory
oligarchy
ominous

omnipotent
omnipresent
omniscient
omnivorous
onerous
onomatopoeia
onslaught
onus
opalescent
opaque
opiate
opportune
opportunist
opprobrium
optician
optimist
optimum
optional
optometrist
opulence
opus
oracular
orator
oratorio
ordain
ordeal
ordinance
ordination
orgy
orient
orientation
orifice
ornate
ornithologist
orthodox
orthography
oscillate
osseous
ossify
ostensible
ostentatious
ostracize

oust
outlandish
outmoded
outskirts
outspoken
outstrip
outwit
ovation
overbearing
overt
overweening
overwrought
ovoid

P

pachyderm
pacifist
pacify
paean
painstaking
palatable
palate
palatial
paleontology
palette
palimpsest
pall
pallet
palliate
pallid
palpable
palpitate
paltry
pan
panacea
panache
pandemic
pandemonium
pander
panegyric
panoramic
pantomime

papyrus
parable
paradigm
paradox
paragon
parallelism
parameter
paramount
paramour
paranoia
paraphernalia
paraphrase
parasite
parched
pariah
parity
parlance
parley
parochial
parody
paroxysm
parquet
parry
parsimony
partial
partiality
partisan
partition
passé
passive
pastiche
pastoral
patent
pathetic
pathological
pathos
patina
patois
patriarch
patrician
patronize
paucity

pauper
peccadillo
pecuniary
pedagogue
pedagogy
pedant
pedantic
pedestrian
pediatrician
peerless
pejorative
pell-mell
pellucid
penance
penchant
pendant
pendulous
penitent
pensive
penumbra
penury
peon
perceptive
percussion
perdition
peregrination
peremptory
perennial
perfidious
perforate
perfunctory
perigee
perimeter
peripatetic
peripheral
periphery
perjury
permeable
pernicious
peroration
perpetrate
perpetual

perpetuate
perquisite
personable
perspicacious
perspicuity
perspicuous
pert
pertinacious
pertinent
perturb
peruse
pervasive
perverse
perversion
pessimism
pestilential
pestle
petrify
petty
petulant
pharisaical
phenomena
philanderer
philanthropist
philatelist
philistine
philology
phlegmatic
phobia
phoenix
phylum
physiognomy
physiological
piebald
piecemeal
pied
piety
pigment
pillage
pillory
pine
pinion

pinnacle
pious
piquant
pique
piscatorial
pitfall
pith
pithy
pittance
pivotal
placate
placebo
placid
plagiarize
plaintive
plait
plasticity
platitude
platonic
plaudit
plausible
plebeian
plenary
plenitude
plethora
pliable
pliant
plight
pluck
plumage
plumb
plummet
plutocracy
podiatrist
podium
poignancy
polarize
polemic
polemical
politic
polity
polygamist

polyglot
pomposity
ponderous
pontifical
pore
porous
portend
portent
portly
poseur
posterity
posthumous
postulate
posture
potable
potent
potentate
potential
potion
potpourri
poultice
practicable
practical
pragmatic
pragmatist
prate
prattle
preamble
precarious
precedent
precept
precipice
precipitant
precipitate
precipitous
précis
precise
preclude
precocious
precursor
predator
predecessor

predetermine
predicament
predilection
predispose
preeminent
preempt
preen
prefatory
prehensile
prelate
prelude
premeditate
premise
premonition
premonitory
preponderance
preposterous
prerogative
presage
prescience
presentiment
prestige
presumptuous
pretentious
preternatural
pretext
prevail
prevalent
prevaricate
prey
prim
primogeniture
primordial
primp
pristine
privation
privy
probe
probity
problematic
proclivity
procrastinate

procurement
prod
prodigal
prodigious
prodigy
profane
profligate
profound
profusion
progenitor
progeny
prognosis
prognosticate
prohibitive
projectile
proletarian
proliferate
prolific
prolixity
prologue
prolong
prominent
promiscuous
promontory
promote
prompt
promulgate
prone
propagate
propellant
propensity
prophetic
prophylactic
propinquity
propitiate
propitious
proponent
propound
propriety
propulsive
prosaic
proscenium

proscribe
proselytize
prosody
prosperity
prostrate
protean
protégé
protocol
prototype
protract
protrude
protuberance
provenance
provender
provident
provincial
provisional
proviso
provocative
prowess
proximity
proxy
prude
prudent
prune
prurient
pry
pseudonym
psyche
psychiatrist
psychopathic
psychosis
pterodactyl
puerile
pugilist
pugnacity
puissant
pulchritude
pulmonary
pulsate
pulverize
pummel

punctilious
pundit
pungent
punitive
puny
purchase
purgatory
purge
purport
purported
purse
purveyor
pusillanimous
putative
putrid
pylon
pyromaniac

quack
quadruped
quaff
quagmire
quail
quaint
qualified
qualms
quandary
quarantine
quarry
quash
quay
queasy
quell
quench
querulous
query
queue
quibble
quiescent
quietude
quintessence

quip
quirk
quisling
quiver
quixotic
quizzical
quorum
quotidian

rabid
raconteur
ragamuffin
rail
raiment
rakish
rally
ramble
ramification
ramify
ramp
rampant
rampart
ramshackle
rancid
rancor
random
rankle
rant
rapacious
rapport
rapt
rarefied
raspy
ratify
ratiocination
rational
rationalize
raucous
ravage
rave
ravel

ravenous
ravine
raze
reactionary
realm
reaper
rebate
rebuff
rebuke
rebus
rebuttal
recalcitrant
recant
recapitulate
recast
receptive
recession
recidivism
recipient
reciprocal
reciprocate
recluse
reconcile
recondite
reconnaissance
recount
recourse
recrimination
rectify
rectitude
recumbent
recuperate
recurrent
redolent
redoubtable
redress
redundant
reek
refectory
refraction
refractory
refrain

refulgent
refurbish
refute
regal
regale
regatta
regeneration
regicide
regime
regimen
rehabilitate
reimburse
reiterate
rejoinder
rejuvenate
relegate
relent
relevant
relic
relinquish
relish
remediable
reminiscence
remiss
remission
remnant
remonstrance
remorse
remunerative
rend
render
rendezvous
rendition
renegade
renege
renounce
renovate
renown
rent
reparable
reparation
repartee

repast
repeal
repel
repellent
repercussion
repertoire
repine
replenish
replete
replica
replicate
repository
reprehensible
repress
reprieve
reprimand
reprisal
reprise
reproach
reprobate
reprobation
reprove
repudiate
repugnance
repulsion
reputable
reputed
requiem
requisite
requite
rescind
resentment
reserve
residue
resignation
resilient
resolution
resolve
resonant
respiration
respite
resplendent

responsiveness
restitution
restive
restraint
resumption
resurge
resuscitate
retain
retaliation
retentive
reticent
retinue
retiring
retort
retract
retrench
retribution
retrieve
retroactive
retrograde
retrospective
revelry
reverberate
reverent
reverie
revert
revile
revoke
revulsion
rhapsodize
rhetoric
ribald
riddle
rider
rife
rift
rig
rigid
rigor
rile
riveting
rivulet

robust
rococo
roil
roseate
roster
rostrum
rote
rotunda
rotundity
rousing
rout
rubble
rubric
ruddy
rudimentary
rue
ruffian
ruminate
rummage
runic
ruse
rustic
rusticate
ruthless

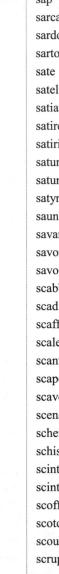

saboteur
saccharine
sacrilegious
sacrosanct
sadistic
saga
sagacious
sage
salacious
salient
saline
sallow
salubrious
salutary
salvage
sanctimonious

sanction
sanctuary
sanguinary
sanguine
sap
sarcasm
sardonic
sartorial
sate
satellite
satiate
satire
satirical
saturate
saturnine
satyr
saunter
savant
savor
savory
scabbard
scad
scaffold
scale
scanty
scapegoat
scavenge
scenario
schematic
schism
scintilla
scintillate
scoff
scotch
scourge
scruple
scrupulous
scrutinize
scuffle
scurrilous
scurry
scurvy

scuttle	shackle	slapdash	sophisticated	statutory
seamy	sham	sleazy	sophistry	steadfast
sear	shambles	sleeper	sophomoric	stealth
seasoned	shard	sleight	soporific	steep
secession	shaving	slew	sordid	stellar
seclusion	sheaf	slight	spangle	stem
secrete	sheathe	slipshod	sparse	stem from
sect	sherbet	slither	spartan	stentorian
secular	shimmer	sloth	spasmodic	stereotype
sedate	shirk	slothful	spat	stickler
sedentary	shoddy	slough	spate	stifle
sedition	shrew	slovenly	spatial	stigma
sedulous	shrewd	sluggard	spatula	stilted
seedy	shun	sluggish	spawn	stint
seemly	shunt	sluice	specious	stipend
seep	shyster	slur	spectral	stipple
seethe	sibling	smattering	spectrum	stipulate
seine	sibylline	smelt	spendthrift	stock
seismic	sidereal	smirk	sphinx-like	stockade
semblance	silt	smolder	splice	stodgy
seminal	simian	snicker	spontaneity	stoic
seminary	simile	snivel	spoonerism	stoke
senility	simper	sobriety	sporadic	stolid
sensitization	simplistic	sodden	sportive	stratagem
sensual	simulate	sojourn	spruce	stratified
sensuous	sinecure	solace	spry	stratum
sententious	sinewy	solder	spurious	strew
sentient	singular	solecism	spurn	striated
sentinel	sinister	solemnity	squabble	stricture
septic	sinuous	solicit	squalor	strident
sepulcher	skeptic	solicitous	squander	stringent
sequester	skiff	soliloquy	squat	strut
sere	skimp	solitude	staccato	studied
serendipity	skinflint	solstice	stagnant	stultify
serenity	skirmish	soluble	staid	stupefy
serpentine	skittish	solvent	stalemate	stupor
serrated	skulduggery	somatic	stalwart	stygian
servile	skulk	somber	stamina	stymie
servitude	slacken	somnambulist	stanch	suavity
sever	slag	somnolent	stanza	subaltern
severity	slake	sonorous	static	subdued
sextant	slander	sophist	statute	subjective

subjugate
sublimate
sublime
subliminal
submissive
subordinate
suborn
subpoena
subsequent
subservient
subside
subsidiary
subsidy
subsistence
substantial
substantiate
substantive
subsume
subterfuge
subtlety
subversive
succinct
succor
succulent
succumb
suffragist
suffuse
sully
sultry
summation
sumptuous
sunder
sundry
superannuated
supercilious
supererogatory
superficial
superfluous
superimpose
supernumerary
supersede
supine

supplant
supple
suppliant
supplicate
supposition
supposititious
suppress
surfeit
surly
surmise
surmount
surpass
surreptitious
surrogate
surveillance
susceptible
sustain
sustenance
suture
swarthy
swathe
swelter
swerve
swill
swindler
sybarite
sycophant
syllogism
sylvan
symbiosis
symmetry
synchronous
synoptic
synthesis
synthetic

T

tacit
taciturn
tactile
taint
talisman

talon
tangential
tangible
tanner
tantalize
tantamount
tantrum
taper
tarantula
tarry
tatty
taut
tautological
tawdry
taxonomist
tedium
teetotalism
temerity
temper
temperament
temperate
tempestuous
tempo
temporal
temporize
tenacious
tenacity
tendentious
tender
tenet
tensile
tentative
tenuous
tenure
tepid
termination
terminology
terminus
terrestrial
terse
tertiary
tessellated

testator
testy
tether
thematic
theocracy
theoretical
therapeutic
thermal
thespian
thrall
threadbare
thrifty
thrive
throes
throng
throttle
thwart
tightwad
tiller
timbre
timidity
timorous
tipple
tirade
titanic
tithe
titillate
title
titter
titular
toady
toga
tome
tonsure
topography
torpor
torque
torrent
torrid
torso
tortuous
totter

touchstone
touchy
tout
toxic
tract
tractable
traduce
trajectory
tranquillity
transcendent
transcribe
transfigure
transgression
transient
transition
transitory
translucent
transmute
transparent
transpire
transport
trappings
traumatic
travail
traverse
travesty
treatise
trek
tremor
tremulous
trenchant
trepidation
tribulation
tribunal
tribute
trident
trifling
trigger
trilogy
trinket
trite
trivia

troth
trough
truculence
truism
truncate
tryst
tumid
tumult
tundra
turbid
turbulence
tureen
turgid
turmoil
turncoat
turpitude
tutelage
tutelary
tycoon
typhoon
tyranny
tyro

U

ubiquitous
ulterior
ultimate
ultimatum
umbrage
unaccountable
unanimity
unassailable
unassuaged
unassuming
unbridled
uncanny
unconscionable
uncouth
unction
unctuous
underlying
undermine

underscore
undulating
unearth
unearthly
unequivocal
unerringly
unexceptionable
unfaltering
unfeigned
unfettered
unfledged
unfrock
ungainly
unguent
uniformity
unilateral
unimpeachable
uninhibited
unintimating
unique
unison
universal
unkempt
unmitigated
unobtrusive
unpalatable
unprecedented
unprepossessing
unravel
unrequited
unruly
unsavory
unscathed
unseemly
unsightly
unsullied
untenable
untoward
untrammeled
unwarranted
unwieldy
unwitting

unwonted
upbraid
uproarious
upshot
urbane
urchin
ursine
usurp
usury
utopia
uxorious

V

vacillate
vacuous
vagabond
vagary
vagrant
vainglorious
valedictory
valid
validate
valor
vampire
vanguard
vantage
vapid
vaporize
variegated
vassal
vaunted
veer
vegetate
vehement
velocity
venal
vendetta
vendor
veneer
venerable
venerate
venial

venison
venom
vent
ventral
ventriloquist
venture
venturesome
venue
veracious
veracity
verbalize
verbatim
verbiage
verbose
verdant
verdigris
verge
verisimilar
verisimilitude
veritable
verity
vernacular
vernal
versatile
vertex
vertigo
verve
vestige
vex
viable
viand
vicarious
vicissitude
victuals
vie
vigilant
vignette
vigor
vilify
vindicate
vindictive
vintner

viper
virile
virtual
virtue
virtuoso
virulent
virus
visage
visceral
viscid
viscous
vise
visionary
vital
vitiate
vitreous
vitriolic
vituperative
vivacious
vivisection
vixen
vociferous
vogue
volatile
volition
voluble
voluminous
voracious
vortex
vouchsafe
voyeur
vulnerable
vulpine

W

waffle
waft
waggish
waif
waive
wake
wallow

wan	welt	winnow	wrangle
wanderlust	welter	winsome	wrath
wane	wheedle	wispy	wreak
wangle	whelp	wistful	wrench
wanton	whet	withdrawn	wrest
warble	whiff	wither	writ
warranted	whimsical	withhold	writhe
warranty	whinny	withstand	wry
warren	whit	witless	
wary	whittle	witticism	
wastrel	whorl	wizardry	
wax	willful	wizened	
waylay	wily	woe	
wean	wince	wont	
weather	windfall	worldly	

yield
yoke
yokel
yore

Z

zany
zeal
zealot
zenith
zephyr

X

xenophobia

Y

yen
yeoman

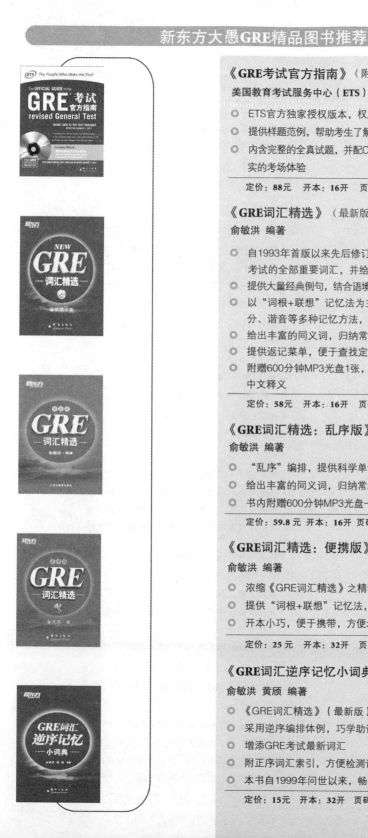

《GRE考试官方指南》（附CD-ROM）

美国教育考试服务中心（ETS）编著

◎ ETS官方独家授权版本，权威解析GRE考试

◎ 提供样题范例，帮助考生了解各题型的命题形式和要求

◎ 内含完整的全真试题，并配CD-ROM 1张，带给考生真实的考场体验

定价：88元　开本：16开　页码：448页

《GRE词汇精选》（最新版）（附MP3）

俞敏洪 编著

◎ 自1993年首版以来先后修订9次，收录迄今为止GRE考试的全部重要词汇，并给出精准释义

◎ 提供大量经典例句，结合语境加深对单词的理解与记忆

◎ 以"词根+联想"记忆法为主，辅以组合词、单词拆分、谐音等多种记忆方法，配以插图，轻松记忆

◎ 给出丰富的同义词，归纳常考搭配

◎ 提供返记菜单，便于查找定位

◎ 附赠600分钟MP3光盘1张，由专业人员朗读单词及中文释义

定价：58元　开本：16开　页码：488页

《GRE词汇精选：乱序版》（附MP3）

俞敏洪 编著

◎ "乱序"编排，提供科学单词记忆方法

◎ 给出丰富的同义词，归纳常考搭配

◎ 书内附赠600分钟MP3光盘一张

定价：59.8元 开本：16开 页码：512页

《GRE词汇精选：便携版》

俞敏洪 编著

◎ 浓缩《GRE词汇精选》之精华，收词全面

◎ 提供"词根+联想"记忆法，实用有趣，轻松记忆

◎ 开本小巧，便于携带，方便考生随时随地记忆单词

定价：25 元　开本：32开　页码：448页

《GRE词汇逆序记忆小词典》

俞敏洪 黄颀 编著

◎ 《GRE词汇精选》（最新版）的姊妹篇

◎ 采用逆序编排体例，巧学助记

◎ 增添GRE考试最新词汇

◎ 附正序词汇索引，方便检测记忆效果

◎ 本书自1999年问世以来，畅销不衰

定价：15元　开本：32开　页码：308页

《GRE考试官方指南词汇必备》（附MP3）

余仁唐 编著

◎ 页码为序，合理编排方便查找
◎ 选词科学，根据语境精准释义
◎ 重点单词，循环出现加深记忆
◎ 一书多用，全面攻克GRE词汇

定价：25元 开本：32开 页码：264页

《GRE核心词汇考法精析》

陈琦 周书林 主编

◎ 7年实战经验沉淀，精炼3000必考词汇
◎ 直击GRE同反考法，星号标注最新词汇
◎ 权威韦氏英文解释，辅以经典英文例句
◎ 高分学员励志推荐，GRE考试高分必备

定价：55元 开本：16开 页码：464页

《新GRE高频词汇：句子填空》

杜昶旭 侯宇轩 编著

定价：48元 开本：16开 页码：384页

《新GRE高频词汇：阅读理解》

杜昶旭 侯宇轩 编著

定价：59元 开本：16开 页码：568页

◎ 科学统计20年GRE考试句子填空与阅读理解真题词汇
◎ 按照单词在考试中出现的频次从高到低排序
◎ 提供单词在GRE考试中考到的中、英文释义
◎ 提供与真题难度相当的例句及高质量中文翻译

《GRE阅读必备专业词汇》

包凡一 编著

◎ 真题为准，重点难点专业词汇一网打尽
◎ 直击考点，有的放矢掌握高频易考单词
◎ 话题分类，按照学科全面罗列各科词汇
◎ 小巧便携，方便随时随地复习与记忆

定价：15元 开本：32开 页码：280页

《词以类记：GRE词汇》（附MP3）

张红岩 编著

◎ 词以类记，按学科和意群精心归纳57个Word List
◎ 收词新、全，收集整理最新GRE重要词汇8400多个
◎ 多重记忆法综合运用，提高了有序储存的效率
◎ 听觉辅助记忆，1000分钟超长录音，另含词汇讲座内容

定价：55元 开本：16开 页码：532页

《GRE备考策略与模拟试题》（附CD-ROM）

[美] Sharon Weiner Green, M.A., and Ira K. Wolf, Ph.D. 编著

◎ 根据新GRE考试趋势编写，全面展现新GRE考试特点

◎ 内含1套与考试难度相符的诊断试题，帮助考生定位薄弱环节

◎ 2套模拟题高度仿真，所有练习及模拟题均附参考答案及详解

◎ CD-ROM内含2套机考模拟题

定价：78元 开本：16开 页码：536页

《GRE 8套题》（附CD-ROM）

[美] 杜兰 编著

◎ 提供8套高仿真模拟试题，并附有答案与详解

◎ 针对GRE写作、语文和数学讲解考试重点，分析备考策略

◎ 为GRE国际考生提供考试相关的重要信息

定价：78元 开本：16开 页码：500页

《GRE 6套题》

[美] 扎勒，[美] 托马斯 编著

◎ 提供6套GRE模拟测试题，体现新GRE考试趋势与特点

◎ 所有试题均附有参考答案和详细的解析

◎ 针对12道分析性写作题目，提供12篇高分写作范文

定价：65元 开本：16开 页码：408页

《GRE语文与写作》

[美] 扎勒，[美] 安林 编著

◎ 深度介绍了新GRE考试语文和分析性写作各题型

◎ 提供各题型的解题技巧和写作指导以及大量自测练习

◎ 附写作高分范文

定价：45元 开本：16开 页码：236页

《GRE数学》

[美] 莫耶 编著

◎ 介绍了新GRE考试所涉及的数学概念，包括算术、代数和几何知识

◎ 涵盖新GRE数学全部题型及考查内容，针对每一类问题提供解答策略

◎ 提供大量练习题供考生进行自测，有助于考生领会解题关键，掌握高分技巧

定价：48元 开本：16开 页码：332页

《GRE官方题库范文精讲》

[美] Mark Alan Stewart 编著

◎ 提供200多道GRE作文真题及其范文

◎ 精讲其中的近100篇

◎ 分析、总结了Issue和Argument高分写作技巧

定价：48元　开本：16开　页码：408页

《GRE写作论证论据素材大全》

韦晓亮 编著

◎ 全面涵盖英文论证和论据素材

◎ 中西方文化大荟萃

◎ 精选权威刊物文章

◎ 汇集数年教学经验，指导考生有效备考

定价：35元　开本：16开　页码：424页

《GRE作文大讲堂——方法、素材、题目剖析》

韦晓亮 编著

◎ 详细阐述Issue和Argument写作策略与步骤

◎ 完整收录GRE写作题库，剖析题目要求

◎ 提供丰富的论证、论据素材，拓展思路

◎ 浓缩多年教学精华，指导考生高效备考

定价：48元　开本：16开　页码：388页

《GRE数学高分快速突破》

陈向东 编著

◎ 详尽归纳数学考点，全面总结数学术语、解题窍门

◎ 强化训练GRE数学考题，帮助考生考前突破，高效备考

定价：40元　开本：16开　页码：300页

《GRE&GMAT阅读难句教程》

杨鹏 编著

◎ 精选GRE、GMAT历年考题中的阅读难句

◎ 以结构分析法，采用各种特定标识，剖析每段难句

◎ 以实战要求为目的，利用语法，学练结合，以练为主

定价：32元　开本：16开　页码：272页

读者反馈表

尊敬的读者：

　　您好！非常感谢您对**新东方大愚图书**的信赖与支持，希望您抽出宝贵的时间填写这份反馈表，以便帮助我们改进工作，今后能为您提供更优秀的图书。谢谢！

　　为了答谢您对我们的支持，我们将对反馈的信息进行随机抽奖活动，当月将有 20 位幸运读者可获赠**《新东方英语》**期刊一份。我们将定期在新东方大愚图书网站 www.dogwood.com.cn 公布获奖者名单并及时寄出奖品，敬请关注。

来信请寄：

　　　　北京市海淀区海淀东三街 2 号新东方南楼 19 层

　　　　北京新东方大愚文化传播有限公司

　　　　　　　　图书部收

　　　　邮编：100080　　　　　　　　E-mail：bj62605588@163.com

姓名：_____　年龄：_____　职业：_____　教育背景：_____

邮编：_____　通讯地址：_____

联系电话：_____　E-mail：_____

您所购买的书籍的名称是：_____

1. **您是通过何种渠道得知本书的（可多选）：**

　　□书店　□新东方网站　□大愚网站　□朋友推荐　□老师推荐

　　□@新东方大愚图书（http://weibo.com/dogwood）　□其他_____

2. **您是从何处购买到此书的？**

　　□书店　□新东方大愚淘宝网　□其他网上书店　□其他_____

3. **您购买此书的原因（可多选）：**

　　□封面设计　□书评广告　□正文内容　□图书价格　□新东方品牌

　　□新东方名师　□其他_____

4. 您对本书的封面设计满意程度：

　□很满意　□比较满意　□一般　□不满意

　改进建议_____

5. 您认为本书的内文在哪些方面还需改进？

　□结构编排　□难易程度　□内容丰富性　□内文版式　□其他_____

6. 本书最令您满意的地方：□内文　□封面　□价格　□纸张

7. 您对本书的推荐率：□没有　□1人　□1—3人　□3—5人　□5人以上

8. 您更希望我们为您提供哪些方面的英语类图书？

　□四六级类　□考研类　□IELTS类　□TOEFL类　□GRE、GMAT类

　□SAT、SSAT类　□留学申请类　□BEC、TOEIC类　□英语读物类

　□初高中英语类　□少儿英语类　□其他_____

　您目前最希望我们为您出版的图书是：_____

9. 您在学习英语过程中最需要哪些方面的帮助？（可多选）

　□词汇　□听力　□口语　□阅读　□写作　□翻译　□语法　□其他_____

10. 您最喜欢的英语图书品牌：_____

　理由是(可多选)：□版式漂亮　□内容实用　□难度适宜　□价格适中

　□对考试有帮助　□其他_____

11. 您对新东方图书品牌的评价：_____

12. 您对本书(或其他新东方图书)的意见和建议：_____

_____

_____

_____

_____

_____

_____

_____

13. 填表时间：_____年_____月____日